Formulation and Treatment in Clinical Health Psychology

Formulation and Treatment in Clinical Health Psychology brings together leading experts in the fields of clinical health psychology and behavioural medicine with the aim of illustrating the formulation and treatment design procedures which they employ in their specialist areas.

Each chapter covers the key biopsychosocial parameters, assessment methods, empirically based treatment strategies and formulation procedures for specific problems. Areas covered include:

- cognitive-behavioural case formulation in the treatment of alcohol problems
- psychological treatment of hypertension
- cognitive therapy for irritable bowel syndrome
- miscarriage: conceptualisation and treatment of the psychological sequelae.

Case studies are employed throughout to demonstrate a link between case formulation, treatment planning and outcome. The practical guidance provided in this volume will prove invaluable for all practising clinicians working in the context of health-related problems.

Ana V. Nikčević is Senior Lecturer in Psychology at Kingston University, a chartered health psychologist and a cognitive behaviour therapist.

Andrzej R. Kuczmierczyk is Senior Lecturer in Clinical & Health Psychology and Director of Health Psychology Postgraduate Training at City University, London. He is currently also a Consultant Clinical Psychologist and cognitive behaviour therapist with the Hertfordshire Partnership (NHS) Trust.

Michael Bruch is Senior Lecturer in Psychology and consultant cognitive behaviour therapist at University College, London.

Contributors: Sallie A. Baxendale, Edward B. Blanchard, Phillip J. Brantley, Michael Bruch, Michael P. Carey, Trudie Chalder, Vincent Deary, Alan M. Delamater, Gareth R. Dutton, Karen B. Grothe, Richard W. Hanson, Jeffrey M. Lackner, Wolfgang Linden, Elizabeth R. Lombardo, Charles M. Morin, Robert L. Newton Jr., Arthur M. Nezu, Christine Maguth Nezu, Ana V. Nikčević, Antonio Prioglio, Josée Savard, Kerri M. Schneider, Sébastien Simard, Marcantonio M. Spada, Peter A. Vanable, Heather M. Walden, Donald A. Williamson.

Formulation and Treatment in Clinical Health Psychology

Edited by Ana V. Nikčević, Andrzej R. Kuczmierczyk & Michael Bruch

Routledge
Taylor & Francis Group

LONDON AND NEW YORK

First published 2006 by Routledge
27 Church Road, Hove, East Sussex BN3 2FA

Simultaneously published in the USA and Canada
by Taylor & Francis Inc
270 Madison Avenue, New York, NY 10016

Routledge is an imprint of the Taylor & Francis Group, an informa business

Typeset in Times by RefineCatch Ltd, Bungay, Suffolk
Printed and bound in Great Britain by
TJ International, Padstow, Cornwall

British Library Cataloguing in Publication Data
A catalogue record for this book is available from the British Library

Library of Congress Cataloging-in-Publication Data
Formulation and treatment in clinical health psychology / edited by
Ana V. Nikčević, Andrzej R. Kuczmierczyk & Michael Bruch.
       p.   cm.
    Includes bibliographical references and index.
ISBN10: 1–58391–284–3 (hbk)
ISBN10: 1–58391–285–1 (pbk)
ISBN13: 9–78–1–58391–284–3 (hbk)
ISBN13: 9–78–1–58391–285–1 (pbk)
    1. Clinical health psychology.   2. Psychiatry—Case
formulation.   3. Psychiatry—Differential therapeutics.   I. Nikčević,
Ana V.   II. Kuczmierczyk, Andrzej R.   III. Bruch, Michael.
    [DNLM: 1. Psychology, Clinical—methods.   2. Disease—
psychology.   3. Psychology, Medical—methods   4. Cognitive Therapy—
methods.   WM 105 F726 2006]
R726.7.F66 2006
616.892—dc22   2005027395

ISBN13: 978–1–583–91284–3 (hbk)
ISBN13: 978–1–583–91285–1 (pbk)
ISBN13: 978–1–583–91200–0 (ebk)

ISBN10: 1–583–91284–3 (hbk)
ISBN10: 1–583–91285–1 (pbk)
ISBN10: 1–583–91000–0 (ebk)

To Marcantonio and Yasna. AN

To my children Ala and Alex who are the wind beneath my wings. ARK

To Victor Meyer, the pioneer of case formulation, in memoriam. MB

Contents

Contributors

Editors

Ana V. Nikčević, PhD, Unit of Psychology, Kingston University, Kingston-upon-Thames, UK.

Andrzej R. Kuczmierczyk, PhD, Department of Psychology, City University, London, UK.

Michael Bruch, PhD, Cognitive-Behavioural Psychotherapy Unit, Department of Psychiatry and Behavioural Sciences, University College, London, UK.

Chapter authors

Sallie A. Baxendale, PhD, Institute of Neurology, University College, London, UK.

Edward B. Blanchard, PhD, ABPP, Center for Stress and Anxiety Disorders, State University of New York at Albany, New York, USA.

Phillip J. Brantley, PhD, Primary Care Studies, Pennington Biomedical Research Center, Louisiana State University, Louisiana, USA.

Michael P. Carey, PhD, Center for Health and Behavior, Syracuse University, Syracuse, New York, USA.

Trudie Chalder, PhD, Department of Psychological Medicine, Institute of Psychiatry, Guy's, King's and St. Thomas' School of Medicine, London, UK.

Vincent Deary, MSc, Chronic Fatigue Treatment Research Unit, Astley Ainsley Hospital, Edinburgh, UK.

Alan M. Delamater, PhD, Department of Pediatrics, University of Miami School of Medicine, Miami, Florida, USA.

Gareth R. Dutton, MA, Primary Care Studies, Pennington Biomedical Research Center, Louisiana State University, Louisiana, USA.

Karen B. Grothe, MA, Primary Care Studies, Pennington Biomedical Research Center, Louisiana State University, Louisiana, USA.

Richard W. Hanson, PhD, VA Long Beach Healthcare System, Long Beach, California, USA.

Jeffrey M. Lackner, PhD, Behavioral Medicine Clinic, Department of Medicine, UB Medical School, Buffalo, New York, USA.

Wolfgang Linden, PhD, Department of Psychology, University of British Columbia, Vancouver, British Columbia, Canada.

Elizabeth R. Lombardo, PhD, private practice, Dallas, Texas, USA.

Charles M. Morin, PhD, School of Psychology, Université Laval, Québec, Canada.

Robert L. Newton Jr., PhD, Pennington Biomedical Research Center, Baton Rouge, Louisiana, USA.

Arthur M. Nezu, PhD, ABPP, Center for Behavioral Medicine, Department of Psychology, Drexel University, Philadelphia, Pennsylvania, USA.

Christine Maguth Nezu, PhD, ABPP, Center for Behavioral Medicine, Department of Psychology, Drexel University, Philadelphia, Pennsylvania, USA.

Antonio Prioglio, MA, Department of Psychology, London Metropolitan University, London, UK.

Josée Savard, PhD, School of Psychology, Université Laval, Québec, Canada; Laval University Cancer Research Center, L'Hôtel-Dien de Québec, Québec, Canada.

Kerri M. Schneider, PhD, Department of Pediatrics, University of Miami School of Medicine, Miami, Florida, USA.

Sébastien Simard, MPs, School of Psychology, Université Laval, Québec, Canada; Laval Cancer Research Center, L'Hôtel-Dien du Québec, Québec, Canada.

Marcantonio M. Spada, MA, Clinical and Health Psychology Research Centre, School of Human and Life Sciences, Roehampton University, London, UK.

Peter A. Vanable, PhD, Center for Health and Behavior, Syracuse University, Syracuse, New York, USA.

Heather M. Walden, MS, Pennington Biomedical Research Centre, Baton Rouge, Louisiana, USA.

Donald A. Williamson, PhD, Pennington Biomedical Research Center, Baton Rouge, Louisiana, USA.

Preface

Over the last few decades the role and importance of psychosocial processes in the experience of health and illness have become widely recognised. As a result, psychologists are now increasingly involved as active members of multidisciplinary clinical and research teams in cardiology, oncology, gastro-enterology, and other medical fields. These developments can be taken as growing evidence that the biopsychosocial model of health and disease is becoming a viable alternative to the biomedical model.

The biopsychosocial approach lies at the core of the disciplines of clinical health psychology and behavioural medicine. It emphasises the interactive influence of biological, psychological and social factors in the development and maintenance of health and illness (Engel, 1977). The model has led to the establishment of a significant knowledge base concerning the role of psychosocial factors in the aetiology and treatment of medical problems.

Although the biopsychosocial model emphasises the importance of idio-syncratic problem conceptualisation and treatment design (Schwartz, 1982), it falls short in providing practical guidance on the processes involved in carrying these out. This is why practitioners working from within the biopsy-chosocial perspective need frameworks that will enable them to tailor assess-ment, formulation and treatment procedures to the idiosyncratic presentation of their clients' problems.

The goals of this book are twofold. First, we aim to provide practitioners working in the context of health-related problems with a conceptual frame-work to enable adequate formulation and treatment design. Second, we aim to illustrate case formulation procedures across a range of different medical conditions. To achieve these goals, we have asked some of the most experi-enced practitioners in the field of clinical health psychology and behavioural medicine to describe the case formulation and treatment design procedures which they employ in their respective specialist areas.

In the initial chapter a well-established cognitive-behavioural framework, the UCL case formulation model, is presented. Central to this approach is a clinical-experimental procedure enabling hypotheses generation regarding the aetiology and maintenance of the presenting problems. This procedure results in the 'problem formulation', a clinical theory linking all problems under investigation. This theory is expected to have explanatory and predictive power, thus allowing for the development and selection of individualised treatment interventions. The UCL case formulation model is designed to encourage integration of biological, psychological and social factors in the conceptualisation of problems. As it is an idiographic approach to treatment, it enables the practitioner to understand and treat difficult and complex problems.

In the subsequent chapters, the authors review the key biopsychosocial parameters, assessment modalities, empirically based treatment strategies and formulation procedures for specific disorders. A variety of approaches to case formulation is adopted. For the majority of disorders the main framework guiding formulation and treatment planning is cognitive-behavioural, but with some disorders the authors have made use of a broader knowledge base. Clinical case material is included in each chapter in order to illustrate the direct link between assessment, problem formulation, treatment planning and outcome. The complexities that exist for clinicians in formulating individual problems and in implementing treatment are highlighted in many of the chapters.

We hope that this text will provide clinicians, working within the biopsychosocial framework, with practical guidance on problem formulation and treatment development.

Ana V. Nikčević

Andrzej R. Kuczmierczyk

Michael Bruch

References

Engel, G.L. (1977). The need for a new medical model: A challenge for biomedicine. *Science, 196*, 129–136.

Schwartz, G. E. (1982). Testing the biopsychosocial model: The ultimate challenge facing behavioural medicine? *Journal of Consulting and Clinical Psychology, 50*, 1040–1053.

Chapter 1

The case formulation procedure

Michael Bruch and Antonio Prioglio

Introduction

Formulating cases on the basis of an idiographic assessment was originally proposed by Victor Meyer (Meyer and Chesser, 1970) when attempting to treat difficult and complex cases in the psychiatric setting. According to Meyer, with such cases standard techniques of behaviour therapy, which became fashionable in the 1960s, were largely ineffective as they were not properly addressing the mechanism of the disorder. He would argue that an individualised understanding of a problem behaviour in learning terms, the 'problem formulation', should be attempted mainly for two reasons:

- Even seemingly similar presenting complaints can involve great individual variations regarding development, presentation, and maintenance.
- It proved unsatisfactory if not impossible to understand and conceptualise more severe, complex disorders on the basis of the diagnostic model, particularly when either multiple or unfocused complaints were reported.

In developing this approach, Meyer emphasised two aspects: the direct application of experimental methodology, as well as learning principles (as developed in the field of empirical learning psychology) to clinical problems. This approach was designed to enhance understanding of the more severe and complex cases that were seen in clinical practice, and to facilitate new innovative treatments where other approaches had failed. Obviously, in those pioneering days of behaviour therapy knowledge about disorders and suitable treatment methods was limited. It is hardly surprising that in due course such a case formulation method proved to be far more useful to therapists (and patients) than a superficial 'symptom–technique' matching approach. The present format does not allow a full discussion regarding assumptions, foundations and historical development of case formulation approaches, particularly in relation to nosological approaches in psychiatry. This can be found elsewhere (e.g. Bruch and Bond, 1998)

Although originally developed for conceptualisation and treatment of complex behavioural disorders, case formulation appears equally suited for the management of health-related problems as is performed in the field of behavioural medicine or health psychology. It is clear that over the past two decades the methodologies of the behavioural and cognitive therapies were increasingly adopted in this field (e.g. Feuerstein *et al.*, 1986), as health problems may mainly differ from behavioural problems in their dimensional profiles of behavioural components. For example, with health problems a stronger representation of somatic responses can be expected in relation to cognitive and motoric responses, but identical dimensions of behaviour and thus similar assessment procedures would still apply. To understand behaviour in terms of such response systems is a major contribution for the assessment of behaviour (originally introduced by Lang, 1971 as *tripartite response system analysis*) as it enables specific operationalising. This procedure has become a cornerstone in the case formulation approach (e.g., Bruch and Bond, 1998). From here, it can be argued that case formulation is a useful tool for any clinician to enhance understanding and treatment of health-related problems, and that the case against standard methods would equally apply. As clinical evidence shows, health problems are often related to a variety of dysfunctional behaviours and/or cognitions, and thus will be subject to individual differences in development and manifestation, in a similar way as with behavioural disorders. For these reasons we would prefer an idiographic approach to 'cookbook' type treatment techniques.

A case formulation approach that allows the clinician to understand the individual mechanism of a disorder will be outlined in this chapter. This process is aided by a clinical-experimental procedure which goes beyond symptomatic complaints. It is hoped that this will lead to an individually meaningful analysis of problems, and thereby provide clients with the most effective help possible. For example, there can be a number of reasons and circumstances that may lead to the manifestation of symptomatic complaints or there may be no clearly visible symptoms at all. On the other hand, narrow focus on symptoms or syndromes according to the diagnostic model is unlikely to explain why problems have developed in the first place, and what maintains them. Clinical evidence shows that it is important to address underlying conditions such as vulnerability factors which may continue to trouble patients or cause relapse. Case formulation guided treatments are designed to avoid such shortfalls.

The UCL case formulation model: the clinical process

General considerations

The main purpose of case formulation is to develop a model of explanation and prediction for any behavioural disorder under investigation. Clearly, this seems especially important for complex problems, which can present a challenge regarding identification of target behaviours and treatment goals, as well as client motivation and the therapeutic relationship. A case formulation will provide guidance with these matters provided by evidence-based hypotheses regarding the mechanism of a disorder. Further, the sharing of such information with the patient will also create transparency in the therapeutic process, and is likely to enhance motivation for treatment. This in turn assists greatly the building of appropriate therapeutic relationships, and fosters adherence in therapy. Obviously, in comparison to a standardised form of assessment, a case formulation procedure can be lengthy and more demanding for the clinician. However, given the long-term impact that therapeutic interventions may have on an individual's life, we feel this effort is more than justified, especially with more complex issues.

Case formulation is an experimental method of investigation, driven by clinical hypotheses derived from cognitive-behavioural knowledge and other relevant experience. The aim is to understand the presented problem in question in terms of its causal history and present conditions of maintenance. It should also allow predictions. All of this is expected to guide treatment interventions comprehensively, as shall be outlined in the remainder of this chapter.

Another major assumption in the case formulation model is individual differences in problem behaviours, both regarding learning history and current maintaining conditions. In other words, seemingly similar symptomatic complaints (according to psychiatric diagnosis) may assume different roles and may be driven by different mechanisms. For example, a social phobia may be related to lack of social skills or, alternatively, to fear of negative evaluation. Or, in relation to health problems, non-compliance with medication may be related to intentionally missing or modifying prescriptions, or to deficits in memory or concentration. Obviously, in recognising such differences, the clinician would determine different treatment priorities and employ individually tailored treatment methods.

Finally, the case formulation approach is flexible and designed to integrate knowledge from beyond the framework of learning principles. This seems especially important for complex disorders involving high levels of comorbidity where creative and innovative thinking may be called for. For example, the self-schema model of complex disorders can be cited as such a development (Bruch, 1988). However, in distinction to methodical eclecticism, we suggest that any such method must be developed within the experimentally guided learning-based approach, and should be subject to empirical evaluation. The overriding concern and interest are focused on the therapeutic application to the individual case.

As already outlined above, case formulation is designed to apply the scientific-experimental approach to clinical problems. Analyses arising from here are designed to investigate the presenting complaint but also link with previously learned behaviours, which may have promoted the onset of problem behaviours in the first place. Such enquiries have to be guided by reasoned hypotheses in the learning framework. Obviously, in the clinical context it is hardly possible to conduct controlled experiments due to methodological and ethical restraints. As the clinical considerations assume priority, the clinician acts in a pseudo-experimental fashion when developing and testing hypotheses. This somewhat subjective process can nevertheless operate satisfactorily if the clinician makes himself account for origins of hypotheses, as well as evidence available in support of these. For less experienced therapists or trainees it would be paramount to introduce intensive supervisory guidance to enable the reflection of this process until experience-based routines (Dreyfus and Dreyfus, 1986) are established.

To conclude, case formulation methodology involves two important issues: first, the process of investigation that follows experimental principles; second, the outcome of that process aiming at an evidence-based model of explanation and prediction (i.e. intervention hypotheses). In other words, unlike psychiatric diagnosis, case formulation is not limited to some form of conceptualisation or categorisation of a problem behaviour. It is an integral part of this process to arrive at a workable treatment programme as guided by the intervention hypotheses and any clinical experimentation inspired by that. To date, the effectiveness of this method, employing learning principles and related knowledge in an idiographic context, has been demonstrated without doubt (e.g. Meyer and Chesser, 1970; Turkat, 1985, 1990; Lane, 1990; Bruch and Bond, 1998). The case formulation method has indeed often revealed significant differences regarding predisposing factors and learning histories with seemingly similar complaints. Obviously, treatment strategies should be adjusted accordingly. We shall illustrate this procedure in more detail below.

The initial interview

The initial interview assumes a crucial role in the case formulation procedure. Here, relevant data are collected in a purposeful manner, which are eventually integrated to formulate a clinical model of explanation accounting for all presenting problems. The interview is guided by a number of critical questions which determine the structure of the interview:

*   What problems is the patient experiencing?
*   Are these predominantly psychological or medical in nature and are there any interactions?
*   Why and how have these problems developed?
*   What factors maintain these problems?
*   What kind of intervention may produce change?

Subsequently, a valid case formulation is expected to comprehensively answer such questions.

During the interview we adopt an empathetic-directive style to enable the clinical-experimental approach in pursuit of the above questions. This is also done in recognition of the fact that patients mostly seek active help and guidance when looking for a therapy to enable change. Sadly, such a style is still being frowned upon by dynamic and humanistic approaches who treat this issue as something not being open to scientific enquiry. Most assertions, for example, patients being too fragile for a directive approach, cannot be substantiated by either research or clinical evidence (for review see AuBuchon and Malatesta, 1998). On the contrary, our own clinical experience demonstrates that patients mostly favour a directive and transparent style in therapy which is designed to share all relevant information with them. Obviously, there are those patients who are merely looking for support and who may benefit mostly from a client-centred non-directive approach. We feel this issue should be clarified at the very beginning of the interview. The patient should be encouraged to give a clear description of any goals he wants to attain in therapy.

The interview is conducted in an open and natural style. Patients are encouraged to ask questions about the procedure and the clinician tries to create a relaxed atmosphere, even allowing for jokes to 'break the ice'. For these reasons it is advisable to avoid professional jargon and to encourage the patient to talk in his or her own language. According to case formulation, we treat the patient as an active partner in achieving the cognitive-behavioural analysis, the problem formulation, and the treatment programme.

To enable discussion, teaching and supervision we consider it a useful option to conduct the initial interview in a small group format. Considerable time is spent explaining the rationale and the patient's role in the therapeutic process. Unlike in psychiatric interviewing, the patient is encouraged to participate actively in the interview, to ask questions and contribute to the assessment. Such discussions may point to more than one way of understanding a problem. All questions during the interview need to be explained in terms of explicit hypotheses. In turn, hypotheses will either be verified or rejected by gathered information. A blackboard or some other medium is used to collect and display all relevant data. Contrary to conventional opinion, most patients enjoy this experience of sharing a range of views, being able to participate in any discussion, and experiencing the construction of a problem formulation.

Developing hypotheses

The generation of appropriate hypotheses of cause and maintenance is central in case formulation as it drives the process in a reasoned and logical manner. Hypotheses should be developed as early as possible and may extend to non-verbal behaviours. For example, body language and interpersonal style during first contact may provide valuable clues about problems and deficits. This may be especially important with individuals who initially find it difficult to verbalise their problems. Obviously, the clinician should rely predominantly on information provided by the patient. However, under certain circumstances it may be necessary to rely on other sources. Once an initial hypothesis has been developed, however crude initially, further questions are designed to verify or reject the hypothesis. Subsequent outcome may further stimulate hypotheses which are scrutinised in the same manner, leading to a shaping process of increasing refinement. In this way, any initial hypotheses will gradually be developed into a comprehensive knowledge base regarding the disorder under investigation.

We have already pointed out that experimental rigour (as proposed by Shapiro, 1957) can neither be possible nor desirable in a clinical context. What options are left to the clinician who operates as a highly subjective agent? Clinical experiences accumulated by therapists working with this model seem to suggest that reasoned systematic questioning involving continuous review of the process is most realistic. Therapists with relevant interpersonal and clinical experience, as well as substantial knowledge in cognitive-behavioural principles, are best equipped for this approach. The experimental approach requires logical reasoning which is best trained and developed in peer supervision or small group teaching. For example, each question should be scrutinised regarding its source and intention. Questions whose purpose and knowledge base cannot be clearly established are unacceptable. Obviously, such interview logic requires much discipline and reflection as the clinician has to perform three roles at the same time: to define reasoned hypotheses on the information provided; to formulate suitable questions; and to test all hypotheses. Ideally, all information given by the patient can be accounted for by a network of hypotheses which form the basis for problem formulation.

Any discrepancies or contradictions require further investigation and in some cases the process has to be restarted. Understandably, inexperienced therapists find it a daunting task to develop appropriate hypotheses in this way and tend to develop over-inclusive strategies: that is, too many questions are being asked in a rather erratic fashion. In this way enormous amounts of information are gathered that are often quite irrelevant and difficult to organise and understand. This can lead to great confusion as we have often witnessed in supervision. Conversely, very experienced clinicians may think 'I have seen it all before' and be tempted to shape the interview according to their prejudged views without looking for substantiating evidence. Rigid preconceived judgement can also encourage selective perception and questioning techniques, which may even shape the patients' behaviours.

In sum, case formulation can be considered a highly complex task requiring exceptional clinical and experimental skills without having the benefit of a proper laboratory. Obviously, it is important to stay flexible and open minded as hypotheses may be false and may require reworking. For better transparency or structure, it is advisable to use a blackboard or some other medium. The added benefit is illustration and explanation of the method both for clinicians and patients.

Clinical steps

For better transparency and guidance, we have adapted Lane's stepwise procedure (Lane, 1990) which is presented in Box 1.1. Five basic phases are suggested which are interconnected by feedback loops to allow verification and correction of the process. Phases one to three are covered by the initial interview. These steps shall be explained in some more detail below.

Box 1.1 Clinical steps: five basic phases

Phase one: Definition of problems

1   Obtain statement of the problem from those involved.
2   Clarify initial objectives of those involved.
3   On the basis of initial information received, specify problems.

Theme: A process of growing awareness aimed at a therapeutic consensus.

Phase two: Exploration

4   Hypotheses of cause and maintenance are generated.
5   Multilevel cognitive-behavioural assessment is conducted.
6   Data are collected to test hypotheses.

Theme: The process is one of increasingly refined observations.

Phase three: Formulation

7   A formulation and intervention hypotheses are established.
8   Discussion with participants and redefinition of objectives takes place.
9   The adequacy of the hypotheses are checked and verified.

Theme: The process is one of testing the hypotheses until an adequate explanation is available.

Phase four: Intervention

10   The procedures to be used are specified.
11   An intervention contract is established.
12   The agreed programme is enacted and monitored.

Theme: The process is one of structured practice.

Phase five: Evaluation

13 Accomplished outcomes are evaluated.
14 Any gains made are supported and enhanced, the programme is optimised and further objectives, if suggested, are pursued.
15 Continuing evaluation and review. Generation of further ideas to consolidate progress.

Theme: The process is one of monitored achievement and support.

Defining problems

We begin the interview by exploring with the patient his or her general views and expectations about therapy and cognitive-behavioural therapy (CBT) in particular. With rather unprepared subjects, it may be useful to explain differences between psychiatric and psychological approaches. If necessary, we may then go on to explain the rationale and procedure of CBT, stressing in particular active participation, goal orientation, time schedule, and therapy as a continuous learning process. The patient is assured that he or she can ask questions about the process at any time. Finally, we may take some biographical details. However, in contrast to psychiatric assessment, this is normally kept to a minimum.

The first phase is entirely client centred and designed to obtain a comprehensive subjective statement of the patient's current problems. This entails enquiry about desired outcomes of treatment, as well as reasons for seeking therapeutic help at this time. The patient is encouraged to report in his or her own language, and to avoid recycling of any previous diagnosis or professional jargon he or she may have acquired in previous contacts with professional helpers. At this stage, the clinician will encourage self-exploration and will use any information to develop hypotheses regarding the nature and mechanism of the problem.

There may be circumstances when other means of assessment are necessary or other sources of information are required. First, patients may find it difficult to express themselves verbally, especially when no clear-cut symptomatic complaints are present. In such cases the therapist may attempt Socratic dialogue style questioning or use suitable questionnaires for screening purposes. In case the interview situation is initially too demanding, the therapist may ask the patient to attempt a detailed list and description of current problems as a homework assignment. Turkat (1986) has provided an example of how such a list can assist the clinician's reasoning:

Assume the following list of problems is generated: (1) Depression, (2) Lack of friends, (3) Excessive hand washing, (4) Inability to leave the house, (5) Difficulty sleeping, (6) Excessive cleaning. The therapist attempts to find an explanatory hypothesis for all of these complaints. A striking hypothesis from the problems listed in this case is a *fear of contamination*. Such a hypothesis is derived from the following type of thinking: The patient probably *washes her hands* and *cleans her house* excessively to prevent possible contamination by dirt, germs, and so forth. Further, she *avoids leaving her home* in order to prevent exposure to more contaminating stimuli. This results in *social isolation*, rumination about her predicament at night (which produces sleep onset *insomnia*) and thus, *depression*. Other problems predicted from the general mechanism of 'fear of contamination' might include: avoidance of touching others, sexual problems, hosing down or vacuuming others when they enter her house (this is not as uncommon as it might sound), preventing others from entering her house, and so forth.

(Turkat, 1986, p. 123)

Second, in case other individuals are involved with the patient's problem, steps may be taken to interview these at a later stage. We also encourage patients to express their expectations for therapy as early as possible. Patients who become aware of clear goals at the beginning of the process will enhance their motivation, and tend to become more active in the therapeutic process. Providing there is agreement with the patient, it may be desirable to get the views of other individuals involved to avoid conflicting interests and adherence problems. For example, consider the case of an obsessive compulsive disorder (OCD) sufferer whose disturbing rituals prompt the partner to arrange therapy for him. Here, a consensus has to be reached whether therapy is acceptable and what format it should take. Obviously, whether any goals are realistic in terms of supporting environment and resources available can only be determined in a collaborative review after completion of the assessment process.

To conclude, the information provided in phase one should facilitate an operationalised description of the problem behaviour(s) as well as initial hypotheses regarding the mechanism of the disorder. These will be investigated in the next phase.

Exploring problems

This phase is led and structured by the clinician who is now attempting to refine hypotheses further. The aim is to achieve a comprehensive formulation of problems. As a first step, an operationalised description of all problem behaviours (i.e. descriptive analysis) should be developed with the patient on the basis of the initial statements. This forms the basis for all further assessments. We consider conducting both functional and developmental analyses as necessary for most problems which can be analysed according to learning principles. Additional assessments should be supported by hypotheses arising from the interview. These may relate to social, interpersonal, intrapersonal, sexual, family aspects, and so on. The goal hereby is to gain full understanding of cause and maintenance of problems as well as their interrelationship. It is important that all further steps in the analysis are justified by reasoned clinical hypotheses to enable building a clinical theory as opposed to mechanistic pigeon holing.

Functional and response system analysis

Unfortunately, this well-established method in behavioural assessment, guided by the 'learning equation', is now regarded by some cognitive therapists as obsolete. In contrast, we would argue strongly that functional analysis is indispensable if one accepts a learning view of behavioural disorders. This analysis was substantially enhanced with the incorporation of tripartite response system analysis as suggested by Peter Lang (1971). This was an important addition, as response systems within a behavioural response were demonstrated to be highly interactive. A graphic outline of the complete model is provided in Figure 1.1.

We begin with the assessment of typical stimulus conditions likely to trigger the problem behaviour. Hereby, it may be of interest whether one can identify a hierarchy of stimuli and the extent to which the stimulus generation may have taken place. The organism link indicates to what extent predisposing factors (e.g. biological factors like habitual level of physiological arousal) may have a moderating role. Both short- and long-term consequences are investigated, as they can serve as possible indicators for problem maintenance and long-term maladjustment.

Of particular value is a detailed response system analysis as illustrated in Figure 1.1. For example, the detection of a dominant response modality which may have a causative effect on other systems allows us to understand how behavioural patterns are unfolding and promoting each other. Obviously, it would make sense to match treatment modalities with the dominant system, that is, the system that responds first and has influence over the

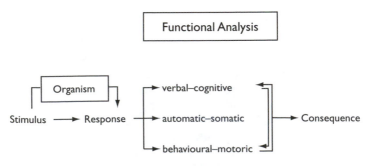

Figure 1.1 Functional and response system analysis.

others. For example, a calming technique for an individual suffering from anxiety-provoking cognitions could address these cognitions as a priority, as opposed to progressive muscular relaxation. Research and clinical evidence have also pointed to predisposed response preferences, that is, individuals may be habitual 'cognitive' or 'autonomic' responders in anxiety-provoking situations (e.g. Bandura, 1977; Bruch, 1988). Clearly, such information would influence the planning of any treatment. Other useful knowledge refers to the state of synchrony of response systems (Rachman and Hodgson, 1974). As high levels of anxiety are usually associated with synchrony of response systems, it may be attempted to decouple response systems. For example, the patient may be encouraged to reappraise autonomic arousal cognitively when this is being reported as anxiety.

Turkat (1979) has proposed the *behaviour analysis matrix* (Table 1.1) for a more systematic and comprehensive assessment which incorporates examination of response systems, both for stimulus situations and consequences of any problem behaviour, in addition to the environmental perspective. To conclude, response system analysis can provide extremely useful information regarding the mechanism of a disorder and may be of great heuristic value for an intervention programme.

Finally, the consequences of any problem behaviours are examined. This is to establish maintaining factors (usually a short-term consequence) and issues regarding life style and general adjustment (usually a long-term consequence). This analysis can provide valuable insight into self-regulation processes. For example, avoidance behaviour provides short-term relief but may prevent adequate problem solving and adjustment in the long term, thus indicating deficient self-regulation. This can be illustrated with social phobia often leading to avoidance of imagined anxiety-provoking situations. Obviously, long term, this may lead to complete social isolation and possibly depression. The analysis of consequences is likely to provide clues for the development of adaptive self-regulation.

Developmental analysis

In traditional behaviour therapy the need for a historical analysis of problems was rather rejected. Possibly as a reaction of what was perceived as

Table 1.1 The Behaviour analysis matrix

	Antecedent	Behaviour	Consequence
Cognitive	X	X	X
Autonomic	X	X	X
Motoric	X	X	X
Environmental	X		X

over-indulgence in psychodynamic therapies, the 'here' and 'now' focus was most strongly upheld. In recognising this still somewhat controversial issue, case formulation argues for a focused and learning-oriented analysis of each problem behaviour as opposed to a broad and generalised biography guided by speculative theories of abnormal behaviour. Again, we attempt to guide our questions by hypotheses arising from prior information or clinical reasoning. The object is to learn as much as possible about predisposing factors, circumstances of onset as well as triggers and maintenance factors of each problem behaviour. For example, we may ask when the problem first occurred and what happened in that situation. We then go on to scan the complete biography of the patient regarding significant occurrences of that problem to determine generalisation effects and if and how learning contingencies may have changed. Typically, this analysis can reveal substantial differences between onset and later manifestations of the problem behaviour. In passing, it may be of interest to note that behavioural research (Staddon, 2001) has shown that individual learning histories are related to corresponding patterns of extinction, thus highlighting the importance of historical analysis. In case more than one problem is reported, development analysis would also focus on possible interactions between problem areas. This may help to determine the role and relative importance of individual problems.

We have also found that etiologic information is a rich source for making observations and developing hypotheses about earlier learned, deeply seated cognitions and behaviours. For example, in the context of complex disorders, we have frequently detected early established maladaptive self-schemata which appeared to be promoting both negative automatic thoughts, as well as behavioural disorders consistent with underlying schemata. Such schemata have also been shown to affect processing tasks such as self-evaluation or self-efficacy expectations. We have described this mechanism as a deficient self-regulation process (Bruch, 1988) and have suggested a specific schema analysis if compelling hypotheses are in evidence.

Additional investigations

The assessment procedures described above can serve as typical examples for case formulation. Ultimately, the selection of assessment methods is driven by hypotheses according to the clinical-experimental strategy. Generally, we prefer to keep routines to a minimum, and prefer a flexible and problem-focused approach. Thus, with some cases the above given procedures may be obsolete (i.e. a functional analysis may not be useful for generalised depression), whilst with other cases, circumstances may inspire inventive explorations. The above given example of schema analysis is testimony to this.

Needless to say, in case formulation we do not recommend 'mechanistic' and 'over-inclusive' analysis procedures (e.g. Kanfer and Phillips, 1970) that may undermine the dynamic flow of the interview, which should be driven by clinical hypotheses. In our opinion, too detailed and systematic assessment schemes are not only laborious and time consuming but can create a vast array of data which may become unmanageable or even confusing when attempting a problem formulation. Acceptance by patients can also be a problem. Nevertheless, standard methods may be selected as prototypes for suitable adaptation in a case formulation procedure. As a note of caution, any behaviours being explored ought to be seen in context. In order to examine relevant parameters, it may be useful to take a 'snapshot' of problem behaviour. However, it is important to recognise that behaviours are continuous in nature, that is, responses may become stimuli and so on.

No assessment should be complete without addressing resources and assets in the behaviour of the patient as this may provide us with vital clues regarding their role in an active treatment programme. For example, we may be interested in areas of positive adjustment in the patient's life style. In the context of problem behaviour evidence of any coping abilities with particular focus on self-control competence may be explored.

As already stated, the patient is regarded as the principal provider of information in the assessment process. At times, though, this may be complemented with other sources, if and when appropriate. For example, partners, family members, etc. may be interviewed if there is substantial involvement with the presenting problem(s). Direct observation in the environment where the problem occurs may be another option. This method can greatly assist clinical experiments aimed to test hypotheses developed during the interview. The clinician selects and explains any additional assessment procedure in collaboration with the patient and must obtain his or her full consent.

Finally, any data being gathered that are not consistent with hypotheses being developed during the interview must be accounted for: the hypothesis may be wrong, the interview procedure flawed, or there could be a lack of patient cooperation who may provide contradictory information.

The problem formulation

Systematic information gathering and development of hypotheses enhance each other in a reciprocal process which promotes gradual building of a comprehensive 'clinical theory', the problem formulation. The clinician attempts to integrate all available data here and all further steps in therapy will be guided by this process. A problem formulation attempts to explain how the patient's complaints are related to each other, why and how they have developed, and what maintaining factors can be identified. Further, it aims to establish in what way the reported problems are related to the patient's upbringing, general development and life style. The formulation also allows predictions regarding the problem behaviour(s) in specified situations, and from here an intervention hypothesis may be formulated. Such prediction ought to be tested in clinical experiments as we shall describe later on.

After completion of the initial interview, the clinician attempts a (provisional) problem formulation which should be further refined during the therapeutic process, if and when new data become available. It is important to share and discuss the formulation, including any intervention hypothesis, before embarking on further steps in treatment. This is done to increase motivation through transparency and hopefully lay the ground for the patient to become an active partner in the therapeutic process. We recommend the following guidelines for this:

1   Begin by explaining the purpose and rationale of a problem formulation.
2   Give a summary of the presenting problems.
3   Explain the mechanism of the disorder as seen in terms of learning principles and cognitive theory.
4   Illustrate how this mechanism is causing and maintaining all the current complaints.
5   Explain why these problems have developed using examples from the developmental history.
6   Emphasise that all described problem behaviours are understood as predominantly learned responses which can be subject to modification employing the same principles.
7   Outline the range of treatment options arising from the intervention hypothesis, including the pros and cons for each option. Raise awareness of possible obstacles during treatment.
8   Conclude whether or not an appropriate treatment programme can be offered and organised by the therapist and outline the expected role of the patient.
9   Invite comments from the patient on all above points, especially regarding possible treatment options.
10 Ask the patient to spend a week or so considering the formulation and treatment implications.
11 Answer any questions the patient may want to ask.

To conclude, apart from being an explanatory model, a case formulation is designed to provide active guidance for all further steps in treatment, in particular regarding an intervention hypothesis and selection of treatment methods. For example, a formulation can advise whether we are dealing with an isolated problem or whether there may be more deeply seated complications (i.e. maladaptive schemata) involved. Why is a particular individual vulnerable to stressful conditions when others may not be? With more complex problems, how are we to determine priorities and organise timing of selected treatment methods? And so on.

Assuming highly individual patterns of behaviour and learning, clinicians using cognitive-behavioural formulations do not rely on 'one cap fits all' diagnostic decision trees or lists of environmental stressors. The formulation enables us to understand how individual predisposition, learning processes and environmental factors interact with each other and form unique behavioural patterns. Multilevel analysis as described above assists this task. The experimental method applied throughout the case formulation process serves as a guiding and integrating tool. Obviously, there may be circumstances when necessary information cannot be readily obtained to formulate a case as required. In such circumstances a pragmatic usually symptom-focused approach may become necessary. Monitoring this process may provide suitable data to allow retrospective construction of a formulation; for example, when evaluating whether the proposed treatment has worked or not, and for what possible reasons. In cases of failure, such evaluation may inspire hypotheses regarding alternative intervention programmes which can hopefully be embedded in a more comprehensive formulation. In any case, case formulations should always be subject to continuous confirmation or modification by data gathered during the ongoing therapeutic process.

Clinical experimentation

Because of the central importance of the formulation, we believe it is important to employ research-oriented methods for further verification. Clinical experimentation is designed accordingly and serves four main purposes:

- to allow testing the predictive power of the case formulation;
- to validate the patient's statement or account for any discrepancies;
- to provide a frame for selection or development of measures of change;
- to inspire prototypes for intervention techniques.

Clinical experimentation requires precisely formulated hypotheses about behaviours to occur under specified stimulus conditions. As this is a clinical situation, the therapist is bound to adjust his research efforts to practical and ethical requirements. It is important to create a realistic scenario in order to be able to evoke genuine responses across all response modalities. For evaluation purposes it is important to develop or select suitable measures which match any hypothesised responses in precise detail. This is of particular importance when investigating specific response systems. Results may shed light on complex interactions and provide clues about 'faulty' labelling or processing tasks. Obviously, in a clinical context such investigations will be limited as it is not always possible to measure all responses directly in the appropriate modality (e.g. physiological arousal). Some patients may find in vivo situations unacceptable or even frightening, in which case the clinician must try to explore other possibilities with the patient to test the formulation, for example, by using imaginary exposure, audio or video tapes.

Obviously, clinical experimentation should not be confused with psychometric assessments for screening or diagnostic purposes.

Clinical experimentation may be illustrated with a travel phobia as follows. The patient reported that, following a severe panic attack, she had been unable to travel on underground trains or even to go near any station for many years. On the basis of this information the clinician can create a scenario to test any predictions developed on the basis of the information provided by the patient. After having obtained consent, the patient may then be asked to approach the fearful situation in a graduated manner. At the same time, the patient's performance is continuously evaluated by suitable measures relating to the described problem behaviour. These may involve subjective ratings on indicators of anxiety across all response systems, or observational measures taken by the therapist or independent assessors. If the original statement is confirmed, the task chosen for the experiment, as well as selected measures, may be considered as prototypes for treatment planning. According to our clinical experience, such 'reality checks' may yield surprising therapeutic results: that is, in some cases exposure is facilitated leading to immediate habituation of previously imagined feared situations. If predictions cannot be confirmed, any related evidence ought to lead to modification of the problem formulation and subsequent intervention hypothesis. To conclude, albeit not being a precise science, clinical experimentation is a useful clinical research tool to assist the case formulation process. A problem formulation that cannot be supported requires revision guided by reformulated hypothesis and respective assessment procedures.

Baselines and measures of change

The process of selecting or developing suitable measures is already piloted in the clinical experimentation phase. Further refinements and additions may then be required after conclusion of a treatment strategy. To enable a comprehensive evaluation of the complete treatment intervention we have recommended to organise measures at three levels. These refer to short-term vs long-term improvements, specific vs global adjustment, and client vs expert estimates. In other words, baselines and outcomes ought to be evaluated both by therapists and patients. Furthermore, they should be judged in the short term (in session), as well as the long term (e.g. follow-up). Finally, there should be an assessment as to whether any changes are relating to symptomatic complaints as well as to life adjustment indicators.

Measures for these dimensions can range from subjective ratings to questionnaires or observation by trained experts. All measures should be closely matched with defined target behaviours. Depending on complexity and length of any intervention programme, a chosen set of measures is employed before, during and after treatment, as well as for several follow-up occasions. Obviously, the emphasis on measurement is on evaluation of *therapeutic change* as opposed to diagnostic or psychometric assessment. When using standardised measures, it may be an added benefit to compare individual data with relevant groups.

Multidimensional measurements are useful in determining a profile for outcome and change. For example, converging evidence for 'positive' changes may indicate overall sustained improvements, whereas discrepant measures may indicate isolated or even disputable gains. Obviously, there must be concern when improvements with symptomatic complaints do not correlate with improved life adjustment, or when patients and therapists do not agree on crucial outcome measures. On the other hand, convergence on all measures would strongly endorse the problem formulation and the intervention programme.

Conclusion

We have outlined the case formulation approach as a clinical-experimental procedure designed to achieve a comprehensive model of explanation. This model requires systematic collection of appropriate information guided and driven by reasoned clinical hypotheses based on cognitive-behavioural principles. During the course of treatment all further clinical decisions are made on the basis of the problem formulation.

As with behavioural disorders, we believe that this approach is equally suitable for health-related problems associated with emotional problems and cognitive dysfunctioning. This case is strengthened by the fact that CBT treatment methodology has already been applied successfully in behavioural medicine and health psychology for some time (see Feuerstein *et al.*, 1986; Baum *et al.*, 1997). Obviously, in realising that human behaviour and its associated problems can be incredibly complex and difficult to understand, a narrow focus on singular symptomatic complaints is rarely helpful. Case formulation is no magic solution. However, it offers a practical framework for the management of health-related problems. Indeed our clinical data have consistently demonstrated the efficacy of this approach (Bruch *et al.*, 1996, 1999, 2000).

We have highlighted the active role of the patient within this approach as we aim to promote adaptive self-regulation as early as possible. To motivate, the patient's view is fully taken into account. All aspects of the treatment procedure are extensively discussed and one proceeds only after full agreement has been reached. This is especially crucial for the problem formulation. Strong emphasis is also given to full explanation of the treatment rationale as we encourage the patient to become his own therapist at an intermediate stage in treatment. More detailed accounts of the UCL case formulation approach and clinical transcripts of the initial interview can be found elsewhere (e.g. Turkat, 1986; Meyer and Liddell, 1977; Bruch and Bond, 1998).

References

Aubuchon, P., & Malatesta, V. (1998). Managing the therapeutic relationship: The need for a case formulation. In M. H. Bruch & F. W. Bond (Eds.), *Beyond diagnosis: Cognitive-behavioural case formulation*. Chichester: Wiley.

Bandura, A. (1977). Self-efficacy: Toward a unifying theory of behavioural change. *Psychological Review, 84*, 2, 191–215.

Baum, A., Newman, S., Weinman, J., West, R., & McManus, C. (1997). *Cambridge handbook of psychology, health and medicine*. Cambridge: Cambridge University Press.

Bruch, M. (1988). *The self-schema model of complex disorders*. Regensburg: Roederer.

Bruch, M., & Bond, F. W. (1998). *Beyond diagnosis. Case formulation approaches in CBT*. Chichester: Wiley.

Bruch, M. *et al.* (1996/1999/2000). *Cognitive-behavioural case formulation I. II. III.* Symposia held at the 26th, 29th and 30th annual EABCT meetings in Budapest, Hungary, Dresden, Germany, and Granada, Spain.

Dreyfus, H. L., & Dreyfus, S. E. (1986). *Mind over machine: The power of human intuition and expertise in the area of the computer*. New York: McGraw-Hill.

Feuerstein, M., Labbé, E. E., & Kuczmierczyk, A. R. (1986). *Health psychology: A psychobiological perspective*. New York: Plenum.

Kanfer, F. H., & Phillips, J. S. (1970). *Learning foundations of behaviour therapy*. New York: Wiley.

Lane, D. (1990). *The impossible child*. Stoke on Trent: Trentham.

Lang, P. J. (1971). The application of psychophysiological methods to the study of psychotherapy and behaviour modification. In A. Bergin & S. Garfield (Eds.), *Handbook of psychotherapy and behaviour change*. New York: Wiley.

Meyer, V., & Chesser, E. S. (1970). *Behaviour therapy in clinical psychiatry*. Harmondsworth: Penguin.

Meyer, V., & Liddell, A. (1977). Behavioural interviews. In A. R. Ciminero, K. S. Calhoun, & H. E. Adams (Eds.), *Handbook of behavioural assessment*. New York: Wiley.

Rachman, S., & Hodgson, R. (1974). I. Synchrony and desynchrony in fear and avoidance. *Behaviour Research and Therapy, 12*, 311–318.

Shapiro, M. B. (1957). Experimental methods in the psychological description of the individual psychiatric patient. *International Journal of Social Psychiatry, 111*, 89–102.

Staddon, J. (2001). *The new behaviourism. Mind, mechanism and society*. Philadelphia: Psychology Press.

Turkat, I. D. (1979). The behaviour analysis matrix. *Scandinavian Journal of Behaviour Therapy, 8*, 187–189.

Turkat I. D. (1985). *Behavioural case formulation*. New York: Plenum.

Turkat, I. D. (1986). The behavioural interview. In A. R. Ciminero, K. S. Calhoun, & H. E. Adams (Eds.), *Handbook of behavioural assessment* (2nd.). New York: Wiley.

Turkat, I. D. (1990). *The personality disorders. A psychological approach to clinical management*. New York: Pergamon

Chapter 2

Cognitive-behavioural case formulation in the treatment of alcohol problems

Marcantonio M. Spada

Introduction

The World Health Organisation (WHO) estimates that worldwide alcohol misuse caused 1.8 million deaths in the year 2000, compared with 0.2 million from the use of illicit drugs (WHO, 2002). After smoking and high blood pressure, alcohol misuse is the global leading factor of preventable death and disability (WHO, 2002).

Alcohol problems are heterogeneous in nature, ranging in severity from heavy social drinking that may occasionally result in a day off work to severe and chronic alcoholism. Although the prevalence of alcohol problems is higher in younger than in older adults, and in males rather than in females, these problems affect individuals from all sociodemographic, ethnic, racial and occupational backgrounds.

In mental health settings at least 30 to 40 per cent of clients are likely to report alcohol problems as part of their presenting problems (Helzer & Pryzbeck, 1988; Wilson, 1988; Kushner *et al.*, 1990; Stewart, 1996; Graham *et al.*, 2001). It is for this reason that clinicians need to be competent in identifying, assessing and planning effective treatment interventions for tackling alcohol problems. This chapter describes a cognitive-behavioural case formulation approach for the conceptualisation and treatment of alcohol problems.

Diagnostic and idiographic perspectives on alcohol problems

The diagnostic perspective

The contemporary psychiatric approach to the diagnosis of alcohol problems centres on a hypothetical construct, the 'alcohol dependence syndrome' (Edwards & Gross, 1976). This is a collection of problematic behavioural patterns resulting from drinking that are hypothesised to represent a diagnostic entity. The alcohol dependence syndrome involves two separate dimensions: alcohol dependence and alcohol abuse. In order to be diagnosed with alcohol dependence an individual must satisfy at least three of seven criteria that relate to impaired control, physical tolerance, physical withdrawal, neglect of other activities, increased time spent using alcohol, and continued use despite awareness of recurrent physical or psychological problems related to use. Diagnosis of alcohol abuse is based on problem use. This includes failing to meet major social role obligations at work, home or school, drinking repeatedly in a way that creates potential for harm (e.g. drinking and driving), incurring frequent alcohol-related legal consequences, or continuing to drink regardless of known social or interpersonal problems arising from drinking.

The idiographic perspective

In contrast to the diagnostic definition of alcohol problems, behavioural researchers and clinicians have advocated that alcohol problems should be represented idiographically on a continuum of alcohol use, ranging from abstinence to non-problem use to different types and degrees of problem use. From this standpoint, alcohol problems may present in a variety of forms, some of which are consistent with a formal diagnosis, and some of which are not (e.g. milder or more intermittent problems). As such treatment should be tailor-made rather than manual-based. This may involve identifying detailed idiographic drinking patterns, targeting concomitant psychosocial problems, working on motivation for change, and looking at personal resources and preferences. From this perspective formal diagnosis is helpful in identifying and defining the severity of a client's alcohol problems but not in the design of treatment. The approach to clinical practice outlined in this chapter will attend to the idiographic conceptualisation of alcohol problems.

Cognitive-behavioural approach to treatment of alcohol problems

The cognitive-behavioural approach to the treatment of alcohol problems is based on the assumption that alcohol problems are learned, maladaptive patterns of behaviour emanating from the interactive processes of classical and operant conditioning, instrumental learning and cognitive mediation (Gorman, 2001). This entails that alcohol problems are complex and involve a variety of determinants which interact in a systematic fashion during development, maintenance and treatment. From the cognitive-behavioural standpoint, problematic drinking behaviour is maintained by a bi-phasic reinforcement dynamic. Alcohol use provides immediate gratification through feelings of pleasure (positive reinforcement) and/or the reduction or elimination of negative states, such as anxiety, low mood or anger (negative reinforcement). Delayed negative consequences (both at a physical and psychological level) arise from continued use, but attempts to abstain in the absence of viable alternative coping behaviours leads to increased distress. This usually triggers the resumption of excessive alcohol use and the reinstatement of the problem. Over time excessive alcohol use becomes an overlearned habit that may be performed with little conscious awareness or attention.

The cognitive-behavioural approach to the treatment of alcohol problems attempts to promote a sense of co-operation, openness, detachment and objectivity in the way clients manage their problems, encouraging them to take an active role in formulation and treatment planning and to progressively assume personal responsibility for the outcome of their treatment. The fundamental goals are: (a) to help the clients learn to recognise that their excessive drinking is something they do rather than an indication of someone they are; (b) to engender self-control and self-management.

In practice, cognitive-behavioural treatment incorporates a wide variety of interventions. The key areas of focus are:

- motivation for change;
- situational antecedents of excessive drinking, such as time of day, place, people, activities;
- internal states, such as anxiety, depression or other unpleasant emotions or painful sensations that may increase the likelihood of excessive drinking;
- cognitive processes, such as expectancies about the rewarding effects of alcohol and attributions infusing alcohol with the capacity to alter moods;
- the reinforcing consequences that serve to maintain the drinking behaviour at an excessive level;
- relapse prevention.

Empirical support for the efficacy of cognitive-behavioural therapy for alcohol use problems is robust (Hester & Miller, 1995; Nathan & Gorman, 1998). Some of the key cognitive-behavioural therapy interventions for alcohol problems will now be briefly reviewed.

Motivational interventions

Effective cognitive-behavioural treatment for alcohol problems requires that both clinician and client understand that individuals go through a series of predictable stages of change when trying to alter their drinking behaviour (Marlatt & Gordon, 1985). Cognitive-behavioural interventions should be relevant to the stage of change a client is experiencing in order to be maximally effective. It is thus paramount to assess on an ongoing basis the client's motivation at various phases of treatment (Baer et al., 1999). Techniques for enhancing motivation include: monitoring and discussing the discrepancy between actual and ideal drinking behaviour, empathic listening, eliciting self-motivating statements, and mutual goal setting and decision making. For a comprehensive review of motivational interventions see Miller and Heather (1998).

Behavioural interventions

A variety of behavioural interventions can be used in the treatment of alcohol problems. Aversive therapies (both in vivo and imaginal) are designed to moderate the reinforcing properties of alcohol by altering the valence of alcohol-related cues (from positive to negative) through counter-conditioning procedures. Cue exposure paired with response prevention is employed for tackling conditioned craving responses to alcohol-related antecedent stimuli (Drobes et al., 2001). Relaxation training (Monti et al., 1989) aims to foster general stress reduction through a variety of techniques including focusing on pleasant imagery, developing breathing skills and muscle relaxation. In addition to relaxation training, exercise has been shown to have similar stress-reducing properties.

Contingency management techniques help clients in restructuring their immediate environments in order to decrease the rewards and increase the costs associated with excessive alcohol use. The principles of contingency management are based on operant learning theory. Techniques include providing incentives for compliance with alcohol treatment as well as positive reinforcement for sobriety (from spouses or friends, for example). This approach is combined with punishment, in the form of withdrawal of attention and approval, contingent on the resumption of excessive alcohol use.

Clients with a history of heavy drinking are likely to be deficient in a variety of coping skills, ranging from rational thinking and problem solving to assertiveness and effective conflict resolution. A variety of behavioural interventions, such as communication and assertiveness training, creating and maintaining social support networks, vocational training, and learning how to pace or refuse drinks, can help to enhance coping and self-control.

Cognitive interventions

Cognitive interventions are aimed at helping the client to build an awareness of the link between internal emotional states, ways of thinking and alcohol use. These interventions primarily target those beliefs, attributions, expectations and metacognitions that are related to excessive alcohol use (Beck et al., 1993; Leigh & Stacy, 1993; Oei & Baldwin 1994; Spada & Wells, 2005, 2006a, 2006b). The client's characteristic appraisal of situations that pose a risk for excessive drinking is assessed (Lazarus et al., 1974; Sanchez-Craig et al. 1987). This is done through identifying cognitions regarding drinking and their relationship to the emotions and behavioural intentions which the client experiences. Once the information on the appraisal process is gathered, the client is taught to generate new, more effective appraisal strategies and to rehearse these strategies in both treatment and real life until mastery is achieved.

As noted previously, maintaining abstinence from alcohol or moderating drinking is dependent, amongst other things, on possessing a wide range of coping skills. Difficulties may arise, however, when the coping skills acquired do not generalise across novel settings and situations. In these instances the client will need to be equipped with a framework for generating novel coping strategies. Problem-solving training can provide this framework and give clients the flexibility and adaptability needed in those instances where specific coping skills may not work (D'Zurilla & Goldfried, 1971).

Relapse prevention

There is a variety of strategies that can be employed for relapse prevention. At the outset it is important to understand past relapses because these may provide important clues to future high-risk situations and deficits with coping skills. Going through a 'relapse fantasy' where the client imagines as vividly as possible what it would take to resume drinking can provide valuable information. For clients who are still drinking, self-monitoring will shed light on the situational contexts in which a relapse may occur and the immediate consequences of the behaviour. Coping skills training (e.g. Chaney et al., 1978), relapse rehearsal, challenging positive outcome expectancies, stimulus control techniques, analogue or assisted in vivo cue exposure, coping imagery, and craving cards are the key strategies used to help clients avoid relapse.

However, simply teaching clients to cope with one high-risk situation after another may not be enough to cement long-term behavioural change. In order to develop a wider ranging and successful programme of habit change it is also necessary to help clients attain a more balanced life style which will increase the overall capacity to cope with stress. This may include, for example, the introduction of regular exercise, novel pastimes, vocational training or new employment.

Overview of assessment

Once the client has agreed to enter treatment a thorough biopsychosocial assessment needs to be undertaken. This will focus on social and medical history, levels of alcohol dependence and consumption, alcohol-related problems, drinking behaviours, drinking-related cognitions, coping skills and deficits, comorbid problems and availability of social support.

Drinking assessment

This involves obtaining detailed information on current and historic levels of drinking as well as the client's perceptions of his or her current drinking. A variety of self-report measures can be used to assess the patterns and severity of the drinking problem. (The instruments described in this section comprise only a partial list of the many assessment instruments available. More information about these and other assessment techniques may be found at http://www.niaaa.gov/.) Two of the most useful measures are AUDIT and QFS.

The Alcohol Use Disorders Identification Test (AUDIT; Babor *et al.*, 1992) was developed as a screening tool by the World Health Organisation (WHO) for early identification of problem drinkers. AUDIT consists of ten questions regarding recent alcohol consumption, alcohol dependence symptoms and alcohol-related problems. Respondents are asked to choose one of five statements (per question) that most applies to their use of alcohol beverages over the past year. Responses are scored from 0 to 4 in the direction of problem drinking. The summary score for the total AUDIT ranges from 0, indicating no presence of problem drinking behaviour, to 40 indicating marked levels of problem drinking behaviour and alcohol dependence. The threshold for indicating drinking pathology is a score of 8.

The Quantity Frequency Scale (QFS; Cahalan *et al.*, 1969) is a measure of alcohol consumption levels, with items assessing the dimensions of quantity and frequency of alcohol beverages consumed over a period of 30 days. The QFS consists of three questions ('Have you been drinking any beer/wine/spirits over the last 30 days?'; 'About how often do you consume beer/wine/spirits?'; and 'About how much beer/wine/spirits did you drink on a typical day when you drink beer/wine/spirits?'). These are repeated for each of the major alcohol beverage categories (beer, wine and distilled spirits). The total scores from the different alcohol beverage categories are then added together and an estimated daily (or weekly) level of alcohol consumption can be computed.

Other key measures include the Comprehensive Drinking Profile, the Brief Drinking Profile and the Timeline Follow-back Method (Donovan & Marlatt, 1988; Sobell & Sobell, 1993).

Self-monitoring of drinking behaviour is an additional and fundamental assessment technique. The client is required to keep a record of the times when he or she is drinking, noting down how much is consumed, when, where and with whom. This is important for two reasons: (a) it will give the clinician a more tangible idea of the severity of the problem by providing continuous rather than snapshot information on drinking patterns; (b) it will give the client a better insight into their problem – the first step in learning how to manage it.

Motivation for change

The clinician must become aware of: (a) whether and why the client would consider it desirable to change his or her life style and pattern of alcohol use; (b) the client's drinking and other treatment goals; (c) the client's stage of change; (d) the degree to which the client perceives negative consequences of his or her current drinking pattern and potential consequences of change.

A variety of measures can be used to assess the client's stage of change and expectancies about alcohol use. Two key ones are:

- the Stages of Change and Treatment Eagerness Scale (SOCRATES; Miller *et al.*, 1995), which assesses recognition, ambivalence, and taking steps relative to the client's problem;
- the Alcohol Outcomes Expectancy Scale (AOES; Leigh & Stacy, 1993), which assesses the client's reasons for drinking, phrased in terms of expected positive and negative effects obtained by drinking.

Perception of negative and positive consequences of drinking can also be assessed through the clinical interview or through the development of a decisional balance sheet with the client (Marlatt & Gordon, 1985).

Other problem areas

At the early stage of assessment it is useful to establish the gravity of concomitant psychosocial and physical problems. This may be undertaken through unstructured interviews and the use of simple problem checklists or via formal interviewing techniques such as the Addiction Severity Index (ASI; McLellan *et al.*, 1992). The ASI is a widely used measure of client functioning across multiple domains (medical, psychological, family/social, legal and employment).

Partner assessment

It is important to assess how the client's partner is coping with the drinking as well as other aspects of the couple's relationship such as problems, satisfaction and shared drinking patterns.

Need for detoxification

If a client is physically dependent on alcohol, then he or she will experience alcohol withdrawal symptoms when decreasing or stopping drinking. A number of signs may suggest that the client may be physically dependent on alcohol. These include daily drinking, drinking regularly and intermittently throughout the day, and morning drinking. If a client reports awakening with fears, trembling or nausea these are also suggestive of dependence. Furthermore, cessation or substantial decrease in drinking will result in the appearance of minor withdrawal symptoms such as tremulousness, nausea, vomiting, irritability and temperature. Such symptoms usually begin within 5 to 12 hours. More severe withdrawal symptoms (such as seizures, delirium or hallucinations) may also occur, usually within 24 to 72 hours of the cessation of drinking.

If the client has stopped drinking within the last three days the clinician will need to enquire about and observe for signs of withdrawal. If the client is currently drinking the clinician must rely on drinking history, pattern, and the results of previous attempts to stop drinking to determine whether detoxification is necessary.

Cognitive-behavioural assessment

The foundation of cognitive-behavioural assessment is the functional analysis. This involves observing and measuring drinking behaviour and its consequences. Through this tool both client and clinician will develop a detailed understanding of the 'mechanics' of the alcohol problem in question: the most frequent and potent antecedents of drinking behaviour, the short-term positive consequences that serve to maintain it, and the long-term costs of continuing to drink. Emphasis is also placed on the role played by internal events (e.g. thoughts, images and expectancies) in determining the selection and meaning of drinking situations. A variety of tools such as the Daily Record of Cravings scale (Beck *et al.*, 1993), the Alcohol Outcome Expectancies questionnaire (Leigh & Stacey, 1993), the Positive Alcohol Metacognitions scale (Spada & Wells, 2006b) and the Negative Alcohol Metacognitions scale (Spada & Wells, 2006b), can help clinician and client to assess cognitive and metacognitive factors related to excessive alcohol use.

The case formulation approach in practice

In this section the University College London (UCL) case formulation approach to the understanding and treatment of a client's alcohol problem and depression is presented. The effectiveness of this method has been extensively demonstrated (Lane, 1990; Bruch & Bond, 1998).

Case study

Biographic details

Karl (pseudonym) was a single, 41-year-old man. His general practitioner referred him for alcohol counselling. He had been prescribed antidepressants

(Prozac 20mg per day), which he was regularly taking. Karl was born in Manchester and moved to London in his late teens. He lived alone and was not working. Several years prior to seeking treatment, when on holiday in Asia, he was knocked down by a truck and severely injured. As a result of this his face became lopsided and he developed chronic back pains. Prior to the accident Karl was a successful carpenter and owned his own business. Following the accident he found it difficult to find regular employment. He has an older sister and two younger brothers, one of which is reported to have an alcohol problem.

Presenting problems as stated by the client

The case formulation process began by asking the client to summarise, in his own words, the difficulties he was experiencing. He was encouraged to explain how he saw his problems, not how others (e.g. family, friends and professionals) perceived them. Specific problem statements were sought because they form the foundation upon which the client's goals of treatment are operationalised. Karl stated that his main problems were:

- *Problem 1: Depression* – Karl reported that he was feeling 'very down' and constantly 'tired'. He said that at best he was 'depressed' 60 per cent of the time, 'middling' 30 per cent of the time and 'euphoric' 10 per cent of the time. He reported that he felt 'useless', 'empty' and 'helpless' and had frequent thoughts such as 'what I attempt I will surely fail', 'there is so much to do . . . where do I start?', 'I feel like a parasite', 'I am ill'. He spent most of the day sleeping and had difficulties getting out of bed before lunchtime or early afternoon. He spent the remainder of the day watching television or lying around.
- *Problem 2: Drinking* – Karl reported that he binged three or four times per week. During each binge he consumed approximately 20 to 30 units of alcohol. He also stated that his drinking was becoming less 'social' and more 'private'. He said he did not start drinking until late in the evening but felt that this pattern may be changing as he was starting to experience cravings during the day. He felt an urge to drink when he was feeling 'low', 'depressed' and 'nervous'.

Treatment goals as stated by the client

At this point the client was encouraged to outline what changes he may envisage.

- *Goal 1: Reduce depression.* Karl explained that he would like to feel 90 per cent of the time neither depressed nor elated and would want to return to feel as he did prior to the accident. He also stated that he would like to find a job or activity (e.g. vocational training) to fill his day as he believed that not working had a 'big negative impact' on his mood.

- *Goal 2: Reduce drinking.* Karl stated he would like to significantly reduce his alcohol consumption to 'social drinking' levels. He thought that 30 to 40 units per week would be ideal.

Functional analysis of the individual problems

At this juncture, a functional analysis (Bruch & Bond, 1998) of the individual problems was carried out (see Figure 2.1). The aim of this stage is: (a) to isolate the stimuli that trigger the client's responses; (b) to analyse the modality of the responses; and (c) to identify the consequences that result from the responses. A quadripartite response system analysis is built into this design to allow the study of individual response modalities in a methodical manner. This is particularly useful in order to identify dominant response modes which may act as a stimulus for another set of problem responses. Understanding such sequences is of pivotal importance in providing clues for the design of an effective treatment programme. The assessment of consequences is designed to shed light on the operant maintaining factors of the problem responses that are being investigated. It is important to identify whether there are conflicting short-term versus long-term consequences as maladaptive self-regulation is usually present when immediate gratification is preferred to long-term benefits.

Based on Karl's account of his difficulties, it appeared that depression was typically triggered by two sets of different stimuli. For reasons of clarity two distinct functional analyses were presented: the first (Table 2.1) depression as a response to environmental and cognitive stimuli; the second (Table 2.2) depression as a response to physiological and behavioural stimuli.

At this stage, the 'circularity' of the client's problems started to become apparent. From the first two functional analyses it was evident that depression arose as a response to a variety of environmental, cognitive, physiological and behavioural cues, and that in turn it acted as a stimulus for drinking (this was termed 'Type 1 drinking'). Depression could thus be

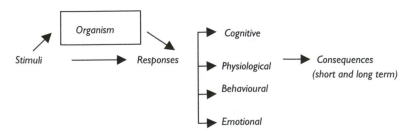

Figure 2.1 Components of a functional analysis.

Table 2.1 Functional analysis of depression as a response to environmental and cognitive stimuli

Component	Stimuli	Primary responses	Secondary responses
Environmental	Being at home, watching TV, talking to strangers at the pub.		
Cognitive	'My flat looks shabby and dirty.' 'If only I could work my life would be better.' 'I am a parasite.'	'My situation will never change.' 'What I attempt I will surely fail.'	'I will feel better after a drink.' 'I will relax after a drink.' 'Let's forget about it and have a drink.'
Physiological			
Behavioural		Staying in bed, watching TV, laying around doing nothing.	**Type 1 drinking.**
Emotional		Low mood and irritability (i.e. **depression**).	

Maintaining consequences	Problem consequences
Temporary reduction in depressive symptoms.	Increase in depressive symptoms.
Socialising.	Problem drinking.

Note. Primary responses can also be interpreted as stimuli for secondary responses. Thus primary responses can be seen as the 'dominant' responses.

conceptualised as the dominant response mode or the 'mediator' between the initial cues and Type 1 drinking. The latter was employed as a short-term strategy for regulating depressive symptomatology. In the long term it exacerbated negative affect and brought further increases in alcohol use.

The third functional analysis (Table 2.3) served to separate drinking that was a response to the underlying depressive symptomatology (functional analyses 1 and 2) which was termed Type 1 drinking, from drinking that was a response to the problem consequences of drinking itself (hangover, alcohol craving, low mood and irritability) which was defined as 'Type 2 drinking'. It appeared useful to break down drinking behaviour in these two typologies because it would help Karl see how all behaviours, emanating from the original depression cues, were interlinked.

Figure 2.2 presents a preliminary model of the cause and maintenance of the client's presenting problems derived from integrating the different functional analyses.

Table 2.2 Functional analysis of depression as a response to physiological and behavioural stimuli

Component	Stimuli	Primary responses	Secondary responses
Environmental			
Cognitive		'My situation will never change.' 'What has happened to me?'	'I will forget how I look after a drink.' 'I will relax after a drink.' 'My pains will go after a drink.'
Physiological	Back pains.		
Behavioural	Looking at facial disfigurement.	Staying in bed, watching TV, laying around doing nothing.	**Type I drinking.**
Emotional		Low mood and irritability (i.e. **depression**).	

Maintaining consequences	Problem consequences
Temporary reduction in depressive symptoms.	Increase in depressive symptoms.
Socialising.	Problem drinking.

Note. Primary responses can also be interpreted as stimuli for secondary responses. Thus primary responses can be seen as the 'dominant' responses.

Historical development of the presenting problems

This stage is aimed at understanding the circumstances and conditions in which the problems started and their 'evolution' to present date.

Karl stated that he had always had ups and downs in mood, but he did not remember feeling depressed for any significant period of time prior to a road traffic accident he suffered 14 years previously when on holiday in Asia. As a consequence of this accident he developed chronic back pain and his face was lopsided. Karl reported that the back pain he experienced had prevented him from returning to his original line of work (carpentry). He had also twice attempted to get a permanent job on building sites but was dismissed on the grounds that he was not 'quick enough' and 'fit enough' for the jobs. Karl recalled that at this point he began experiencing 'lots of disturbing thoughts' regarding his lost physical abilities, the disfigurement that resulted from the accident and his general inadequacy at coping with life. His energy levels began to drop and he found himself spending an increasing amount of time sleeping, lying in bed and watching television. At this stage Karl also started

Table 2.3 Functional analysis of Type 2 drinking as a response to the problem consequences of Type 1 drinking

Component	Stimuli (problem consequences of Type 1 drinking)	Responses
Environmental		
Cognitive	'I am a wanker.' 'I am nothing other than my drinking.' 'I am a parasite.' 'I spend all my money on drink.'	'I will feel better after a drink.' 'I will relax after a drink.' 'Let's forget about it and have a drink.'
Physiological	Hangover. Alcohol craving.	
Behavioural	Waking up after a binge the previous day.	**Type 2 drinking.**
Emotional	Very low mood and irritability.	

Maintaining consequences	Problem consequences
Reduction of Type 1 drinking symptoms.	Increase in depressive symptoms. Escalation of problem drinking into alcohol dependence.

drinking in the region of 50–60 units per week, 'peaking' after two years at over 120 units per week. He decided at that point to seek counselling. He received individual counselling for a period of nine months, and this proved to be a useful experience. For the subsequent eight years Karl's alcohol consumption levels decreased steadily and he was abstinent for two years. This period of reduced drinking/abstinence coincided with a marked improvement in mood. He went back into education and successfully passed an A level and a university access course. He then started university (on a full-time undergraduate degree course in history) but dropped out after the first term because he experienced the workload as 'too demanding'. He immediately reattempted to return to manual work but found it too physically taxing. As a consequence of these experiences he started feeling 'very down' and 'depressed' again. The heavy drinking resumed (with the situation worsening until present). He was referred for alcohol counselling by his general practitioner.

It is important to note that prior to the accident drinking did not appear to have been a problem for Karl (though bingeing episodes were not uncommon). From the age of 15 onwards his alcohol consumption levels varied but overall remained well below the 21 units per week threshold. During the 'critical' age of excess drinking (18 to 25 years of age) he was mostly abstinent (these periods lasted for up to three or four months).

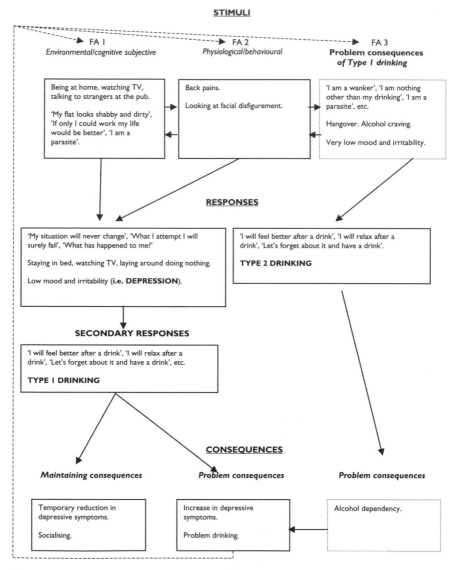

Figure 2.2 An idiosyncratic model of the interaction between depression and problem drinking.

Problem formulation

Information from the preceding sections is brought together in the problem formulation. This is a clinical theory that: (a) relates all the client's complaints to one another; (b) explains why the client developed these problems; and (c) provides predictions concerning the client's behaviour given any stimulus conditions. The integrated model of the cause and maintenance of the client's problems is shared with the client and amended accordingly.

Prior to the road traffic accident Karl appeared to be functioning adaptively. He did not drink excessively nor did he remember displaying any depressive symptomatology. Following the accident he lost the 'physical fitness' needed to perform successfully his trade as a carpenter. After attempting to return to work, and being dismissed for being unable to meet standards, he started experiencing powerful feelings of inadequacy and helplessness. These were dealt with by drinking alcohol. The latter initially provided negative reinforcement through the reduction of depressive symptomatology. Karl learned that, at least as a short-term coping strategy, his depressive symptoms could be curbed by drinking alcohol. As a longer term consequence he developed problematic drinking behaviour which further worsened the underlying depressive symptomatology. Seeing a counsellor helped Karl to improve and rebuild confidence, resulting in a significant period of abstinence and improved mood. However, the recent abortive attempt at returning to manual work, coupled with dropping out of university, reactivated powerful feelings of inadequacy and helplessness. These in turn triggered a relapse in alcohol use as a maladaptive means for regulating negative affect. The self-perpetuating cycle had started again.

The problem formulation was presented to Karl. It was also explained to him that it was a working hypothesis which needed to be tested out in order to prove its validity. Karl thought that it 'accurately' reflected the 'intuitive understanding' he had about the nature of his problems.

Collaborative definition of treatment goals

Following the outlining of the problem formulation the treatment goals were agreed with the client.

- *Goal 1: Reduction in depression*

    (a) To find a job or activity (e.g. vocational training).
    (b) To learn to challenge negative thoughts.
    (c) To get fitter so as to reduce back pains.

- *Goal 2: Reduction in alcohol consumption*

    (a) To reduce alcohol consumption to a maximum of 40 units per week.

Development of the treatment programme

In this phase, consistent with the problem formulation and treatment goals, the rationale for treatment and components of the treatment programme were presented to the client.

From the information gathered it appeared that Karl had managed to drink moderately or be abstinent for long stretches of time over the past 14 years despite significant life setbacks. This demonstrated that he possessed, to a degree, effective coping skills. It was thus hypothesised that treatment should primarily tackle depression rather than problematic drinking, since the former appeared to be the main trigger of the client's problem 'concatenation'. This line of reasoning was supported by the observation of current drinking patterns, which were heavy but irregular (i.e. bingeing), thus providing windows of opportunity for developing alternative inhibitory behaviours for dealing with negative affect. If Karl's drinking had been continuous (i.e. daily), targeting it first may have played a more central role in the treatment programme.

STAGE 1: TREATMENT OF DEPRESSION

To begin with behavioural strategies would be employed (Hawton *et al.*, 1989). These would focus primarily on monitoring activities and introducing graded mood-enhancing tasks.

In the second phase of treatment cognitive strategies (e.g. learning to identify and restructure negative automatic thoughts, Socratic dialogue, verbal reattribution exercises and challenging dysfunctional assumptions) would be introduced to help the client restructure maladaptive cognitions (Hawton *et al.*, 1989).

As the final part of treatment, relapse prevention strategies would be employed. These would include reviewing the functional analysis of depression, re-running through the problem formulation and practising adaptive responses to depressogenic scenarios.

STAGE 2: TREATMENT OF PROBLEM DRINKING

This phase of treatment would begin by asking the client to self-monitor his drinking behaviour. In the first few sessions the negative physical and psychological effects of problem drinking would be illustrated. Subsequently Karl would be informally solicited to list the advantages and disadvantages of drinking alcohol.

During this initial phase it would be important to focus on the therapeutic relationship and facilitate the gradual emergence of motivation to change. It would be anticipated that the benefits of the interventions for depression would filter through and affect mood to such an extent that Karl would realise that further improvements in mood could be attained if he were to reduce or stop drinking.

If Karl were to stop or reduce drinking, relapse prevention strategies would be introduced. These would include re-listing the advantages and disadvantages of drinking, assessing if and how life had improved without drinking, looking at the interlink between depression and problem drinking, and challenging alcohol-related beliefs. In addition strategies for talking lapses would be reviewed (e.g. putting the lapse in context, focusing on what has been achieved, changing alcohol violation beliefs, etc.).

Measures

A variety of measures were employed to monitor change. These would initially allow for the assessment of the gravity of each problem, and help the client shift to a self-monitoring mode. During the treatment phase the measures would help to determine whether the changes were pointing in the right direction.

The Beck Depression Inventory (BDI; Beck *et al.*, 1961) and a weekly activity schedule (Young *et al.*, 2001) were used to monitor changes in depression. The Quantity Frequency Scale (QFS; Cahalan *et al.*, 1969) and a drinking diary were used to monitor changes in alcohol use.

Course of treatment

This section briefly explains the course of treatment to provide a picture of the progress and pitfalls of this case.

ASSESSMENT, PROBLEM FORMULATION AND OUTLINE OF TREATMENT PROGRAMME (SESSIONS 1–4)

During the first four sessions we progressed swiftly through the various stages of assessment, problem formulation and delineation of the treatment programme. The client appeared motivated to engage in treatment and had a natural understanding and affinity with the CBT rationale. Prior to starting treatment he had managed to be abstinent for three weeks. During the course of these initial sessions Karl started drinking again (bingeing on average three times per week and consuming approximately 20 units of alcohol per binge). This was expected to a certain extent, as we had been exploring a variety of topics (e.g. the accident, failures at work, dropping out of university) that were very distressing. This distress was, in turn, being dealt with through drinking.

TREATMENT (SESSIONS 5–10)

During these sessions Karl was encouraged to start monitoring his activities (weekly activity schedule and drinking diary) and look at mood-elevating tasks he may want to engage in. He filled his weekly activity schedule and drinking diary consistently and agreed to write a list of 'things to do with his time'. In this list he emphasised the desire to find a job or retrain in a new field (i.e. not manual work). He wanted to do something that made him feel as though he was using his time constructively. He said that he had always been interested in IT and thought that training/working in this field could be challenging and rewarding. Amongst his weekly tasks we decided to make it a priority to contact any organisation that offered basic training in this area. Karl discovered that Mind (a mental health organisation) was offering a two-hour per week introductory course for the duration of ten weeks. After the end of this course he would be able to progress to more advanced and specialised training which would give him the opportunity to work (albeit voluntarily) in IT. He was also aware that he needed to purchase a computer and get a phone line in order to be able to do the work and added these tasks to his weekly list.

Karl began the IT course at Mind and felt very motivated. He also had several career assessment interviews to identify what career he would like to retrain in. These supported his view that IT was an appropriate choice irrespective of his age. Towards session eight we began spending some time discussing the harmful physical and psychological aspects of problematic drinking. We also listed (using a board) the advantages and disadvantages of drinking alcohol.

During this same period Karl started appreciating that engaging in behavioural tasks was starting to impact on some of his negative cognitions and make him feel 'increasingly positive about the future'. One week he reported he had not felt depressed at all and had been 'too busy' most days to 'think of feeling down'. By the end of the tenth session he spontaneously concluded that he had to stop drinking if he was 'to get a life back'. During this phase Karl continued to binge, consuming between 30 and 80 units of alcohol per week.

TREATMENT (SESSIONS 11–15)

During the course of the eleventh week Karl managed to be abstinent for five consecutive days and then went on a binge which lasted two days (he consumed 60 units). He felt very bad about this, especially because it resulted in him missing his IT class and not completing any homework (i.e. weekly activity schedule and weekly tasks exercise). He did not fill the weekly activity schedule because 'nothing happened' and did not manage to buy the computer and get a phone line (some of his original targets). We spent most of the session putting in context his 'lapse' by looking at all of what he had achieved to date. We went again through the functional analyses and problem formulation. This helped Karl to realise that he had actually done quite a lot of work over the course of the previous sessions and that even if he did have a bad week the 'trend' was towards significant improvement. It is at this point that Karl reached the conclusion that he would have to remain abstinent if he was to 'really improve'.

Karl decided to target abstinence as part of his weekly tasks (he actually wrote it on the list of weekly tasks). The following week he achieved most of the tasks set (computer purchase, telephone line, meeting with doctor, IT training, etc.) and discussed how he saw his problem as 'contextual'. By contextual he meant that it was partly rooted in his social environment (drinking partners that play a significant role in the maintenance of the problem) and that he needed to exercise some control over it if he was to achieve his target of not drinking. We therefore agreed as a target to drink only non-alcoholic drinks if he went out socially so as to test whether his negative cognitions regarding 'being boring if not drunk' were founded. We practised drinking refusal skills and introduced cognitive restructuring exercises aimed at tackling urges and cravings.

Over the course of the following three sessions Karl remained abstinent. He reported feeling 'very well' most of the time. He also completed his homework assignments and found that he actually got bored rather than felt boring when he went out with his drinking pals. We discussed the possibility of looking at cognitive rather than exclusively behavioural strategies for dealing with low mood.

TREATMENT (SESSIONS 16–20)

Karl remained abstinent during the course of the following sessions. He said he had not felt as good for a long time and that he was concerned about 'coping' with potential 'lows' or 'obstacles' as well as his own irrational, maladaptive and obsolete thoughts. At this stage two cognitive strategies aimed at identifying and questioning negative cognitions were introduced: daily records of dysfunctional thoughts and Socratic dialogue exercises. In doing so it was hoped that Karl would learn to find counter-evidence for his negative cognitions and spot errors in logic.

At this juncture Karl started considering the possibility of ceasing to take Prozac. His mood was much improved and he said that he was considering the option of returning to university, on a part-time basis, to study IT. He said he wanted to think of a strategy that would allow him to gain financial independence within three or four years. He reported he was now very aware of the 'destructive power' of alcohol in his life and firmly believed he would have to be abstinent for a substantial amount of time if he were to return to lead a 'constructive' life. As a further behavioural task he decided to start swimming and do t'ai chi once a week.

TREATMENT (SESSIONS 21–27)

Karl's abstinence continued throughout the course of the last seven sessions. He managed to pass a further examination in IT. His mood was variable but he had accepted that it was not 'fixed' and that alcohol was 'definitely not a good solution' for regulating it.

We started looking at preventative strategies by focusing again on the functional analyses of the presenting problems and reviewing adaptive versus maladaptive responses to given stimuli. We also took some time to look at core dysfunctional beliefs, alcohol-related beliefs as well as coping strategies for potential lapses.

Outcome of treatment

Earlier it had been hypothesised that treatment should primarily tackle depression rather than problematic drinking because the former appeared to be the main trigger of the client's problem 'concatenation'. In addition, because the client's drinking pattern was heavy but irregular (i.e. bingeing), windows of opportunity for developing alternative inhibitory behaviours for dealing with negative affect would be available. The data at hand (see Figure 2.3) supports the hypothesis in that a marked improvement in depressive symptomatology was followed by a reduction in problematic drinking.

Weekly activity schedules at the beginning of treatment showed that though pleasure ratings were on average high (roughly 6/10), 25 per cent of them (10/39) were under the 5 threshold. In addition Karl spent most of the day sleeping (50 per cent). Towards the end of treatment Karl gained an extra 25 hours of 'awake time' in the week (sleeping only 5 per cent of the day). His pleasure ratings rose to an average of 7/10, with all but one score at or above 5. These results indicate a significant change in behavioural patterns, supporting the BDI data.

According to the BDI score and the weekly activity schedules, depressive

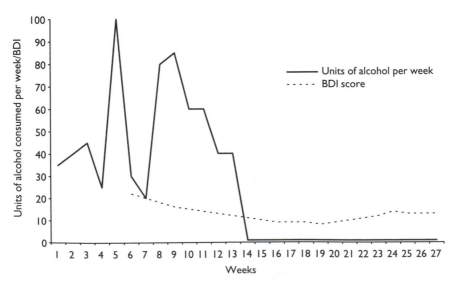

Figure 2.3 Treatment outcome measures.

symptoms had already been in remission (for about two months) by the time the client spontaneously decided to become abstinent. Though there was a 'hike' in the BDI score (weeks 23–26) the client did not resume drinking. By then he had: (a) learned that alcohol would not work as a coping strategy for his depressive symptomatology; and (b) developed a variety of alternative responses to deal with negative affect.

Conclusion

The provision of treatment to people with alcohol problems is a multifaceted process. This chapter has sought to provide an overview of the cognitive-behavioural approach to the assessment and treatment of alcohol problems, and to introduce the UCL case formulation procedure as applied to a client presenting with depression and alcohol problems. It goes without saying that human behaviour is extremely complex and that any psychological approach or model will have a plurality of limitations in explaining and predicting specific behaviours. Nevertheless the case formulation approach provides a unique methodology for helping the clinician make sense of the complexities of clinical reality, allowing for a coherent and tailor-made choice of treatment modality and intervention sequence.

References

Babor, T. F., de la Fuente, J. R., Saunders, J., & Grant, M. (1992). *The Alcohol Use Disorders Identification Test: Guidelines for use in primary healthcare*. Geneva: World Health Organisation.

Baer, J. S., Kivlahan, R., & Donovan, D. M. (1999). Integrating skills training and motivational therapies: Implications for the treatment of substance dependence. *Journal of Substance Abuse Treatment, 17*, 1–2, 15–24.

Beck, A. T., Ward, C. H., Mendelson, M., Mock, J., & Erbaugh, J. (1961). An inventory for measuring depression. *Archives of General Psychiatry 4*, 561–571.

Beck, A. T., Wright, F.D., Newman, C. F. & Liese, B. S. (1993). *Cognitive therapy of substance abuse*. New York: Guildford Press.

Bruch, M. H., & Bond, F. W. (Eds.). (1998). *Beyond diagnosis: Case formulation approaches in CBT*. Chichester: Wiley.

Cahalan, D., Cisin, I., & Crossley, H. (1969). *American drinking practices: A national survey of drinking behaviours and attitudes*. New Brunswick, NJ: Rutgers Centre for Alcohol Studies.

Chaney, E. F., O'Leary, M. R., & Marlatt, G. A. (1978). Skills training with alcoholics. *Journal of Consulting and Clinical Psychology, 46*, 1092–1104.

Donovan, D. M., & Marlatt, C. A. (1988). *Assessment of addictive behaviors*. New York: Guilford Press.

Drobes, D. J., Saladin, M. E., & Tiffany, S. T. (2001). Classical conditioning mechanisms in alcohol dependence. In N. Heather. T. J. Peters, & T. Stockwell (Eds.), *International handbook of alcohol dependence and problems* (pp. 257–280). Chichester: Wiley.

D'Zurilla, T. J., & Goldfried, M. R. (1971). Problem solving and behavior modification. *Journal of Abnormal Psychology, 78*, 107–126.

Edwards, G., & Gross, M. M. (1976). Alcohol dependence: Provisional description of a clinical syndrome. *British Medical Journal, 1*, 1058–1061.

Gorman, D. M. (2001). Developmental processes. In N. Heather. T. J. Peters, & T. Stockwell (Eds.), *International handbook of alcohol dependence and problems* (pp. 339–356). Chichester: Wiley.

Graham, H. L., Maslin, J., Copello, A., Birchwood, M., Mueser, K., McGovern, D., & Georgiou, G. (2001). Drug and alcohol problems amongst individuals with severe mental health problems in an inner city area of the UK. *Social Psychiatry and Psychiatric Epidemiology, 36*, 448–455.

Hawton, K., Salkovskis, P. M., Kirk, J., & Clark, D. M. (1989). *Cognitive behaviour therapy for psychiatric problems*. Oxford: Oxford University Press.

Helzer, J. E., & Pryzbeck, T. R. (1988). The co-occurrence of alcoholism with other psychiatric disorders in the general population and its impact on treatment. *Journal of Studies on Alcohol, 49*, 3, 219–224.

Hester, R. K., & Miller, W. R. (1995). *Handbook of alcoholism treatment approaches: Effective alternatives*. Needham Heights: Allyn & Bacon.

Kushner, M. G., Sher, K. J., & Beitman, B. D. (1990). The relation between alcohol problems and anxiety disorders. *American Journal of Psychiatry, 147*, 6, 685–695.

Lane, D. (1990). *The impossible child*. Stoke on Trent: Trentham.

Lazarus, R. S., Averill, J. R., & Opton, E. M. (1974). The psychology of coping: Issues of research and assessment. In G. V. Coelbo, D. A. Hamburg, & J. E. Adams (Eds.), *Coping and adaptation* (pp. 131–162). New York: Basic Books.

Leigh, B.C., & Stacy, A.W. (1993). Alcohol outcome expectancies: Scale construction and predictive utility in higher order confirmatory models. *Psychological Assessment, 5*, 216–229.

McLellan, A. T., Kashner, H., Metzeger, D., Peters, R., Smith, I., Grissom, G., Pettinati, H., & Argeriou, M. (1992). The fifth edition of the Addiction Severity Index. *Journal of Substance Abuse Treatment, 9*, 199–213.

Marlatt, G. A., & Gordon, J. R. (Eds.). (1985). *Relapse prevention: Maintenance strategies in the treatment of addictive behaviors*. New York: Guilford Press.

Miller, W. R. & Heather, N. (1998). *Treating addictive behaviors: Processes of change*. New York: Plenum Press.

Miller, W. R., Tonigan, J. S., & Longabaugh, R. (1995). *The Drinker Inventory of Consequences: An instrument for assessing adverse consequences of alcohol abuse*. Rockville, MD: National Institute on Alcohol Abuse and Alcoholism.

Monti, P. M., Abrams, D. B., Kadden, R. M., & Cooney, N. L. (1989). *Treating alcohol dependence: A coping skills training guide*. New York: Guilford Press.

Nathan, P. E., & Gorman. I. M. (1998). *A guide to treatments that work*. New York: Oxford University Press.

Oei, T. P. S., & Baldwin, A.R. (1994). Expectancy theory: A two-process model of alcohol use and abuse. *Journal for the Studies of Alcohol, 55*, 525–534.

Sanchez-Craig, M., Wilkinson, D. A., & Walker, K. (1987). Theory and methods for secondary prevention of alcohol problems: A cognitively based approach. In W. M. Cox (Eds.), *Treatment and prevention of alcohol problems* (pp. 287–331). Orlando, FL: Academic Press.

Sobell, M. B., & Sobell. L. C. (1993). *Problem drinkers: Guided self-change treatment*. New York: Guilford Press.

Spada, M. M., & Wells, A. (2005). Metacognitions, emotion and alcohol use. *Clinical Psychology and Psychotherapy*, *12*, 2, 150–155.

Spada, M. M., & Wells, A. (2006a). Metacognitions about alcohol use in problem drinkers. *Clinical Psychology and Psychotherapy, 13, 2*, 138–143.

Spada, M. M., & Wells, A. (2006b). Metacognitive beliefs about alcohol use: Development and preliminary validation of two self-report scales. Manuscript submitted for publication.

Stewart, S. H. (1996). Alcohol abuse in individuals exposed to trauma: A critical review. *Psychological Bulletin, 120*, 83–112.

Wilson, G. T. (1988). Alcohol and anxiety. *Behavioural Research and Therapy 26*, 5, 369–381.

World Health Organisation (WHO) (2002). *World health report 2002: Reducing risks, promoting healthy life*. Geneva: WHO.

Young, J. E., Weinberger, A. D., & Beck, A. T. (2001). Cognitive therapy for depression. In D. H. Barlow (Ed.), *Clinical handbook of psychological disorders* (pp. 264–308). New York: Guilford Press.

Chapter 3

Obesity

*Donald A. Williamson, Robert L. Newton, Jr. and
Heather M. Walden*

Introduction

Definition of obesity

Obesity refers to excess body fat or excessive body mass for stature (Bray *et al.*, 1998). The best definition of obesity has been a subject of intense study. Excess fatness (or adiposity) in the abdomen is most strongly associated with increased health risks (Bray *et al.*, 1998). The most widely accepted method for defining obesity uses body mass index (BMI), which is the body weight in kilograms divided by the square of the height in meters (kg/m^2). Table 3.1 summarizes the most commonly used definitions of obesity, using BMI; these values are a modification of those used by the World Health Organization (Bray *et al.*, 1998).

Measurement of obesity

Many methods have been developed for estimating adiposity. These include the measurement of height and weight, with conversion to BMI. This widely used approach is easily applied and is the most common metric that is used in the modern scientific literature pertaining to obesity. Use of the body mass index is flawed because it does not directly measure fatness or take into consideration body build or shape. More accurate estimates of body fatness

Table 3.1 Modified WHO classification of overweight and obesity

	BMI
Normal range	18.50–24.99
Grade I overweight	25.00–29.99
Grade IIa overweight	30.00–34.99
Grade IIb overweight	35.00–39.99
Grade III overweight	≥ 40.00

Source: Bray; Bouchard and James (1998).

that are relatively inexpensive and easily applied are skinfold thickness measures, body circumference measures, and body impedance analysis (Heymsfield
et al., 2002). These methods are not as accurate as the current "gold standard"
which is called dual energy X-ray absorptiometry (DEXA), which replaced
hydrodensitometry (or underwater weighing) as the most accurate estimate of
total or regional body fat. Imaging methods such as magnetic resonance
imaging and computed tomography are two additional methods that can be
used for body composition assessment at the tissue-system level (Heymsfield
et al., 2002). These latter methods are quite expensive and not generally
available to most clinicians.

Obesity epidemic

Over the past 30 years, epidemiologists have recognized a steady trend toward
increased prevalence of obesity in Europe, the United States, Asia, and the
Middle East (Seidell & Rissanen, 2002). While the baseline levels of overweight and obesity may differ across countries and regions, the rate of
increased prevalence appears to be quite similar. This observation has been
called the "obesity epidemic" (Surgeon General's Report, 2001). In the United
States, 64.5 per cent of adults are overweight, 30.9 per cent are obese (Flegal
et al., 2002), and the prevalence of obesity has increased 7.6 per cent between
1994 and 2000. Furthermore, the problem is especially prevalent in minority
populations where almost three-quarters of African-American and Hispanic
women are overweight or obese (Flegal *et al.*, 2002). There is a general
conclusion that the obesity epidemic is caused by an "obesigenic" (Allison
et al., 1997) or toxic (Horgan & Brownell, 2002) environment that promotes
overeating and sedentary behavior. One implication of this conclusion is
that the solution to the epidemic will require behavioral and environmental
approaches that modify eating behavior and physical activity.

Impact of obesity on health and quality of life

Over the past 20 years, there has been a growing recognition that obesity
is associated with a diverse set of health problems, ranging from medical
symptoms such as hypertension to syndromes such as type 2 diabetes. Epidemiological research has found strong positive correlations between BMI
and the following health problems:

- cardiovascular disease
- type 2 diabetes
- cancers
- gallstones
- osteoarthritis
- benign prostatic hyperplasia (Field *et al.*, 2002).

Obesity is also correlated with overall lower quality of life, including lower vitality, greater fatigue, and disturbances of mood (Williamson & O'Neil, 2002). Therefore, the health and psychosocial consequences of obesity are considerable. Furthermore, the costs to society are also considerable. For example, in the USA the economic costs of obesity have been estimated to account for 7 per cent of all healthcare expenditures (Field *et al.*, 2002). Therefore the development of effective interventions for the treatment of obesity is viewed as a very significant priority from the public health perspective. The following sections describe the details of what has been learned about behavioral interventions for obesity over the past 30 years.

History of behavioral treatment of obesity

Research testing the efficacy of behavioral therapy for obesity was first introduced in 1967 with a study published by Richard B. Stuart. This study sample had eight participants, who remained in the treatment program for a period of 12 months. Weight loss averaged 17 kg, ranging from 12 kg to 21 kg. The treatment methods used by Stuart (1967) were: frequent visits during the first part of the program, modification of eating and exercise habits, and use of cognitive interventions. This study produced a "wave" of behavioral treatment programs and research in this area beginning in the early 1970s. Stuart's initial studies led him to publish a behavioral treatment manual, *Slim Chance in a Fat World* (Stuart & Davis, 1972).

Components of behavioral therapy for obesity emphasized during treatment have changed over the last few decades. As reported by Wing (2002), behavioral treatment programs used in the 1970s usually included minimally overweight individuals participating in treatment for approximately ten weeks. No specific goals for calorie intake or exercise were prescribed; instead participants were instructed to incorporate new habits into their eating routine. Treatment strategies included: (a) restricting eating to one location; (b) abstaining from other activities while eating; (c) monitoring situational and emotional cues related to eating. The average weight loss reported for these studies was approximately 4.5 kg. (Wing, 2002). More recent studies have included: self-monitoring, problem solving, stimulus control, preplanning of eating and exercise, and relapse prevention. Another important component added to current studies is the prescription of specific goals for both calories and exercise.

Jeffery *et al.* (2000) reported that from 1974 to 1994 not only did the duration of treatment double, but the average weight loss reported had also doubled. Perri (1998) reviewed research done before the late 1990s and concluded that greater weight loss was achieved when participants were in treatment for an extended period of time. As noted by Williamson and Perrin (1996), previously attempted behavioral programs produce good results for mildly obese persons, but not for moderately or seriously obese persons.

Theory of behavioral treatment for obesity

The general principle underlying behavior therapy of obesity is that obese patients have learned eating and exercise patterns that are contributing to weight gain and/or maintenance of obesity. Consequently, these behaviors can be unlearned and the patient's behaviors can be modified in order to produce weight loss. Ultimately, behavioral treatment of obesity seeks to alter the environment, since environmental reinforcement contingencies shape behavior.

Classical conditioning is one of the learning theories applied to treatment. According to the theory, a neutral stimulus (e.g. reading) is repeatedly paired with a stimulus (e.g. hunger) followed by eating that normally elicits a response (e.g. salivation). After repeated associations, reading will begin to elicit the salivation/hunger response. Just as this behavior is learned, it can be unlearned by breaking the association. The other learning theory that is applicable to obesity is operant conditioning. According to this theory, behaviors such as eating or exercise are shaped by environmental reinforcement or punishment. Eating food is positively reinforced because it usually tastes good and it is negatively reinforced because it decreases feelings of hunger. On the contrary, physical activity can lead to muscle soreness, can be considered boring, and usually requires being removed from pleasurable experiences. Behavioral therapy is, in part, designed to alter the consequences of these behaviors.

According to behavioral theory, obesity results from caloric intake exceeding caloric expenditure (positive energy balance), and the excess calories produce weight gain because they are stored as fat. Eating is the primary source of caloric intake and spontaneous physical activity is a major source of energy expenditure. Therefore, they are the two targets of treatment. In addition, both are largely learned behaviors and thus are modifiable. Behavioral weight control therapies assume that other factors (i.e. biological, metabolic, and physiological) contribute to the development and maintenance of obesity. However, obesity fundamentally results from energy intake exceeding energy expenditure. Conversely, weight loss occurs from negative energy balance, i.e. energy expenditure exceeds energy intake.

Psychological and behavioral assessment of obesity

Psychological and behavioral assessments are used to design individualized treatment plans. This evaluation requires assessment of the patient's weight history, food intake, physical activity, and contributing psychosocial factors. Both interview and paper-and-pencil questionnaires can be used to obtain this information.

Weight history

A detailed weight history should describe weight changes and influences on these changes, from childhood to the present. The counselor should determine the initial onset of obesity, any substantial weight fluctuations, and the patient's highest and lowest adult weight. In addition, all weight loss efforts should be discussed in order to determine the types of treatments attempted (e.g. commercial weight loss programs, over the counter or prescribed medications). Large weight losses due to behavioral efforts are usually indicative of a good prognosis for success in the current treatment. Small weight losses may be the result of behavioral or biological factors (i.e. limited weight loss effort versus metabolic factors) and carries a poorer prognosis.

A family history will also help to shed light on the etiology of the patient's obesity. Parental obesity is highly correlated with offspring obesity. For example, only 8 per cent of children of normal weight parents are obese, whereas 40 per cent of children with one obese parent and 70 per cent of children with two obese parents become obese as adults (Wadden & Phelen, 2002).

Eating habits

Eating habits consist of the types of foods eaten, food preparation methods, and patterns of eating. By assessing the types of foods that are typically eaten, a counselor can determine the patient's average daily caloric intake and problem foods. When assessing caloric intake, it is important to remember that obese individuals typically underestimate their caloric intake anywhere from 30 per cent to 40 per cent (Lichtman et al., 1992). Food preparation methods are also important to assess because they can add substantially to caloric intake. It is important to understand if the participant has regular eating patterns, versus irregular eating patterns that may cause episodic intense hunger (e.g. skipping meals).

Physical activity

Assessment of the patient's level of physical activity will allow the counselor to determine the contribution of energy expenditure to the patient's weight status. There are four aspects of physical activity to be assessed: the type, duration, frequency, and intensity of the activity. Physical activity can take the form of programmed (exercise) or life style activity (i.e. using the stairs more frequently). Current and previous levels of activity should be assessed to determine the types of physical activity that the individual enjoys and that have contributed to weight loss in the past.

Psychosocial factors

Social support can help to directly shape the patient's environment to make behavior change more or less difficult. For example, other people can help cook low-fat meals and accompany the patient on exercise bouts, or sabotage changes in behavior. Though not universal, obese individuals experience many negative psychosocial outcomes, including decreased quality of life, lower self-esteem, body dissatisfaction, ridicule, discrimination, and prejudice (Williamson & O'Neil, 2002). Furthermore, patients often have unrealistic ideas concerning the outcomes of weight loss. Many patients expect to achieve an unrealistic "ideal" or normal weight status or anticipate that their social lives will improve substantially following weight loss.

Psychopathology

Mental health problems usually complicate obesity treatment. Binge eating and mood disorders are commonly seen in obese patients seeking treatment. Binge eating can make it difficult for participants to adhere to their caloric goals. Mood disorders can result in isolation (missing group meetings) and cognitive impairments (difficulty concentrating).

Questionnaires

There is a variety of measures to assess disordered eating patterns. The Eating Disorders Inventory-II (EDI-II; Garner, 1991), Bulimia Test-Revised (BULIT-R; Thelen et al., 1991), and the Eating Questionnaire Revised (EQ-R; Williamson et al., 1989) can be used to assess binge eating. One main value of the EDI-II in obesity assessment is that it measures bulimic behaviors and beliefs. Another test designed to measure the symptoms of bulimia is the BULIT-R (Thelen et al., 1991). The BULIT-R assesses the binge eating, loss of control, and purgative behaviors associated with bulimia. The EQ-R (Williamson et al., 1989) is a 15-item measure of the symptoms of bulimia based on DSM-III criteria. The concepts of binge eating, purgative habits, and loss of control over eating are assessed. More recently, the Weight Loss Behavior Scale (WLBS; Smith et al., 2000) was developed specifically for weight loss outcome research.

The two most commonly used semi-structured interviews are the Eating Disorder Examination (EDE; Cooper & Fairburn, 1987), and the Interview for Diagnosis of Eating Disorders, fourth version (IDED-IV; Kutlesic et al., 1998). Both interviews assess symptoms of eating disorders and binge eating.

Concerns related to body image can be assessed using the Body Shape Questionnaire (BSQ; Cooper et al., 1987). Williamson and colleagues developed the Body Image Assessment for Obesity (BIA-O; Williamson et al., 2000). The measure assesses body satisfaction using 18 silhouettes of women (or men) ranging from an emaciated figure to a severely obese figure. Satisfaction is calculated by subtracting the ideal from the current. More recently, a computerized body image assessment has been developed (Body Morph Assessment, BMA), and uses the same calculation for body dissatisfaction (Stewart *et al.*, 2001).

Psychopathology is typically measured using questionnaires such as the Beck Depression Inventory-II (BDI-II; Beck *et al.*, 1996), the State Trait Anxiety Inventory (STAI; Spielberger *et al.*, 1970), and the Symptom Checklist 90 (SCL-90; Derogatis, 1977). The most widely used measure of personality is the Minnesota Multiphasic Personality Inventory-II (MMPI-II; Butcher, 1990).

The Food Frequency Questionnaire (Block *et al.*, 1990) is a paper-and-pencil measure of typical diet composition. A 24-hour dietary recall can be used for the same purpose. This procedure requires a trained interviewer to assist the patient in recalling all food and drink consumed within the last 24 hours.

The Physical Activity Recall (PAR; Sallis *et al.*, 1985) is an interview-based recall of physical activity during the past week. Frequency, intensity, duration, and type of activity can be assessed and estimated energy expenditure can be derived. The Paffenbarger Physical Activity Questionnaire (PAQ; Paffenbarger *et al.*, 1978) provides a brief assessment of physical activity.

Behavioral treatment of obesity

As described previously, behavioral treatment of obesity is based on theories of learning. Principles from classical and operant conditioning are used to reshape the individual's environment, thereby making behavioral change increasingly likely. The primary targets for behavioral treatment typically include eating and exercise behavior. Treatment is designed to create a negative energy balance whereby caloric expenditure exceeds caloric intake. Common components of treatment are described below.

Nutrition education

Patients are educated concerning the nutritional aspects of weight loss. They are taught the caloric content of fat, protein, and carbohydrates per gram and are provided with a text that contains the caloric content of food. Participants are typically prescribed an overall calorie and fat goal. Typical treatments prescribe caloric goals between 1200 and 1800 kilocalories per day and a dietary fat goal between 20 per cent and 30 per cent.

Self-monitoring

Self-monitoring is the process in which the patient keeps a written record of their eating and exercise behaviors. It is designed to help the patient become more aware of their eating and exercise patterns and allows for feedback from the counselor. The self-monitoring form will allow the patient to record all foods eaten, the time, date, type of meal, the patient's emotional state, and calculate the caloric/ fat content of each meal. In monitoring exercise, the patient will record the type, frequency, duration, and the intensity of the activity.

Stimulus control

Stimulus control is designed to alter the environmental antecedents that control behavior. In the case of weight loss, the technique is designed to change the environment from one that supports weight gain behaviors to one that does not, by replacing cues that stimulate weight gain behaviors to ones that stimulate weight loss behaviors (Williamson & Perrin, 1996). Stimulus control techniques include eating the same meal at the same time each day, banishing problematic foods from the home, and placing exercise equipment in plain view.

Behavior contracting

Behavioral contracting is designed to set appropriate goals that will lead to weight loss. The process involves defining a goal, breaking the overall goal into small steps, and rewarding the participant for attaining each small goal.

Obtaining social support

Social support helps to directly shape the participant's immediate environment. For example, significant others can cook low-calorie meals or accompany participants on walks. Treatment is designed to teach patients skills to increase and/or obtain social support, including emotional support.

Meal planning

The main purpose of meal planning is to have patients eat regularly scheduled meals. Most meal plans will be structured so that the patient eats three meals per day, scheduled no more than three to five hours apart. This lessens the possibility of overeating by decreasing hunger and by preventing meals from being ambiguous. Meal planning allows the patient to pre-plan meals, which will help the patient to anticipate and overcome high-risk situations. Finally, the caloric content of meals can be calculated prior to consumption, which assists with adherence to overall caloric goals.

Meal replacements

Meal replacements (e.g. Slimfast, Optifast, Boost) assist in weight loss in a number of ways. They have a known caloric content, are low calorie, nutritionally balanced, do not require much preparation, are easy to purchase, are less expensive than the meal they replace, and do not put the patient around food that may stimulate eating. When prescribing meal replacements, it is normally suggested that two meals and one snack are replaced, per day. Meal replacements are typically used for a short period of time during active treatment, but use can be extended.

Physical activity

Exercise can assist in weight loss by preserving lean body mass during weight loss, decreasing appetite, improving self-efficacy for exercise, and/or by improving mood. Physical activity can be increased either through life style (e.g. using the stairs rather than the elevator, riding a bike to work versus taking a car) or programmed activity (e.g. health clubs). Most participants in weight loss programs are prescribed moderate intensity exercises (e.g. brisk walking). In addition, patients are allowed to exercise in one continuous bout, or in multiple bouts of at least ten minutes.

Maintenance strategies

The primary maintenance strategy is to extend the length of treatment. The purpose of extended treatment is to provide a longer period of time that the individual receives active treatment. Participants should stay in contact with a counselor (i.e. behavioral therapist, nutritionist), either through individual or group sessions. The increased length of contact should result in continuous use of weight loss strategies, and thus, weight maintenance.

Relapse prevention techniques, adapted from the work of Marlatt and Gordon (1985), have been incorporated into behavioral treatment. According to this theory, any individual attempting to change behavior will encounter a "high-risk situation" that threatens their current behavior change. An individual's ability to cope effectively with the situation decreases the likelihood of relapse through a greater sense of control and increased self-efficacy to cope. Relapse prevention techniques include identifying high-risk situations, setting up a warning system, building confidence, and reframing and countering negative thoughts.

Cognitive restructuring involves educating participants about the effect of negative and dysfunctional thoughts and how they can serve as cues for overeating and sedentary behavior. For example, a patient may skip a day of exercise and think "I've blown my exercise program, I knew I couldn't do it, I'll never lose weight!" Patients are taught how to identify and counter these negativistic thoughts. The primary benefit of countering these thoughts is that it will help participants to decrease self-defeating statements, feelings, and behaviors (Perri *et al.*, 1992).

Problem solving, as it applies to obesity (Williamson & Perrin, 1996), teaches patients to overcome problematic situations. Participants are taught a specific problem-solving method by which the patient defines the problem, generates solutions (brainstorming), evaluates the potential solutions, implements a solution, and then evaluates the outcome of the solution.

Empirical studies of behavioral treatment

Hundreds of studies have reported that the behavioral approach for weight management is more effective than various control conditions and that it yields average weight losses of about 5 per cent to 12 per cent of total body weight. Since the late 1980s, most studies have tested the efficacy of combining standard behavior therapy with other weight loss approaches. These studies tested the efficacy of behavioral treatment plus: (a) very low calorie diets; (b) meal replacements; (c) structured meal plans; (d) exercise; (e) pharmacotherapy, upon long-term weight loss and maintenance.

Behavioral treatment and very low calorie diets

Several studies were conducted in the late 1980s and early 1990s that combined very low calorie diets (VLCDs) with standard behavioral treatment. These diets typically ranged from 400–800 kcal/day. Wadden and Stunkard (1986) assessed the effectiveness of a combined program using VLCDs and behavior therapy vs. each of these alone. Weight losses for the group receiving the combined treatment (mean = 19.3 kg) were significantly greater than losses for the other two conditions (VLCD mean = 14.1 kg; behavior therapy mean = 14.3 kg). Similar results were found by other studies combining behavior therapy with VLCDs (Lindner & Blackburn, 1976; Wadden *et al.*, 1984).

Later studies investigating the effectiveness of VLCDs combined with behavioral therapy found no significant benefits of VLCDs when compared with a more balanced and less restrictive diet of 1000–1500 kcal/day (Wadden *et al.*, 1994; Wing *et al.*, 1994). In conclusion, VLCDs may indeed promote rapid initial weight loss, which will most likely result in rapid weight gain. A less restrictive diet will also produce weight loss, and may decrease the probability of rapid weight gain following treatment.

Behavioral therapy and the use of meal replacements

An alternative approach is the combination of behavioral therapy and meal replacements, i.e. pre-packaged meals and/or liquid meals designed to yield a

900 to 1100 kcal/day caloric intake. These programs are implemented to produce similar weight loss effects as those found in VLCDs, but avoid the need for medical supervision, which is necessary when using VLCDs.

Studies using the combination of behavioral therapy and meal replacements typically substitute two meals per day with a meal replacement and instruct participants to either consume a pre-packaged meal replacement for dinner or to eat a healthy meal within a specific calorie range. This method simplifies the dietary portion of the behavioral program and results in increased dietary adherence (Wadden *et al.*, 1997, 1998; Ditschuneit *et al.*, 1999).

Behavioral therapy and structured meal plans

Another method used to ensure a healthy, low-calorie diet is to provide participants with a structured meal plan, often including grocery lists or actually providing the participant with the food to be eaten, in appropriate serving sizes. The results of two studies suggest that those participants who were given food provisions did not lose more weight then those who were provided with meal plans, shopping lists, and recipes (Jeffery *et al.*, 1993; Wing *et al.*, 1996).

Behavioral therapy and exercise

Several studies have investigated the effects of behavioral therapy combined with exercise on weight loss. In a review of long-term weight loss in six studies containing a one-year or longer follow-up, Wing (1999) concluded that there was greater long-term weight loss in all six studies for groups receiving diet plus exercise treatment, although only two of these found significant differences.

Behavioral therapy and pharmacotherapy

A combination of behavioral treatment with pharmacotherapy generally yields greater weight loss than behavioral treatment alone (Phelan & Wadden, 2002). Two medications, sibutramine and orlistat, have been approved for long-term (two-year) treatment (Phelan & Wadden, 2002). Sibutramine, a weight loss medication currently approved by the FDA, affects the central nervous system by inhibiting the reuptake of both norepinephrine and serotonin. In their review of studies lasting one to two years, Phelan and Wadden (2002) concluded that sibutramine combined with behavioral therapy increased initial weight loss (~ 4kg greater than placebo), and also resulted in greater maintenance of weight loss than those administered placebo. Orlistat is an inhibitor of the digestion of lipases and therefore causes "wasting" of dietary fat that is consumed. Combined with behavioral treatment, orlistat can yield weight losses of about 7 per cent of total body weight (Phelan & Wadden, 2002).

Individualizing treatment

Though the previous section reports on the typical behavioral strategies that are used to treat obesity, all treatments have to be individualized to some degree. The type of treatment that the participant receives typically dictates the degree to which treatments can incorporate individual modifications. Group-based behavioral treatments allow for the least level of individual flexibility, whereas individual treatment with a professional provides the greatest level of individualized treatment. As with group-based treatment, these sessions will occur more frequently at the outset of treatment and more infrequently as treatment continues.

Individualization of treatment can occur at any one or all of the different treatment components. For example, some patients may have developed a habit of eating while watching television, and others may struggle more with emotional eating. Although group-based treatments include components to address both of these issues, stimulus-control techniques will be emphasized in the former case, while problem-solving and cognitive strategies will be emphasized in the latter. At a more complex level, some patients may be dealing with psychopathological issues while others may not. For example, many obese individuals are depressed and/or engage in binge eating. Patients with psychopathological issues may require medications, therapy, or a combination of the two, to specifically address the pathology prior to actual weight loss treatment. The case of Susan will help illustrate how comorbid psychopathology necessitates additional treatment beyond standard behavioral therapy for weight loss, and thus, how to individualize therapy based on patient need.

Case formulation

The case of Susan illustrates the relationship between case formulation and treatment design for weight management. Susan was a very severe case of obesity that was complicated by binge eating and depression.

Presenting problems

At the time of admission to the hospital-based research clinic for obesity, Susan weighed 125 kg (275 lb) at a height of 1.65 m (65 in), which converts to a body mass index of 45.8 and a classification of Grade III overweight (see Table 3.1). She was 25 years old, living alone, working at night delivering papers. She seldom left her home due to feelings of inadequacy and shame about her body size. She had been overweight as a child and adolescent. She had very limited support from her parents who were divorced and living in another region of the United States.

Psychological evaluation

Susan was interviewed for history, eating habits, weight management strategies, and eating disorder symptoms using the IDED-IV (Kutlesic *et al.*, 1998). This assessment found that Susan had a ten-year history of episodic binge eating at least once per day with only minimal efforts to counteract the weight gain caused by binge eating (e.g., by dieting or exercise). She denied ever using self-induced vomiting or laxative/diuretic abuse to control her weight. Psychological testing using the IDED-II (Garner, 1991), the BULIT-R (Thelen *et al.*, 1991), and the EQ-R (Williamson *et al.*, 1989) indicated that she met diagnostic criteria for binge eating disorder (Williamson & Martin, 1999), but did not meet criteria for bulimia nervosa, nonpurging type (American Psychiatric Association, 1994) because she did not report excessive exercise or extreme fasting as a means of compensating for the binge eating. Assessment of psychopathology using the BDI-II (Beck *et al.*, 1996) and the SCL-90 (Derogatis, 1977) indicated that she was clinically depressed and that she was socially anxious.

Case formulation

A functional analysis of binge eating, based upon interview and self-monitored eating behavior, suggested that the antecedent conditions for binge eating were: negative affect and/or dietary restriction. Susan tended to binge when she was upset and binge eating had the effect of making her feel less disturbed for a brief period of time, thus negatively reinforcing binge eating. She was significantly overweight and reported considerable dissatisfaction with body size and shape. In response to this body dissatisfaction, she was "always on a diet" which resulted in skipping meals and excess hunger in the early evening. She often engaged in eating binges in response to this hunger. Thus, binge eating was negatively reinforced by reduction of hunger. This case formulation led to a treatment plan that contained multiple components, including a standard protocol for behavioral treatment of obesity and more specific treatment for binge eating and depressed mood.

Treatment plan

Based upon this assessment, individual therapy with a clinician trained in the application of behavioral therapy for obesity was recommended. The standard treatment program followed the treatment manual developed by Williamson *et al.*, (1996). This program, called Lifestyle Change, provides a treatment protocol for a 52-week life style behavior modification program.

The initial phase of treatment requires meeting on a weekly outpatient basis for 12 consecutive weeks. During this phase, Susan learned to accurately self-monitor food intake and physical activity and to recognize the social and emotional cues that were associated with healthy eating, binge eating, healthy exercise, and inactivity. During therapy sessions, Susan learned to develop behavioral contracts to increase physical activity and to eat three healthy meals per day without binge eating. She was strongly encouraged to avoid skipping meals since this habit appeared to cause increased hunger and subsequent binge eating.

She was encouraged to initiate a trial of antidepressant medication beginning in the fourth week of treatment and she began taking fluoxetine, which had the effect of improved mood and decreased motivation to binge eat (Williamson & Martin, 1999). Treatment after week eight focused more directly on binge eating. The treatment program focused upon helping her develop alternative responses to negative mood states, including increased physical activity, relaxation training, and assertiveness to resolve interpersonal conflict. After week 12 until week 36, the frequency of therapy was reduced to once every other week. From week 36 to week 52 she was seen only once per month. During this final phase of treatment, the focus shifted to the development of social support and relapse prevention.

Treatment outcome

Over the course of the 52-week treatment program, Susan lost a total of 28 kg (61.6 lb) or 22.4 per cent of her total body weight. She was still overweight, as indicated by a BMI of about 35, but was now classified as Grade IIb Overweight (see Table 3.1). Binge eating was significantly improved. Before treatment, binge eating occurred approximately five times per week. After one year of behavioral and pharmacological therapy, binge eating occurred less than once per month, on average. Also, she was no longer clinically depressed and her overall health and quality of life was much improved. She was followed over the next four years with quarterly (every three months) visits and though her weight fluctuated, she never regained a significant amount of weight for a lengthy period. Furthermore, binge eating was never a clinically significant problem. She continued to eat a healthy diet and improved physical fitness. She eventually married and now has two children.

Treatment rationale

Susan's weight loss treatment was individualized based on the diagnoses of depression and binge eating. Susan's depression and maintenance of binge eating were conceptualized to be contributing factors to her obesity. Susan was depressed in part due to the fact that she was obese and felt ashamed of her body. In an effort to feel less ashamed of her body, Susan would diet (skip meals) in order to reduce her weight. Skipping meals would frequently result in excess hunger later in the day, which would result in binge eating. Thus, by treating the obesity it was likely that both the depression and binge eating would decrease substantially. One reason for the decrease would be the removal of cues (shame of body, excess hunger) that would lead to depressed mood and/or binge eating. As can be seen, in such cases, a multi-pronged approach is often the best treatment plan. Therefore, in Susan's case, depression, binge eating, and obesity were targets of treatment.

There is a variety of methods to treat depression. In Susan's specific case, the severe level of depression warranted the use of medications. Studies have shown that the combination of medications plus cognitive behavioral therapy (CBT) work best (Walsh *et al.*, 1997; Mitchell *et al.*, 2003). Many of the main components of CBT were being taught (identifying and modifying automatic negative thoughts) in the standard behavioral treatment. Medication was included to facilitate adherence to the behavioral treatment plan for eating and physical activity. Oftentimes, depressed patients do not have the concentration necessary to retain information that is presented in treatment sessions. Antidepressant medications assist with the patient's ability to attend to and recall the information provided in therapy. In addition, medications assist in improving the patient's energy level so that they are able to engage in the cognitive strategies required by CBT.

As stated earlier, Susan's binge eating was maintained by reduction of hunger and negative mood and her excess body weight was caused, in part, by the excessive energy intake associated with frequent binge eating. Therefore, by establishing a regular eating pattern (decreasing hunger) and by promoting weight loss behaviors (increasing body image and mood), the antecedents leading to binge eating and resulting in obesity were removed. Had we believed that the binge eating was a separate syndrome from the obesity, the treatment would have been conceptualized differently. For example, Susan could have reported that the binge eating preceded her obesity by several years, or that there could have been times when she lost weight and the binge eating continued at the same frequency. This situation would have required an alternative treatment option, such as specifically treating the binge eating prior to or after the obesity treatment.

Conclusions

Behavioral therapy for obesity is well established and is a primary medical recommendation for adults who are overweight. The greatest strength of the behavioral approach is that it can be used to safely induce clinically significant weight losses. As noted by Williamson and Perrin (1996), however, those strategies that are used to induce weight loss may be the same strategies that must be used for weight maintenance, which is one reason that most people tend to regain much of the weight that was lost during the treatment. Current research evidence suggests that long-term weight management may require continued therapeutic contact (Perri *et al.*, 1988; Perri & Corsica, 2002). This conceptualization of obesity views the problem as a long-term, chronic health problem as opposed to a short-term cosmetic problem. This modern perspective appears to be yielding much better changes in behavior and health.

References

Allison, D. B., Nezin, L. E., & Clay-Williams, G. (1997). Obesity among African-American women: Prevalence, consequences, causes, and developing research. *Women's Health Research, 2*, 243–274.

American Psychiatric Association (1994). *Diagnostic and statistical manual of mental disorders* (4th ed.). Washington, DC: APA Press.

Beck, A. T., Brown, G. K., & Steer, R. A. (1996). *Beck Depression Inventory-II*. San Antonio, TX: Psychological Corporation.

Block, G., Woods, M., Potosky, A., & Clifford, C. (1990). Validation of a self-administered diet history questionnaire using multiple diet records. *Journal of Clinical Epidemiology, 43*, 1327–1335.

Bray, G.A., Bouchard, C., & James, W.P.T. (Eds.). (1998). *Handbook of obesity*. New York: Marcel Dekker.

Butcher, J. N. (1990). *MMPI-2 in psychological treatment*. New York: Oxford University Press.

Cooper, P. J., Taylor, M. J., Cooper, Z., & Fairburn, C. G. (1987). The development and validation of the body shape questionnaire. *International Journal of Eating Disorders, 6*, 485–494.

Cooper, Z., & Fairburn, C. (1987). The eating disorder examination: A semi-structured interview for the assessment of the specific psychopathology of eating disorder. *International Journal of Eating Disorders, 6*, 1–8.

Derogatis, L. (1977). *Manual for the Symptom Checklist-90, Revised*, Baltimore: Johns Hopkins University Press.

Ditschuneit, H.H., Fletchtner-Mors, M., Johnson, T.D., & Adler, G. (1999). Metabolic and weight loss effects of a long-term dietary intervention in obese patients. *American Journal of Clinical Nutrition, 69*, 198–204.

Field, A. E., Barnoya, J., & Colditz, G. A. (2002). Epidemiology and health and economic consequences of obesity. In T. A. Wadden & A. J. Stunkard (Eds.), *Handbook of obesity treatment* (pp. 186–226). New York: Guilford Press.

Flegal, K. M., Carroll, M. D., Ogden, C. L., & Johnson, C. L. (2002). Prevalence and trends in obesity among US adults, 1999–2000. *Journal of the American Medical Association, 288*, 1723–1727.

Garner, D. M. (1991). *Eating Disorder Inventory-2 manual*. Odessa, FL: Psychological Assessment Resources.

Heymsfield, S. B., Allison, D. B., Wang, Z., Baumgartner, R. N., & Ross, R. (2002). Evaluation of total and regional body composition. In G. A. Bray & C. Bouchard (Eds.), *Handbook of obesity* (2nd ed.). New York: Marcel Dekker.

Horgan, K. B., & Brownell, K. D. (2002). Confronting the toxic environment:

Environmental public health actions in a world crisis. In T. A. Wadden & A. J. Stunkard (Eds.), *Handbook of obesity treatment* (pp. 186–226). New York: Guilford Press.

Jeffery, R.W., Wing, R.R., Thorson, C., Burton, L.R., Raether, C., Harvey, J., & Mullen, M. (1993). Strengthening behavioral interventions for weight loss: A randomized trial of food provision and monetary incentives. *Journal of Consulting and Clinical Psychology, 61*, 1038–1045.

Jeffery, R.W., Epstein, L.H., Wilson, G.T., Drewnowski, A., Stunkard, A.J., & Wing, R.R. (2000). Long-term maintenance of weight loss: Current status. *Health Psychology, 19*, 5–16.

Kutlesic, V., Williamson, D. A., Gleaves, D. H., Barbin, J. M., & Murphy-Eberenz, K. P. (1998). The Interview for the Diagnosis of Eating Disorders IV: Application to DSM-IV diagnostic criteria. *Psychological Assessment, 10*, 41–48.

Lichtman, S. W., Pisarka, K., Berman, E. R., Pestone, M., Dowling, J., Offenbacher, E., Weisel, H., Heshka, S., Matthews, D. E., & Heymsfield, S. B. (1992). Discrepancy between self-reported and actual caloric intake and exercise in obese subjects. *New England Journal of Medicine, 327*, 1893–1898.

Lindner, P.G., & Blackburn, G.L. (1976). Multidisciplinary approach to obesity utilizing fasting modified by protein-sparing therapy. *Obesity/Bariatric Medicine, 5*, 198–216.

Marlatt, G. A., & Gordon, J. R. (1985). *Relapse prevention: Maintenance strategies in addictive behavior change*. New York: Guilford Press.

Mitchell, J. E., de Zwann, M., & Roerig, J. L. (2003). Drug therapy for patients with eating disorders. *Current Drug Targets, 2*, 17–29.

Paffenbarger, R. S., Wing, A. L., & Hyde, R. T. (1978). Physical activity as an index of heart attack risk in college alumni. *American Journal of Epidemiology, 108*, 161–175.

Perri, M.G. (1998). The maintenance of treatment effects in the long-term management of obesity. *Clinical Psychology: Science and Practice, 5*, 526–543.

Perri M.G., & Corsica, J.A. (2002). Improving the maintenance of weight lost in behavioral treatment of obesity. In T.A. Wadden & A.J. Stunkard (Eds.), *Handbook of obesity treatment*. New York: Guilford Press.

Perri, M.G., McAllister, D.A., Gange, J.J., Jordan, R.C., McAdoo, W.G., & Nezu, A.M. (1988). Effects of four maintenance programs on the long-term management of obesity. *Journal of Consulting and Clinical Psychology, 56*, 529–534.

Perri, M. G., Nezu, A. M., & Viegener, B. J. (Eds.). (1992). *Improving the long-term management of obesity: Theory, research, and clinical guidelines*. New York: Wiley.

Phelan, S., & Wadden, T.A. (2002). Combining behavioral and pharmacological treatments for obesity. *Obesity Research, 10*, 560–574.

Sallis, J. F., Haskell, W., & Wood, P. (1985). Physical activity assessment methodology in the Five-City Project. *American Journal of Epidemiology, 121*, 91–106.

Seidell, J. C., & Rissanen, A. M. (2002). Time trends in the worldwide prevalence of obesity. In G. A. Bray & C. Bouchard (Eds.), *Handbook of obesity* (2nd ed.). New York: Marcel Dekker

Smith, C. F., Williamson, D. A., Womble, L. G., Johnson, J., & Burke, L. E. (2000). Psychometric development of a multidimensional measure of weight-related attitudes and behaviors. *Eating and Weight Disorders, 5*, 73–86.

Spielberger, C. D., Gorsuch, R. L., & Lushene, R. E. (1970). *Manual for the State Trait Anxiety Inventory*. Palo Alto, CA: Consulting Psychologists.

Stewart, T. M., Williamson, D. A., Smeets, M. A. M., & Greenway, F. L. (2001). The Body Morph Assessment: Development of a computerized measure of body image. *Obesity Research, 9*, 43–50.

Stuart, R. (1967). Behavioral control of overeating. *Behavioral Research and Therapy, 5*, 357–365.

Stuart, R., & Davis, B. (1972). *Slim chance in a fat world*. Champaign, IL: Research Press.

Thelen, M. H., Farmer, J., Wonderlich, S., & Smith, M. (1991). A revision of the Bulimia Test: The BULIT-R. *Psychological Assessment, 3*, 119–124.

Wadden, T. A., & Phelan, S. (2002). Behavioral assessment of the obese patient. In T. Wadden & A. J. Stunkard (Eds.), *Handbook of obesity treatment* (pp. 186–226). New York: Guilford Press.

Wadden, T.A., & Stunkard, A.J. (1986). Controlled trial of very low calorie diet, behavior therapy, and their combination in the treatment of obesity. *Journal of Consulting and Clinical Psychology, 54*, 482–488.

Wadden, T.A., Stunkard, A.J., Brownell, K.D., & Day, S.C. (1984). Treatment of obesity by behavior therapy and very low calorie diet: A pilot investigation. *Journal of Consulting and Clinical Psychology, 52*, 692–694.

Wadden, T.A., Foster, G.D., & Letizia, K.A. (1994). One-year behavioral treatment of obesity: Comparison of moderate and severe caloric restriction and the effects of weight maintenance therapy. *Journal of Consulting and Clinical Psychology, 62*, 165–171.

Wadden, T.A., Vogt, R.A., Anderson, R.E., Bartlett, S.J., Foster, G.D., Kuehnel, R.H., Wilk, J., Weinstock, R., Buckenmeyer, P., Berkowitz, R.I., & Steen, S.N. (1997). Exercise in the treatment of obesity: Effects of four interventions on body composition, resting energy expenditure, appetite, and mood. *Journal of Consulting and Clinical Psychology, 65*, 269–277.

Wadden, T.A., Vogt, R.A., Foster, G.D., & Anderson, D.A. (1998). Exercise and maintenance of weight loss: 1-year follow-up of a controlled clinic trial. *Journal of Consulting and Clinical Psychology, 66*, 429–433.

Walsh, B. T., Wilson, G. T., Loeb, K. L., Delvin, M. J., Pike, K. M., Roose, S. P., Fliess, J., & Waternaux, C. (1997). Medication and psychotherapy in the treatment of bulimia nervosa. *American Journal of Psychiatry, 154*, 523–531.

Williamson, D. A., & Martin, C. K. (1999). Binge eating disorder: A review of the literature after publication of DSM-IV. *Eating and Weight Disorders, 4*, 103–114.

Williamson, D. A., & O'Neil, P. M. (2002). Obesity and quality of life. In G. A. Bray & C. Bouchard (Eds.), *Handbook of obesity* (2nd ed.). New York: Marcel Dekker.

Williamson, D.A., & Perrin, L.A. (1996). Behavior therapy for obesity. *Endocrinology and Metabolism Clinics of North America, 25*, 943–954.

Williamson, D. A., Davis, C. J. Goreczny, A. J., Bennett, S. M., & Watkins, P. C. (1989). The Eating Questionnaire-Revised: A new symptom checklist for bulimia. In P. A. Keller & L. G. Ritt (Eds.), *Innovations in clinical practice: A sourcebook*. Sarasota, FL: Professional Resource Exchange.

Williamson, D. A., Champagne, C. M., Jackman, L. P., & Varnado, P. J. (1996). Lifestyle change: A program for long-term weight management. In V. B. Van Hasselt & M. Hersen (Eds.), *Sourcebook of psychological treatment manuals of adult disorders*. New York: Plenum Press.

Williamson, D. A., Womble, L. G., Zucker, N. L., Reas, D. L., White, M. A.,

Blouin, D. C., & Greenway, F. (2000). Body Image Assessment for Obesity (BIA-O): Development of a new procedure. *International Journal of Obesity, 24,* 1326–1332.

Wing, R.R. (1999). Physical activity in the treatment of the adulthood overweight and obesity: Current evidence and research issues. *Medicine and Science in Sports and Exercise, 31,* S547–S552.

Wing, R.R. (2002). Behavioral weight control. In T.A. Wadden & A.J. Stunkard (Eds.), *Handbook of obesity treatment.* New York: Guilford Press.

Wing, R.R., Blair, E., Marcus, M., Epstein, L.H., & Harvey, J. (1994). Year-long weight loss treatment for obese patients with Type II diabetes: Does including an intermittent very-low calorie diet improve outcome? *American Journal of Medicine, 97,* 354–362.

Wing, R.R., Jeffery, R.W., Burton, L.R., Thorson, C., Sperber Nissinoff, K., & Baxter, J.E. (1996). Food provision vs. structured meal plans in the behavioral treatment of obesity. *International Journal of Obesity, 20,* 56–62.

Chapter 4

Insomnia

Josée Savard, Sébastien Simard and Charles M. Morin

Insomnia is a problem frequently reported by patients in various clinical settings, a problem that may have important clinical implications. Insomnia is particularly prevalent in patients with medical illnesses such as cancer. In this chapter a clinical case of a woman with insomnia secondary to breast cancer will be described using a case formulation approach. This will be preceded by a brief literature review on the nature, assessment, and treatment of insomnia.

Literature review

Definition of insomnia

Insomnia is a heterogeneous complaint typically reflecting an unsatisfactory duration, efficiency, or quality of sleep. This includes difficulties falling asleep at bedtime (i.e. initial or sleep onset insomnia), trouble staying asleep with prolonged nocturnal awakenings (i.e. middle or maintenance insomnia), early morning awakening with inability to resume sleep (i.e. terminal or late insomnia), and non-restorative sleep. These difficulties are not mutually exclusive, as a person may present with mixed difficulties initiating and maintaining sleep.

Insomnia varies greatly in terms of frequency, severity, duration, and daytime sequelae. The person can only present with some insomnia symptoms or can meet the criteria for an insomnia syndrome. When combining criteria of the International Classification of Sleep Disorders (American Sleep Disorders Association, 1997), the DSM-IV (American Psychiatric Association, 1994), and those typically used in clinical research, the insomnia disorder (or insomnia syndrome) can be defined as:

- difficulty initiating (i.e. 30 min or more to fall asleep) or maintaining sleep (i.e. 30 min or more of nocturnal awakenings), with a corresponding sleep efficiency (i.e. ratio of total sleep time to time spent in bed) lower than 85 per cent

- the sleep problem occurs at least three nights per week
- the sleep disturbance causes significant daytime impairment (e.g. fatigue, mood disturbances) or marked distress.

The insomnia disorder is considered transient when its duration is one month or less, subacute when its duration is more than one month but less than six months, and chronic when its duration is more than six months.

Prevalence, risk factors, longitudinal course, and potential consequences of insomnia

Prevalence

Insomnia is the most common of all sleep disorders (Bixler *et al.*, 1979). Prevalence rates for insomnia vary considerably across surveys, with an average of approximately 20 per cent (Ohayon *et al.*, 1998). Based on the most cited epidemiological surveys, insomnia affects one-third of the adult population, including between 9 per cent and 12 per cent on a chronic basis (Ford & Kamerow, 1989; Gallup Organization, 1991; Mellinger *et al.*, 1985).

Risk factors

Studies, although mostly cross-sectional, suggest that the risk to develop insomnia increases with aging, and is higher in women, unemployed, separated, and widowed individuals, as well as in people living alone (Bixler *et al.*, 1979; Mellinger *et al.*, 1985; Ford & Kamerow, 1989; Ohayon *et al.*, 1997). Insomnia is also more prevalent in patients with psychiatric symptomatology, particularly those with depression and anxiety disorders (Morin & Ware, 1996), and individuals with medical disorders (Katz & McHorney, 1998). A past personal history and a family history of insomnia are other factors increasing the risk for insomnia (Vollrath *et al.*, 1989). Finally, stressful life events such as personal losses (e.g. death of a loved one), family stressors (e.g. marital difficulties), health-related difficulties (e.g. hospitalization), and work and financial problems (e.g. job overload) are other important risk factors for insomnia (Cernovsky, 1984).

Longitudinal course

Insomnia can begin at any time during the course of the life span, but onset of the first episode is most common in young adulthood (Kales *et al.*, 1984). The first episode of insomnia can also occur late in life, although it must be distinguished from normal age-related changes in sleep patterns and from sleep disturbances due to medical problems or prescribed medications. For the large majority of insomnia sufferers, sleep difficulties are transient in nature, lasting a few days, and resolving themselves once the initial precipitating event (e.g. stressful life event) has subsided or the individual has adapted to it. Its course may also be intermittent, with repeated brief episodes of sleep difficulties following a close association with the occurrence of stressful events (Vollrath *et al.*, 1989). Even when insomnia has developed a chronic course, typically there is extensive night-to-night variability in sleep patterns, with an occasional restful night's sleep intertwined with several nights of poor sleep.

According to a cognitive-behavioural conceptualization of insomnia (see Figure 4.1; Morin, 1993), the most salient conditions maintaining insomnia over time are maladaptive sleep habits and dysfunctional cognitions that the person develops and entertains in reaction to sleep disturbance. Both types of factors exert their negative effects by increasing arousal (i.e. physiological, cognitive, and emotional arousal) and performance anxiety (i.e. the pressure to sleep), which are in direct opposition to the relaxation state required for sleep.

Individuals with chronic insomnia tend to spend excessive time in bed, nap during the day, and have an irregular sleep–wake schedule to compensate for sleep loss. Although these sleep habits can be effective in the short term to cope with sleep loss and fatigue, they desynchronize the sleep–wake cycle in the long run. In addition, individuals with persistent insomnia tend to engage in sleep-interfering activities in the bedroom that serve as cues for staying awake rather than inducing sleep (e.g. watching television, listening to music, eating, working or reading in the bed or bedroom). These behaviours tend to

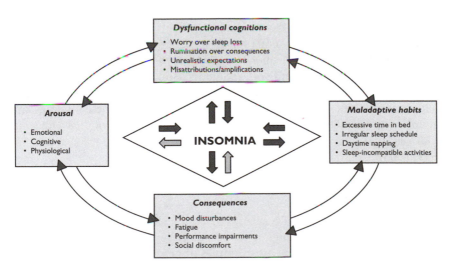

Figure 4.1 A cognitive-behavioural model of chronic insomnia (reprinted with permission from Morin, C.M. *Psychological Assessment and Management.* New York: Guilford Press, 1993).

weaken the association (i.e. deconditioning) between certain normally sleep-inducing stimuli (e.g. bed, bedtime and bedroom) and sleep (Morin, 1993). Individuals with chronic insomnia also entertain a number of faulty beliefs and attitudes about sleep and sleeplessness that may contribute to maintain their problem over time (Morin, 1993; Morin et al., 2000). These cognitions can be grouped in the following categories:

*   unrealistic sleep requirement expectations
*   faulty appraisals of sleep difficulties
*   misattributions of daytime impairments
*   misconceptions about the causes of insomnia.

Potential consequences

Fatigue is one of the most common complaints of patients with insomnia (Lichstein et al., 1997). Individuals with insomnia also frequently report daytime impairments such as poor concentration and memory, difficulties accomplishing simple tasks, and drowsiness (Gallup Organization, 1991). Research also validates the widespread assumption that insomnia is associated with an overall decrease in quality of life (Chevalier et al., 1999; Zammit et al., 1999). Psychological disturbances (e.g. depression, anxiety, irritability) are other potential consequences of insomnia. In fact, there is increasing evidence that insomnia can lead to the subsequent development of psychiatric disorders, including depressive, anxiety, and substance use disorders (Breslau et al., 1996; Chang et al., 1997; Ford & Kamerow, 1989; Gillin, 1998; Livingston et al., 1993; Weissman et al., 1997). There is also some evidence suggesting that sleep disturbance negatively affects health. In cross-sectional studies, individuals with insomnia report a higher frequency of health problems, medical consultations, and hospitalizations relative to good sleepers (Kales et al., 1984; Mellinger et al., 1985; Gislason & Almqvist, 1987; Simon & VonKorff, 1997). Also, some psychoneuroimmunological research suggests that insomnia can alter immune functioning, although these findings are based on cross-sectional studies and the clinical impact of this effect on health is unknown (Irwin et al., 1992; Cover & Irwin, 1994; Savard et al., 1999, 2003).

Insomnia assessment

There are a large number of measures assessing sleep disturbances and it is beyond the scope of this chapter to exhaustively review them. The instruments reviewed in this section are examples of modalities that are very useful in clinic to assess insomnia. Each of these measures was used in the clinical case described hereafter.

Insomnia Interview Schedule (IIS)

The clinical interview is certainly the most important component of the insomnia assessment. The IIS (Morin, 1993) is a semi-structured interview that gathers a wide range of information about the nature (i.e. problems falling asleep, staying asleep, waking up too early in the morning, problem staying awake during the day) and severity of the sleep problem, and the current sleep–wake schedule. The IIS also assesses the onset (e.g. gradual or sudden, precipitating events), course (e.g. persistent, episodic, seasonal), and duration of insomnia, past and current use of sleeping aids (i.e. prescribed and over-the-counter medications, alcohol), as well as health habits that might influence sleep (i.e. exercise, caffeine intake, smoking, alcohol use). Information is also gathered about environmental factors (e.g. bed partner, mattress, noise level, temperature), as well as on sleep habits (e.g. watching television in the bedroom, staying in bed when awake) and other factors (e.g. stress, vacation) that impair/facilitate sleep. In addition, the IIS assesses the impact of insomnia on daytime functioning and quality of life. Finally, symptoms of other sleep disorders and psychiatric disorders are evaluated for differential diagnosis. In sum, the IIS provides all relevant clinical information to conduct a functional analysis of insomnia and provide a diagnosis based on ICSD or DSM-IV classifications.

Sleep diary

Sleep diary monitoring is the most widely used method for assessing insomnia (Bootzin & Engle-Friedman, 1981). It is a practical and economical method to assess patients' perception of their sleep difficulties in their natural environment. Sleep diary monitoring gives a general overview of the patient's sleep patterns for an entire week. At a glance, the clinician can quickly gain an understanding of the nature, frequency, and intensity of insomnia, as well as nightly variations of sleep difficulties, and the presence of certain perpetuating factors (e.g. naps, spending too much time in bed). The sleep diary is also very useful to monitor changes associated with treatment. A typical daily sleep diary form collects information about bedtime, arising time, sleep-onset latency, number and duration of awakenings, time of last awakening, sleep duration, naps, medication intake, and indices of sleep quality and daytime functioning. The diary can be simplified or adapted to patient's specific needs. Sleep variables that are derived from this information are as follows: sleep-onset latency, wake time after sleep onset, early morning awakening, time in bed, total time awake, total time asleep, and sleep efficiency. Usually, the sleep diary is completed for a period of at least two weeks before treatment initiation, and throughout treatment thereafter. This procedure allows the clinician to establish baseline insomnia severity and to monitor progress over the course of treatment. Daily estimates of sleep-onset latency and waking after sleep onset obtained by the diary yield a reliable and valid relative index of insomnia, even though they do not reflect absolute values obtained from polysomnography (Coates *et al.*, 1982).

Insomnia Severity Index (ISI)

The ISI (Morin, 1993) yields a quantitative index of insomnia severity. The ISI is composed of seven items assessing, on a five-point scale, the perceived severity of problems with sleep onset, sleep maintenance, and early morning awakenings, the degree of dissatisfaction with the current sleep pattern, the degree of interference with daily functioning, the noticeability of impairment due to the sleep disturbance, and the degree of worry or concern caused by the sleep problem. The total ISI score, obtained by summing the seven ratings, ranges from 0 to 28, a higher score indicating more severe insomnia. Two parallel versions, a clinician and a significant other (e.g. spouse, roommate) versions, are available to provide collateral validation of patients' perception of their sleep difficulties. Empirical validation studies have revealed excellent psychometric properties (Bastien *et al.*, 2001).

Dysfunctional Beliefs and Attitudes about Sleep scale (DBAS)

The DBAS (Morin, 1994) is a 30-item, self-report scale designed to assess sleep-related beliefs and attitudes that are believed to be instrumental in maintaining sleep difficulties (Morin *et al.*, 1993, 2002). The patient indicates the extent to which he or she agrees or disagrees with each statement on a visual analogue scale ranging from 0 (strongly disagree) to 100 (strongly agree). The content of the items reflects several themes such as faulty causal attributions (e.g. "I feel that insomnia is basically the result of aging"), misattribution or amplification of the perceived consequences of insomnia (e.g. "I am concerned that chronic insomnia may have serious consequences for my physical health"), unrealistic sleep requirement expectations (e.g. "I need eight hours of sleep to feel refreshed and function well during the day"), diminished perception of control and predictability of sleep (e.g. "I am worried that I may lose control over my abilities to sleep"), and faulty beliefs about sleep-promoting practices (e.g. "When I have trouble getting to sleep, I should stay in bed and try harder"). The DBAS is a useful tool for clinicians to select relevant targets for cognitive therapy sessions.

Polysomnography (PSG)

A polysomnographic evaluation involves all-night electrophysiological monitoring of sleep as measured by electroencephalography (EEG), electro-oculography (EOG), and electromyography (EMG). These three parameters provide the necessary information to distinguish sleep from wake and to determine the specific sleep stages. Respiration, electrocardiogram, oxygen desaturation, and leg movements are also often assessed, at least during the first night, to detect the presence and severity of sleep pathologies other than insomnia (e.g. sleep apnea, periodic limb movement). It is the only sleep measure that allows quantification of sleep stages and can confirm or rule out the presence of another form of sleep pathology. However, although it is largely considered the "gold standard", laboratory PSG is limited by the fact that individuals may sleep differently in the laboratory then they do at home (i.e. measure reactivity). Ambulatory PSG may attenuate this problem. Nevertheless, PSG is quite expensive, which precludes its routine use. Moreover, although PSG evaluation may be helpful for determining the level of discrepancy between the subjective complaint and actual sleep disturbances, PSG is not always necessary to assess insomnia in clinical settings, especially when the clinician has no suspicion about the presence of an underlying sleep disorder such as sleep apnea (Jacobs *et al.*, 1988; Edinger *et al.*, 1989).

Treatment of insomnia

Pharmacotherapy

Hypnotic medications, particularly benzodiazepines, are by far the most commonly used treatment for insomnia. These include benzodiazepines that are specifically marketed as hypnotics (e.g. flurazepam, temazepam, triazolam), but several other benzodiazepines marketed as anxiolytics (e.g. lorazepam, clonazepam, oxazepam). More recently, nonbenzodiazepine hypnotics (e.g. zolpidem, zopiclone, zaleplon) have been marketed and are increasingly used. These latest medications are believed to have more selective/specific hypnotic effects and less residual effects the next day. Some antidepressant medications (those with sedating properties such as trazodone, amitriptyline, doxepin) can also be of some utility in the treatment of insomnia in depressed patients.

Placebo-controlled studies have suggested that benzodiazepines are an efficacious treatment for the acute and short-term management of insomnia, as indicated by reduced sleep latency and awakenings and increased total sleep duration and sleep efficiency (Roth & Roehrs, 1991; Parrino & Terzano, 1996; Kupfer & Reynolds, 1997; Nowell *et al.*, 1997). However, because placebo-controlled studies have typically not included follow-ups (median duration of treatment seven days), the long-term efficacy of hypnotic medications is unknown (Nowell *et al.*, 1997). Furthermore, a recent meta-analysis of benzodiazepine efficacy expressing therapeutic benefits in clinically interpretable units suggested that benzodiazepines only significantly improve sleep duration and that patients generally overestimate the efficacy of these medications (Holbrook *et al.*, 2000).

In addition, the usage of hypnotic medications is associated with a number of risks and limitations. Individuals using hypnotic medications, especially long-acting agents (e.g. flurazepam, quazepam), can feel residual effects the next day, the most frequent being daytime drowsiness, dizziness or lightheadedness, and cognitive and psychomotor impairments (Johnson & Chernik, 1982; Hall, 1998; Holbrook *et al.*, 2000). Because of their slower drug metabolism, elderly people are more vulnerable to experience these effects. Other important limitations associated with prolonged usage of hypnotic medications are their risks of tolerance, that is the reduction of efficacy over time and the need to increase the dosage to maintain therapeutic effects, as well as dependence, particularly psychological dependence ("I need medication to sleep"), that contribute in maintaining sleep problems (Morin, 1993; Hall, 1998).

These limitations have led sleep experts to recommend using hypnotic medications primarily for situational insomnia and to use the lowest effective dosage of hypnotics for the shortest period of time. Further, the treatment should start with a small dosage, with a subsequent gradual increment only if necessary. Although this recommendation needs empirical validation, treatment duration should not exceed four weeks in order to avoid tolerance and minimize the risk of dependency. Then, if the problem persists or is recurrent, the main intervention should be nonpharmacological and a hypnotic medication may be used as adjunctive therapy (National Institutes of Health, 1984, 1991, 1996).

Psychological therapies

Several nonpharmacological interventions have been used for the treatment of insomnia. Research efforts have mainly been devoted to evaluating the efficacy of behavioural and, more recently, cognitive-behavioural treatments. Two meta-analyses of the existing literature (based on approximately 60 studies) revealed that these interventions treat efficaciously insomnia (Morin *et al.*, 1994; Murtagh & Greenwood, 1995). Specifically, most of the effect sizes obtained fell in the moderate to large effect sizes spectrum, with larger therapeutic effects obtained on sleep-onset latency (0.87 and 0.88), sleep quality ratings (0.94), and duration of awakenings (0.65), and medium size effects obtained on total sleep time (0.42 and 0.49) and number of awakenings (0.53 and 0.63). Interestingly, the magnitude of these changes is comparable to those obtained with hypnotic medications (Nowell *et al.*, 1997) and, overall, between 70 per cent and 80 per cent of patients benefit from a psychological treatment (Morin *et al.*, 1994). Of special importance are the findings showing that sleep improvement derived from psychological management of insomnia is well maintained up to 24 months after the initial treatment (Morin *et al.*, 1999).

Stimulus control, sleep restriction, and multimodal treatments (i.e. combining several approaches) have generally been found to be the most effective psychological interventions. Sleep hygiene education produces only modest gains when used alone (Morin *et al.*, 1994), but can be useful as part of a multicomponent treatment. Other commonly used strategies include relaxation and cognitive therapy. Recent studies indicated that relaxation alone was less effective than sleep compression (Lichstein *et al.*, 2001) or a multimodal therapy (Edinger *et al.*, 2001). The efficacy of cognitive therapy as a single treatment for insomnia has never been evaluated, but studies that have incorporated this intervention to a multicomponent treatment have shown some therapeutic benefits associated with its use (Morin *et al.*, 2000). The goals and procedures of stimulus control therapy, sleep restriction, cognitive therapy, and sleep hygiene will be further described in the clinical case section.

Matching the case formulation with the intervention

Several general principles can guide practitioners when selecting optimal treatment strategies. These guidelines are functions of several factors including the nature (primary vs. secondary), duration (acute vs. chronic) and course of insomnia, the presence of comorbid psychological or medical conditions, prior use of hypnotic medications, and the patient's treatment preference.

For acute and situational insomnia, treatment should focus first on alleviating the precipitating factors when possible (i.e. stress, medical illness). In some instances (e.g. bereavement, divorce, jet lag), a hypnotic medication may be necessary and very useful to alleviate sleep difficulties. As mentioned earlier, for chronic and primary insomnia, cognitive-behavioural treatment should be the main intervention, with hypnotic medications serving as an adjunct.

The presence of comorbid medical or psychological disorders is another factor to consider when selecting the most appropriate treatment for insomnia. For instance, hypnotic medications are contra-indicated during pregnancy, when there is a history of alcohol or substance abuse, and with patients who present with renal or hepatic diseases. When insomnia is associated with another form of psychopathology or with another medical condition, the general principle is to treat the underlying condition first. However, this is not always possible. Nor does this approach always resolve the concurrent sleep difficulties. For example, treatment of chronic pain or major depression does not always alleviate an associated sleep disturbance. In such instances, it may be necessary to add treatment (cognitive-behavioural or pharmacological) that focuses directly on the sleep disturbance.

Prior use of hypnotic drugs is another important consideration for selecting the most appropriate treatment for insomnia. Two different scenarios are likely to arise in clinical practice. The first one, most commonly encountered by psychologists, involves a patient who has already been using sleep medications for a prolonged period and is unable to discontinue their use. The most appropriate intervention for this type of hypnotic-dependent insomnia would involve a gradual tapering of the sleep medication, accompanied by cognitive-behavioural therapy. Another possible scenario is that of a patient who may have used hypnotic medications only infrequently or not at all in the past. In this case, a short-term trial on hypnotic medications could be useful during the initial course of treatment in order to provide some immediate relief and reduce performance anxiety. Cognitive-behavioural therapy would be initiated simultaneously and continued upon drug withdrawal.

The patient's preference is another important, although often neglected, factor for selecting among psychological and pharmacological therapies. Regardless of how effective a treatment is, if a patient fails to comply with the treatment regimen (because of side effects or for other reasons), this treatment will be of little benefit. Thus, if a patient is unwilling to use a sleep medication, behavioural interventions may be the only alternative available. Likewise, if a patient is unwilling to invest time and effort in a cognitive-behavioural approach, medication may be a better choice of treatment. Although cognitive-behavioural approaches are often more acceptable to patients than medication, this issue of treatment preference needs to be addressed systematically when discussing the various treatment options with a patient.

Secondary insomnia

Most of the research literature has focused on primary insomnia, that is insomnia etiologically unrelated to any other coexisting psychological or medical condition. Conversely, a diagnosis of secondary insomnia is established when the trouble sleeping is judged to be due to another psychiatric disorder (e.g. mood disorder), a medical illness, substance use, or another sleep disorder. Secondary insomnia is receiving increasing attention along with the recognition that a significant proportion of insomniacs belong to this group (McCrae & Lichstein, 2001). Physical illnesses that may be etiologically responsible for insomnia include, but are not restricted to, cerebrovascular disease, congestive heart failures and chronic pulmonary diseases, degenerative neurological conditions, hyperthyroidism, gastrointestinal diseases, chronic bronchitis, and degenerative neurological conditions. Also, almost any condition producing pain or physical discomfort is likely to cause insomnia. These conditions include low back pain, arthritis, osteoporosis, headaches, and cancer.

Insomnia secondary to cancer

Studies conducted among heterogeneous samples of cancer patients suggest that between 30 per cent and 50 per cent of newly diagnosed or recently treated cancer patients report sleep difficulties (Savard & Morin, 2001). Two studies conducted by our research team revealed that 19 per cent and 18 per cent of breast cancer and prostate cancer survivors, respectively, met diagnostic criteria for an insomnia syndrome, which is considerably higher than the rate of 9–12 per cent found in the general population. In most cases (95 per cent) the insomnia was chronic (Savard *et al.*, 2001; Savard *et al.*, 2005a). Thus, it would appear that a large proportion of cancer patients display clinical levels of insomnia that warrant clinical attention.

There are several factors that may contribute in increasing the risk of cancer patients to suffer from insomnia. First, cancer is a highly stressful experience characterized by a succession of severe stressors, each of which can serve as a precipitating factor for insomnia (Hodgson, 1991). Moreover, oncological treatments may increase the risk to develop insomnia, either because of their emotional impact (some treatments are more distressing than others), their direct physiological effects, or their side effects. This includes surgery, particularly when involving esthetic adverse effects or a functional loss (e.g. mastectomy, colostomy), the hospitalization in itself, radiotherapy, chemotherapy, probably due to the influence of anti-emetic treatments used (i.e. corticosteroids), and bone marrow transplant. In addition, hormonal changes associated with some cancer treatments (e.g. chemotherapy and hormone therapy), both in women and men, can also trigger insomnia through the induction or aggravation of menopausal/andropausal symptoms such as hot flashes and night sweats. Insomnia can also be precipitated by pain (Savard & Morin, 2001).

These are all factors that may trigger the insomnia onset. However, as in primary insomnia, factors that are believed to contribute most importantly to the maintenance of insomnia over time are the maladaptive behaviours and dysfunctional cognitions about sleep that the person develops in reaction to sleep difficulties (Savard & Morin, 2001). Maladaptive sleep behaviours (e.g. day napping, excessive amounts of time lying down) are particularly frequent in cancer patients who are encouraged to get rest and sleep to recuperate from their cancer treatments (Graydon *et al.*, 1995; Richardson & Ream, 1997; Irvine *et al.*, 1998). Cancer patients often receive an hypnotic medication at crucial moments (e.g. surgery, diagnosis; Derogatis *et al.*, 1979; Stiefel *et al.*, 1990) that may become difficult to stop afterwards. In addition, cancer patients who suffer from insomnia often report dysfunctional cognitions specific to cancer that may have been instrumental in the maintenance of their sleep problem. These thoughts include: "If I don't sleep well, my cancer will come back"; "My doctor told me to rest and I can't do it. This is catastrophic"; "I have to do everything possible to cure my cancer, so I must sleep well"; "If I don't sleep well, I'll get fatigued and stressed out, which could make me sick."

The treatment of insomnia secondary to cancer, after it has became chronic, must hence involve the same behavioural and cognitive strategies that have been found useful for chronic primary insomnia. However, very few studies have been conducted on the efficacy of psychological therapies for insomnia secondary to cancer. Two studies, including a case study, have assessed the efficacy of relaxation, which revealed only modest improvements (Cannici *et al.*, 1983; Stam & Bultz, 1986). More recently non-randomized studies showed positive outcomes associated with multimodal psychological interventions for insomnia, including improved subjective sleep and some aspects of quality of life (Davidson *et al.*, 2004). We also found positive findings in women with breast cancer associated with the administration of cognitive-behavioural therapy for insomnia in a pilot study using a multiple-baseline design (Quesnel *et al.*, 2003) and a randomized controlled study (Savard *et al.*, 2005b). The clinical case hereafter described received the same intervention.

Case study

Demographics and psychiatric antecedents

Diane (a pseudonym) is a 50-year-old Caucasian female. She has been married for 20 years and is mother of a 16-year-old son. She completed her high school degree and has been an aesthetician for 16 years. Diane is the third of a family of 14 children. Her mother died several years ago from uterus cancer and her father has recently died from prostate cancer. Four of her sisters survived from breast cancer and two of her sisters have sleep difficulties.

At the time of evaluation (June 2002), Diane has no DSM-IV axis I disorder other than insomnia, as assessed using the Structured Clinical Interview for DSM-IV (Spitzer *et al.*, 1997). However, she mentions having chronic marital difficulties. Four years ago, she had a major depressive episode, partly related to these difficulties, with accompanying symptoms of insomnia. Both depression and insomnia went into complete spontaneous remission (i.e. without treatment) within a few months. She has no other significant personal or family history of psychiatric disorder.

History of sleep difficulties and breast cancer

Diane was diagnosed with Stage II breast cancer in September 1999. Her treatment included a lumpectomy, causing transitory pain, followed by chemotherapy. Besides inducing an early menopause, chemotherapy was associated with several side effects, including nausea, anorexia, and fatigue. She developed significant anxiety at the time her cancer was diagnosed and, when the treatment ended, she became very fearful of cancer recurrence, due to her strong familial history of cancer. Sleep difficulties occurred soon after the breast cancer diagnosis and she then rapidly changed her sleep schedule and began doing more day napping. At the surgery, she received a prescription of zopiclone, which strengthened her belief that she had lost control over her ability to sleep. Later on, she used trazodone, 250 mg h.s. (from April to

November 2000), with limited beneficial effect on sleep and started zaleplon, 5 mg h.s., in December 2000.

Patient's description of sleep difficulties and treatment goals

At the time of assessment, Diane complains of mixed difficulties initiating and maintaining sleep, occurring every night. She is still using zaleplon (twice a week) and, for the past four months, has used a natural product (Nervinol) every night. Usually, she goes to bed at 10:00 PM after reading a while in the living room. She reports no difficulty falling asleep when taking Nervinol, but taking up to 120 min to fall asleep otherwise. More often than not, she awakes after one hour of sleep and stays awake for 60 to 90 min before going back to sleep. She claims sleeping about 3 to 4 hours a night, although a close examination at her sleep diaries indicate that she actually sleeps at least 6 hours, with a sleep efficiency of 72 per cent. She occasionally naps during the day and has a different sleep schedule during weekends to compensate for her sleep loss.

Diane is very dissatisfied and frustrated about her sleep quality and quantity. She does not understand why she cannot sleep like everybody else. She is convinced that insomnia is responsible for all the fatigue she experiences and that insomnia significantly impairs her daytime functioning. She even believes that insomnia contributes to her marital difficulties, her husband getting irritated when she pleads fatigue for missing social activities or refusing sexual relationships. She also fears that insomnia could lead to a breast cancer recurrence. Considering: (a) that the time awake during the night was higher than 30 min at least three nights a week; (b) the sleep efficiency was lower than 85 per cent; (c) that the sleep difficulties were associated with impaired daytime functioning and significant distress; (d) the duration of insomnia was longer than six months; and (e) there was a temporal relationship between the insomnia onset and breast cancer diagnosis, as well as a patient's subjective report of an association between both events, a diagnosis of chronic insomnia secondary to breast cancer was made.

She hopes therapy will help her achieve her goal consisting of falling asleep in less than 15 min without medication, being awake during the night for less than 10 min and getting a total of 7h30 of refreshing sleep on a regular basis.

Functional analysis of sleep difficulties

Stimuli

On the IIS, Diane reports that stress, busy day at work, fatigue, marital conflicts, worrying about cancer and the consequences of insomnia are all factors that may be associated with more difficulties sleeping.

Responses

When she is unable to sleep during the night, about half of the time she stays in bed trying to get back to sleep. The other times, she gets out of the bed after approximately 45 min and reads in another room. She tends to compensate for sleep loss by staying longer in bed in the morning (she gets up about an hour after her final awakening), by staying in bed even longer during the weekend and by occasionally napping during the day. In addition, Diane has always relied on prescribed medications and natural products to improve her sleep.

Besides these behaviours that contribute to maintaining her sleep difficulties over time, Diane entertains several dysfunctional beliefs about sleep that may also exert an influence through performance anxiety. Indeed, at pretreatment, she obtains elevated scores (> 70) on the following items of the DBAS: "I need 8 hours of sleep to feel refreshed and function well during the day"; "When I don't get a proper amount of sleep on a given night, I need to catch up on the next day by napping or on the next night by sleeping longer"; "I am concerned that chronic insomnia may have serious consequences for my physical health" (score of 100); "By spending more time in bed, I usually get more sleep and feel better the next day"; "When I feel irritable, depressed, or anxious during the day, it is mostly because I did not sleep well the night before"; "Because my bed partner falls asleep as soon as his head hits the pillow and stays asleep through the night, I should be able to do so too"; "When I sleep poorly on one night, I know it will disturb my sleep schedule for the whole week"; and "Without an adequate night's sleep, I can hardly function the next day".

These faulty beliefs were associated with the occurrence of a variety of negative automatic thoughts that Diane entertained when she was unable to sleep or get back to sleep, such as "If I don't sleep, I'll be a mess tomorrow", "If I am not able to sleep well, my cancer will come back". These cognitive responses were associated with physiological activation as indicated by Diane's reports of restlessness (tossing and turning in her bed) and muscular tension.

Consequences

Because she had once heard about sleep hygiene rules in the media, Diane was partially aware of the negative impact of her behaviours (i.e. spending too much time in bed, day napping) on sleep. In addition, she intuitively knew that worrying about insomnia and its consequences could only result in more sleep difficulties. However, she felt unable to change her behaviours by herself and did not know how to stop being overwhelmed by these negative thoughts.

Cognitive-behavioural formulation

Diane's insomnia was precipitated by her breast cancer diagnosis and treatment. Although she did not meet criteria for an anxiety disorder, Diane was very anxious about her prognosis. With anxiety and pain related to the surgery, sleep became more impaired. These difficulties were exacerbated with the chemotherapy side effects (nausea, anorexia, fatigue). Chemotherapy also induced menopause, but given that Diane reported only mild hot flashes, this factor did not significantly contribute to insomnia. Thus, it was hypothesized that anxiety, pain, and side effects of chemotherapy precipitated Diane's insomnia.

Diane was convinced that spending time awake in bed and napping during the day were helpful strategies to cope with insomnia and fatigue. However, these behaviours resulted in disturbed wake–sleep rhythm, lowered the association between the bed (and bedroom) and sleep, and, in the long run, contributed in the maintenance of insomnia over time. Also, because she believed that she had lost control over her ability to sleep, Diane relied exclusively on medications to treat her insomnia. However, these medications had limited benefits for Diane, which encouraged her to keep trying new agents, including natural products of which efficacy remains to be demonstrated. This resulted in increased psychological dependency and reinforced the perception that she could not do anything to improve her sleep.

Besides encouraging Diane in adopting maladaptive sleep behaviours, it was hypothesized that her faulty beliefs about sleep also produced physiological and cognitive arousal, thereby aggravating the sleep disturbance. When awake at night, Diane ruminated about the consequences of sleep loss on her daily functioning and mood, as well as on the potential impact on breast cancer recurrence. These cognitive distortions enhanced performance anxiety (i.e. wanting too much to sleep) and further sleep disturbances.

Treatment goals

The intervention offered to Diane pursued the following goals:

- to reassociate temporal (bedtime) and environmental (bed and bedroom) stimuli with sleep
- to establish a regular circadian sleep–wake rhythm
- to curtail the time spent in bed to the actual amount of sleep she obtained
- to restructure her erroneous beliefs about sleep and about the consequences of insomnia.

Stimulus-control therapy was used to achieve the first two goals, sleep restriction was used to attain the third goal, and cognitive therapy was used for the last goal.

Outline of treatment programme

The treatment involved eight weekly sessions of approximately 90 min, administered in a group of five women with insomnia secondary to breast cancer. Patients completed a daily sleep diary for two weeks before intervention, during the intervention (i.e. seven weeks), as well as for three additional periods of two weeks at post-treatment, three- and six-month follow-up. Each session followed a structured format, beginning with a summary of the previous treatment session, followed by a review of sleep diaries and compliance with the behavioural procedures, a discussion of difficulties encountered in the application of treatment strategies, and the adjustment of an individualized sleep window. Then, a didactic presentation and a group discussion, led by the clinician, took place on the main topic of the session. At the end of each session, patients were encouraged to provide feedback on the session and the therapy in general. A homework was given at each treatment session, which minimally included the reading of a handout summarizing the treatment procedures, in preparation for the next session.

Details of treatment programme

Session 1

This session was devoted to discussing basic facts about sleep such as the sleep stages, circadian rhythms, and normal changes with aging. Then, the different insomnia types, the definition of chronic insomnia, and the etiology of insomnia (i.e. predisposing, precipitating, and maintaining factors) were explained. This was followed by the presentation of a cognitive-behavioural conceptual model of insomnia (Morin, 1993; see Figure 4.1). Based on this model, Diane was asked to identify at home the particular behavioural and cognitive factors that might have been instrumental in the maintenance of her sleep difficulties over time.

Session 2

The conceptual model of insomnia was reviewed, with a special focus on the behavioural factors that contributed to perpetuate insomnia. Then, the stimulus control and sleep restriction procedures were presented with their rationale. Specifically, patients were instructed: (a) to go to bed only when sleepy; (b) when unable to fall asleep or go back to sleep within 15 to 20 minutes, get out of bed and leave the bedroom, and return to bed only when sleepy; (c) use the bed/bedroom for sleep and sexual activities only (e.g. do not watch television, listen to the radio, eat, or read in the bed); (d) arise at the same time every morning; (e) do not nap during the day or, if necessary, do naps of less than 60 min, in the bed, and before 3:00 PM; and (f) keep at least an hour to unwind before going to bed. Rules (b), (d), and (e) were particularly emphasized for Diane. Finally, a sleep window for sleep restriction was defined for each patient based on sleep diary data. The general principle was to allow patients to stay in bed for a period corresponding to the actual total sleep time the first week and to progressively increase it by 20–30 min for each week sleep efficiency exceeded 85 per cent. Because Diane slept an average of 381 min (6.4 hrs) during the preceding three weeks, her sleep window was established at 6.5 hrs. To respect this sleep window, Diane decided it would be easier for her to go to bed later than usual (at 12:00 AM rather than 10: 00 PM) and to get up at 6:30 AM.

Session 3

After reviewing sleep diaries, compliance and difficulties with homework assignment were reviewed. Diane reported that it was difficult to adhere to some of those strategies, particularly to get up at 6:30 AM and to consistently get out of bed when awake at night. She also reported difficulties postponing her bedtime until 12:00 AM because of acute somnolence. However, she also recognized important positive effects, particularly the shorter duration of her nocturnal awakenings. Then, the clinician normalized the experience of somnolence at this stage of treatment, emphasized the important distinctions between somnolence and fatigue, and designed with Diane strategies to cope with somnolence that occurred at other moments than bedtime (e.g. do more stimulating activities). Strategies were also suggested to help Diane getting up when awake at night (e.g. set up a comfortable area in the living room, do relaxing activities, such as reading, to induce somnolence). Diane was reinforced for her efforts and encouraged to continue the application of behavioural strategies. Because her sleep efficiency exceeded 85 per cent (86 per cent) in the preceding week, her sleep window for the following week was extended to 7hr (11:30 PM to 6:30 AM).

Session 4

Diane expressed a high level of satisfaction with the progress made. She still experienced somnolence during the day, but was able to cope with it more efficiently. The clinician reviewed again the cognitive-behavioural model of insomnia, but this time emphasized the deleterious effect of dysfunctional beliefs about sleep and the concept of performance anxiety an its effect on sleep. The general cognitive model of emotions based on Beck's model (Beck *et al.*, 1979; Beck, 1995) was explained, as well as the concept of cognitive distortions and general cognitive restructuring procedures. Besides being encouraged to continue the application of behavioural strategies during the following week, Diane was also instructed to monitor automatic thoughts on the typical three-column grid (situation-automatic thoughts-emotions). Her sleep window was increased to 7.5 hrs (11:15 PM to 6:45 AM), since her sleep efficiency in the preceding week was again greater than 85 per cent (86 per cent).

Session 5

The cognitive model was first reviewed. Then, two very common cognitive distortions about sleep were discussed: that is, unrealistic expectations about sleep and false causal attributions of insomnia. It was then the opportunity to challenge Diane's beliefs that eight hours of sleep are necessary to function well during the day and that because her husband could fall asleep rapidly and would never wake up during the night, she should be able to do the same. Standard cognitive restructuring techniques (probing questions) were used to make Diane realize that there are individual differences in sleep needs and in sleep patterns. Diane was encouraged to become more aware of her thoughts about sleep, as well as to monitor and challenge them using a five-column form (situation-automatic thoughts-emotions-alternative thoughts-emotions). Her sleep window was increased further to 7.75 hrs (from 11:15 PM to 7:00 AM), since her sleep efficiency of the previous week remained above 85 per cent (87 per cent).

Session 6

First, Diane's dysfunctional sleep cognitions were reviewed and challenged. On one night, she spent much time awake during the night and found herself thinking "I need to sleep well, otherwise my cancer will recur", a thought she could not eliminate although she recognized that it increased her perform-ance anxiety to sleep. The lack of evidence linking insomnia and cancer was discussed, along with an explanation of a multifactorial model of cancer risk. In other words, she was brought to understand that if sleep were associated with an increased risk of cancer recurrence, which has not been scientifically demonstrated yet, it would be part of a more complex picture including several other risk factors (e.g. genetic, hormonal, health behaviours). Hence, it would be very unlikely that insomnia would constitute the only or the most influential factor causing a cancer recurrence. Another belief challenged was the idea that one should try harder when unable to sleep. This was accom-plished by simply pointing out that sleep is a phenomenon that cannot be controlled and trying harder only generates more performance anxiety. Finally, the belief that insomnia negatively impairs daytime functioning and mood was placed in a more realistic perspective. This was done by emphasizing that bad nights of sleep are not always followed by poor daytime functioning (or mood disturbances) and poor daytime functioning (or mood disturbances) may follow good nights of sleep as well and may be explained by other factors. Thus, Diane then realized that it was erroneous to blame insomnia for everything that went wrong in her life. She was instructed to continue monitoring her automatic and alternative thoughts on a five-column form and to continue using behavioural strategies.

Session 7

The patient's cognitive restructuring exercises were again reviewed by the clinician. Then, sleep hygiene education principles were presented. This included information on the effect of caffeine, nicotine, and alcohol use, nutrition, physical exercises, and environmental factors (e.g. bedroom temperature, lightness, noise) on sleep. The patient was encouraged to continue implementing both behavioural and cognitive strategies during the week.

Session 8

This session was devoted mainly to relapse prevention. First, a summary of treatment procedures learned was done. When asked to identify future high-risk situations that could potentially cause a relapse of insomnia, Diane mentioned cancer recurrence. Based on strategies that had been shown effective for Diane, a "treatment plan" was established for this possible situation. Importantly, it was emphasized that temporary insomnia is a normal reaction to stressful situations, that it does not necessarily indicate a relapse, and that the focus should be on avoiding the return to old maladaptive sleep habits and cognitions, such as spending too much time in bed and catastrophizing about the consequences of insomnia, that might contribute to the return of chronic insomnia.

Treatment evaluation

Diane's progress was evaluated by comparing total wake time, sleep efficiency and total sleep time parameters, derived from her sleep diaries, across study phases. As shown in Figure 4.2, her mean total wake time at pre-treatment was 150 min (2.5 hrs), with a sleep efficiency of 72 per cent. Total sleep time averaged 392 min (6.5 hrs) per night, of a total of 542 min (9 hrs) spent in bed. Hence, her sleep was impaired significantly at pre-treatment. Figure 4.2 also shows that sleep improved rather drastically during week two, when stimulus control and sleep restriction were introduced. Total wake time was reduced to 54 min per night, with sleep efficiency increased to 86 per cent. However, as could be expected because of the short-term "side effect" of sleep restriction (i.e. light sleep deprivation), sleep duration was decreased to 339 min (5.6 hrs) at that time. Total wake time and sleep efficiency remained stable throughout the remaining of the intervention, at post-treatment and at

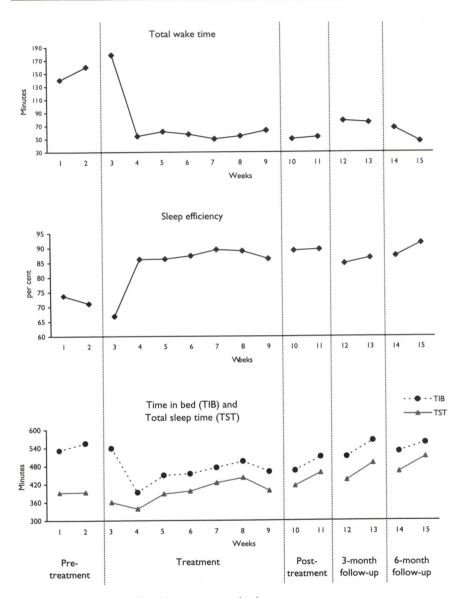

Figure 4.2 Diane's sleep diary data across study phases.

three- and six-month follow-up. Total sleep time gradually increased during the intervention and continued to do so throughout follow-up phases. Indeed, Diane's sleep duration averaged 414 min (6.9 hrs) per night during the last week of the intervention, 436 min (7.3 hrs) at post-treatment, 461 min (7.7 hrs) at 3-month and 486 min (8.1 hrs) at six-month follow-ups. It is also noteworthy that Diane stopped the use of Nervinol at week two and remained drug free throughout treatment and follow-up phases.

Laboratory polysomnographic data corroborated these subjective findings. Total wake time decreased from 65 min per night at pre-treatment to 26 min at post-treatment. In addition, sleep efficiency increased from 86 per cent to 94 per cent with treatment, and total sleep time increased from 403 min (6.7 hrs) to 418 min (7.0 hrs). Scores obtained on the DBAS provided further evidence of Diane's improvement. At post-treatment she indicated a score of 30 or less on each item. Importantly, the largest pre- and post-treatment difference was on the item "I am concerned that chronic insomnia may have serious consequences for my physical health".

In summary, the intervention was associated with significant improvement of sleep. As is often the case after psychological intervention for insomnia, Diane only partly met criteria commonly used to identify good sleepers. She was still awake approximately 60 min each night when combining time to fall asleep and the time awake during the night. However, her sleep efficiency consistently exceeded the cut-off score of 85 per cent. Although she has not completely reached her initial treatment goals, Diane was very satisfied with the treatment outcome, in part because she realized during the treatment course that these goals were unrealistic. Her satisfaction is evidenced by an ISI total score of one at all assessment periods following the intervention. She also reported a significant improvement of her quality of life.

Conclusion

Insomnia is a very common problem, particularly in patients with cancer. Although insomnia secondary to cancer is often precipitated by physical or psychological factors associated with the cancer diagnosis or treatment, sleep difficulties are often maintained by the development of maladaptive behaviours and dysfunctional beliefs about sleep. Cognitive-behavioural therapy, which has been shown effective for chronic primary insomnia, appears to also be effective in patients with insomnia secondary to cancer.

Acknowledgements

Preparation of this chapter was supported in part by grants from the Medical Research Council of Canada (MT-14039) and by the National Institute of Mental Health (#MH55469), as well as a young investigator award conferred to Josée Savard by the Canadian Institutes of Health Research.

References

American Psychiatric Association (1994). *Diagnostic and statistical manual of mental disorders* (4th ed.). Washington, DC: APA.

American Sleep Disorders Association (1997). *The international classification of sleep disorders: Diagnostic and coding manual.* Rochester, MN: American Sleep Disorders Association.

Bastien, C. H., Vallières, A., & Morin, C. M. (2001). Validation of the Insomnia Severity Index as an outcome measure for insomnia research. *Sleep Medicine, 2,* 297–307.

Beck, J. S. (1995). *Cognitive therapy: Basics and beyond.* New York: Guilford Press.

Beck, A. T., Rush, A. J., Shaw, B. F., & Emery, G. (1979). *Cognitive therapy of depression.* New York: Guilford Press.

Bixler, E. O., Kales, A., & Soldatos, C. R. (1979). Sleep disorders encountered in medical practice: A national survey of physicians. *Behavioral Medicine, 6,* 1–6.

Bootzin, R. R., & Engle-Friedman, M. (1981). The assessment of insomnia. *Behavioral Assessment, 3,* 107–126.

Breslau, N., Roth, T., Rosenthal, L., & Andreski, P. (1996). Sleep disturbance and psychiatric disorders: A longitudinal epidemiological study of young adults. *Biological Psychiatry, 39,* 411–418.

Cannici, J., Malcom, R., & Peek, L. A. (1983). Treatment of insomnia in cancer patients using muscle relaxation training. *Journal of Behavior Therapy and Experimental Psychiatry, 14,* 3, 251–256.

Cernovsky, Z. Z. (1984). Life stress measures and reported frequency of sleep disorders. *Perceptual and Motor Skills, 58,* 39–49.

Chang, P. P., Ford, D. E., Mead, L. A., Cooper-Patrick, L., & Klag, M. J. (1997). Insomnia in young men and subsequent depression. *American Journal of Epidemiology, 146,* 2, 105–114.

Chevalier, H., Los, F., Boichut, D., Bianchi, M., Nutt, D. J., Hajak, G., Hetta, J., Hoffmann, G., & Crowe, C. (1999). Evaluation of severe insomnia in the general population: Results of a European multinational survey. *Journal of Psychopharmacology, 13,* 4, S21–S24.

Coates, T. J., Killen, J. D., George, J., Marchini, E., Silverman, S., & Thoresen, C. (1982). Estimating sleep parameters: A multitrait-multimethod analysis. *Journal of Consulting and Clinical Psychology, 50,* 3, 345–352.

Cover, H., & Irwin, M. (1994). Immunity and depression: Insomnia, retardation, and reduction of natural killer cell activity. *Journal of Behavioral Medicine, 17,* 2, 217–223.

Davidson, J. R., Waisberg, J. L., Brundage, M. D., & MacLean, A. W. (2001). Nonpharmacologic group treatment of insomnia: A preliminary study with cancer survivors. *Psychooncology, 10,* 389–397.

Derogatis, L. R., Feldstein, M., Morrow, G., Schmale, A., Schmitt, M., Gates, C., Murawski, B., Holland, J., Penman, D., Melisaratos, N., Enelow, A. J., & Adler, L. M. (1979). A survey of psychotropic drug prescriptions in an oncology population. *Cancer, 44,* 1919–1929.

Edinger, J. D., Hoelscher, T. J., Webb, M. D., Marsh, G. R., Radtke, R. A., & Erwin, C. W. (1989). Polysomnographic assessment of DIMS: Empirical evaluation of its diagnostic value. *Sleep, 12,* 4, 315–322.

Edinger, J. D., Wohlgemuth, W. K., Radtke, R. A., Marsh, G. R., & Quillian, R. E. (2001). Cognitive behavioral therapy for treatment of chronic primary insomnia: A randomized controlled trial. *Journal of the American Medical Association, 285,* 14, 1856–1864.

Ford, D. E., & Kamerow, D. B. (1989). Epidemiologic study of sleep disturbances and psychiatric disorders: An opportunity for prevention? *Journal of the American Medical Association, 262*, 11, 1479–1484.

Gallup Organization. (1991). *Sleep in America.* Princeton, NJ: Gallup.

Gillin, J. C. (1998). Are sleep disturbances risk factors for anxiety, depressive and addictive disorders? *Acta Psychiatrica Scandinavica, 98*, 39–43.

Gislason, T., & Almqvist, M. (1987). Somatic diseases and sleep complaints: An epidemiological study of 3201 Swedish men. *Acta Medica Scandinavica, 221*, 475–481.

Graydon, J. E., Bubela, N., Irvine, D., & Vincent, L. (1995). Fatigue-reducing strategies used by patients receiving treatment for cancer. *Cancer Nursing, 18*, 1, 23–28.

Hall, N. (1998). Taking policy action to reduce benzodiazepine use and promote self-care among seniors. *Journal of Applied Gerontology, 17*, 3, 318–351.

Hodgson, L. A. (1991). Why do we need sleep? Relating theory to nursing practice. *Journal of Advanced Nursing, 16*, 1503–1510.

Holbrook, A. M., Crowther, R., Lotter, A., Cheng, C., & King, D. (2000). Meta-analysis of benzodiazepine use in the treatment of insomnia. *Canadian Medical Association Journal, 162*, 2, 225–233.

Irvine, D. M., Vincent, L., Graydon, J. E., & Bubela, N. (1998). Fatigue in women with breast cancer receiving radiation therapy. *Cancer Nursing, 21*, 2, 127–135.

Irwin, M., Smith, T. L., & Gillin, J. C. (1992). Electroencephalographic sleep and natural killer activity in depressed patients and control subjects. *Psychosomatic Medicine, 54*, 10–21.

Jacobs, E. A., Reynolds, C. F., Kupfer, D. J., Lovin, P. A., & Ehrenpreis, A. B. (1988). The role of polysomnography in the differential diagnosis of chronic insomnia. *American Journal of Psychiatry, 145*, 3, 346–349.

Johnson, L. C., & Chernik, D. A. (1982). Sedative-hypnotics and human performance. *Psychopharmacology, 76*, 101–113.

Kales, J. D., Kales, A., Bixler, E. O., Soldatos, C. R., Cadieux, R. J., Kashurba, G. J., & Vela-Bueno, A. (1984). Biopsychobehavioral correlates of insomnia, V: Clinical characteristics and behavioral correlates. *American Journal of Psychiatry, 141*, 11, 1371–1376.

Katz, D. A., & McHorney, C. A. (1998). Clinical correlates of insomnia in patients with chronic illness. *Archives of Internal Medicine, 158*, 1099–1107.

Kupfer, D. J., & Reynolds, C. R. (1997). Management of insomnia. *New England Journal of Medicine, 336*, 341–346.

Lichstein, K. L., Means, M. K., Noe, S. L., & Aguillard, N. (1997). Fatigue and sleep disorders. *Behaviour Research and Therapy, 35*, 8, 733–740.

Lichstein, K. L., Riedel, B. W., Wilson, N. M., Lester, K. W., & Aguillard, R. N. (2001). Relaxation and sleep compression for late-life insomnia: A placebo-controlled trial. *Journal of Consulting and Clinical Psychology, 69*, 2, 227–239.

Livingston, G., Blizard, B., & Mann, A. (1993). Does sleep disturbance predict depression in elderly people? A study in inner London. *British Journal of General Practice, 43*, 445–448.

McCrae, C. S., & Lichstein, K. L. (2001). Secondary insomnia: Diagnostic challenges and intervention opportunities. *Sleep Medicine Reviews, 5*, 1, 47–61.

Mellinger, G. D., Balter, M. B., & Uhlenhuth, E. H. (1985). Insomnia and its treatment: Prevalence and correlates. *Archives of General Psychiatry, 42*, 225–232.

Morin, C. M. (1993). *Insomnia: Psychological assessment and management.* New York: Guilford Press.

Morin, C. M. (1994). Dysfunctional beliefs and attitudes about sleep: Preliminary scale development and description. *The Behavior Therapist, 17*, 163–164.

Morin, C. M., & Ware, J. C. (1996). Sleep and psychopathology. *Applied and Preventive Psychology, 5*, 211–224.

Morin, C. M., Stone, J., Trinkle, D., Mercer, J., & Remsberg, S. (1993). Dysfunctional beliefs and attitudes about sleep among older adults with and without insomnia complaints. *Psychology and Aging, 8*, 3, 463–467.

Morin, C. M., Culbert, J. P., & Schwartz, S. M. (1994). Nonpharmacological interventions for insomnia: A meta-analysis of treatment efficacy. *American Journal of Psychiatry, 151*, 8, 1172–1180.

Morin, C. M., Hauri, P. J., Espie, C. A., Spielman, A. J., Buysse, D. J., & Bootzin, R. R. (1999). Nonpharmacologic treatment of chronic insomnia. *Sleep, 22*, 8, 1134–1156.

Morin, C. M., Savard, J., & Blais, F. C. (2000). Cognitive therapy. In K. L. Lichstein & C. M. Morin (Eds.), *Treatment of late-life insomnia* (pp. 207–230). Thousand Oaks: Sage.

Morin, C. M., Blais, F., & Savard, J. (2002). Are changes in beliefs and attitudes about sleep related to sleep improvements in the treatment of insomnia? *Behaviour Research and Therapy, 40*, 741–752.

Murtagh, D. R. R., & Greenwood, K. M. (1995). Identifying effective psychological treatments for insomnia: A meta-analysis. *Journal of Consulting and Clinical Psychology, 63*, 79–89.

National Institutes of Health (1984). Drugs and insomnia: The use of medication to promote sleep. *Journal of the American Medical Association, 18*, 2410–2414.

National Institutes of Health (1991). Consensus development conference statement: The treatment of sleep disorders of older people. *Sleep, 14*, 169–177.

National Institutes of Health (1996). NIH releases statement on behavioral and relaxation approaches for chronic pain and insomnia. *American Family Physician, 53*, 1877–1880.

Nowell, P. D., Mazumdar, S., Buysse, D. J., Dew, M. A., Reynolds, C. F., & Kupfer, D. J. (1997). Benzodiazepines and zolpidem for chronic insomnia: A meta-analysis of treatment efficacy. *Journal of the American Medical Association, 278*, 24, 2170–2177.

Ohayon, M. M., Caulet, M., Priest, R. G., & Guilleminault, C. (1997). DSM-IV and ICSD-90 insomnia symptoms and sleep dissatisfaction. *British Journal of Psychiatry, 171*, 382–388.

Ohayon, M. M., Caulet, M., & Lemoine, P. (1998). Comorbidity of mental and insomnia disorders in the general population. *Comprehensive Psychiatry, 39*, 4, 185–197.

Parrino, L., & Terzano, M. G. (1996). Polysomnographic effects of hypnotic drugs: A review. *Psychopharmacology, 126*, 1–16.

Quesnel, C., Savard, J., Simard, S., Ivers, H., & Morin, C. M. (2003). Efficacy of cognitive-behavioral therapy for insomnia in women treated for non-metastatic breast cancer. *Journal of Consulting and Clinical Psychology, 71*, 189–200.

Richardson, A., & Ream, E. K. (1997). Self-care behaviours initiated by chemotherapy patients in response to fatigue. *International Journal of Nursing Studies, 34*, 1, 35–43.

Roth, T., & Roehrs, T. A. (1991). A review of the safety profiles of benzodiazepine hypnotics. *Journal of Clinical Psychiatry, 52*, 38–41.

Savard, J., & Morin, C. M. (2001). Insomnia in the context of cancer: A review of a neglected problem. *Journal of Clinical Oncology, 19*, 3, 895–908.

Savard, J., Miller, S. M., Mills, M., O'Leary, A., Harding, H., Douglas, S. D., Mangan, C. E., Belch, R., & Winokur, A. (1999). Association between subjective sleep quality and depression on immunocompetence in low-income women at risk for cervical cancer. *Psychosomatic Medicine, 61*, 496–507.

Savard, J., Simard, S., Blanchet, J., Ivers, H., & Morin, C. M. (2001). Prevalence, clinical characteristics, and risk factors for insomnia in the context of breast cancer. *Sleep, 24*, 5, 583–589.

Savard, J., Laroche, L., Simard, S., Ivers, H., & Morin, C. M. (2003). Chronic insomnia and immune functioning. *Psychosomatic Medicine, 65*, 211–221.

Savard, J., Simard, S., Hervouet, S., Ivers, H., Lacombe, L., & Fradet, Y. (2005a). Insomnia in men treated with radical prostatectomy for prostate cancer. *Psycho-Oncology, 14*, 147–156.

Savard, J., Simard, S., Ivers, H., & Morin, C. M. (2005b). Randomized study on the efficacy of cognitive-behavioral therapy for insomnia secondary to breast cancer: Part I – Sleep and psychological effects. *Journal of Clinical Oncology, 23*, 6083–6096.

Simeit, R., Deck, R., & Conta-Marx, B. (2004). Sleep management training for cancer patients with insomnia. *Support Care Cancer, 12*, 176–183.

Simon, G. E., & VonKorff, M. (1997). Prevalence, burden, and treatment of insomnia in primary care. *American Journal of Psychiatry, 154*, 10, 1417–1423.

Spitzer, R. L., Williams, J. B. W., & Gibbon, M. (1997). *Structured Clinical Interview for DSM-IV (SCID)*. New York: New York State Psychiatric Institute, Biometrics Research Department.

Stam, H. J., & Bultz, B. D. (1986). The treatment of severe insomnia in a cancer patient. *Journal of Behavior Therapy and Experimental Psychiatry, 17*, 1, 33–37.

Stiefel, F. C., Kornblith, A. B., & Holland, J. C. (1990). Changes in the prescription patterns of psychotropic drugs for cancer patients during a 10-year period. *Cancer, 65*, 1048–1053.

Vollrath, M., Wicki, W., & Angst, J. (1989). The Zurich study. VIII. Insomnia: Association with depression, anxiety, somatic syndromes, and course of insomnia. *European Archives of Psychiatry and Neurological Sciences, 239*, 113–124.

Weissman, M. M., Greenwald, S., Nino-Murcia, G., & Dement, W. C. (1997). The morbidity of insomnia uncomplicated by psychiatric disorders. *General Hospital Psychiatry, 19*, 245–250.

Zammit, G. K., Weiner, J., Damato, N., Sillup, G. P., & McMillan, C. A. (1999). Quality of life in people with insomnia. *Sleep, 22*, S379–S385.

Chapter 5

Psychological treatment of hypertension

Wolfgang Linden

Objectives of this chapter

The treatment approach described here has gradually shaped over a 20-year period and moved from case studies to a completed clinical trial (Linden *et al.*, 2001) and further ongoing controlled intervention trials. This chapter therefore represents a very personal account of this development process and its contents are not claimed to represent an "industry standard". Guidance in the development of this approach has come from the early writing of Meyer and Liddell (1975) and Meyer and Turkat (1979) on case formulation in behaviour therapy at large, and from periodic reviews of the literature on etiology and on the treatment of hypertension in particular (Linden, 1984, 1988, Linden & Chambers, 1994; McGrady & Linden, 2003). For the purpose of this chapter, I will refer to the case formulation approach described here as the **H**ypertension **I**ndividually-tailored **T**reatment approach (acronym HIT).

It is posited that the three most unique features of HIT are:

1   The extensive integration of assessment in the treatment process.
2   The deliberate use of all baseline assessment information for individual tailoring of treatment steps and contents
3   The emancipated "student and self-healer" role that is given to patients.

Each of these features is described in more detail as this chapter progresses. The critical elements of the HIT approach have evolved from blending clinical observations with available research, and are guided by a theoretically eclectic view that is more responsive to individual patient background than it is prescriptive; most importantly, it does not assume universal etiological mechanisms.

Note that it will be presumed below that the therapist is a clinical psychologist simply because it is the author's "home turf" and because this is the most likely scenario. It does not imply that members of another profession could not also provide effective non-drug treatments for hypertension.

Etiology and definition of "high" blood pressure

Throughout this chapter, the terms "hypertension" and "high blood pressure" are treated as interchangeable. I consider it imperative that the psychological practitioner working with hypertensives has a sound basic understanding of the physiology of blood pressure (Vander *et al.*, 1994) for sensible treatment planning, and she or he will need to provide related education to his or her patient (usually very early in therapy) in a manner appropriate for the educational level of the patient. This chapter cannot serve as a thorough review of the literature on blood pressure regulation (for such a review see Linden, 1988 for example) but some basic information is provided nevertheless. Appreciation of the complexities of neural and endocrine influences on blood pressure is not essential for this chapter.

In a very small subgroup of patients (an estimated 5 per cent of all hypertensives), the blood pressure elevation is due to a known physiological or anatomical abnormality like kidney dysfunction. In these cases medical treatment is indicated and there may be little opportunity for psychological treatments to have an effect. However, the great, great majority of hypertensives are referred to as "primary" or "essential", which means that the cause is unknown. The common belief is that primary hypertension develops because of interacting factors, namely genetics, high stress levels, and poor diet/lack of exercise (Light *et al.*, 1999). The fact that these well-known contributing factors are not equally present in all hypertensive patients provides the first important clue as to why HIT favours individually tailored treatment where therapist and patient together build and test an etiological model that is specific to this one patient.

Of further use for this chapter is a summary of the difficulties with accurate blood pressure (BP) measurement and the diagnosis of hypertension. Blood pressure is expressed by describing two features, namely systolic/ diastolic, in millimeters of mercury. Systolic blood pressure (SBP) is the maximum pressure during ejection of blood from the heart (i.e. the heart muscle contraction phase, and diastolic blood pressure (DBP) is the minimum pressure during cardiac muscle relaxation. Mean arterial pressure (MAP) is the average blood pressure driving blood through tissues. Cardiac output and total peripheral resistance determine blood pressure. One calculates cardiac output by multiplying heart rate (beats per minute) by stroke volume output. The latter is the amount of blood ejected with each beat of the heart. While heart rate is very easy to measure (and is actually a built-in provision in all automatic blood pressure monitors), stroke volume is difficult to determine and usually beyond the technical capacity of the typical psychologist's office. Factors controlling heart rate and stroke volume include sympathetic and parasympathetic nerve activity, and it is currently believed that the best functioning cardiac system is characterized by a fluid "balancing act" of sympathetic and parasympathetic activity. Total peripheral resistance refers to the flow characteristics of blood and is a function of the width of blood vessels which are normally elastic and can dilate to reduce overall pressure in the system.

It is the very nature of hypertensive disease that in the early stages blood pressure elevation is most likely due to heightened sympathetic arousal and excessive cardiac output whereas in chronic hypertension a shift occurs such that heightened peripheral resistance is a stronger contributor to high pressure levels. At least in part, heightened peripheral resistance is maintained by the deposition of plaque in blood vessels (i.e. arteriosclerosis) which reduces the flexibility and its inherent self-regulatory, dilating potential of blood vessels. At the level of measurement, the underlying hemodynamic pattern is reflected in the absolute levels of SBP and DBP as well the difference score between the two (the latter is also referred to as pulse pressure). In a healthy individual, pulse pressure is likely in the 40–50 point range (example SBP = 120, DBP = 80 mmHg), whereas sympathetic hyperarousal is probably the primary contributor to a blood pressure reading of 160/90 mmHg where pulse pressure is large. A review of the subcategories used for diagnosing hypertension and their cutoff values may be of use and is provided in Table 5.1. The information is based on the recommendation of the Joint National Committee (JNC VI, 1997).

The role of medication

Once hypertension is diagnosed by a physician, treatment is often quickly initiated and the psychologist working with hypertensives should be aware of some basic facts of pharmacological treatment regimens. In medical practice, no single rigid criterion is used to decide on initiation of a drug treatment regimen although readings over 140/90 mmHg are considered elevated and in urgent need of attention. Patients with other heart disease risk factors present (like diabetes, smoking, positive family history, etc.) are more likely to be placed on antihypertensive medication at lower levels of blood pressure than those patients for whom only high blood pressure is a present risk.

Another important question is that of the suitability of patients who are

Table 5.1 Classification of blood pressure in adults aged 18 or older

Category	Systolic mmHg	Diastolic mmHg
Normal	<130	<85
High normal	130–139	85–89
Mild hypertension	140–159	90–99
Moderate hypertension	160–179	100–109
Severe hypertension	180–209	110–119

already drug treated for additional psychological treatment. There is no disagreement in the medical literature that antihypertensive medications effectively reduce blood pressure for almost all patients even if the first drug chosen may not turn out to be sufficient or the best choice. Often, multi-drug "cocktails" are needed, or two or three different drug classes may have to be tried. Although clinical trials of antihypertensive drugs strongly support their BP-lowering propensities, it should be noted that true BP control in community-living hypertensives is achieved in less than 30 per cent of hypertensives (JNC VI). Cause for this low success rate is frequently poor compliance with taking medication which in turn is due to a lack of willingness to accept side effects, a typical lack of subjective perception of improvement, and poor follow-up by the healthcare system. Whatever the reason may be for poor success with traditional hypertension treatment, it provides a strong justification to also consider non-drug approaches that are more readily tolerated. Considering psychological interventions therefore makes most sense when one or more of the following conditions apply:

- blood pressure is in the borderline or mild hypertension range
- antihypertensive drugs do not show the full expected effect
- side effects are present that the patient is not willing to tolerate
- there is a perceived high stress level that may contribute to hypertension
- the patient is at least somewhat psychologically minded and willing to see a psychologist.

In the Linden *et al.* (2001) study, patients on medication (provided they were still hypertensive prior to psychological treatment) benefited just as much from psychological therapy as those off medication. Hence, there is no need (nor is it recommended) to reduce or cut out all medications when working with psychological therapy. On the other hand, there are frequent case reports and even controlled studies (Shapiro *et al.*, 1997) showing that patients who underwent psychological treatment can reduce their medication load after therapy without fear of blood pressure going out of control. In fact, that is the explicit goal of many of the hypertensives that I have worked with. Note also that hypertensives who seek out psychologists are often the type who dislike all medications and may be prone to reduce medications on their own, often without the knowledge or approval of their physician. When perceiving this kind of attitude, it is highly recommended to discuss with the patient that treatment should involve all parties, and it is usually not in the best interest of patients to change the treatment regime without their physician's knowledge.

Furthermore, in the standard HIT approach, copies of the 24-hr blood pressure reports (pre and post treatment) are routinely shared with the family physician because: (a) this information sharing underlines the desire to consider treatment a collaborative effort; (b) parallel treatments without informing all parties involved are potentially counterproductive; (c) it is extremely rare that family physicians use 24-hr monitors, although they do consider the 24-hr blood pressure information vital and are usually grateful to have copies of these reports in their patients' charts.

Relationship of blood pressure to patient personality and emotional responding

Although there is a rich body of studies linking BP to psychological factors, the findings are complex, inconsistent, and not as helpful for making treatment decisions as the psychological therapist would like (for reviews see Byrne, 1992; Jorgensen et al., 1996; Rutledge & Hogan, 2002). There is a particular dearth of studies that allow prospective evaluation of personality and hypertension (Rutledge & Hogan, 2002a, 2002b). A full review of this extensive literature is beyond the scope of this chapter but a distillation of critical findings is clearly needed. Given its documented effects on blood pressure, particular problems appear to be lack of social support (Linden et al., 1993), high levels of trait anger and hostility as well as inflexible patterns of either unassertive or overly aggressive responding (Everson et al., 1999; Hogan & Linden, 2004), anxiety and depression (Byrne, 1992), and self-deception (Rutledge & Linden, 2000a, 2000b). Hence, appropriate targets for intervention appear to be reduction of anxiety, depression, and hostility, modification of self-deceptive responding, as well as the teaching of assertive and diplomatic anger response styles (Davidson et al., 1999; Linden et al., 2001)

Evaluation and measurement

HIT uses extensive and ongoing measurement of physiological and psychological functions: (a) to evaluate pre- to post-treatment changes; (b) to facilitate treatment target selection; (c) to motivate patients; (d) to track progress. Blood pressure measurement uses office and ambulatory determinations. Psychological functions are also monitored and focus on anxiety, depression, self-reported stress, hostility, anger level, and anger coping styles. If at all possible, patients complete 24-hr blood pressure monitoring and psychological tests prior to the first treatment session. All measures are scored and made available to the therapist for use in the first session.

Blood pressure measurement

The psychologist interested in working with HIT needs to have available simple-to-use and trustworthy blood pressure monitors and needs to know about the meaning of blood pressure variation as well accurate diagnostic methods. Ideally, office and ambulatory monitors should be accessible and be made use of.

For office professional use, relatively inexpensive automatic BP monitors can be purchased. Ease of use and clear displays are critical if the tool is used more or less continuously throughout therapy sessions. Inexpensive electronic monitors can provide reliable measures of SBP, DBP, and heart rate but the quality of the underlying validation work should be carefully evaluated prior to its purchase (Mattu *et al.*, 2001). Even if the basic measurement methodologies are similar, devices can differ substantially in their accuracy. It is very important to remember that office readings may falsely lead to a positive diagnosis because of measurement apprehension (the so-called white-coat hypertension), or they miss a substantial portion of patients who have high blood pressure all day but present with normal readings in the clinic (Liu *et al.*, 1999; Selenta *et al.*, 2000). These diagnostic errors are unfortunately very frequent (estimates are that 30–50 per cent of office diagnoses are wrong; Selenta *et al.*, 2000), but can be avoided when a 24-hour ambulatory device is used. However, ambulatory monitoring is quite a bit more costly and noticeably more inconvenient for patients. These obstacles notwithstanding, HIT relies on effective use of BP monitoring outside of the office. It is not unusual that patients who seek non-medical help are also the type of hypertensive who own their own BP monitor and often take their pressures at home. The HIT therapist welcomes this self-measurement as long as the patient has been trained to use a standard measurement protocol that averages multiple measures taken in comparable situations. Occasionally, patients take excessive numbers of readings and this should be discouraged to avoid obsessive attention to their own health status.

Psychological tools

Standardized tools are used in HIT for hostility (or trait anger), preferred anger coping styles (BARQ), anxiety and depression. The tools most often used in our clinic are the Beck Depression Inventory (1978), the Perceived Stress Scale (Cohen *et al.*, 1983), the Spielberger Trait Anger Inventory (Spielberger *et al.*, 1983), and the Behavioral Anger Response Questionnaire Scale (BARQ; Linden *et al.*, 2003). While all tools except the last are well known and have been in extended use, the BARQ is new and needs some description. The BARQ is a 37-item, self-report tool that taps six empirically derived and extensively validated subscales: namely Direct Anger Out, Assertion, Support Seeking, Diffusion, Avoidance, and Rumination. The BARQ had been used in the Linden *et al.* (2001) clinical trial and decreases in hostility scores (on the Cook-Medley scale, 1954) as well as increases in BARQ assertion use were positively correlated with blood pressure reduction thus serving as a criterion validation process for BARQ. The HIT therapist should be knowledgeable about norms for all scales that are used and provide relevant interpretations of the resulting scores meaning to the patient.

The intake interview

The first treatment session is explicitly designed to serve as an intake inter-view that blends history taking, analysis of 24-hr data, education, rapport building, and discussion of topic blocks (presented in discrete time epochs) together with joint attempts at interpreting observed blood pressure vari-ability. The term "topic block" reflects an attempt to ask questions about a particular topic or theme (like work stress or availability of social supports) within a well-defined time block (let's say five minutes) so that at least two or three BP readings can be taken during each such block.

A BP monitor is attached to the patient's arm early in the session after a full explanation of the monitor's purpose. The monitor is placed so that the therapist can easily activate the device and record all readings. In addition, the resulting readings should be visible to the patient so that unresolved curiosity does not disrupt the flow of the session. Nevertheless, it is best not to place the display right in front of the patient to prevent preoccupation with the BP measurement results. Therapists promptly point out how they inter-pret the readings and provide basic instruction on typical phenomena of measurement habituation, differentiation of rest-related activity from speech with affectively loaded content. For purposes of measurement reliability and the ability to make trustworthy inferences about blood pressure changes in response to distinct themes, the intake session should proceed by sequencing topics in distinct blocks of five to ten minutes each where BP is sampled every two or three minutes and can be averaged to maximize reliability. A sample of a recording from patient X that reflects BP changes as a function of interview topics is provided as Table 5.2.

The decision to sample BP throughout the session and relate it to interview content was triggered by the pioneering work of Lynch (1985) who showed how various social interactions (pleasant and unpleasant) of cardiac inpa-tients with staff and family triggered distinct heart rhythm irregularities. The very first time this parallel biology–psychology measurement approach was used with a hypertension case was also an exceedingly striking example of this approach's advantage as the case description shows:

A 62-year-old farmer (F) was referred for insomnia and hypertension which he refused to take medications for. Both hypertension and insomnia had been first noticed about 18 months prior. The intake session was structured to have theme blocks of (1) health concerns, (2) potential economic stressors inherent in farming (dependence on weather, sudden shifts in crop prices, etc.), and (3) the patient's social life and support network. Throughout topics 1 and 2, F had BPs that were around 160/ 100 mmHg and these were at least 10 points higher than a few readings taken during rest. To open up the assessment of topic 3, he was asked about his marital status and he revealed to be married with two daughters

Table 5.2 Sample of a recording of BP measures and corresponding themes in an intake session

Timing	Theme	Blood pressure reading
Min 0–5	No theme, instruments were set up and process was explained	no BP available
Min 5–15	Problem history and current health concerns	148/97
Min 15–30	Discussion of work environment and inherent stressors	145/94
Min 30–45	Patient revealed that she had a crack cocaine addicted daughter who prostituted herself to sustain her habit. Patient greatly worried for her safety, felt helpless as well	169/115
Min 45–55	Discussed support system and she expressed great comfort in having a very supportive husband	150/92
Min 55–60	Quick layout of a possible etiological model and treatment options	142/88

who were grown up and no longer lived with the parents. When he was asked what his marriage was like, F responded, "I guess it is OK." Which, if taken on its own, would have most likely made me stop to pursue the topic in greater detail. However, his BP readings shot up from 100 mmHg diastolic to 130 mmHg diastolic within two minutes of touching on the topic of marriage. When this BP jump was pointed out to F and tentatively linked to marital unhappiness, he responded by saying that he was actually miserable in his marriage, and had known on the day of the wedding that this was not going to be a happy union.

Next he was asked whether preceding his first diagnosis of insomnia and hypertension, there had been any salient life events. This question triggered the revelation that F's best and only friend had died from cancer at that time, and that his youngest daughter (to whom he had a strong attachment) left the small farm community to go to university 300 km away. These two parallel events had in one blow destroyed his positive social support and he now felt alone with a spouse who he perceived as quarrelsome and cold. As is predictable, the therapy consisted mainly of attempts to improve the marital situation and rebuild a positive social support system. Unfortunately, the great distance of the small farming town where he lived and the university town where we met prevented completion of therapy as planned and no pre-post outcome data were available. Nevertheless, the case of F left a striking and lasting impression with the author who might have missed (or at least taken much longer) to identify F's primary life stressors.

For further illustration of the tools used in HIT, samples are provided of a fairly typical 24-hr blood pressure monitor output (Figure 5.1), of a diary page that patients complete with each measurement (Figure 5.2), and a recording sheet sample is also provided that shows how intake session themes and BPs may correspond (Table 5.2). The diary recordings of mood and

```
ABP Hourly Averages·              A.C.                        Page 1 of 1
============================================================================
       Day &                                          Heart
       Hour            Readings    Systolic   Diastolic   Rate
----------------------------------------------------------------------------
    1-13:31 - 14:30       1          148        100        100
    1-14:31 - 15:30       3          146         98         83
    1-15:31 - 16:30       2          165        110         87
    1-16:31 - 17:30       3    A     172        120         80
    1-17:31 - 18:30       3          147         92         86
    1-18:31 - 19:30       3          140         93         93
    1-19:31 - 20:30       3          127         77         78
    1-20:31 - 21:30       3          149        106        105
    1-21:31 - 22:30       3          154         99         92
    1-22:31 - 23:30       3          140         94         81
    1-23:31 - 00:30       2          153        104         79
    1-00:31 - 01:30       1    B     151         98         75
    1-01:31 - 02:30       1          113         75         77
    1-02:31 - 03:30       1          119         78         79
    1-03:31 - 04:30       1           93         61         81
    1-04:31 - 05:30       1          104         63         78
    1-05:31 - 06:30       2          118         73         74
    1-06:31 - 07:30       3          126         80         73
    1-07:31 - 08:30       3          132         89         75
    1-08:31 - 09:30       3          150        107         88
    1-09:31 - 10:30       3          149        107         86
    1-10:31 - 11:30       3          146        106         79
    1-11:31 - 12:30       3          144         95         86
    1-12:31 - 13:30       3          135         91         99
    2-13:31 - 14:30       2          111         72         85
----------------------------------------------------------------------------
    Mean Averages                    137         92         84
```

A - STUCK IN HEAVY TRAFFIC DUE TO ACCIDENT AHEAD, GET VERY IMPATIENT, COULD NOT USE CELLPHONE DUE TO BAD RECEPTION

B - DIFFICULT TO FALL ASLEEP, MIND STILL RACING WITH REVIEW OF DAY'S EVENTS & WORRIED ABOUT LONG LIST OF THINGS TO DO FOR THE NEXT DAY

Figure 5.1 A typical data display from the ambulatory monitor.

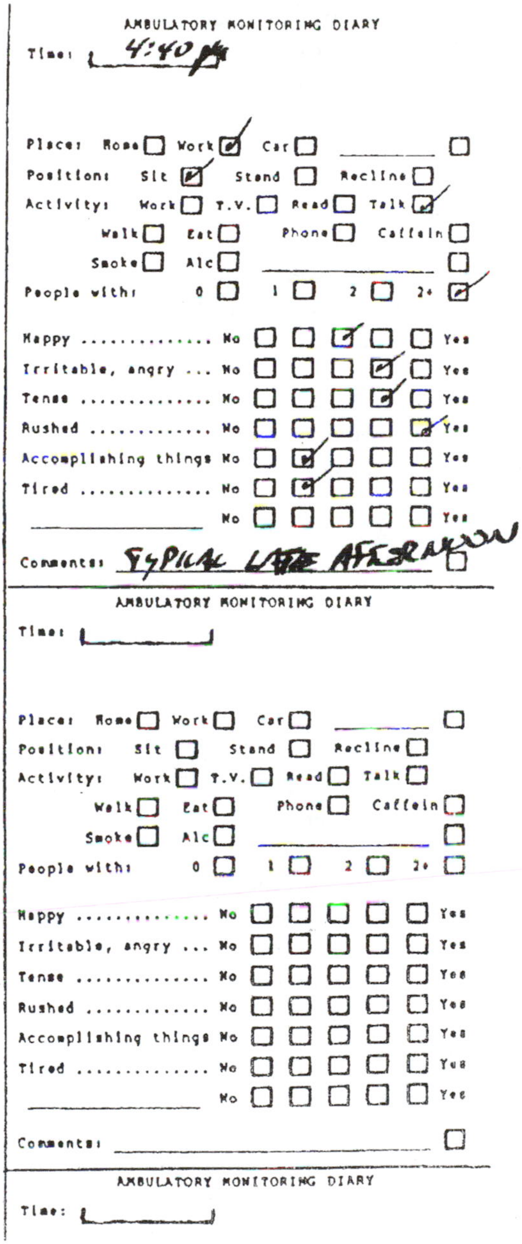

AMBULATORY MONITORING DIARY

Time: ⌊ 4:40 pm ⌋

Place: Home ☐ Work ☑ Car ☐ _____ ☐
Position: Sit ☑ Stand ☐ Recline ☐
Activity: Work ☐ T.V. ☐ Read ☐ Talk ☑
        Walk ☐ Eat ☐ Phone ☐ Caffein ☐
        Smoke ☐ Alc ☐ _____ ☐
People with: 0 ☐ 1 ☐ 2 ☐ 2+ ☑

Happy .... No ☐ ☐ ☑ ☐ ☐ Yes
Irritable, angry ... No ☐ ☐ ☐ ☑ ☐ Yes
Tense .... No ☐ ☐ ☐ ☑ ☐ Yes
Rushed .... No ☐ ☐ ☐ ☐ ☑ Yes
Accomplishing things No ☐ ☐ ☑ ☐ ☐ Yes
Tired .... No ☐ ☑ ☐ ☐ ☐ Yes
_____ No ☐ ☐ ☐ ☐ ☐ Yes

Comments: TYPICAL LATE AFTERNOON ☐

AMBULATORY MONITORING DIARY

Time: ⌊ _____ ⌋

Place: Home ☐ Work ☐ Car ☐ _____ ☐
Position: Sit ☐ Stand ☐ Recline ☐
Activity: Work ☐ T.V. ☐ Read ☐ Talk ☐
        Walk ☐ Eat ☐ Phone ☐ Caffein ☐
        Smoke ☐ Alc ☐ _____ ☐
People with: 0 ☐ 1 ☐ 2 ☐ 2+ ☐

Happy .... No ☐ ☐ ☐ ☐ ☐ Yes
Irritable, angry ... No ☐ ☐ ☐ ☐ ☐ Yes
Tense .... No ☐ ☐ ☐ ☐ ☐ Yes
Rushed .... No ☐ ☐ ☐ ☐ ☐ Yes
Accomplishing things No ☐ ☐ ☐ ☐ ☐ Yes
Tired .... No ☐ ☐ ☐ ☐ ☐ Yes
_____ No ☐ ☐ ☐ ☐ ☐ Yes

Comments: _____ ☐

AMBULATORY MONITORING DIARY

Time: ⌊ _____ ⌋

Figure 5.2 A completed sample diary page to accompany the blood pressure recording.

activity displayed in Figure 5.2 are to be completed for every BP recording that is taken (except during sleep, of course) and are used to help understand BP variability throughout the day. The information provided herein is also useful to help explain the emotional component and its effect on BP changes.

The blood pressure recordings in Figure 5.1 reflect the averages of two to three readings per hour and this display is preferred because the averaging increases test reliability. The patient monitored here (Figure 5.1) had a fairly hectic day. His BP peaked in the late afternoon when he got stuck in traffic, his cell phone did not work, and he was late for a meeting without being able to inform anybody. He described himself as very impatient and upset at that time. In addition, there are some high readings after midnight when he tried to sleep but struggled with falling asleep, still rehearsing his day and unresolved problems.

Note that attempts to connect BP changes with psychologically or physically salient events is not an exact science and involves guesswork, and trial and error. If the therapist's questions do not lead to prompt insight on the part of the patient, there is little use to argue with patients that there must have been some upsetting event anyway. When patients don't know, then such events can also not be discussed.

Decision making for treatment planning

Development of rationale

The initial assessment provides the therapist with a rich database that can be used for treatment planning. The exploration of the 24-hour blood pressure monitor data together with the activity diary, and the joint assessment of themes and parallel blood pressure changes in the intake session helps to identify times, activities, environments, and emotional responses that may be critical for understanding patient stress exposure and coping. The coping aspect is further enhanced by the information derived from standardized self-report tools regarding anxiety, anger level, and anger coping habits. At the end of the intake session, the therapist provides the patient with factual information regarding factors that influence blood pressure, and will have proposed a therapy rationale and sequence of steps that the patient is asked to agree to. Wherever reasonable, treatment options can be presented as choices to the patient. For example, a patient may be instructed that relaxation training is probably useful and that either temperature biofeedback or autogenic training would be good choices to achieve this. After receiving a description of the methods, the patient can then choose the method which appears more appealing and which has more inherent credibility.

Given the emphasis on an educational approach and the individual tailoring of targets, there is little concern over motivational problems that may undermine adherence. The one aspect that is most likely to be difficult is adherence to home practices of breathing and other relaxation training. The provision of clear rationales, use of a simple diary for record keeping, and repeated (but not overly invasive) questioning by the therapist about progress are meant to maximize compliance. More detail on suggestions for compliance with relaxation homework instructions can be found in Linden's (1990) clinical guidebook for autogenic training.

In the section on intervention, the reader will find two case illustrations that demonstrate how assessment information is used to weave an etiological model for each of these patients, and how a treatment approach is then derived from there.

Intervention

Especially in the age of managed care and healthcare cuts, all clinicians should be prepared to show and defend the efficacy of their work. In this light, HIT can be considered to have a solid empirical basis. The biobehavioural or psychological therapies used for treating hypertension are typically described as adjuncts to standard pharmacological treatments in the more severe hypertensive patient or as an alternative to medication in the mild or borderline (Stage 1 or 2) hypertensive patient. The consensus report of JNC VI (1997) stated that relaxation and biofeedback therapies have not been sufficiently tested to lead to firm conclusions, and that "the role of stress management techniques . . . is uncertain". More recently, a Canadian Consensus group (Spence *et al.*, 1999) has concluded that individualized stress management may be an effective intervention after all. This conclusion was partly based on Linden and Chambers' (1994) argument that the classification of biofeedback and relaxation as "mere" adjuncts may be unfairly based on research protocol peculiarities in that non-drug studies typically start with much lower blood pressures than drug studies. This is important because Jacob *et al.* (1991) have shown a high positive correlation between BP at entry and subsequent degree of BP change. Adjustment for different BP levels at baseline in the Linden and Chambers meta-analysis (1994) indicated that the best non-drug treatments were as efficacious as a variety of different drug regimens. In a recent trial, using a combination of techniques including temperature biofeedback and autogenic training, HIT reduced 24-hr means for SBP and DBP. The results were even stronger at follow-up (Linden *et al.*, 2001).

As mentioned above, the originality of HIT lies in individualizing treatment rationale and technique sequencing and this process has already been described. Specific techniques to be used are not particularly original but are largely based on well-established, empirically validated approaches that are typically applied with the aid of standardized manuals (Bernstein & Borkovec, 1973; Linden, 1990; Suinn, 1990; Greenberger & Padesky, 1995; McGrady & Linden, 2003). The therapist should have a solid foundation in a fairly wide range of theoretical approaches with particular skill and experience in cognitive-behavioural therapies and autonomic self-regulation approaches (i.e. autogenic training, muscular relaxation, temperature biofeedback, and breathing training). This chapter cannot provide detailed descriptions of these methods for novice therapists. Each one of them would require one or more books for mere presentation of materials as well as hands-on training and supervision.

Early in the intervention, typically in session two, a demonstration is given of how good breathing and relaxation acutely affect BP. This is done by providing quick instructions in elementary breathing techniques and then a practice. It is set up like a classic A-B-A experiment such that at least two BP readings are available prior to relaxation. BP is also recorded two or three times during the brief relaxation, and then compared to another two readings taken post relaxation when the therapist–patient discourse continues. This little experiment often leads to substantial variations in BP, with as much as 20 point drops in SBP and 10 point drops in DBP. Display and discussion of these results are then used to convince the patient that BP is indeed under his or her control and is very much affected by physical and mental activity. This quick demonstration lends credibility to the therapy approach and serves as a powerful motivating agent that can create a growing sense of self-efficacy.

A fairly typical layout of session content for a ten-session (at 60 minutes each) therapy with a hypertensive who reported lots of work stress and occasional anger outbursts, might look like this:

- *Session 1*: intake session that ends with the development of an etiological model for a given patient, and a resulting treatment plan.
- *Session 2*: teaching of breathing and/or a relaxation method; identification of irrational thought patterns that may perpetuate impatience and frequent angry reactions; homework is diary keeping of stressful events and corresponding thoughts.
- *Session 3*: review of the homework on relaxation practice, and working through diary information provided by the patient; attempt to identify maladaptive thought patterns.
- *Session 4*: additional instructions for relaxation, expansion of cognitive therapy, more diary-keeping homework.
- *Session 5*: continuation of cognitive therapy for frequent anger responding.
- *Session 6*: teaching time-management skills and diary keeping on time usage as homework.
- *Session 7*: review of time management homework, teaching relaxation transfer skills to real-life situations.
- *Session 8*: review of current social support network, sources for frustration and underutilized opportunities for emotional support.

- *Session 9*: review of pleasant activities, strategies to increase pleasant activities and related homework.
- *Session 10*: review of all therapy phases, identification of new skills learned and their usefulness, and development of plans and goals for the next few months.

Especially when reviewing social networks, relationship problems may come to the surface, and the therapist may invite the spouse to join for one or two sessions. Throughout the therapy, the therapist will use opportunities to continue teaching skills (like time management) or pass on knowledge (for example, how exercise affects blood pressure).

As the above example of the farmer with the very unhappy marriage indicated, the initial assessment often reveals a distinct concern or aspect of everyday life that has blood pressure raising stimulus properties and these features become an obvious target for intervention.

Clinical experience, however, has also shown that neither the blood pressure measurement during the intake session nor the clinical interview will necessarily reveal any aspect of salient concern to the patient. In such a case, a generic arousal reduction program is usually implemented. The treatment of a young mother who had developed hypertension during pregnancy is now described:

> Jane P had given birth to her first child six months ago and was happy with her new mother's role. However, she had developed hypertension during pregnancy, and had to be hospitalized for two months to guarantee a safe pregnancy. She had been understandably scared and upset about the pregnancy-induced hypertension. In many such patients, the hypertension quickly dissipates post-birth. However, in her case BP continued to be high (BP average in the first session was 138/95 mmHg. The continuing BP assessment during the intake interview revealed very little variability in her BP and no salient theme could be identified that triggered noticeable BP changes. In this case, the therapy approach was largely educational and directed at learning basic arousal reduction techniques (i.e. autogenic training) and she was encouraged to gradually build up an exercise program. Furthermore, she was greatly relieved to learn that pregnancy-induced hypertension is not as infrequent as she had thought and that she had nothing for which she would deserve to be blamed. Within six sessions her BP level (averaged across 12 readings taken within the session) dropped by -10 mmHg SBP and -17 mmHg DBP.

If one accepts the basic notion that a variety of stressors (whether concrete and external like work overload, or more internal like stress-enhancing thought patterns) can contribute to hypertension, then it also stands to reason that the therapist need not be limited to a narrow theoretical approach. A good example is the case now described where biobehavioural strategies (i.e. arousal reduction techniques) were paired with a more interpersonal-psychodynamic approach:

> Max C was a 63-year-old male referred for hypertension and self-reported high anxiety. He presented with long hair and a ponytail, routinely wearing black jeans, cowboy boots and a black T-shirt. Not only was his dress code unusual for a man in his age group, but it was even more striking that he worked as an office manager/technician although he had earned a PhD in biology from a prestigious university. It was learned that his whole life had consisted of mocking the world, bucking authority, and not committing to close relationships. At the time of therapy he was in his third marriage and this marriage was not doing well either, which he solely attributed to lack of commitment on his part, marked by occasional extramarital affairs. The first discovery in Mr C's therapy was that he qualified as a genuine white-coat hypertensive given that his 24-hr BP mean was 142/93 whereas readings in the physician's office and in our session typically ranged from 180/100 to 200/110. While the BP average during the first treatment session was 185/115, the time epoch during which we discussed his marriage and close relationships in general was marked by a BP average of 209/136 mmHg, i.e. strikingly elevated. In order to engage in concrete progress quickly and have an opportunity to build a strong rapport, treatment initially focused on temperature biofeedback and autogenic training. From about the third session on, topics were more directed at interpersonal relationships and it was learned that he had grown up in a chaotic, aloof family and had learned not to trust anybody. Hence, the topic of trust and intimacy became the focus of the therapeutic work over the next few sessions. Mr C made a real emotional breakthrough when a colleague whom he knew moderately well, sought out his support in dealing with severe marital problems. The discovery that somebody else was willing and able to trust him, opened Mr C's eyes and provided a stimulus to test the results of increasing his own openness, especially with his wife. At the end of session nine, i.e. the end of therapy, he reported a much higher comfort level around his wife and they had begun to have more common activities, namely going out with friends and travel. His 24-hr BP had gone down from 142/93 mmHg to 132/87 mmHg and his family physician no longer saw a need to place Mr C on medication.

Unresolved questions

The treatment response (i.e. magnitude of blood pressure change) to any kind of psychological treatment, or HIT in particular, is highly varied and likely even more varied than the response to medication would have been. It is unknown at this time whether distinct subgroups of patients exist for whom psychological stress is not connected in any causal way to blood pressure, or whether insufficient length of treatment or inappropriate choice of technique accounts for treatment failure. Judging treatment success by only studying pre-post changes may also mask effects because we have found interesting "sleeper effects" when carefully studying the treatment response curve in patients who returned for six-month follow-ups. While it was unusual that treatment gains (as measured immediately post treatment) were lost at follow-up, there was a substantial group of patients who appeared unchanged at post-test but improved from post-test to follow-up (Linden *et al.*, 2001). This was interpreted as therapy having "planted a seed" that did not come to sprout in the typical three-month, active therapy period. Furthermore, it was considered good news because it supports the notion that patients may have learned lasting skills for stress coping, and that initial treatment success is not just an artifact or the result of transient therapist attention.

Acknowledgments

I greatly appreciate the feedback on earlier drafts provided by Martine Habra, Susan Holtzman, and Sandra Young. I am also indebted to the Medical Research Council of Canada, the Canadian Institutes of Health Research, and the Heart and Stroke Foundation of British Columbia and Yukon who provided financial support for the work described here.

References

Beck, A.T. (1978). *Depression Inventory*. Philadelphia, PA: Center for Cognitive Therapy.

Bernstein, D. A., & Borkovec, I. O. (1973). *Progressive relaxation training: A manual for helping professions*. Champaign, IL: Research Press.

Byrne, D. G. (1992). Anxiety, neuroticism, depression, and hypertension. In E. H. Johnson, W. D. Gentry, & S. Julius (Eds.), *Personality, elevated blood pressure, and essential hypertension* (pp. 67–85). Washington: Hemisphere.

Cohen, S., Kamarck, I. & Mermelstein, R. (1983). A global measure of perceived stress. *Journal of Health and Social Behavior, 24*, 385–396.

Cook, W.W., & Medley, D.M. (1954). Proposed hostility and pharisaic-virtue scales for the MMPI. *Journal of Applied Psychology, 38*, 414–418.

Davidson, K., MacGregor, M.W., Stuhr, J., & Gidron, Y. (1999). Increasing constructive anger verbal behavior decreases resting blood pressure: A secondary analysis of a randomized controlled hostility intervention. *International Journal of Behavioral Medicine, 6*, 268–278.

Everson, S.A., Goldberg, D.E., Kaplan, G.A., Julkunen, J., & Salonen, J.T. (1999). Anger expression and incident hypertension. *Psychosomatic Medicine, 60*, 730–735.

Greenberger, D., & Padesky, C.A. (1995). *Mind over mood: Change how you feel by changing the way you think*. New York: Guilford Press.

Hogan, B.E., & Linden, W. (2004). Anger response styles and blood pressure: At least don't ruminate about it. *Annals of Behavioral Medicine, 27*, 38–49.

Jacob, R.G., Chesney, M.A., Williams, D.M., Ding, Y., & Shapiro, A.P. (1991). Relaxation therapy for hypertension: Design effects and treatment effects. *Annals of Behavioral Medicine, 13*, 5–17.

Jorgensen, R.S., Johnson, B.T., Kolodziej, M.E., & Schreer, G.E. (1996). Elevated blood pressure and personality: A meta-analytic review. *Psychological Bulletin, 120*, 293–320.

Light, K.C., Girdler, S.S., Sherwood, A., Bragdon, E.E., Bronwley, K.A., West, S.G., & Hinderliter, A.L. (1999). High stress responsivity predicts later blood pressure only in combination with positive family history and high life stress. *Hypertension, 33*, 1458–1464.

Linden, W. (1984). *Psychological perspectives of essential hypertension.* Basel: S. Karger.

Linden, W. (1988). Biopsychological barriers to the behavioral treatment of essential hypertension. In W. Linden (Ed.), *Biological barriers in behavioral medicine.* New York: Plenum.

Linden, W. (1990). *Autogenic training: A clinical guide.* New York: Guilford Press.

Linden, W. (2003). Psychological treatment can be an effective treatment for hypertension. *Preventive Cardiology, 6*, 48–53.

Linden, W., & Chambers, L.A. (1994). Clinical effectiveness of non-drug therapies for hypertension: A meta-analysis. *Annals of Behavioral Medicine, 16*, 35–45.

Linden, W., Chambers, L., Maurice, J., & Lenz, J.W. (1993). Sex differences in social support, self-deception, hostility, and ambulatory cardiovascular activity. *Health Psychology, 12*, 376–380.

Linden, W., Lenz, J.W., & Con, A.H. (2001). Individualized stress management for primary hypertension: A controlled clinical trial. *Archives of Internal Medicine, 161*, 1071–1080.

Linden, W., Hogan, B.E., Rutledge, I., Chawla, A., Lenz, J.W., & Leung, D. (2003) There is more to anger coping than 'in' or 'out'. *Emotion, 3*, 12–29.

Liu, J.E., Roman, M.J., Pini, R., Schwartz, J.E., Pickering, T.G., & Devereux, R.B. (1999). Elevated ambulatory with normal clinic blood pressure ('white coat normotension') is associated with cardiac and arterial target organ damage. *Annals of Internal Medicine, 131*, 564–572.

Lynch, J.J. (1985). *The language of the heart.* New York: Basic Books.

McGrady, A., & Linden, W. (2003). Biobehavioral treatment of essential hypertension. In M. S. Schwartz & F. Andrasik (Eds.), *Biofeedback–A Practitioner's Guide* (3rd ed.). New York: Guilford Press.

Mattu, G.S., Perry, T.L. Jr, & Wright, J.M. (2001). Comparison of the oscillometric blood pressure monitor (BPMI OOBeta) with the auscultatory mercury sphygmomanometer. *Blood Pressure Monitoring, 6*, 153–159.

Meyer, V., & Liddell, A. (1975). Behaviour therapy. In D. Bannister (Ed.), *Issues and trends in psychological therapies.* Chichester: Wiley.

Meyer, V., & Turkatl, D. (1979). Behavioural analysis of clinical cases. *Journal of Behavioral Assessment, 1*, 259–269.

Rutledge, T., & Hogan, B.E. (2002). A quantitative review of prospective evidence linking psychological factors with hypertension development. *Psychosomatic Medicine, 64*, 758–766.

Rutledge, T., & Linden, W. (2000a). Psychological response styles and cardiovascular health: Confound or independent risk factor? *Health Psychology, 19*, 441–451.

Rutledge, T., & Linden, W. (2000b). Defensiveness status predicts 3-year incidence of hypertension. *Journal of Hypertension, 18*, 153–159.

Selenta, C., Hogan, B., & Linden, W. (2000). How often do office blood pressure measurements fail to identify true hypertension? *Archives of Family Medicine, 9*, 533–540.

Shapiro, D., Hui, K.K., Oakley, M.E., Pasic, J., & Jamner, L.D. (1997). Reduction in drug requirements for hypertension by means of a cognitive-behavioral intervention. *American Journal of Hypertension, 10*, 9–17.

Spence, J.D., Bamett, P.A., Linden, W., Ramsden, V., & Tanezer, P. (1999). Nonpharmacologic therapy to prevent and control hypertension: 7. Recommendations on stress management. *Canadian Medical Association Journal, 160*, S46–S50.

Spielberger, C.D., Jacobs, G.A., Russell, S.F., & Crane, R.J. (1983). Assessment of anger: The State-Trait Anger Scale. In J. Butcher & C.D. Spielberger (Eds.), *Advances in personality assessment* (pp. 161–189). Hillsdale, NJ: Lawrence Erlbaum Associates, Inc.

Suinn, R.M. (1990). *Anxiety management training: A behavior therapy.* New York: Plenum Press.

The Sixth Report of the Joint National Committee on Prevention, Detection, Evaluation, and Treatment of High Blood Pressure: (JNC VI) (1997). *Archives Internal Medicine, 157*, 2413–2446.

VA Administration Cooperative Study Group on Anthypertensive Agents. (1975). Return of elevated blood pressure after withdrawal of antihypertensive drugs. *Circulation, 51*, 1107–1113.

Vander, A. J., Sherman, J. H., & Luciano, O. (1994). *Human physiology* (6th ed.). New York: McGraw-Hill.

Chapter 6

Stress, anger, and hostility in coronary heart disease

Phillip J. Brantley, Karen B. Grothe and Gareth R. Dutton

Coronary heart disease (CHD) is the leading cause of death in the USA, accounting for one of every five deaths in this country. The estimated overall prevalence of CHD in the USA is 6.4 per cent, affecting 13 million people, and the prevalence of this disease is similar across most other industrialized countries (American Heart Association, AHA, 2003). The direct and indirect costs of this disease were estimated at $133.2 billion in 2003 (AHA, 2003). CHD is a broad category comprised of a set of conditions resulting from coronary artery disease (CAD), which is the gradual accumulation of plaque in coronary arteries. CAD is a progressive and slow condition that may be asymptomatic for years. Eventual symptoms of CAD can include myocardial ischemia (insufficient oxygen supply to the heart), angina pectoris (chest pain), myocardial infarction (MI; death of heart muscle), and cardiac arrhythmias (Krantz & McCeney, 2002; Smith & Ruiz, 2002). There are a number of well-established risk factors associated with the development of CAD and CHD, such as smoking, hypertension, and hyperlipidemia (Kannel, 1979). However, such risk factors have only moderate value in predicting new cases of CHD (Jenkins, 1988), suggesting other variables may play an important role in the development and outcome of this common disease. Thus, research examining other CHD risk factors has increased tremendously, and several psychological variables, including stress, anger, and hostility, have been implicated for their relationship to CHD.

Stress and CHD

Numerous studies have suggested that various types of stress are associated with cardiac events. Animal research has suggested that social stress and conflict can result in abnormal coronary constriction, increased coronary artery blockage, malignant arrhythmias, and heart failure (Krantz & McCeney, 2002). In humans, natural and man-made disasters have demonstrated an association with increased rates of sudden cardiac events (Meisel *et al.*, 1991). Additionally, stressful life events are related to increased blood pressure (Theorell & Emlund, 1993) and have been found to occur more often in the

24 hours prior to sudden cardiac death (Cottington *et al.*, 1980). Mental stressors induced in laboratory settings have also resulted in increased abnormal cardiac events such as myocardial ischemia (Rozanski *et al.*, 1988). Occupational stress and work demands may confer specific risk, as studies have demonstrated that job demands, job autonomy, and job satisfaction are related to CHD. In particular, job strain, a construct defined by an occupation with both high job demands and low job control, has been implicated for its role in increased risk of CHD (Karasek *et al.*, 1988).

To summarize, animal and human studies suggest that both acute and chronic stressors may influence the development and outcome of various coronary indicators. Such findings highlight the need to attend to such variables in the assessment and treatment of CAD and CHD. It should be noted, however, that several limitations (e.g. small sample sizes, biased recall) to this area of research restrict the generalizability of results, which argues for the importance of individualized assessment for CHD patients (Krantz & McCency, 2002; Smith & Ruiz, 2002).

Anger, hostility and CHD

Examination of anger and hostility as variables related to CHD originated from Friedman and Rosenman's (1959) initial work on Type A behavior pattern (TABP) and CHD. TABP is defined as behavior and affect characterized by a sense of time urgency, achievement striving, competitiveness, impatience, loud and quick speech patterns, controlling behavior, and frequent anger and hostility. Initial research found TABP to be predictive of CHD (Rosenman *et al.*, 1975). However, after subsequent research failed to replicate this relationship, researchers began to examine the contributions of individual components of TABP.

Of the studied components of TABP, anger and hostility have received a significant amount of attention for their relationship with CHD. Hostility is generally defined as an enduring trait characterized by emotional, cognitive, and behavioral subcomponents (Smith & Ruiz, 2002). Cognitive factors include cynicism, mistrust of others, and the frequent interpretation of others' behaviors as malevolent. Affective components are comprised primarily of the emotion of anger, and the behavioral component includes verbal and nonverbal aggressive behaviors. The affective component of anger can be further separated into either a temporary state or a more enduring trait or disposition. Behavioral responses to anger have been summarized as anger-in and anger-out (Spielberger *et al.*, 1985). While anger-in refers to a pattern of withholding expressions of anger, anger-out is characterized by a tendency to express anger via verbal or nonverbal behaviors. Clearly, the affective, behavioral, and cognitive constructs of hostility and anger share many features and in practical measurement can be difficult to separate.

Expression of anger has shown significant relationships with several CAD and CHD indices. For example, it has been suggested that extreme levels (high or low) of anger expression result in negative health consequences such as elevated blood pressure and progression of atherosclerosis (Dembroski et al., 1985; Siegman et al., 1992; Suarez & Williams, 1990). Alternatively, moderate levels of anger expression have demonstrated a protective effect against stroke and nonfatal MI (Mona et al., 2003).

In addition to the expression of anger, the internal experience of anger has also been implicated in the course of CHD. Individuals who exhibit high levels of angry temperament have shown more than a double increase in CHD risk compared to those without angry temperament, even after controlling for other CHD risk factors (Kawachi et al., 1996; Williams et al., 2001). When considered as a stable personality trait (characterized by more frequent, more intense, and longer lasting episodes of anger), anger confers a two- to three-fold increased risk of CHD in addition to a dose response relationship (Kawachi et al., 1996; Williams et al., 2000). Further, normotensives with an angry temperament share a similar level of risk for CHD as hypertensive individuals, suggesting anger may confer a similar level of risk as hypertension (Williams et al., 2001).

It has been suggested that hostility, particularly the cognitive aspect of hostility (cynical mistrust), is the toxic component of TABP. Several large-scale prospective and cross-sectional studies have identified a consistent relationship between hostility and CHD. Hostility has been identified as a risk factor for CHD as well as a predictor of myocardial infarction, CAD, peripheral artery disease, and all-cause mortality, even after controlling for other traditional risk factors (Barefoot et al., 1983; Miller et al., 1996; Smith & Ruiz, 2002). Clinician-based structured interviews often demonstrate a stronger association between CHD and hostility compared to self-report measures of hostility. The strength of the relationship between hostility and CHD may also vary based on gender, age, and ethnicity (Miller et al., 1996; Finney et al., 2002).

Pathways between risk factors and CHD

Growing evidence suggests stress and hostility may have both chronic (progression of CAD) and acute (precipitant of myocardial infarction) effects on the cardiovascular system. Physiological responses to stress and hostility include a number of processes that could exacerbate the development of CAD and CHD. Stress, anger, and hostility often serve to increase heart rate and blood pressure, which over time can damage the lining of the coronary artery and hasten CAD. The stress response is associated with the release of catecholamines and corticosteroids, which can increase blood platelet aggregation and coronary vasoconstriction, subsequently increasing the risk of thrombosis, or clotting of tissue within the artery (Krantz & Manuck,

1984; Muller *et al.*, 1989). Hostility and anger may also be associated with increased risk of acute coronary events (Mittleman *et al.*, 1995).

In addition to the potential physiological processes involved in the experience of stress, anger, and hostility, these psychological variables may also influence CHD via behavioral pathways, including performance or failure to perform both positive and negative health behaviors, for example, smoking, high-fat diet, regular exercise (Smith & Gallo, 1994; Smith & Ruiz, 2002). Individuals with high levels of hostility may also be at increased risk for CHD due to limited social support networks and greater interpersonal conflict related to their personality style (Smith & Ruiz, 2002).

Assessment of CHD risk factors

One of the foundational components of assessment with a CHD patient is the clinical interview, which may be unstructured, semi-structured, or structured in nature. In such an interview, it is important to assess for current and past psychopathology (e.g. depression, anxiety) as well as current and past medical conditions, medications, and treatments, with special emphasis placed on the patient's cardiovascular history. Particular attention should be paid to the timeline of such information, including the onset, duration, intensity, and frequency of physical and/or mental symptoms. Possible interactions between physical symptoms and emotional experiences should also be assessed along with the patient's insight into these interactions. It is important to assess the patient's motivation for engaging in psychological treatments if deemed appropriate, and should such interventions be initiated, it is essential to obtain appropriate medical clearance for the patient's participation. Any medical contra-indications to treatment should be discussed with qualified medical professionals.

In addition to the traditional clinical interview, structured interviews have been developed to assess TABP characteristics. Special emphasis is placed on overt behavior during these interviews, including speech characteristics and manner of responding (e.g. frequent interruption of the interviewer). As the influence of TABP gradually fell out of favor, new scoring systems were created for the structured interview that focused specifically on hostility (Dembroski *et al.*, 1989). Although these structured interviews have been used frequently in CHD research, the interviews are lengthy to administer and have poor inter-observer reliability (Barefoot, 1992). Thus, these interviews are generally impractical in most clinical settings.

The Cook-Medley Hostility (Ho) scale is the most commonly used self-report measure of hostility and is comprised of 50 true–false items from the Minnesota Multiphasic Personality Inventory (MMPI; Cook & Medley, 1954). Ho scores have been consistently linked to CHD outcomes. High scorers on the Ho scale have been identified as persons with frequent anger, lack of hardiness (adaptive appraisal mechanisms), lower levels of and satisfaction with social support, and higher frequency and severity of minor life events (Smith & Frohm, 1985). With the introduction of the MMPI-2, the Anger Content and Cynicism scales also began to be used to assess these constructs (Kawachi *et al.*, 1996; Siegman *et al.*, 2000). The Anger Content scale (16 items) assesses anger-control problems, including irritability, hot-headedness, and feeling like swearing or smashing things. The Cynicism scale (23 items) assesses individuals' tendency to believe others' actions are negative and threatening (Kawachi *et al.*, 1996). The Buss-Durkee Hostility Inventory (BDHI; Buss & Durkee, 1957) is another self-report measure that consists of seven subscales, including Assault, Indirect Hostility, Irritability, Negativity, Resentment, Suspicion, and Verbal Hostility.

Spielberger and colleagues have developed self-report inventories useful for assessing the experience, expression, and control of anger. The State-Trait Anger Expression Inventory (STAXI) was designed to assess the experience of anger as a transient emotional state as well as a more enduring personality trait (Spielberger, 1999). State anger includes subjective feelings of irritation, annoyance, and fury that may vary in intensity across different situations, while trait anger can be conceptualized as the frequent occurrence of state anger. The STAXI yields scores for subscales concerning Anger Expression, Anger Control, and an overall Anger Expression Index. As the name implies, the Anger Expression subscales measure one's tendency to suppress or express anger. The Anger-Control subscales measure respondents' ability to control the outward expression of anger or to calm down once angry. Previous research has found Trait-Anger scores to be associated with CHD and Anger Expression scores with MI and unstable angina pectoris (Spielberger, 1999).

A number of self-report inventories are available to assess the frequency and/or impact associated with stressful life events as well. Such measures can generally be divided into two groups that vary in the type of life event assessed. While some measures specifically address the occurrence of major life events (e.g. divorce, family death), other inventories assess the effects of minor life events, or daily hassles. A commonly used inventory of major life events is the Life Events Schedule (LES; Sarason *et al.*, 1978). The LES is often preferred over earlier measures of life stress because it assesses the respondent's appraisal of the event and its impact on their functioning in addition to the occurrence or non-occurrence of events. There are several measures of minor life events, including the Daily Hassles Scale (Kanner *et al.*, 1981) and the Weekly Stress Inventory (WSI; Brantley *et al.*, 1997). Such measures assess the frequency and perceived impact of everyday stressors, such as arguments at work, upcoming deadlines, having to wait in line, etc. Like the LES, these measures have the advantage of assessing not only the frequency of daily hassles but also the individual's perceived stressfulness of each event.

When feasible, physiological indices can also be used in the assessment of psychological variables associated with CAD and CHD. For example, advances in ambulatory ECG monitoring allow for the measurement of myocardial ischemia, or the insufficient supply of oxygen to the heart. Use of ambulatory monitors can be especially helpful in allowing researchers and clinicians to measure occurrences of myocardial ischemia following stressful life events. Such assessment is especially useful since silent ischemia (i.e. ischemia in the absence of chest pain) has been shown to occur in conjunction with physical activity as well as mental stressors (Rozanski *et al.*, 1988). Physiological measures of the stress response (e.g. assessment of cortisol levels) can also be helpful in determining the degree of stress associated with particular events. However, such procedures are more commonly used in research settings and are generally unavailable or impractical for most clinicians.

Psychological treatment of CHD risk factors

A number of studies have examined various types of psychological interventions utilized with cardiac patients to reduce the recurrence of cardiac events and improve CHD mortality rates. Much of the early intervention research examined the efficacy of psychological treatments specifically targeting TABP, and these studies produced significant findings. For instance, Friedman *et al.* (1986) found treatment including relaxation, cognitive therapy, hostility reduction, and time management resulted in decreased Type A behavior and cardiac mortality in post-MI patients. A meta-analysis of this literature also highlighted the efficacy of psychological interventions aimed at reducing TABP. Treatments including a variety of techniques such as behavioral modification, cognitive interventions, relaxation, and other components showed a significant reduction in Type A behavior and some indices of CHD (Nunes *et al.*, 1987).

While the emphasis has gradually shifted away from TABP, typical psychological interventions have continued to include a variety of techniques such as stress management, relaxation training, anger management, communication skills training, meditation, and cognitive interventions. In one quantitative review of the intervention literature, Linden *et al.* (1996) examined whether the addition of psychosocial interventions would result in better outcomes than that achieved by traditional rehabilitation programs (i.e. medication and/or exercise). They concluded that cardiac patients receiving psychological interventions demonstrated significant reductions in both "hard" (e.g. mortality, cardiac recurrence) and "soft" (e.g. psychological distress) outcomes compared to traditional rehabilitation alone. In fact, psychosocial interventions significantly reduced mortality, cardiac recurrences, psychological distress, blood pressure, and cholesterol up to two years following treatment. Specifically, psychosocial interventions resulted in a 41 per cent reduction in cardiac-related mortality and a 46 per cent reduction in nonfatal cardiac recurrences (Linden *et al.*, 1996).

A more recent meta-analysis also demonstrated the benefit of psychological interventions for CHD patients (Dusseldorp *et al.*, 1999). In fact, stress management and health education techniques resulted in a 34 per cent reduction in cardiac mortality and a 29 per cent reduction in recurrent myocardial infarction. There were also beneficial effects for blood pressure, cholesterol, weight, smoking, exercise, and diet. Dusseldorp *et al.* (1999) also found that the distal effects of interventions (i.e. mortality, cardiac recurrences) were moderated by proximal treatment outcomes, including reductions in psychological symptoms. In other words, the overall impact of interventions was significantly greater when the interventions achieved significant improvement in psychological and biological outcomes (e.g. reduced blood pressure, reduced smoking, and decreased emotional distress).

While reviews of CHD psychosocial interventions point to the efficacy of such treatments in reducing both cardiovascular and psychological symptoms, a number of reviewers also point out the need for more study of specific mechanisms resulting in treatment benefit. Little is known about specific aspects of treatment regimens that are responsible for improved outcome. In addition, more attention is needed to determine which patients stand to gain the most benefit from specific psychosocial interventions. The majority of the intervention research has been conducted with Caucasian men. Therefore, less is known about the efficacy of such interventions for women or ethnic minorities (Schneiderman *et al.*, 2001).

Case study

Assessment and formulation

The following is an overview of the assessment, case formulation, and treatment of a patient with CHD who was referred for psychological treatment post-myocardial infarction. This case is utilized to further illustrate issues regarding assessment and treatment, as well as the process of case formulation specific to this population. While this case provides a synopsis of several general issues involved in working with heart disease patients, it also demonstrates the need for idiographic assessment and case formulation, in addition to a tailored treatment plan.

Identification and referral information

Mr. C was a 54-year-old white, married male with two teenage children who worked in middle management at a local factory for automobile parts. He was referred by his cardiologist following an MI he experienced three weeks ago. At the time of the MI, Mr. C presented to the emergency room with diaphoresis (excessive sweating) and crushing substernal chest pain with radiation to the left arm and jaw. Angiography revealed a blockage in the distal left anterior descending artery and his ejection fraction was at 45 per cent, which indicated Mr. C had experienced a moderate MI. Mr. C underwent angioplasty (to increase the artery opening) and was subsequently hospitalized for three days for monitoring. Mr. C's medications at the time of psychological assessment included metoprolol for hypertension, atorvastatin for hyperlipidemia, clopidogrel for platelet inhibition, and sublingual nitroglycerin as needed for chest pain.

Behavioral observations

Mr. C arrived early for his appointment and was casually dressed. He appeared overweight (medical chart reported a BMI of 29 kg/m^2) and smelled of cigarette smoke. Mr. C appeared restless and impatient throughout the interview, tapping his foot and asking repeatedly how much longer the interview was going to last. His mood was irritable and his affect was labile. Mr. C reacted angrily to personal questions asked by the interviewer and seemed to have a generally pessimistic and hostile attitude. His speech was loud and pressured and his answers to questioning were often short and abrupt, requiring continued questioning to obtain pertinent information. Mr. C denied any previous psychological history.

Problem identification and definition

A semi-structured clinical interview was conducted to obtain information regarding Mr. C's medical history and psychological risk factors potentially affecting his cardiovascular health. Several behavioral health problems were apparent upon Mr. C's presentation to the interview. Weight history revealed that Mr. C was slightly overweight as a teenager, and that he had gradually gained weight since that time. His diet consisted mainly of fried, carbohydrate-rich foods, despite his eight-year history of hypertension and hyperlipidemia. Mr. C did not engage in binge eating, purging or laxative use, but did admit that he often eats larger portions than he probably should. He noted that caffeine is one of his "vices," of which he consumed approximately four cups of coffee and two regular soft drinks per day. Mr. C said that he had "never been an exerciser," but did note that he had attempted walking for exercise on a few occasions at the request of his wife. Mr. C repeatedly stated that he doesn't have enough time with his work schedule to eat right and exercise, even though he knows he should.

Mr. C began smoking cigarettes at the age of 18 when he joined the military. He smoked two packs per day until eight years ago when he was diagnosed with hypertension, and he reduced his smoking to one pack per day. Mr. C had attempted smoking cessation on two previous occasions several years ago. On each attempt he was able to remain abstinent from nicotine for a period of approximately two weeks, but eventually returned to smoking one pack per day. Mr. C said that his wife "gets on me all the time about my smoking," and he seemed irritated by his wife's prompts to improve his health behaviors.

Mr. C had a significant increase in life stress approximately one year ago when he was laterally moved into a middle management position within his company. Mr. C said that this new job allowed him very little control over quotas set for his department, which was very stressful for him. This position also created interpersonal conflict between himself and his supervisors (who demanded higher production), and his supervisees (who felt the pace set by the quotas was unrealistic). In addition, Mr. C and his wife had been experiencing marital distress, as she felt that he was not involved enough in raising their teenage sons. Mr. C noted experiencing problems with one of his sons who was skipping school and failing classes. He was able to enjoy golfing on occasion with a co-worker, but otherwise described himself as becoming isolated from his former social network due to work demands and a generally negative and cynical attitude toward others.

While Mr. C was initially defensive to questions regarding anger and hostility, he eventually endorsed "moodiness" and irritability on a daily basis as a longstanding problem that was exacerbated with the job change. Mr. C reported experiencing "anger blow-ups" most of his adult life that were fairly infrequent until the recent onset of work stress. In the last year these anger episodes had been occurring as often as three to four times per week. Triggers to his anger could be very minor things, such as his sons not picking up their dirty laundry or a complaint from a co-worker. Mr. C endorsed yelling, slamming doors, saying things he regrets later, and occasionally throwing things or punching the wall when he is angry. Mr. C was involved in a handful of "bar fights" in his twenties and thirties, but otherwise denied physical aggression towards others when angry. He had no legal problems related to his anger but did report negative consequences to his anger that included problems in his relationships with family and supervisors at work. Mr. C endorsed some mild depressive symptoms since the MI, denied symptoms of anxiety, and there was no indication of more severe psychopathology, such as a thought disorder.

Mr. C admitted increasing his consumption of alcohol since starting his new position at work. He had no previous history of alcohol abuse or dependence and described himself as an occasional "social drinker" prior to the job change. During the past year, Mr. C reported increasing his drinking from one to two 12-ounce beers per week to drinking one or two beers per day. He was particularly defensive during this line of questioning and repeatedly stated that he needed the beer to "wind down from all the stress in my life." Mr. C did not experience symptoms of tolerance or withdrawal from alcohol consumption, and it had not affected his work. He denied spending significant amounts of time obtaining alcohol or nursing hangovers and did not engage in binge drinking. He had no legal problems related to drinking.

Mr. C did report that his wife "nags me about my drinking." It is possible that Mr. C underestimated his alcohol consumption due to defensiveness, yet he still endorsed consuming up to 14 alcoholic drinks per week (see Box 6.1 for a complete problem list for Mr. C).

Box 6.1 Problem list for Mr. C

1. Overweight
2. Poor diet
3. Sedentary life style
4. Nicotine dependence
5. Lack of control at work
6. Job dissatisfaction
7. Interpersonal conflict at work
8. Hostile temperament
9. Anger outbursts
10. Irritability
11. Marital distress
12. Conflict with child
13. Increased alcohol consumption
14. Social isolation

Developmental analysis

Mr. C is the oldest of three children and was raised by both his parents. He did not experience notable medical problems as a child and his early childhood was unremarkable. Mr. C's mother often criticized him about his weight and his average academic abilities. His father was hostile and demanding, enforcing strict rules and exacting harsh punishment, which was often not contingent on bad behavior. Mr. C said that he never felt particularly close to either of his parents.

Mr. C performed in the average range academically. He was expelled from school on two occasions for fighting during elementary and junior high school. Mr. C had friends and girlfriends during high school, but he was never involved in organized sports or other extracurricular activities. While his parents were strict about his school attendance and academic performance, they displayed cynical and pessimistic attitudes regarding other activities, telling Mr. C that "sports were for dumb jocks." Outside of enforcing the rules regarding attendance and grades, Mr. C's parents were fairly uninvolved in his teenage life.

After high school, Mr. C held a few factory jobs before taking a "line job" with his current company making automobile parts at the age of 25. He worked on the assembly line for four years before he was promoted to line manager. It took him another ten years to be promoted to middle management, where he has remained since the age of 39. Mr. C was initially a hard worker, taking on extra hours and making sure that quotas were met during his shifts. During the ten years it took for him to be promoted to middle management, Mr. C became increasingly cynical about the company and his abilities for upward movement, after being passed up for promotion on two occasions. Once in his middle management position, his general demeanor and attitude regarding work improved mildly, then became gradually more pessimistic and negative. Mr. C was expecting a job promotion one year ago when he was given the lateral move, which he described as "the last straw."

Family background

Mr. C's father was overweight and both of his parents were smokers. His father and paternal grandfather were diagnosed with CHD during their fifties. Neither of Mr. C's parents followed a healthy diet or incorporated exercise into their life styles. His father drank excessively and had anger management difficulties, at times being physically abusive to his mother. Mr. C denied any other family psychological or pertinent medical history.

Collateral information

Mr. C's wife reported that she had noticed him becoming more reclusive over the past few years. She stated that they had been experiencing marital distress for several years and noted that she has difficulty communicating with him, as he usually becomes angry and defensive, and will storm out of the room, slamming doors behind him. Mrs. C said that she is at times fearful of him during his "anger blow-ups," but that he has never been physically violent with her or the children. Mrs. C repeatedly expressed concern regarding Mr. C's health and stated that she had worried about his weight and nicotine dependence long before the MI. Mrs. C also appeared particularly frustrated that her husband did not quit smoking following the MI.

Assessment measures

Weekly stress inventory

Mr. C endorsed experiencing 35 minor stressors in the past week and his impact score was 174. This indicated that Mr. C had experienced about the average number of minor stressful life events during the week prior to interview, but that he perceived the impact of these events to be much higher than the average adult.

Life experiences survey

Mr. C had experienced six major life events in the past year, most of which related to his job change and decreased recreation, as well as marital distress and MI. His negative impact score and total impact score were both 16 because Mr. C did not endorse any items to have a positive impact. This indicated that Mr. C experienced slightly more than the average number of major life events in the past year, and that he rated the negative impact of these events higher than the average adult.

Beck depression inventory

Mr. C scored 14 on the BDI-II, which indicated that he was experiencing a mild level of depressive symptoms. He endorsed items related to sadness, pessimism, punishment, self-criticalness, and irritability, which corroborated symptoms he endorsed and/or demonstrated during clinical interview.

Cook-Medley hostility questionnaire

Mr. C received a raw score of 37 on the Ho, which was equivalent to a T Score of 75, which demonstrates a high level of hostility.

State-trait anger expression inventory-2

Mr. C received a raw score of 29 on the State Anger Scale, which corresponds to a T Score of 68 and is at the ninetieth percentile, meaning he scored higher than 90 per cent of the adults over the age of 30 who took the STAXI. He received a raw score of 31 on the trait anger subscale, which corresponds to a T Score of ≥ 80 and is at the ninety-eighth percentile. Because both scales are high, Mr. C most likely experiences pervasive feelings of anger, frustration, and feeling as though he is treated unfairly by others, rather than anger that is situationally predisposed.

Case formulation

Mr. C's longstanding history of poor health behaviors most likely had a large influence on his CHD. Mr. C's 36-year history of smoking, including approximately 28 years smoking two packs per day, is a major risk factor for CHD and most likely contributed to his MI. His high fat diet and sedentary life style contributed to being overweight (a risk factor for both hypertension and hyperlipidemia) and predisposed him to experience CHD. Mr. C also had a known family history of heart disease in both his father and paternal grand-father, which suggests that there may be a genetic contribution to his medical problems. Mr. C also has a chronic history of an angry and hostile temperament that has negatively influenced his relationships with others, including his family, friends, and co-workers. This has resulted in a reduction in social support and an increase in conflict with others over time. In addition, his temperament may have contributed to CHD through chronic reactivity of the sympathetic nervous system, although appropriate testing to determine this was not conducted.

In the context of these longstanding poor health behaviors and hostile personality style, Mr. C experienced a significant work-related stressor when he was given the lateral middle management position when expecting a promotion. Due to this occupational change, Mr. C experienced regular work-related stress due to lack of control on his job and conflict between himself and upper-level management as well as assembly line workers. Work-related stress led to an increase in his angry and hostile personality style, marital distress, and increased alcohol consumption. The combination of longstanding poor health problems, a hostile temperament, work-related stress, low social support and possible genetic influences culminated in an MI for Mr. C (see Figure 6.1).

Treatment

Mr. C had several problems that could be addressed through various types of cognitive and behavioral intervention. Specific problems to be targeted include nicotine dependence, poor diet and exercise habits, stress, anger and hostility, and minor depressive symptoms. A comprehensive program incorporating treatment for all these areas, such as that used in the Lifestyle Heart Trial (Billings *et al.*, 1998) would be ideal. However, most clinicians do not have access to such interventions and must provide treatment in the context of individual therapy. Components of the treatment utilized in the Lifestyle Heart Trial can provide guidance. Given his numerous risk factors, prioritizing areas for Mr. C's intervention would be a logical first step in treatment, and this might be done on the basis of the strength of risk factor for further cardiac events (i.e. health behaviors may be addressed first).

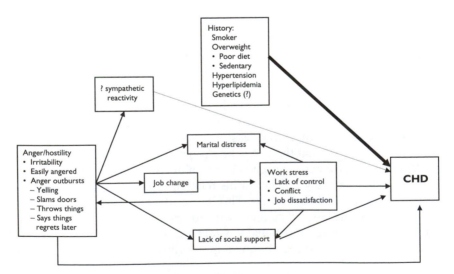

Figure 6.1 Diagram of the formulation for Mr. C.

However, Mr. C's motivation to change certain behaviors and willingness to engage in various aspects of therapy should be considered to enhance treatment adherence and success. Therefore, treatment might begin with education regarding the different risk factors for further cardiac events and discussion of treatment options.

Because tobacco use is such a potent risk factor for cardiac events, smoking cessation should be considered as a primary goal. Mr. C's readiness to change with regard to smoking behavior should be assessed utilizing the stage of change model. If Mr. C is in an earlier stage of change, such as Precontemplation or Contemplation, techniques such as consciousness raising or environmental re-evaluation may be used to help Mr. C progress to the Preparation and Action stages of change (Prochaska *et al.*, 1992). Consciousness raising might involve education about the negative effects of nicotine and basic education regarding CHD, which might be discussed in individual or group therapy, and/or provided through bibliotherapy. Current recommendations regarding smoking cessation encourage total cessation accompanied by nicotine replacement, either through patches, gum, or inhalers (Fiore *et al.*, 2000). Mr. C would be encouraged to utilize stimulus control to reduce the number of cues for smoking both prior to quitting and following cessation. Mr. C could be taught methods to cope with urges to smoke, such as distraction, relaxation, or cognitive restructuring, and his urges to smoke should be monitored. While smoking cessation may be the initial part of Mr. C's treatment program, the issue should be revisited throughout treatment to ensure that he is maintaining abstinence from nicotine (Fiore *et al.*, 2000).

Coinciding with smoking cessation, Mr. C's therapist may wish to encourage the reduction of alcohol intake. Mr. C should be educated regarding the negative health effects of excessive alcohol intake (including disinhibition, which may lead to a lapse in smoking cessation), and his stage of readiness to change should be assessed. A motivational interviewing approach (Miller & Rollnick, 2002) may be necessary to enhance his motivation to reduce alcohol intake, as Mr. C appeared particularly defensive regarding this behavior. For example, a decisional balance could be conducted, examining the pros and cons of his alcohol consumption.

Once Mr. C is successful with nicotine and alcohol reduction, a natural progression toward focusing on his high fat diet and sedentary life style might be considered. It is likely that Mr. C would experience some temporary weight gain with smoking cessation, and this should be discussed with him and monitored. It may be beneficial to enlist the assistance of a dietician and physical therapist at this point for basic nutrition and activity education and guidelines. Mr. C's cardiologist should be consulted regarding the type, frequency, intensity, and duration of exercise recommendations. Most cardiac rehabilitation programs recommend low resistance activities for 20 to 50 minutes at least three days per week at 70 to 85 per cent of maximum intensity (Stein, 1998). Mr. C could be provided with a cognitive-behavioral approach to weight management, such as the LEARN (Lifestyle, Exercise, Attitudes, Relationships, Nutrition) Program for Weight Management (Brownell, 2000), which may be provided on an individual or group basis. The group format could have the added benefit of enhancing his social support.

As Mr. C begins to improve his management of health risk behaviors, cognitive-behavioral stress management could be introduced, as he endorsed experiencing significant impact from current stressors. Relaxation has demonstrated positive effects with regard to stress management (Barlow & Rapee, 1991; Deffenbacher, 1994) and in the reduction of blood pressure and negative psychological symptoms (Friedman *et al.*, 1998). Relaxation training for the CHD patient might include diaphragmatic breathing, progressive muscle relaxation, or the use of imagery (Sirois & Burg, 2003). Additional stress management techniques might involve improving time organization for efficient completion of tasks through prioritizing, and utilizing agendas and decreasing time urgency. Mr. C would also be taught how to avoid overcommitting himself by learning to refuse and delegate tasks (Barlow & Rapee, 1991). Beginning treatment with a focus on stress management might be helpful if Mr. C is resistant to changing health behaviors.

Finally, once rapport is well established and Mr. C is engaged in treatment, anger and hostility reduction might be achieved through education, increased awareness, identification of triggers, and modification of beliefs that promote irritability and cynicism (Deffenbacher, 1994; Bracke & Thoresen, 1998). Mr. C should be taught to monitor his triggers and reactions in both work and family situations. Additionally, Mr. C's mild depressive symptoms should be monitored throughout treatment. If his symptoms remain following therapy, they should be treated specifically, as depression may interfere with adherence to behavior change and is a risk factor for further CHD morbidity in and of itself (Smith & Ruiz, 2002; Sirois & Burg, 2003). Mr. C should be able to apply many of the skills he learned in other contexts (i.e. self-monitoring, cognitive restructuring; Young *et al.*, 2001) in treating depression. Mr. C may also benefit from interpersonal therapy (IPT) for depression, as this is an efficacious therapy (Craighead *et al.*, 1998), and he has several interpersonal issues and role changes contributing to his depressive symptoms.

General remarks

The case of Mr. C demonstrates several biological and psychosocial predisposing factors to CHD. The assessment measures and treatment described are extensive due to the many risk factors delineated in this patient. While any of the behavioral interventions discussed would be appropriate in the treatment of this patient, attempting several interventions at once is not advised. Behavior change is a difficult task and attempting to change more than one behavior at a time may result in failure to achieve treatment goals, potentially leading the patient to feel more despondent. Each CHD patient presenting for treatment should be assessed on an individual basis, and treatment goals should extend from the patient's level of motivation for particular areas of behavior change, as well as current health status, strengths and weaknesses.

Conclusion

Several conclusions can be drawn from this brief review and case conceptualization of the CHD literature. First, evaluation of psychosocial factors such as anger, hostility, and stress is clearly warranted considering their potentially powerful role in the development and outcome of CHD. Second, clinician-administered interviews, self-report inventories, and physiological procedures are available for assessment of psychological variables and should be utilized by the healthcare provider working with cardiac patients. Third, the results of a thorough evaluation should be used to inform treatment recommendations, which may include psychological interventions targeting health behaviors, stress management, anger management, or depression. Finally, such techniques should be incorporated selectively into treatment based on the particular profile of the patient in order to maximize therapeutic benefit.

References

American Heart Association (2003). *Heart disease and stroke statistics — 2004 update.* Dallas, TX: American Heart Association.

Barefoot, J. C. (1992). Developments in the measurement of hostility. In H. S. Friedman (Ed.), *Hostility, coping & health* (pp. 13–31). Washington, DC: American Psychological Association.

Barefoot, J. C., Dahlstrom, W. G., & Williams, R. B. Jr. (1983). Hostility, CHD incidence, and total mortality: A 25-year follow-up study of 255 physicians. *Psychosomatic Medicine, 45*, 59–63.

Barlow, D. H., & Rapee, R. M. (1991). *Mastering stress: A lifestyle approach.* Dallas, TX: American Health Publishing Company.

Billings, J. H., Scherwitz, L. W., Sullivan, R., Sparler, S., & Ornish, D. M. (1998). The lifestyle heart trial: Comprehensive treatment and group support therapy. In R. Allan and S. Scheidt (Eds.), *Heart & mind: The practice of cardiac psychology* (pp. 233–253). Washington, DC: American Psychological Association.

Bracke, P. E., & Thoresen, C. E. (1998). Reducing type A behavior patterns: A structured-group approach. In R. Allan and S. Scheidt (Eds.), *Heart & mind: The practice of cardiac psychology* (pp. 255–290). Washington, DC: American Psychological Association.

Brantley, P. J., Jones, G. N., Boudreaux, E., & Catz, S. (1997). Weekly stress inventory. In C. P. Zalaquett & R. J. Wood (Eds.), *Evaluating stress: A book of resources* (pp. 405–420). Lanham, MD: Scarecrow.

Brownell, K. D. (2000). *The LEARN program for weight management: Lifestyle, exercise, attitudes, relationships, nutrition.* Dallas, TX: American Health Publishing Company.

Buss, A. H., & Durkee, A. (1957). An inventory for assessing different kinds of hostility. *Journal of Consulting Psychology, 21*, 343–349.

Cook, W., & Medley, D. (1954). Proposed hostility and pharisaic-virtue scales for the MMPI. *Journal of Applied Psychology, 238*, 414–418.

Cottington, E. M., Matthews, K. A. Talbott, E., & Kuller, L. H. (1980). Environmental agents preceding sudden death in women. *Psychosomatic Medicine, 42*, 567–574.

Craighead, W. E., Hart, A. B., Craighead, L. W., & Ilardi, S. S. (1998). Psychosocial treatments for major depressive disorder. In P. E. Nathan & J. M. Gorman (Eds.), *A guide to treatments that work* (2nd ed., pp. 245–261). New York: Oxford University Press.

Deffenbacher, J. L. (1994). Anger reduction: Issues, assessment, and intervention strategies. In A. W. Siegman & T. W. Smith (Eds.), *Anger, hostility, and the heart* (pp. 239–269). Hillsdale, NJ: Lawrence Erlbaum Associates, Inc.

Dembroski, T. M., MacDougall, J. M., Williams, R. B., Haney, T. L., & Blumenthal, J. A. (1985). Components of type A, hostility, and anger-in: Relationship to angiographic findings. *Psychosomatic Medicine, 47*, 219–233.

Dembroski, T. M., MacDougall, J. M., Costa, P. T., & Grandits, G. A. (1989). Components of hostility as predictors of sudden death and myocardial infarction in the Multiple Risk Factor Intervention Trial. *Psychosomatic Medicine, 51*, 514–522.

Dusseldorp, E., van Elderen, T., Maes, S., Meulman, J., & Kraaij, V. (1999). A meta-analysis of psychoeducational programs for coronary heart disease patients. *Health Psychology, 18*, 506–519.

Finney, M. L., Stoney, C. M., & Engebretson, T. O. (2002). Hostility and anger expression in African American and European American men is associated with cardiovascular and lipid reactivity. *Psychophysiology, 39*, 340–349.

Fiore M. C., Bailey, W. C., Cohen, S. J., *et al.* (2000). *Treating tobacco use and dependence: Quick reference guide for clinicians.* Rockville, MD: US Dept of Health and Human Services.

Friedman, M., & Rosenman, R. H. (1959). Association of a specific overt behavior pattern with blood and cardiovascular findings. *Journal of the American Medical Association, 169*, 1286–1296.

Friedman, M., Thoreson, C. E., Gill, J. J., Ulmer, D., Powell, L. H., Price, V.A., *et al.* (1986). Alteration of type A behavior and its effect on cardiac recurrences in post myocardial infarction patients: Summary results of the recurrent coronary prevention project. *American Heart Journal, 112*, 653–665.

Friedman, R., Myers, P., Krass, S., & Benson, H. (1998). The relaxation response: Use with cardiac patients. In R. Allan and S. Scheidt (Eds.), *Heart & mind: The practice of cardiac psychology* (pp. 363–384). Washington, DC: American Psychological Association.

Jenkins, C. D. (1988). Epidemiology of cardiovascular diseases. *Journal of Consulting and Clinical Psychology, 56*, 324–332.

Kannel, W. B. (1979). Cardiovascular disease: A multifactorial problem. In M. L. Pollack & D. H. Schmidt (Eds.), *Heart disease and rehabilitation* (pp. 15–31). New York: Wiley.

Kanner, A. D., Coyne, J. C., Schaefer, C., & Lazarus, R. S. (1981). Comparison of two modes of stress measurement: Daily hassles and uplifts versus major life events. *Journal of Behavioral Medicine, 4*, 1–39.

Karasek, R. A., Theorell, T., Schwartz, J. E., Schnall, P. L., Pieper, C. F., & Michela, J. L. (1988). Job characteristics in relation to the prevalence of myocardial infarction in the US Health Examination Study (HES) and the Health and Nutrition Examination Study (HANES). *American Journal of Public Health, 78*, 910–918.

Kawachi, I., Sparrow, D., Spiro, A., Vokonas, P., & Weiss, S. T. (1996). A prospective study of anger and coronary heart disease. *Circulation, 94*, 2090–2095.

Krantz, D. S., & McCeney, M. K. (2002). Effects of psychological and social factors on organic disease: A critical assessment of research on coronary heart disease. *Annual Review of Psychology, 53*, 341–369.

Krantz, D. S., & Manuck, S. B. (1984). Acute psychophysiologic reactivity and risk of cardiovascular disease: A review and methodological critique. *Psychological Bulletin, 96*, 435–464.

Linden, W., Stossel, C., & Maurice, J. (1996). Psychosocial interventions for patients with coronary artery disease: A meta-analysis. *Archives of Internal Medicine, 156*, 745–752.

Meisel, S. R., Kutz, I., Dayan, K. I., Pauzner, H., Chetboun, I., Arbel, Y., & David, D. (1991). Effect of Iraqi missile war on incidence of acute myocardial infarction and sudden death in Israeli civilians. *Lancet, 338*, 660–661.

Miller, W. R., & Rollnick, S. (2002). *Motivational interviewing: Preparing people for change* (2nd ed.). New York: Guilford Press.

Miller, T. Q., Smith, T. W., Turner, C. W., Guijarro, M. L., & Hallet, A. J. (1996). A meta-analytic review of research on hostility and physical health. *Psychological Bulletin, 119*, 322–348.

Mittleman, M. A., Maclure, M., Sherwood, J. B., Mulry, R. P., Tofler, G. H., Jacobs, S. C., Friedman, R., Benson, H., & Muller, J. E. (1995). Triggering of acute myocardial infarction onset by episodes of anger. *Circulation, 92*, 1720–1725.

Mona, P., Fitzmaurice, G., Kubzansky, L. D., Rimm, E. B., & Kawachi, I. (2003). Anger expression and risk of stroke and coronary heart disease among male health professionals. *Psychosomatic Medicine, 65*, 100–110.

Muller, J. E., Tofler, G. H., & Stone, P. H. (1989). Circadian variation and triggers of onset of acute cardiovascular disease. *Circulation, 79*, 733–743.

Nunes, E. V., Frank, K. A., & Kornfield, D. S. (1987). Psychological treatment for the type A behavior pattern and for coronary heart disease: A meta-analysis of the literature. *Psychosomatic Medicine, 48*, 159–173.

Prochaska, J. O., DiClemente, C. C., & Norcross, J. C. (1992). In search of how people change: Applications to addictive behaviors. *American Psychologist, 47*, 9, 1102–1114.

Rosenman, R. H., Brand, R. J., Jenkins, C. D., Friedman, M., Strauss, R., & Wurm, M. (1975). Coronary heart disease in the Western Collaborative Group Study: Final follow-up experience of 8.5 years. *Journal of the American Medical Association, 223*, 872–877.

Rozanski, A., Bairey, C. N., Krantz, D. S., Friedman, J., Resser, K. J., Morell, M., et al. (1988). Mental stress and the induction of silent myocardial ischemia in patients with coronary artery disease. *New England Journal of Medicine, 318*, 1005–1012.

Sarason, I. G., Johnson, J. H., & Siegel, J. M. (1978). Assessing the impact of life changes: Development of the Life Experiences Survey. *Journal of Consulting and Clinical Psychology, 46*, 932–946.

Schneiderman, N., Antoni, M. H., Saab, P. G., & Ironson, G. (2001). Health psychology: Psychosocial and biobehavioral aspects of chronic disease management. *Annual Review of Psychology*, 52, 555–580.

Siegman, A. W., Anderson, R. A., Herbst, J., Boyle, S., & Wilkinson, J. (1992). Dimensions of anger-hostility and cardiovascular reactivity in provoked and angered men. *Journal of Behavioral Medicine, 15*, 257–272.

Siegman, A. W., Kubzansky, L. D., Kawachi, I., Boyle, S., Vokonas, P. S., & Sparrow, D. (2000). A prospective study of dominance and coronary heart disease in the normative aging study. *American Journal of Cardiology, 86*, 145–149.

Sirois, B. C., & Burg, M. M. (2003). Negative emotion and coronary heart disease. *Behavior Modification, 27*, 83–102.

Smith, T. W., & Frohm, K. D. (1985). What's so unhealthy about hostility? Construct validity and psychosocial correlates of the Cook and Medley Ho Scale. *Health Psychology, 4*, 6, 503–520.

Smith, T. W., & Gallo, L. C. (1994). Psychosocial influences on coronary heart disease. *Irish Journal of Psychology, 15*, 8–26.

Smith, T. W., & Ruiz, J. M. (2002). Psychosocial influences on the development and course of coronary heart disease: Current status and implications for research and practice. *Journal of Consulting and Clinical Psychology, 70*, 548–568.

Spielberger, C. D. (1999). *Professional manual for the State-Trait Anger Expression Inventory-2 (STAXI-2)*. Lutz, FL: Psychological Assessment Resources.

Spielberger, C.D., Johnson, E.H., Russell, S. F., Crane, R.J., Jacobs, G.A., & Worden, T. J. (1985). The experience and expression of anger: Construction and validation of an anger expression scale. In M.A. Chesney & R.H. Rosenman (Eds.), *Anger and hostility in cardiovascular and behavioral disorders* (pp. 5–30). New York: Hemisphere/McGraw-Hill.

Stein, R. A. (1998). Exercise and the patient with coronary heart disease. In R. Allan & S. Scheidt (Eds.), *Heart & mind: The practice of cardiac psychology* (pp. 385–396). Washington, DC: American Psychological Association.

Suarez, E. C., & Williams, R. B. (1990). The relationships between dimensions of hostility and cardiovascular reactivity as a function of task characteristics. *Psychosomatic Medicine, 52*, 558–570.

Theorell, T., & Emlund, N. (1993). On physiological effects of positive and negative life changes – a longitudinal study. *Journal of Psychosomatic Research, 37*, 653–659.

Williams, J. E., Paton, C. C., Siegler, I. C., Eigenbrodt, M. L., Nieto, F. J., & Tyroler, H. A. (2000). Anger proneness predicts coronary heart disease risk: Prospective analysis from the atherosclerosis in communities (ARIC) study. *Circulation, 101*, 2034–2039.

Williams, J. E., Nieto, F. J., Sanford, C. P., & Tyrolet, H. A. (2001). Effects of an angry temperament on coronary heart disease risk: The atherosclerosis risk in communities study. *American Journal of Epidemiology, 154*, 230–235.

Young, E. Y., Weinberger, A. D., & Beck, A. T. (2001). Cognitive therapy for depression. In D. H. Barlow (Ed.), *Clinical handbook of psychological disorders* (3rd ed., pp. 264–308) New York: Guilford Press.

Chapter 7

Case formulation in type 1 diabetes

Kerri M. Schneider and Alan M. Delamater

Type 1 diabetes mellitus is a chronic illness that affects about one in 700 children (Arslanian *et al.*, 1994). The daily treatment regimen for type 1 diabetes is complex, requiring careful insulin administrations, monitoring of blood glucose, and modification of diet and exercise. The maintenance of optimal blood glucose is necessary to prevent the onset of a variety of short-term complications, for example, hypoglycemia, hyperglycemia, and long-term complications, for example, retinopathy, neuropathy, nephropathy, and cardiovascular disease (Diabetes Control and Complications Trial, DCCT, 1993).

One of the most commonly used indicators of patient's blood glucose control is a glycosylated hemoglobin assay test (HbA_{1c}), which reflects average blood glucose levels of the preceding two to three months. The HbA_{1c} test is generally considered to be the best and most widely used measure of long-term glycemic control (Gonen *et al.*, 1977). The DCCT goal for optimal glycemic control was $HbA_{1c} < 7$ per cent (DCCT, 1993). Study participants were able to achieve an average HbA_{1c} of 7.5 per cent. However, adolescents in the study typically averaged higher levels (DCCT, 1994). This finding points to the challenges in attaining optimal glycemic control for adolescents with type 1 diabetes.

In this chapter, we highlight the challenge of achieving good glycemic control in an adolescent with type 1 diabetes. Before presenting the case material, we first review key findings from the literature on psychosocial and behavioral factors related to diabetes management in children and adolescents. Much of this research has focused on the relationship of behavioral and psychosocial factors to diabetes-related outcomes such as regimen adherence and metabolic control, although some studies have also focused on the impact of diabetes on psychosocial functioning (Delamater *et al.*, 2001). This section will highlight some of the most important findings in this area, including the role of socio-demographic, family and psychological factors, as well as psychosocial intervention research.

Psychosocial factors and diabetes management

Socio-demographic factors

Regimen adherence tends to decline over time, and is especially poor among many adolescents (Jacobson *et al.*, 1990; Johnson *et al.*, 1992). Metabolic control is often worse in children from single-parent families, as shown in studies both in the USA (e.g. Overstreet *et al.*, 1995; Thompson *et al.*, 2001) and Sweden (e.g. Forsander *et al.*, 2000). Ethnicity has also been examined in relation to regimen adherence and metabolic control. The results of these studies have consistently shown that African American youths have poorer metabolic control than Caucasian youths (Delamater *et al.*, 1991; Auslander *et al.*, 1997; Delamater *et al.*, 1991a, 1999). These findings may be explained in part by lower adherence to diet and glucose testing and the greater prevalence of single-parent families among African Americans (Auslander *et al.*, 1997).

Family factors

Poor metabolic control is more common among children from families that have more conflict and financial problems, and less cohesion and stability (Anderson *et al.*, 1981; Hanson *et al.*, 1987). Studies indicate that good metabolic control is related to better family communication and conflict resolution skills (Wysocki, 1993), agreement about family responsibilities and appropriate involvement of parents in diabetes management tasks (Anderson *et al.*, 1990, 1997) and more structured and controlling family environments (Weist *et al.*, 1993). Clinical studies of adolescents with chronically poor metabolic control have shown significant family dysfunction for the majority of families (Orr *et al.*, 1983; White *et al.*, 1984).

Regimen adherence has also been examined in relation to family factors. Results of these studies have shown adherence to be related with both general and regimen-specific family support (Schafer *et al.*, 1983; La Greca *et al.*, 1995b) as well as communication skills (Bobrow *et al.*, 1985) and conflict (Miller-Johnson *et al.*, 1994). Parental warmth was predictive of better adherence in young children (Davis *et al.*, 2001). Youths receive instrumental support from their families, and considerable emotional support from their friends (La Greca *et al.*, 1995b).

Research has examined the psychological functioning of parents of children with diabetes. These findings indicate that many mothers are at risk for psychological adjustment problems after their children are diagnosed with type 1 diabetes, with clinically significant depression noted in approximately one-third of mothers. Most of these adjustment problems, however, are resolved within the first year after the child's diagnosis (Kovacs *et al.*, 1985b). The role of fathers in diabetes management has received little research attention. The results of a recent study showed that 24 per cent of mothers and

22 per cent of fathers met diagnostic criteria for post-traumatic stress disorder six weeks after their child had been diagnosed (Landolt *et al.*, 2002). Other recent studies indicate that fathers typically are not very involved in diabetes management tasks (Seiffge-Krenke, 2002), and suggest that psychological maladjustment of fathers predicts poor glycemic control in children five years after diagnosis (Forsander *et al.*, 1998).

Psychological factors

Adjustment after diagnosis

Several longitudinal studies have addressed the issue of psychological adjustment after diagnosis of type 1 diabetes. In one study, 36 per cent of newly diagnosed children had diagnosable psychiatric disorders soon after diabetes onset, most commonly being adjustment disorders with depression and anxiety. However, most children's adjustment problems had resolved within the first year after diagnosis (Kovacs *et al.*, 1985a). In another study, there were no differences between diabetic children and a medical control group on a variety of behavioral and psychological measures five months after diagnosis, with the exception of decreased school-related competence in children with diabetes (Jacobson *et al.*, 1986). Mild adjustment problems were noted in another study, but dissipated by the end of the first year after diagnosis. However, some problems reappeared by the end of the second year (Grey *et al.*, 1995). The results of these studies suggest that while the majority of children's adjustment problems appear to resolve within the first year, children who do not may be at risk for poor adaptation to diabetes, including regimen adherence problems, poor metabolic control, and continued psychosocial difficulties (Grey *et al.*, 1995; Jacobson *et al.*, 1994; Kovacs *et al.*, 1995).

Long-term adjustment

Recent findings suggest that children with diabetes, like children with other chronic diseases, may be at increased risk for psychological problems (Lavigne & Faier-Routman, 1992). One-third of a study sample of 93 diabetic adolescents had psychiatric disorders (mostly internalizing symptoms), compared with 10 per cent of the subjects in a control group (Blanz *et al.*, 1993). In a ten-year follow-up study of newly diagnosed youth, nearly half of the study sample had a psychiatric diagnosis, the most frequent being major depression, conduct disorder, and generalized anxiety disorder (Kovacs *et al.*, 1997). In another ten-year follow-up study of newly diagnosed children and adolescents, it was observed that as young adults patients reported lower self-esteem compared to control participants (Jacobson *et al.*, 1997). Poorer adjustment to diabetes during adolescence may persist into early adulthood (Wysocki *et al.*, 1992). In a recent longitudinal study of 76 adolescents, patients with behavioral problems during their teen years had significantly poorer glycemic control as young adults (Bryden *et al.*, 2001).

Psychological functioning and glycemic control

Studies have found increased anxiety and lower self-concept in youths with poor glycemic control (Anderson *et al.*, 1981). Research has also shown that girls are more likely than boys to be depressed, and that depression is associated with poorer glycemic control (La Greca *et al.*, 1995a). There is evidence that diabetic girls are at increased risk for eating disorders, and that eating disorders are associated with poor glycemic control (Daneman *et al.*, 1998; Bryden *et al.*, 1999; Jones *et al.*, 2000; Meltzer *et al.*, 2001; Neumark-Sztainer *et al.*, 2002). It is estimated that at least 10 per cent of adolescent girls with type 1 diabetes may meet diagnostic criteria for an eating disorder, a rate twice as common as in girls without diabetes (Jones *et al.*, 2000). Without intervention, disordered eating and insulin manipulation may worsen over time and increase the risk of serious health complications (Rydall *et al.*, 1997). Disordered eating in girls with diabetes has been associated with problems in the mother–daughter relationship (Maharag *et al.*, 2001) and less perceived control (Schwartz *et al.*, 2001).

Psychosocial and behavioral interventions

The efficacy of various psychosocial and behavioral interventions for children and adolescents with type 1 diabetes has been examined in controlled studies. Review of this literature indicates positive effects of these interventions (Hampson *et al.*, 2000; Delamater *et al.*, 2001, 2003). The family has been an integral part of treatment in most of these interventions. It is important to include the family in diabetes management interventions, because studies have shown that when parents allow older children and adolescents to have self-care autonomy without sufficient cognitive and social maturity, youths are more likely to have problems with diabetes management (Ingersoll *et al.*, 1986; Wysocki *et al.*, 1996).

Controlled intervention studies indicate that family-based behavioral intervention techniques such as goal setting, self-monitoring, positive reinforcement, behavioral contracts, supportive parental communications, and appropriately shared responsibility for diabetes management have improved regimen adherence and glycemic control (Satin *et al.*, 1989; Anderson *et al.*, 1999). Such interventions have also been shown to improve the parent–adolescent relationship (Delamater *et al.*, 1991b; Anderson *et al.*, 1999; Wysocki *et al.*, 1999, 2000, 2001). A family-focused teamwork intervention increased family involvement without impacting family conflict or youth quality of life, and helped prevent worsening of glycemic control (Laffel *et al.*, 2003). Psychosocial interventions that promote problem-solving skills and increase parental support early in the disease course have been shown to improve long-term glycemic control of children (Delamater *et al.*, 1990). Children who received psychosocial interventions at regular outpatient visits were shown to increase visit frequency and have reduced acute adverse outcomes such as hypoglycemia and emergency department visits (Svoren *et al.*, 2003).

Peer group interventions for diabetic youth have also been studied. Research findings have shown that peer group support and problem solving have improved short-term glycemic control (Kaplan *et al.*, 1985; Anderson *et al.*, 1989). Group coping skills training has been shown to improve glycemic control and quality of life for adolescents involved in intensive insulin regimens (Grey *et al.*, 1998; Boland *et al.*, 1999), effects which were maintained after the intervention was completed (Grey *et al.*, 2000). A peer group intervention study targeting problem solving found that problem solving and glucose monitoring increased, while glycemic control improved (Cook *et al.*, 2002). Studies have also demonstrated that stress management and coping skills training delivered in small groups of youths has reduced diabetes-related stress (Boardway *et al.*, 1993; Hains *et al.*, 2000) and improved social interaction (Mendez & Belendez, 1997).

Summary and clinical implications

Review of research findings indicates that psychological and family factors are essential to consider for optimal diabetes management for children and adolescents. Besides achieving good metabolic control, it is important to ensure that youth develop optimally in all areas of their life: psychologically, socially, academically, and physically. Clinicians should therefore routinely assess youths' developmental status in these areas, as well as disease-related skills, regimen adherence, and metabolic control. It is important to maintain consistent contact with families, as studies have shown that children who have infrequent and irregular visits with the healthcare team are more likely to have significant problems with metabolic control (Jacobson *et al.*, 1997; Kaufman *et al.*, 1999). Efforts to intensify regimens with insulin pumps, multiple daily injections, and more frequent glucose monitoring are very important for achieving good glycemic control, but many youths and their families may be unable to commit to and succeed with this type of regimen. Results from a recent study suggests that regimen intensification should not be limited to youth with high self-care competence, as those with low self-care competence may derive the most benefit in terms of glycemic control (Wysocki *et al.*, 2003).

Studies indicate that youths who do not manage diabetes well are more likely to have family conflict, decreased parental involvement and support for diabetes tasks, psychological problems, and eating disorders. Interventions must therefore consider these psychosocial issues. As children become older, many are given self-care autonomy without sufficient cognitive and emotional maturity. Research has shown that 25 per cent of youths admitted to missing insulin injections, 29 per cent fabricated blood glucose test results, and 81 per cent ate inappropriately (Weissberg-Benchell *et al.*, 1995). Parental involvement in children's diabetes care should be evaluated routinely, and interventions delivered to promote teamwork so that good control of diabetes can be achieved.

The results of controlled studies have shown that interventions to improve parent–adolescent teamwork in diabetes management can reduce family conflict (Anderson *et al.*, 1999). Family-based behavioral intervention focusing on communication skills, goal setting with behavioral contracts, and problem-solving strategies has resulted in improvements in parent–teen relationships, regimen adherence, and glycemic control (e.g. Schafer *et al.*, 1982; Carney *et al.*, 1983; Satin *et al.*, 1989; Delamater *et al.*, 1991b; Anderson *et al.*, 1999; Wysocki *et al.*, 2001). Interventions to improve these psychosocial factors are also likely to improve the quality of life of children and adolescents with diabetes.

Case study

The current case study focuses on poor regimen adherence and glycemic control in an adolescent girl with type 1 diabetes. This case illustrates the process by which case formulation with an empirically validated treatment approach can be applied to everyday practice with a challenging family.

Pertinent history

The patient was a 17-year-old Hispanic female, who was diagnosed with type 1 diabetes when she was 6 years old. She was in her senior year of high school and had declining grades over the past two years. She lived with both of her biological parents and her younger brother, and had an older sister who was away at college.

When the patient was initially diagnosed, her parents were very involved in her treatment. During her early childhood, she reportedly maintained adequate to good glycemic control. However, as she approached adolescence, she began acquiring increased responsibility for her diabetes care. Over time, her glycemic control worsened and conflict with her parents increased, as she and her parents had developed a negative pattern of communication regarding her diabetes care. By the time the patient was referred by her endocrinologist for psychological services, her HbA_{1c} results were 16 per cent (recommended treatment goal is typically $HbA_{1c} < 7$ per cent), indicating extremely poor glycemic control.

Initial evaluation

The patient attended the intake interview along with both of her biological parents. During an individual interview, the patient was friendly and answered all questions asked of her in an open manner. She displayed above average insight as she described the situation regarding her poor diabetes self-management and her problematic relationship with her parents. At the time of intake, the patient verbalized a strong motivation to modify her behaviors, including obtaining better glycemic control so that she could eventually be considered for placement on the insulin pump, as well as obtaining better grades so that she would be able to graduate from high school at the end of the school year.

Measures

The following psychosocial measures were obtained prior to treatment and five months later, when treatment was concluded. The patient and both parents completed all of the measures at intake. Only patient report and mother report were available when treatment was concluded. Therefore, these are the only scores discussed. In addition, measures of the patient's glycemic control were obtained prior to treatment, during treatment, at treatment termination, at seven-month follow-up, and at one-year follow-up.

Conflict Behavior Questionnaire (CBQ)

Conflict and quality of communication in the parent–teen relationship was assessed with the 20-item brief version of the CBQ (Robin & Foster, 1989). Scores can be converted to t-scores. Parents and teens are provided with parallel versions of the measure in which they are asked to rate perceived communication and conflict within the parent–adolescent relationship over the past few weeks. Studies have demonstrated that CBQ scores discriminated between distressed and non-distressed families and were sensitive to a behavioral family therapy program consisting of communication and problem-solving skills training (Robin & Foster, 1989).

Diabetes Self-Care Inventory (SCI)

The SCI is a 14-item measure in which parents and children are asked to rate the child's typical adherence (on a 5-point Likert scale) over the preceding month for each of 14 regimen behaviors (La Greca et al., 1990). The SCI provides an overall adherence score and three rationally derived subscales: blood glucose regulation, insulin and food regulation, and exercise. Concurrent validity of the SCI has been documented with regard to 24-hour recall interview measures of glucose testing frequency and eating frequency in adults with diabetes (Greco et al., 1990). A recent study demonstrated acceptable internal consistency for this measure (Wysocki et al., 2000).

Diabetes Family Behavior Checklist (DFBC)

The DFBC (Schafer et al., 1983) was designed to assess the perceived frequency of both supportive and non-supportive behaviors directed toward children with diabetes by their family members. The measure consists of 16 items with nine of these items consisting of supportive behaviors regarding diabetes regimen requirements and seven items consisting of non-supportive behaviors. Children are asked to rate both of their parents on these items. Similarly, there is a parent version of this measure in which children's parents are asked to rate themselves on each of these items. Ratings are based on a 5-point scale ranging from 1 (never) to 5 (at least once a day). The DFBC has been shown to be a reliable measure (Schafer et al., 1982).

Diabetes Quality of Life for Youths (DQOL)

The DQOL (Ingersoll & Marrero, 1991) is a child-completed measure that includes a 17-item Diabetes Life Satisfaction scale, a 26-item Disease Impact scale, and a 13-item Disease-related Worries scale. In addition, there is a one-item general self-rating of overall health. This measure has acceptable psychometric properties (Ingersoll & Marrero, 1991) and has been shown to be sensitive to the effects of treatment (Grey et al., 1998).

Glycosylated Hemoglobin A_{1c} (HbA$_{1c}$)

The HbA$_{1c}$ reflects average blood glucose levels of the preceding two to three months and is generally considered to be the best and most widely used measure of long-term glycemic control (Gonen et al., 1977). The normal non-diabetic range for the assay used in this report was 3.9 per cent–5.9 per cent.

Case formulation and approach to treatment

The case formulation approach identified factors associated with the patient's non-adherence to her regimen, including parental criticism which functioned to decrease self-care behaviors as well as unrealistic parental expectations for glycemic control. As her parents noted her increased blood glucose values, they would typically become accusatory and punitive. In addition, they would often engage in lecturing the patient about the potential long-term health risks of poor glycemic control, with which they were very concerned and anxious because of their experience with their own parents who had diabetes. As a result, the patient decreased the frequency of her blood glucose monitoring.

She also began lying to her parents about the frequency and results of her daily glucose values, implying that everything was within the normal range. However, when the family would obtain a HbA_{1c} test during visits to their endocrinologist, the results were inconsistent with the patient's reported daily blood glucose values. This resulted in feelings of betrayal by the parents and subsequent attempts to punish the patient for her misbehavior. Conflict between the patient and her parents increased while the frequency of positive interactions decreased. The patient and her parents became emotionally disengaged. The patient was performing self-care activities independently of her parents, who had little involvement in her daily regimen. Thus, glucose monitoring was avoided by the patient because of the punitive parental responses which followed, and the parents avoided interaction with their daughter around diabetes self-care because of the inevitability of conflict.

The treatment with the patient had several goals: increase the patient's use of self-monitoring of blood glucose; identify barriers to adherence; and increase assertive behavior towards her parents. The treatment with the parents also had several goals: increase supportive parental involvement in the patient's diabetes self-care; decrease the frequency of non-supportive behaviors regarding their daughter's diabetes (e.g. nagging, lecturing, punishing); and modify the mother's irrational thoughts through cognitive restructuring. Goals for the family consisted of improving communication; improving problem-solving skills (i.e. how to address fluctuations in BG values in a calm, rational way without blaming or becoming emotional); and decreasing conflict.

Each treatment session was structured by beginning the meeting with two therapists and the family together. This time period typically consisted of a review of homework assigned from the previous session and a discussion of important events from the previous week (or weeks). This was followed by a separation of the parents and the patient with their identified therapist to address individual issues. Each session was concluded with the patient and parents meeting together to discuss homework and the plan for the upcoming session.

The initial plan was to conduct sessions on a biweekly basis. However, due to scheduling difficulties the sessions were held further apart. A total of seven sessions were conducted over a five-month period (September 1999 to February 2000). The first two sessions involved both parents and the patient. However, the last five sessions were conducted with just the mother and the patient since the father had recently obtained a time-demanding job that precluded him from attending the scheduled sessions. A brief outline of the content of the session follows.

Session #1

Relevant history was obtained and assessment measures were completed. In meeting with the patient, barriers to adherence were identified, such as peer demands (i.e. wanting to fit in, wanting to eat what peers eat and when they eat), body image concerns (i.e. fear of becoming fat if she gets her sugar under better control). Parental concerns about their daughter's health were discussed in light of their family history of diabetes and health complications. The session concluded with a discussion of general goals for treatment, including improved glycemic control and reduced family conflict.

Session #2

This session began with a review of the general goals established during the first session, and refinement of these to be more specific. The following goals were specified: increased blood glucose monitoring; change parental interactions with patient around blood glucose monitoring to be more neutral with respect to less than optimal results, and more positive about values in the target range; increased physical activity and improved dietary adherence; increased parental involvement in daily diabetes self-care behaviors; and increased parental support for the patient's regimen related self-care behaviors.

A discussion with the parents focused on how they had learned to behave with regard to their daughter's diabetes regimen, and how their responses functioned to either increase or decrease the frequency of appropriate self-care behaviors in the patient. The parents were counseled on the effects of reinforcement and punishment on modifying behavior. They were informed of the importance of increasing positive parental involvement in their daughter's self-care regimen, by being present when she tested her blood glucose values, assisting her in determining if insulin adjustments needed to be made based on the results, and praising her for checking herself and taking an active role in her diabetes care. They were also informed of the problems with non-supportive involvement and were instructed to avoid engaging in questioning or criticism when blood glucose values were high. They were asked to respond to high values by utilizing a neutral tone to engage in a problem-solving discussion that would facilitate learning from the event.

The parents were asked to record the number of times they participated in the patient's care in a positive manner. The patient began assertiveness training to help her to effectively express her opinions during family sessions. She was asked to record the number of times her parents praised her.

Session #3

At the beginning of this session, homework was reviewed. Prior to therapy, the patient had not been checking her blood glucose levels at all. By this point, the patient was checking her blood glucose levels more frequently and consistently (i.e. three to four times each day). In addition, her parents were more involved in daily diabetes care, periodically supervising blood glucose monitoring and reviewing values in her glucose meter. They used these opportunities to praise the patient for good self-care behaviors. They also increased other forms of supportive behavior such as exercising regularly with the patient. In addition, they gradually decreased the frequency of nagging and lecturing. The therapist reviewed previous barriers to adherence with the patient and parents and utilized a problem-solving approach to generate potential solutions to these concerns. For example, a weight-loss plan was formulated, involving increasing exercise and meeting with the dietician on the diabetes medical team to learn how to count carbohydrates.

Session #4

Progress with regard to ongoing homework assignments was reviewed. The family had a brief relapse back to old patterns of communication when the mother witnessed the patient eating a nutritious snack at night without first checking her blood glucose levels. The mother reacted by stating that they "were back to square one." Furthermore, she stated that she could not trust her daughter and that her daughter would die young. During this session, communication training was provided (i.e. use of "I" statements as opposed to "you" statements, validation of each other's concerns). Cognitive restructuring was conducted with the mother to modify irrational thoughts (i.e. catastrophizing that a poor blood glucose value would ultimately lead to long-term complications such as blindness and leg amputation). Role plays were completed with the patient regarding assertive communication of her concerns to her parents.

Session #5

The patient admitted that she avoided checking when she thought she was high for fear of her parents' reaction. She and her mother were able to communicate their concerns in an effective manner and generate a plan of action to avoid similar problems in the future. For example, the patient agreed to go to her mother at times when she was aware she was high, but was hungry, so that they could work together and use her sliding scale to increase her insulin an appropriate amount to adjust for her high blood glucose levels as well as the food she was about to eat.

Session #6

The patient's blood glucose values decreased and her overall psychological functioning had improved. She began caring more about her appearance, was doing better in school, and became more involved in social activities.

Session #7

In a session that was conducted about six weeks later, it was determined that the patient had maintained her improved adherence and her family had maintained their positive communication patterns with regard to diabetes-related issues. However, these skills did not generalize to other areas. Specifically, the family returned to old communication patterns regarding the patient's recently declining grades. The patient began lying about her grades, which her parents found out about from a teacher phone call. They punished her, lectured her about the importance of good grades, nagged her about studying, and withdrew emotionally. The patient then withdrew as well. During the therapy session, a parallel was drawn between their communication pattern for this situation and their previous communication patterns regarding diabetes related issues. Once the patient and her mother became aware of this pattern, they were able to generate potential mechanisms to break the pattern in the future.

As a result of her improvements in adherence and glycemic control, her endocrinologist agreed to put the patient on the insulin pump. The family reported that they were able to use their newly acquired communication and problem-solving skills in order to discuss difficult issues regarding the pump.

The same assessment measures administered at the beginning of treatment were completed again. Summary scores were obtained on the SCI based on sums of the frequency ratings, t-scores were obtained on the CBQ, and z-scores were obtained on the DFBC and the DQOL. As can be seen in Table 7.1 and Figure 7.1, the family made meaningful gains during treatment. The patient's overall adherence with her treatment regimen improved, as indicated by both patient report and parent report. Dramatic decreases in overall parent–teen conflict following treatment were reported by both the patient and her mother. At baseline, ratings of the mother's perceived conflict with her daughter and ratings of the daughter's perceived conflict with both parents were in the clinically significant range (t >70). However, following

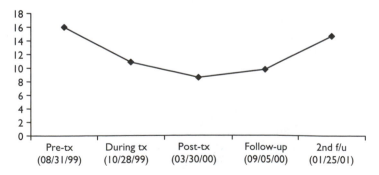

Figure 7.1 Glycosylated hemoglobin A_{1c} (HbA$_{1c}$) results over the course of treatment and follow-up.

Table 7.1 Pre- and post-treatment ratings on behavioral and psychosocial measures

Questionnaire	Informant/scale	Pre-treatment score	Post-treatment score
Self-Care Inventory	Teen	Raw score = 33	Raw score = 47
	Mother	Raw score = 28	Raw score = 45
Conflict Behavior	Teen with Mom	t-score = 79	t-score = 47
Questionnaire	Teen with Dad	t-score = 121	t-score = 59
	Mother	t-score = 84	t-score = 45
Diabetes Family Behavior	Teen with Mom	z-score = 2.22	z-score = -0.18
Checklist-	Teen with Dad	z-score = 1.8	z-score = 0.02
Nonsupportive	Mother	z-score = 1.8	z-score = -1.11
Diabetes Family Behavior	Teen with Mom	z-score = 0.62	z-score = 1.12
Checklist-Supportive	Teen with Dad	z-score = 0.28	z-score = 0.45
	Mother	z-score = 0.86	z-score = 2.35
Diabetes Quality of Life	Impact	z-score = 1.4	z-score = 0.2
for Youths	Worries	z-score = 1.2	z-score = 0.5
	Satisfaction	z-score = -0.53	z-score = 0.2

treatment, all of these ratings were within normal limits. According to both patient report and parent report, parental non-supportive behaviors were in the clinically significant range at baseline, but reduced to be within normal limits following treatment. Although parental supportive behaviors were within normal limits at baseline, there was a slight increase in these behaviors following treatment. Patient report regarding her quality of life indicated that following treatment, diabetes had less impact on her life, she had less worries about her diabetes, and she was more satisfied with her diabetes and her life. Additionally, her glycemic control had improved significantly.

Multiple attempts were made to provide booster sessions and assess long-term treatment affects. The family did not attend several scheduled booster sessions and failed to return telephone calls and emails. Therefore, follow-up measures on indicators of psychosocial functioning could not be obtained. Results of laboratory testing indicated that the patient's glycemic control worsened significantly over the year following the last treatment session (see Figure 7.1). In January 2001, which was almost one year since treatment was terminated, the patient's HbA_{1c} was 14.7 per cent, reflecting very poor glycemic control over the past few months.

Discussion

This case study demonstrated the efficacy of a behavioral intervention that targeted self-care behavior and family functioning. Marked improvements in diabetes self-care, parent–teen conflict, quality of life, and glycemic control were achieved. The improvement regarding self-reported quality of life is consistent with a recent finding of Grey and colleagues (1998, 2000), in which quality of life improved following an intervention addressing coping skills.

Follow-up data obtained almost one full year after termination suggests that without treatment there was a significant relapse in terms of glycemic control. It is important to note that the improvement in glycemic control at the end of treatment was clinically meaningful. This case report illustrates the use of family-based interventions that have already proven effective for improving adherence to diabetes self-management tasks in several case-controlled studies. This was an uncontrolled case study. However, these findings suggest that the intervention was successful because when treatment was discontinued the patient's glycemic control worsened, presumably due to relapse to pre-treatment behaviors. This finding indicates that "booster" sessions may be a necessity for the maintenance of treatment gains.

This study reinforces the findings of a large literature regarding the importance of family functioning in teenagers with diabetes and provides further support for the importance of case formulation in guiding treatment. In this case, formulating the problem in terms of family behaviors led to building more effective communication and teamwork in the parent–teen relationship to promote good self-care behavior. The normative developmental tasks of the teenage years include striving for increased responsibilities and independence. However, teenagers are often unprepared for the unique challenges posed by taking too much responsibility regarding their diabetes self-care. As a result, their glycemic control often worsens. In this case, the patient was taking primary responsibility for her self-care when she was not mature enough to assume this responsibility. When her parents were involved, they typically engaged in non-supportive interactions, thus perpetuating the problem. In addition, the parents had cognitive distortions (e.g. "catastrophizing" about a blood glucose test) that caused them great anxiety and hindered their ability to communicate effectively with their daughter. Once these cognitions were addressed, they were able to become more constructively involved in their daughter's diabetes management tasks. They also began engaging in supportive forms of interaction and treatment goals were achieved. These findings are consistent with the results of an office-based intervention reported by Anderson and colleagues (1999) in which increased supportive parental involvement in insulin administration and blood glucose monitoring was related to decreased parent–teen conflict and improved glycemic control.

Improved glycemic control during adolescence has the potential to prevent and/or delay the onset of long-term complications from diabetes (DCCT Research Group, 1994). Therefore, interventions to improve the glycemic control of adolescents remain an important concern for clinical and research efforts. The findings of this case study illustrate that improvements in regimen adherence and glycemic control can be achieved with behavioral case formulation and tailored behavioral interventions.

Summary and conclusions

This chapter provided a summary of research findings relating psychosocial factors to diabetes management in children and adolescents. Studies have shown that diabetic youth appear to be at increased risk for psychosocial problems, and when present are likely to be associated with difficulties with diabetes management. Better regimen adherence and glycemic control have been consistently observed for children with families that communicate well, provide support, and are appropriately involved in diabetes care. Research has demonstrated the efficacy of psychosocial interventions that have been shown to improve regimen adherence and glycemic control, as well as psychosocial functioning and quality of life.

The case report focused on the treatment of poor regimen adherence and glycemic control in an adolescent girl with type 1 diabetes, illustrating the use of case formulation to guide a behavioral intervention applied to family functioning and self-care behavior. The patient was a 17-year-old Hispanic female, who was diagnosed with type 1 diabetes when she was 6 years old. A total of seven sessions were conducted over a five-month period. Several psychosocial measures were obtained prior to treatment and when treatment was terminated. Measures of glycemic control were obtained prior to treatment, during treatment, at treatment termination, at seven-months follow-up, and at one-year follow-up. Marked improvements in diabetes self-care, parent–teen conflict, quality of life, and glycemic control were achieved by the conclusion of treatment. However, follow-up data indicated that without treatment there was a significant relapse in terms of glycemic control. This finding indicates that booster sessions may be necessary for the maintenance of treatment gains.

References

Anderson, B.J., Miller, J.P., Auslander, W.F., & Santiago, J. (1981). Family characteristics of diabetic adolescents: Relationship to glycemic control. *Diabetes Care, 4*, 586–594.

Anderson, B.J., Wolf, R.M., Burkhart, M.T., Cornell, R.G., & Bacon, G.E. (1989). Effects of peer-group intervention on metabolic control of adolescents with IDDM: Randomized outpatient study. *Diabetes Care, 12*, 179–183.

Anderson, B.J., Auslander, W.F., Jung, K.C., Miller, J.P., & Santiago, J.V. (1990). Assessing family sharing of diabetes responsibility. *Journal of Pediatric Psychology, 15*, 477–492.

Anderson, B.J., Ho, J., Brackett, J., Finkelstein, D., & Laffel, L. (1997). Parental involvement in diabetes management tasks: Relationships to blood glucose monitoring adherence and metabolic control in young adolescents with insulin-dependent diabetes mellitus. *Journal of Pediatrics, 130*, 257–265.

Anderson, B.J., Brackett, J., Ho, J., & Laffel, L.M.B. (1999). An office-based intervention to maintain parent–adolescent teamwork in diabetes management. *Diabetes Care, 22*, 713–721.

Arslanian, S., Becker, D., & Drash, A. (1994). Diabetes mellitus in the child and adolescent. In D. Wilkens (Ed.), *The diagnosis and treatment of endocrine disorders in childhood and adolescence* (4th ed., pp. 969–971). Springfield, MA: Charles C. Thomas.

Auslander, W.F., Thompson, S., Dreitzer, D., White, N.H., & Santiago, J.V. (1997). Disparity in glycemic control and adherence between African-American and Caucasian youths with diabetes: Family and community contexts. *Diabetes Care, 20*, 1569–1575.

Blanz, B., Rensch-Riemann, B., Fritz-Sigmund, D., & Schmidt, M. (1993). IDDM is a risk factor for adolescent psychiatric disorders. *Diabetes Care, 16*, 1579–1587.

Boardway, R.H., Delamater, A.M., Tomakowsky, J., & Gutai, J.P. (1993). Stress management training for adolescents with diabetes. *Journal of Pediatric Psychology, 18*, 29–45.

Bobrow, E.S., AvRuskin, T.W., & Siller, J. (1985). Mother–daughter interaction and adherence to diabetes regimens. *Diabetes Care, 8*, 146–151.

Boland, E.A., Grey, M., Oesterle, Al., Fredrickson, L., & Tamborlane, W.V. (1999). Continuous subcutaneous insuli infusion: A new way to lower risk of severe hypoglycemia, improve metabolic control, and enhance coping in adolescents with type 1 diabetes. *Diabetes Care, 22*, 1779–1784.

Bryden, K.S., Neil, A., Mayou, R.A., Peveler, R.C., Fairburn, C.G., & Dunger, D.B. (1999). Eating habits, body weight, and insulin misuse: A longitudinal study of teenagers and young adults with type 1 diabetes. *Diabetes Care, 22*, 1956–1960.

Bryden, K.S., Peveler, R.C., Stein, A., Neil, A., Mayou, R.A., & Dunger, D.B. (2001). Clinical and psychological course of diabetes from adolescence to young adulthood: A longitudinal cohort study. *Diabetes Care, 24*, 1536–1540.

Carney, R.M., Schechter, K., & Davis, T. (1983). Improving adherence to blood glucose testing in insulin-dependent diabetic children. *Behavior Therapy, 14*, 247–254.

Cook, S., Herold, K., Edidin, D.V., & Briars, R. (2002). Increasing problem solving in adolescents with type 1 diabetes: The choices diabetes program. *Diabetes Educator, 28*, 115–124.

Daneman, D., Olmsted, M., Rydall, A., Maharaj, S., & Rodin, G. (1998). Eating disorders in young women with type 1 diabetes: Prevalence, problems and prevention. *Hormone Research, 50*, 79–86.

Davis, C.L., Delamater, A.M., Shaw, K.H., La Greca, A.M., Eidson, M.S., Perez-Rodriguez, J.E., & Nemery, R. (2001). Parenting styles, regimen adherence, and glycemic control in 4- to 10-year-old children with diabetes. *Journal of Pediatric Psychology, 26*, 123–129.

Delamater, A., Bubb, J., Davis, S., Smith, J., Schmidt, L., White, N., & Santiago, J.V. (1990). Randomized prospective study of self-management training with newly diagnosed diabetic children. *Diabetes Care, 13*, 492–498.

Delamater, A.M., Albrecht, D., Postellon, D., & Gutai, J. (1991a). Racial differences in metabolic control of children and adolescents with Type 1 diabetes mellitus. *Diabetes Care, 14*, 20–25.

Delamater, A., Smith, J.A., Bubb, J., Green-Davis, S., Gamble, T., White, N.H., & Santiago, J.V. (1991b). Family-based behavior therapy for diabetic adolescents. In J.H. Johnson & S.B. Johnson (Eds.), *Advances in child health psychology*. Gainesville, FL: University of Florida Press.

Delamater, A.M., Shaw, K., Applegate, B., Pratt, I., Eidson, M., Lancelotta, G., Gonzalez-Mendoza, L., & Richton, S. (1999). Risk for metabolic control problems in minority youth with diabetes. *Diabetes Care, 22*, 700–705.

Delamater, A., Jacobson, A., Anderson, B., Cox, D., Fisher, L., Lustman, P., Rubin, R., & Wysocki, T. (2001). Psychosocial therapies in diabetes. *Diabetes Care, 24*, 1286–1292.

Delamater, A.M., Alvarez-Salvat, R., & McCullough, J. (2003). Evidenced-based interventions for children and adolescents with type 1 diabetes. In L. Vandecreek (Ed.), *Innovations in clinical practice: Focus on children and adolescents*. Sarasota, FL: Professional Resource Press.

Diabetes Control and Complications Trial (DCCT) Research Group (1993). The effect of intensive treatment of diabetes on the development and progression of long-term complications in insulin-dependent diabetes mellitus. *New England Journal of Medicine, 329*, 977–986.

Diabetes Control and Complications Trial (DCCT) Research Group (1994). Effect of intensive diabetes treatment on the development and progression of long-term complications in adolescents with insulin-dependent diabetes mellitus. *Journal of Pediatrics, 125*, 177–188.

Forsander, G.A., Persson, B., Sundelin, J., Berglund, E., Snellman, K., & Hellstrom, R. (1998). Metabolic control in children with insulin-dependent diabetes mellitus 5 y after diagnosis: Early detection of patients at risk for poor metabolic control. *Acta Paediatrica, 87*, 857–864.

Forsander, G.A., Sundelin, J., & Persson, B. (2000). Influence of the initial management regimen and family social situation on glycemic control and medical care in children with type 1 diabetes mellitus. *Acta Paediatrica, 89*, 1462–1468.

Gonen, B., Rachman, H., Rubenstein, A.H., Tanega, S.P., & Horwitz, D.L. (1977). Hemoglobin A_1C as an indicator of the degree of glucose intolerance in diabetics. *Lancet, 2*, 734–737.

Greco, P., La Greca, A.M., Auslander, W., Spetter, D., Skyler, J.S., Fisher, E., & Santiago, J.V. (1990). Assessing adherence in IDDM: A comparison of two methods. *Diabetes, 40*, 108A.

Grey, M., Cameron, M., Lipman, T., & Thurber, F. (1995). Psychosocial status of children with diabetes in the first 2 years after diagnosis. *Diabetes Care, 18*, 1330–1336.

Grey, M., Boland, E. A., Davidson, M., Yu, C., Sullivan-Bolyai, S., & Tamborlane, W.V. (1998). Short-term effects of coping skills training as adjunct to intensive therapy in adolescents. *Diabetes Care, 21*, 902–908.

Grey, M., Boland, E., Davidson, M., Yu, C., & Tamborlance, W. (2000). Coping skills training for youth on intensive therapy has long-lasting effects on metabolic control and quality of life. *Journal of Pediatrics, 137*, 107–113.

Hains, A.A., Davies, W.H., Parton, E., Totka, J., & Amoroso-Camarata, J. (2000). A stress management intervention for adolescents with type 1 diabetes. *Diabetes Educator, 26*, 417–424.

Hampson, S.E., Skinner, R.C., Hart, J., Storey L., Gage, H., Foxcroft, D., Kimber, A., Cradock, S., & McEvilly, E.A. (2000). Behavioral interventions for adolescents with type 1 diabetes: How effective are they? *Diabetes Care, 23*, 1416–1422.

Hanson, C.L., Henggeler, S.W., Burghen, G.A. (1987). Model of associations between psychosocial variables and health-outcome measures of adolescents with IDDM. *Diabetes Care, 10*, 752–758.

Ingersoll, G.M., & Marrero, D.G. (1991). A modified quality of life measure for youths: Psychometric properties. *Diabetes Educator, 17*, 114–120.

Ingersoll, G.M., Orr, D., Herrold, A., & Golden, M. (1986). Cognitive maturity and self-management among adolescents with insulin-dependent diabetes mellitus. *Journal of Pediatrics, 108*, 620–623.

Jacobson, A.M., Hauser, S.T., Wertlieb, D., Woldsdorf, J., Orleans, J., & Viegra, M. (1986). Psychological adjustment of children with recently diagnosed diabetes mellitus. *Diabetes Care, 9*, 323–329.

Jacobson, A.M., Hauser, S.T., Lavori, P., *et al.* (1994). Family environment and glycemic control: A four-year prospective study of children and adolescents with insulin-dependent diabetes mellitus. *Psychosomatic Medicine, 56*, 401–409.

Jacobson, A.M., Hauser, S.T., Willett, J., Wolfsdor, J., & Herman, L. (1997a) Consequences of irregular versus continuous medical follow-up in children and adolescents with insulin-dependent diabetes mellitus. *Journal of Pediatrics, 131*, 727–733.

Jacobson, A.M., Hauser, S.T., Willett, J., Wolfsdorf, J.I., Herman, L., & de Groot, M. (1997b). Psychological adjustment to IDDM: 10-year follow-up of an onset cohort of child and adolescent patients. *Diabetes Care, 20*, 811–818.

Johnson, S.B., Kelly, M., Henretta, J.C., Cunningham, W.R., Tomer, A., & Silverstein, J.H. (1992). A longitudinal analysis of adherence and health status in childhood diabetes. *Journal of Pediatric Psychology, 17*, 537–553.

Jones, J.M., Lawson, M.L., Daneman, D., Olmsted, M.P., & Rodin, G. (2000). Eating disorders in adolescent females with and without type 1 diabetes: Cross sectional study. *British Medical Journal, 320*, 1563–1566.

Kaplan, R.M., Chadwick, M.W., & Schimmel, L.E. (1985). Social learning intervention to promote metabolic control in type I diabetes mellitus: Pilot experimental results. *Diabetes Care, 8*, 152–155.

Kaufman, F.R., Halvorson, M., & Carpenter, S. (1999). Association between diabetes control and visits to a multidisciplinary pediatric diabetes clinic. *Pediatrics, 103*, 948–951.

Kovacs, M., Feinberg, T.L., Paulauskas, S., Finkelstein, R., Pollock, M., & Crouse-Novak, M. (1985a). Initial coping responses and psychosocial characteristics of children with insulin-dependent diabetes mellitus. *Journal of Pediatrics, 106*, 827–834.

Kovacs, M., Finkelstein, R., Feinberg, T.L., Crouse-Novak, M., Paulauskas, S., & Pollock, M. (1985b). Initial psychologic responses of parents to the diagnosis of insulin dependent diabetes mellitus in their children. *Diabetes Care, 8*, 568–575.

Kovacs, M., Ho, V., & Pollock, M.H. (1995). Criterion and predictive validity of the diagnosis of adjustment disorder: A prospective study of youths with new-onset insulin-dependent diabetes mellitus. *American Journal of Psychiatry, 152*, 523–528.

Kovacs, M., Goldston, D., Obrosky, D., & Bonar, L. (1997). Psychiatric disorders in youths with IDDM: Rates and risk factors. *Diabetes Care, 20*, 36–44.

Laffel, L., Vangsness, L., Connell, A., Goebel-Fabbri, A., Butler, D., & Anderson, B.J. (2003). Impact of ambulatory, family-focused teamwork intervention on glycemic control in youth with type 1 diabetes. *Journal of Pediatrics, 142*, 409–416.

La Greca, A.M., Follansbee, D.S., & Skyler, J.S. (1990). Developmental and behavioral aspects of diabetes management in children and adolescents. *Children's Health Care, 19*, 132–139.

La Greca, A. M., Swales, T., Klemp, S., Madigan, S., & Skyler, J. (1995a). Adolescents with diabetes: Gender differences in psychosocial functioning and glycemic control. *Children's Health Care, 24*, 61–78.

La Greca, A.M., Auslander, W.F., Greco, P., Spetter, D., Fisher, E.B., & Santiago, J.V. (1995b). I get by with a little help from my family and friends: Adolescents' support for diabetes care. *Journal of Pediatric Psychology, 20*, 449–476.

Landolt, M.A., Ribi, K., Laimbacher, J., Vollrath, M., Gnehm, H.E., & Sennhauser, F.H. (2002). Posttraumatic stress disorder in parents of children with newly diagnosed type 1 diabetes. *Journal of Pediatric Psychology, 27*, 647–652.

Lavigne, J., & Faier-Routman, J. (1992). Psychological adjustment to pediatric physical disorders: A meta-analytic review. *Journal of Pediatric Psychology, 17*, 133–157.

Maharag, S., Rodini, G., Olmsted, M., Connolly, J., Daneman, D. (2001). Eating problems and the observed quality of mother–daughter interactions among girls with type 1 diabetes. *Journal of Consulting and Clinical Psychology, 69*, 950–958.

Meltzer, L.J., Johnson, S.B., Prine, J.M., Banks, R.A., Desrosiers, P.M., & Silverstein, J.H. (2001). Disordered eating, body mass, and glycemic control in adolescents with type 1 diabetes. *Diabetes Care, 24*, 678–682.

Mendez, F., & Belendez, M. (1997). Effects of a behavioral intervention on treatment adherence and stress management in adolescents with IDDM. *Diabetes Care, 20*, 1370–1375.

Miller-Johnson, S., Emery, R.E., Marvin, R.S., Clarke, W., Lovinger, R., & Martin, M. (1994). Parent–child relationships and the management of insulin-dependent diabetes mellitus. *Journal of Consulting and Clinical Psychology, 62*, 3, 603–610.

Neumark-Sztainer, D., Patterson, J., Mellin, A., Ackard, D., Utter, J., Story, M., & Sockalosky, J. (2002). Weight control practices and disordered eating behaviors among adolescent females and males with type 1 diabetes: Associations with sociodemographics, weight concerns, familial factors, and metabolic outcomes. *Diabetes Care, 25*, 1289–1296.

Orr, D., Golden, M.P., Myers, G., & Marrero, D.G. (1983). Characteristics of adolescents with poorly controlled diabetes referred to a tertiary care center. *Diabetes Care, 6*, 170–175.

Overstreet, S., Goins, J., Chen, R.S., Holmes, C.S., Greer, T., Dunlap, W.P., & Frentz, J. (1995). Family environment and the interrelation of family structure, child behavior, and metabolic control for children with diabetes. *Journal of Pediatric Psychology, 20*, 435–447.

Robin, A.L., & Foster, S.L. (1989). *Negotiating parent–adolescent conflict: A behavioral family systems approach.* New York: Guilford Press.

Rydall, A.C., Rodin, G.M., Olmsted, M.P., Devenyi, R.G., & Daneman, D. (1997). Disordered eating behavior and microvascular complications in young women with insulin-dependent diabetes mellitus. *New England Journal of Medicine, 336,* 1849–1854.

Satin, W., La Greca, A., Zigo, M., & Skyler, J. (1989). Diabetes in adolescence: Effects of multifamily group intervention and parent simulation of diabetes. *Journal of Pediatric Psychology, 14,* 259–276.

Schafer, L.C., Glasgow, R.E., & McCaul, K.D. (1982). Increasing the adherence of diabetic adolescents. *Journal of Behavioral Medicine, 5,* 3, 353–362.

Schafer, L.C., Glasgow, R.E., McCaul, K.D., & Dreher, M. (1983). Adherence to IDDM regimens: Relationship to psychosocial variables and glycemic control. *Diabetes Care, 6,* 5, 493–498.

Schwartz, S.A., Weissberg-Benchell, J., & Perlmuter, L.C. (2001). Personal control and disordered eating in female adolescents with type 1 diabetes. *Diabetes Care, 25,* 1987–1991.

Seiffge-Krenke, I. (2002). 'Come on, say something, Dad!': Communication and coping in fathers of diabetic adolescents. *Journal of Pediatric Psychology, 27,* 439–450.

Svoren, B., Butler, D., Levine, B., Anderson, B.J., & Laffel, L. (2003). Reducing acute adverse outcomes in youths with type 1 diabetes: A randomized, controlled trial. *Pediatrics, 112,* 914–922.

Thompson, S.J., Auslander, W.F., & White, N.H. (2001). Comparison of single-mother and two-parent families on metabolic control of children with diabetes. *Diabetes Care, 24,* 234–238.

Weissberg-Benchell, J., Glasgow, A.M., Tynan, W.D., Wirtz, P., Turek, J., & Ward, J. (1995). Adolescent management and mismanagement. *Diabetes Care, 18,* 77–82.

Weist, M., Finney, J., Barnard, M., Davis, C., & Ollendick, T. (1993). Empirical selection of psychosocial treatment targets for children and adolescents with diabetes. *Journal of Pediatric Psychology, 18,* 11–28.

White, K., Kolman, M., Wexler, P., Polin, G., & Winter, R.J. (1984). Unstable diabetes and unstable families: A psychosocial evaluation of diabetic children with recurrent ketoacidosis. *Pediatrics, 73,* 749–755.

Wysocki, T. (1993). Associations among teen–parent relationships, glycemic control, and adjustment to diabetes in adolescents. *Journal of Pediatric Psychology, 18,* 4, 441–452.

Wysocki, T., Hough, B.S., Ward, K. M., & Green, L.B. (1992). Diabetes mellitus in the transition to adulthood: Adjustment, self-care, and health status. *Journal of Developmental and Behavioral Pediatrics, 13,* 194–201.

Wysocki, T., Taylor, A., Hough, B., Linscheid, T., Yeates, K., Naglieri, J. (1996). Deviation from developmentally appropriate self-care autonomy: Association with diabetes outcomes. *Diabetes Care, 19,* 119–125.

Wysocki, T., Miller, K., Greco, P., Harris, M.A., Harvey, L., Taylor, A., Elder Danda, C., McDonell, K., & White, N.H. (1999). Behavior therapy for families of adolescents with diabetes: Effects on directly observed family interactions. *Behavior Therapy, 30,* 507–525.

Wysocki, T., Harris, M.A., Greco, P., Bubb, J., Danda, C.E., Harvey, L.M., McDonell, K., Taylor, A., & White, N.H. (2000). Randomized, controlled trial of behavior therapy for families of adolescents with insulin-dependent diabetes mellitus. *Journal of Pediatric Psychology, 25*, 23–33.

Wysocki, T., Greco, P., Harris, M. A., Bubb, J., & White, N. H. (2001). Behavior therapy for families of adolescents with diabetes: Maintenance of treatment effects. *Diabetes Care, 24*, 441–446.

Wysocki, T., Harris, M. A., Wilkinson, K., Sadler, M., Mauras, N., & White, N. (2003). Self-management competency as a predictor of outcomes of intensive therapy or usual care in youth with type 1 diabetes. *Diabetes Care, 26*, 2043–2047.

Chapter 8

Cognitive therapy for irritable bowel syndrome
Improving clinical decision making and treatment efficiency through behavioral case formulation

Jeffrey M. Lackner and Edward B. Blanchard

Irritable bowel syndrome (IBS) is a common gastrointestinal disorder characterized by a cluster of symptoms including abdominal pain or discomfort associated with altered bowel habits (e.g. diarrhea, constipation) in the absence of organic disease. Because the locus of the problem is in how the gut functions, not abnormalities in its physical structure, IBS is considered a functional gastrointestinal (GI) disorder. Of the 25 functional GI disorders, IBS is the most prevalent, costly, and disabling.

Epidemiology

Approximately 40 million individuals in the USA suffer from IBS (Lynn & Friedman, 1993), making IBS not only one of the most prevalent chronic pain disorders (Crombie *et al.*, 1999), but one of the most prevalent chronic illnesses in general. IBS has nearly twice the prevalence rate of hypertension and is more than six times as prevalent as diabetes (Adams & Benson, 1991). Although most (80 per cent) IBS patients do not seek medical attention, the 20 per cent who do represent nearly 30 per cent of all visits to GI practices and 12 per cent of all primary care visits, making IBS one of the most common disorders seen by physicians (Physician Drug and Diagnosis Audit, 1999). In fact, IBS is the most common GI disorder seen in primary care settings.

Therefore, IBS represents a substantial source of morbidity and cost to the community. IBS has been identified as second only to the common cold as a cause of work absenteeism (Drossman *et al.*, 1993). It has been reported that approximately 30 per cent of IBS sufferers take sick leave for this condition, with half of these being absent from work at least two weeks per year. In fact, IBS affects quality of life as much or more than congestive heart failure (Whitehead *et al.*, 1996). IBS also exacts a heavy financial toll, costing the US healthcare system approximately $8 billion annually (Talley *et al.*, 1995).

Although IBS occurs in both genders, and among all age and socio-economic groups, IBS is three times more common in women, especially among those seeking treatment and those most severely affected. Patients with higher education, high income levels, and elevated levels of pain and stress are more likely to seek medical treatment for IBS.

Pathophysiology

IBS is not caused by structural, biochemical or mucosal disease in the GI system. Because IBS lacks a clear organic basis, many healthcare medical professionals whose training has strong philosophical roots in the Cartesian dualism of mind and body see IBS as a physical manifestation of an under-lying psychiatric disorder such as somatization, depression, and anxiety (e.g. Hislop, 1971; Latimer, 1983; Clouse, 1988). Although psychological factors can influence the onset, expression and trajectory of IBS, a sizable subset of patients diagnosed with IBS do not have a clinical psychiatric dis-order (Blanchard, 2000). Therefore, the characterization of IBS as a strictly psychosomatic problem is neither accurate nor constructive.

An understanding of the precise pathophysiologic mechanisms underlying irritable bowel syndrome is evolving, with no underlying physiologic mechan-ism unique to IBS identified. One popular approach has emphasized the role of motility in the expression of symptoms. This conceptualization is based on several lines of evidence. IBS patients whose predominant bowel habit is diarrhea have been found to have a greater number of fast contractions and propagated contractions in the colon compared to normal subjects (Whitehead et al., 1990). Patients whose predominant bowel habit is consti-pation have, on the other hand, fewer high amplitude propagated contractions than normal subjects (Bazzocchi et al., 1990). Additional support for an important role for abnormal motility comes from research showing increased motor reactivity (e.g. increased colonic contractions) to a variety of stimuli, including meals, peptide hormones, mechanical distension and laboratory induced stress and negative emotional states (e.g. Almy et al., 1949; Sullivan et al., 1978) among IBS patients. However, abnormal motor activity is not specific to IBS patients (i.e. occurs in control subjects) and is only weakly correlated with pain.

These data argue against the view that IBS is strictly a disorder of enhanced motility and invite speculation about alternative mechanisms that work in concert with disorder motility to influence IBS. For this reason much recent research has shifted from a focus on normal perception of abnormal motility to abnormal perception of normal motility (i.e. visceral hypersensitivity). The concept of visceral hypersensitivity refers to a state of heightened awareness of and sensitivity to normal intestinal activity (e.g. gas, normal intestinal contractions) that arises within the gut during digestion as well as painful distention of the colon. Visceral hypersensitivity research has been based largely on a series of distension studies, which demonstrate that a significant proportion of IBS patients, particularly those whose bowel habits involve diarrhea, experience pain at lower levels of pressure and volume than controls when their rectum, sigmoid, or small intestine are distended by a balloon. In other words, IBS patients experience discomfort in the GI tract in response to stimuli that do not elicit discomfort in non-IBS patients. This pain sensitivity appears to be relatively specific to the gut and does not characterize thresholds for somatic pain stimuli (e.g. cold pressor test; Whitehead *et al.*, 1990).

The current conceptual model for IBS suggest that it results from dysregulation in interactions among the central nervous system (CNS) and the enteric nervous system (ENS). This neural network is referred to as the "brain–gut axis". The ENS, along with the sympathetic (SNS) and parasympathetic nervous (PNS) systems, comprises the three divisions of autonomic nervous systems (ANS), the part of the nervous system that regulates involuntary actions including smooth muscle, cardiac muscle, and glands. The ANS's enteric division (i.e. ENS) is located in the sheaths of tissue lining the GI tract from the esophagus to the rectum. The ENS is composed of both local sensory neurons that detect and relay information regarding changes in the tension of the gut walls and its chemical environment and motor neurons that control muscle contractions of the gut wall and secretion. The ENS plays a major role in maintaining homeostasis in the body by controlling gastrointestinal blood vessel tone, motility, gastric secretion and fluid transport. Because of its heavy concentration of neurotransmitters (e.g. serotonin, 5-HT, substance P, vasoactive intestinal peptide, and calcitonin gene-related peptide); the fact that it is embryologically derived from the same part of the neural crest that forms the brain; and its unique ability among other parts of the peripheral nervous system to mediate reflex behavior (i.e. gut function) in the absence of input from the brain or spinal cord (Gershon, 1998), the ENS has been referred to as the "second brain". Normal digestive functions involve communication links between the ENS and the CNS. These links take the form of parasympathetic and sympathetic fibers that connect either the central and enteric nervous system or connect the CNS directly with the digestive tract. Through these cross-connections, sensory inputs from the gut are relayed to and processed by higher cortical centers where they modulate affect, pain perception and behavioral response. Because the neural transmission lines of the brain–gut axis are bidirectional and reciprocal, the CNS receives information from the digestive tract and modulates the ENS. The bidirectional relationship of the brain–gut axis means that higher order mental processes (attention, emotion, sensation, taste, thought) can influence GI function, secretion and sensation (Drossman, 1994). Normal GI function is typically characterized by a relatively high degree of coordination of the brain–gut axis. In IBS patients, however, there is a persistent disruption in the interaction of the neuroenteric system that contribute to key pathogenic mechanisms of GI motility abnormalities and visceral hypersensitivity.

Treatment

There is no universally accepted medical option for the full range of symptoms of IBS. No single medication (or class of medications) currently available has been demonstrated in well-designed and well-controlled clinical trials to be consistently superior to placebo treatment for IBS symptoms. Some of the most promising outcome data comes from clinical trials testing psychological treatments. Four different psychological treatments (brief psychodynamic psychotherapy with relaxation, hypnotherapy, cognitive behavioral therapy, and cognitive therapy) each have been shown to be more effective than symptom monitoring or routine medical care in reducing IBS symptoms (Blanchard, 2000; Lackner *et al.*, 2004). Results with cognitive therapy and hypnotherapy have been replicated and found to be superior to attention-placebo control conditions. The psychological treatment with one of the best positive track records is cognitive therapy (CT) for IBS, which was developed by Blanchard (2000). The rationale for treatment is based on research showing that there are bidirectional neural pathways (i.e. afferent and efferent neurons) involved in the CNS modulation of gut function and sensation integrated at peripheral, spinal, and supraspinal levels (DePonti & Malagelada, 1998). Because higher order brain processes (attention, thoughts) have the capacity to influence GI function by modifying signals between the brain and gut (Mayer & Raybould, 1990), it is reasonable that a cognitively oriented treatment which acts on the brain gut axis could improve IBS symptoms.

Therefore, the goal of cognitive therapy is to teach patients a set of information-processing and problem-solving skills to reconfigure "faulty wiring" between the ENS and CNS. Consistent with this hypothesis, high-quality data show that cognitively based treatment is highly effective in that 60 to 80 per cent of IBS patients achieve at post-treatment a clinically significant (>50 per cent or more) reduction in IBS symptoms, maintaining these gains at three-month follow-up. Treatment gains are not limited to a reduction of GI symptoms alone. A significant proportion of patients also show substantial reductions in comorbid psychological distress (e.g. depression, anxiety) at post-treatment. These data are some of the strongest results available supporting the efficacy of psychological treatments.

Diagnosis

The diagnosis of IBS is based on the presence of clinical features and the exclusion of other disorders, but the nonspecific nature of IBS symptoms makes diagnosis difficult. Drossman (1994) has identified 31 disorders across 13 classes of medical diseases (e.g. intestinal disease, pancreatic insufficiency, etc.) whose symptoms are descriptively similar to IBS symptoms. Because IBS symptoms mimic those other GI diseases, the diagnosis of IBS is often established only after the patient undergoes extensive diagnostic work-ups to rule out organic disease. It is not surprising then that the average IBS patient visits three doctors over three years before an IBS diagnosis is confirmed (Chang *et al.*, 2000). This is an inefficient, costly, prolonged and painful exercise, which has prompted the development of a symptom-based classification system (known as the Rome criteria). The Rome criteria are conceptually and operationally similar to the classification method of psychiatric disorders in DSM-IV-R, which organizes disorders into discrete clinical conditions based on defined criteria sets with defining features that typically co-occur or covary across time. By establishing positive clinical features and diagnostic requirements, Rome criteria sought to increase the specificity of IBS diagnosis and, in the process, encourage practitioners to move away from their longstanding reliance on a "diagnostic by exclusion" strategy involving multiple, costly and unnecessary diagnostic studies reserved for organic disease. To meet diagnostic criteria for IBS, Rome criteria require that in the preceding 12 months the patient must experience 12 weeks (need not be consecutive) of abdominal pain or discomfort with two out of three features:

- relieved with defecation; and/or
- onset associated with a change in frequency of stool; and/or
- onset associated with a change in appearance of stool.

Rome criteria represent a major advance in the diagnosis of functional GI disorders in general and IBS in particular. Rome criteria legitimize IBS as a "real" diagnostic entity in the eyes of providers, many of whom have historically considered IBS to be anything from an annoyance to a psychiatric condition. The criteria also summarize a rich body of clinical, epidemiological and basic research, help inform clinical decision making, and facilitate communication among clinicians and researchers. Perhaps most importantly, Rome provides the most accurate description of IBS clinical features (Mertz, 2001). These criteria come closest to comprising a gold standard, and represent a sound step in making research more comparable and a positive diagnosis more likely (Blanchard, 2000).

Rome criteria recognize that IBS is a multifactorial problem whose complexion (e.g. quality, location, frequency) and temporal course differs across – and even within – patients. Such between-patient heterogeneity typically represents a serious threat to the validity and clinical utility of many symptom-based classification system (e.g. DSM-IV-R). Rome criteria address the heterogeneity problem by delineating a set of clinical guidelines that encourage an individualized treatment approach based on either the symptom severity or predominant symptom of the patient. The *predominant symptom classification* method is perhaps the most common approach. In this approach, patients are subclassified into constipation-prominent, diarrhea-prominent, and mixed (i.e. alternating periods of diarrhea and constipation), based on the nature of stool frequency, stool form, and stool passage. According to Rome criteria, diarrhea-prominent IBS patients experience more than three bowel movements per day, loose or watery stools, and urgency. Constipation-predominant IBS patients, on the other hand, are typically characterized by having two or more of the following symptoms: fewer than three bowel movements per week, hard or lumpy stools, and straining during bowel movements. The symptom predominant classification approach recommends a hierarchical treatment approach structured around resolution of the primary symptom (e.g. pain, diarrhea, constipation). According to Drossman, an example of the predominant symptom approach would call for "the use of an antispasmodic for pain, loperamide for diarrhea, and increased fiber for constipation" (Drossman, 1997, p. 24).

This subclassification method has been criticized for its limited clinical utility, since the predominant primary symptom is not necessarily stable over time (Agreus et al., 1998). A patient whose symptom profile is classified as diarrhea-predominant at point A may show a profile classification of constipation-predominant IBS at point B. For this reason, the predominant symptom classification has given way to an alternative stratification method based on the *severity of symptoms* (mild, moderate, severe). Symptoms of the great majority of individuals who merit an IBS diagnosis (70 per cent) can be classified as mild, in that they occur relatively infrequently, do not require medical care, and are not disabling. First-line treatment for mildly affected patients are patient education about IBS, reassurance regarding the condition's benign nature, and life-style changes (e.g. patients encouraged to exercise, eat well-balanced, regular meals, avoid food fads and excess fat, and reduce intake of caffeine, the artificial sweetener sorbitol (present in sugarless gum, dietetic candy, and many other products) and alcohol (Drossman et al., 1997). Treatment for patients with slightly more severe symptoms may require the addition of pharmacotherapy directed at the gut, life-style modification, and behavioral self-management training. In the case of patients with severe symptoms, a tertiary treatment center where psychotropic medications (e.g. antidepressants) and psychological interventions are recommended.

In the context of Rome criteria symptoms, IBS symptom severity is operationalized as a composite index that reflects the intensity and duration of symptoms, psychosocial distress, and treatment seeking (Drossman et al., 1997, Drossman et al., 2000b). The rationale for using symptom severity as a proxy for a patient's symptom experience and illness behaviors comes from research that shows that psychological functioning is strongly associated with the severity of symptoms and patient status (Drossman et al., 2000b). First, psychological variables differentiate patients with IBS from patients without IBS. Second, a set of psychological variables (abuse history, coping, negative pain beliefs) predict worse health outcomes, as defined by increased pain scores, distress, sick days, and healthcare utilization (e.g. physical visits, phone calls, days in bed). Third, in research comparing patients with moderate and severe IBS on physiologic, psychological, and heath status measures, pain complaints were more strongly associated with psychological factors (e.g. depression, coping response, illness behaviors) than physiological parameters (e.g. rectal sensitivity). The subgroups and their accompanying clinical guidelines are an improvement over prior approaches, which were characterized more by their informality, idiosyncratic, and unsystematic qualities, than for their clinical utility and empirical basis. Taken together, these subtype methods recognize that patient complaints are not static nor, topographically speaking, uniform. The course and complexion of IBS is variable and shaped by many factors, including the patient's age and gender, predominant symptoms, severity and duration of symptoms, and psychosocial factors (e.g. Bennet *et al.*, 1998). These data, when integrated with the results of objective medical information, have the potential to increase the clinician's understanding of the patient's illness and promote improved patient management.

That said, both classification systems are imperfect in several important ways. While both suggest potentially relevant causal variables and treatment strategies based on aggregate data, they are burdened by a lack of specificity. The predominant symptom classification system provides limited explicit information regarding the underlying causal mechanisms (e.g. triggers) that give rise to and maintain the symptoms that define the subgrouping. The recommendation in favor of pharmacological treatment is based on the rationale that "these patients have symptoms (e.g. post-prandial pain, diarrhea, constipation) that relate to altered gut physiology" (Drossman, 1999). The presumption of a biological mechanism underlying bowel dysfunction suggests a degree of uniformity that does not necessarily generalize to all patients whose same problem can be governed by very different functional conditions. In patients whose predominant gut symptoms are triggered primarily by situational anxiety, for example, medications and fiber supplements may not target the primary controlling variables, fall short of therapeutic objectives, and may be counter-therapeutic by increasing symptom-exacerbating anxiety, reinforcing disease conviction, and strengthening illness behaviors (e.g. health-seeking behaviors). From a behavioral perspective, identifying more specific information regarding controlling variables is important because of the assumption that treatments are more likely to yield efficacious results when tailored around the causal variables with the greatest magnitude of effect on a target problem (Haynes & O'Brien, 1999). An argument challenging a uniformity myth was recently raised by Whitehead *et al.* (2002), who wrote that "not all IBS patients are alike . . . there may be a subgroup of patients whose IBS symptoms result from predominant biological process and another subgroup whose IBS symptoms reflect predominant psychological etiologies". Interestingly, Wolpe (1989) raised similar concerns about the potential problems of neglecting individual differences in controlling variables of persons belonging to the same diagnostic group when he wrote:

"While response similarity in maladaptive habits provides a convenient basis for placing [patients] in diagnostic pigeonholes ... common pigeonholes do not necessarily imply common treatment, because the stimulus antecedents vary" (p.7).

The symptom severity approach improves upon the predominant symptom classification system approach by specifying a constellation of biological, psychosocial, environmental and developmental factors relating to IBS symptoms. An assumption of the symptom severity model is that psychological factors are causally related to IBS symptoms by influencing "symptom severity, quality of life, disability and global healthcare utilization". The precise directionality among these variables has not been empirically established, however. It is possible that psychological distress is (as in the majority of chronic pain patients) a consequence – not cause – of a chronic, painful, and emotionally unpleasant condition for which there is no medical cure. Beyond the directionality of causal variables, severity models provide limited information about how IBS symptoms relate to controlling variables, and the functional relations among these variables. Haynes and Williams (2003) write that variables that maintain a problem may differ on multiple dimensions, including their modifiability, the extent to which they combine with other causal variables (if any) to influence a problem, and the magnitude of effect both on a problem and among causal variables (i.e. importance). To illustrate, psychosocial variables (passive coping strategies, catastrophizing) may exert a greater impact on diarrhea than dietary factors and would presumably represent a more important causal variable and focus of treatment than dietary interventions designed to alter an underlying biological process in the GI system. Conversely, a dietary approach would be indicated for a patient whose diarrhea was strongly affected by food-related changes in gut motility, but only moderately affected by psychological processes.

Another inherent limitation of the symptom severity stratification approach is its inability to accommodate the clinical reality that patients often present with multiple problems. This may be particularly true of IBS patients, who present with comorbid or nongastrointestinal symptoms, including bladder irritability, chronic fatigue syndrome, TMD, pelvic pain, sleep disturbance, occupational difficulties, diminished quality of life, worry, fibromyalgia, chronic fatigue syndrome, dysmenorrhea, and urinary problems (Whitehead *et al.*, 2002).

These problems are not necessarily orthogonal to IBS symptoms, but may be functionally related in complex ways. Haynes and O'Brien (1999) outline different causal pathways by which variables may influence a problem. For example, in what they characterize as the "keystone" type, for example, a behavior problem functions as a causal variable for two or more other problems – as when IBS symptoms are a cause of work dysfunction (e.g. absenteeism), financial pressures, and marital discord. Another type occurs when two discrete problems (e.g. fibromyalgia, IBS) might share a single causal mechanism (e.g. abnormal processing of pain stimuli). Just as not all IBS patients are alike, the functional relationships among their presenting problems and underlying causal mechanism(s) also differ and cannot be inferred from diagnosis alone. The nature of multiple problems, their causal variables, mechanisms, and their relationship with the presenting problem are important data points that can influence clinical decision making, the treatment planning, and outcome (Haynes *et al.*, 1997). Such information is, however, beyond the scope of the biopsychosocial model, which is essentially a heuristic model, based on nomothetic research findings and designed to illustrate the integration of potential developmental, biological and psychological factors. The model reflects what we know about IBS patients in general and is not intended to capture the idiographic features of a single patient. While the biopsychosocial model and its clinical guidelines promotes individualized treatment "based on the severity of the symptoms, the physiologic and psychosocial determinants of the patient's illness behavior, and the degree of functional impairment" (Drossman, 1994, pp. 52–53), it provides practitioners with limited information about which target problems or goals need to be prioritized, what biobehavioral processes their interventions must modify, and what treatment strategies they must use to reduce GI symptoms.

One potentially useful approach draws upon the principles and practice of behavioral case formulation research. During the past ten years a number of authors have offered different models of behaviorally based case formulations (Turkat, 1985; Persons, 1989; Nezu 1996; Haynes & O'Brien, 1999) that differ in their conceptual foundations, component parts, and methodology. However, they all attach importance to the assessment process in detailing a sufficiently comprehensive problem list, specifying the clinically relevant controlling variables and their interrelationships with the target behavior(s), and using these data to construct an efficient and effective treatment program informed by nomothetic research but tailored to the characteristics of the individual client. One of the most theoretically grounded, sophisticated and comprehensive case formulation approaches is the functional case formulation approach (Haynes & O'Brien, 1999). Key elements of this approach include (a) obtaining a detailed description of the problem behavior; and (b) executing a functional analysis. A guiding principle of the problem behavior description phase of the formulation is the triple response system theory of emotion (Lang, 1968). Generally speaking, the triple response system theory holds that behavioral activity consists of three response systems, which include overt-motor behavior, physiological-emotional responses, and verbal-cognitive channels. These components are loosely coupled, correlated, and partially independent (Rachman, 1998). In other words, the three components do not always correspond (Lang *et al.*, 1983). Changes in one response system are not necessarily followed by changes in another response system. Further, any one of the three response systems can predominate across time and place, a phenomenon that Rachman and Hodgson (1974) characterize as "desynchrony".

Although Lang's three-component approach has been most fully developed in the context of anxiety disorders, it is also relevant to the assessment of irritable bowel syndrome. One implication is that IBS is not a unitary phenomenon, but consists of three major response components (i.e. physiological, cognitive, behavioral). The physiological component refers to peripheral or central nervous system arousal associated with GI symptoms or related arousal (e.g. autonomic arousal due to anxiety). The verbal-cognitive component corresponds with higher order mental processes that are represented by a patient's expectations, attributions, coping self-statements, mental images, problem-solving strategies, and attentional focus. The behavioral component corresponds with the different strategies that patients use to respond to aversive symptoms which, when maladaptive, may include excessive escape/avoidance behaviors and/or disruption of functional activities. A second implication is that proper measurement and treatment cannot reliably depend on a diagnosis or a single measure from one response domain (e.g. self-report). As noted above, a diagnostic category per se provides limited information regarding "the most salient mode of a . . . problem because a diagnosis can involve any or all responses" (Haynes, 1998) systems. Furthermore, because of desynchrony among response systems, a single measure or response component is not necessarily a reliable proxy for other data obtained through other measures or response systems. For this reason, an assessment strategy involving several instruments (e.g. diagnostic interview, self-report, medical examination data) tapping the behavioral, cognitive, and physiological-emotional dimension is ideal for obtaining the most comprehensive evaluation. A multimethod, multimodal assessment dovetails with the biopsychosocial model, which views IBS as having a strong learned response with specific affective, cognitive, behavioral features. The goal of assessment is to confirm a diagnosis of IBS, to assess comorbidity, and define the nature, severity and natural history of the presenting problem as well as its antecedent, concurrent, and consequent events (Wilson & O'Leary, 1987). The following section will review the assessment methods that support these goals.

Assessment

The selection of assessment measures that comprise our testing protocol reflects the biopsychosocial model of IBS (Drossman, 1998). The biopsychosocial model holds that individual biology (e.g. genetic predisposition, GI physiology), behaviors, and higher order cognitive processes (coping, illness beliefs) influence IBS through their interaction with each other, with early life factors (e.g. trauma, modeling) and with the individual's social and physical environments (e.g. reinforcement contingencies). Consistent with this conceptualization, our core testing battery includes measures that tap the major components of the model, including psychological distress, coping resources, negative cognitions, pain, behavioral functioning, quality of life, abuse, and illness behaviors.

The first step in the evaluation is to assess the nature and severity of symptoms, their natural history, the circumstances, patterns, determinants, and consequences of symptoms, as well as the patient's treatment history (current and lifetime). The Albany GI History (Blanchard, 2000) is a three-part semi-structured interview that supports these goals. Part One covers history and description of GI symptoms. Symptoms of pain, bowel disturbance, and associated symptoms (e.g. flatulence, bloating) are assessed in terms of their severity, frequency, and duration. The GI symptom is sufficiently detailed to support a diagnosis using Rome criteria once physical pathology has been medically ruled out. Because the GI symptom history covers situational factors that precede the onset of a symptom and consequent events, it lends itself to executing a functional analysis and generating a case formulation. Part Two is devoted to exploring the history of GI disorders in the extended family, a psychosocial history, and description of psychosocial functioning and related problem areas in the patient's life (relationship with peers, job strain, marital relations, etc.). Part Three includes a brief mental status examination.

Information obtained through the GI symptom history is supplemented with daily self-monitoring using the GI symptom diary. Following the initial assessment, patients begin monitoring their symptoms of abdominal pain and tenderness, diarrhea, constipation, flatulence, belching, and bloating on a five-point scale ranging from "not a problem" = 0 to "debilitating" = 4. There are a number of advantages with self-monitoring data. Because of its accuracy (Meissner et al., 1997), sensitivity to temporal variations, and objectivity, the GI symptom diary is seen as the "gold standard" in IBS research.

The somatic symptom assessment component of the testing battery includes a number of questionnaires such as the McGill Pain Questionnaire and the Pain Coping Skills Questionnaire that are designed to tap aspects of the pain experience associated with IBS. Although IBS is not strictly a pain disorder, a majority of IBS patients identify pain as their most bothersome symptom, with 39 per cent describing it as "intolerable" (Cheng et al., 2000). To measure different aspects of patients' pain experience, we use the McGill Pain Questionnaire (MPQ; Melzack, 1975). The MPQ contains 78 pain words grouped in 20 subclasses of 3 to 5 descriptive words. Within these subclasses, the patient ranks the three to five words according to the implied pain intensity. The 20 subclasses are grouped into four sections: sensory (e.g. cramping), affective (agonizing), evaluative, and miscellaneous. In addition to the 78 pain words, the course of time is assessed with 9 words. The location of pain is assessed with a drawing of the body with the words "external/internal" added. We also administer the Pain Coping Skills Questionnaire

(PCSQ; Rosenstiel & Keefe, 1983). The PCSQ measures the frequency of use of seven pain coping strategies, six of which are cognitive (diverting attention, reinterpreting pain sensations, coping self-statements, ignoring pain sensations, praying and hoping, and catastrophizing) and one of which is behavioral (increasing behavioral activity). The PCSQ also includes two ratings of coping efficacy: one rating of perceived efficacy of coping in decreasing pain and one rating of perceived efficacy of coping in controlling pain. Our incorporation of the PCSQ into the testing protocol is based on recent reports that over-reliance on passive pain coping response, particularly a negatively skewed thinking pattern termed "catastrophizing", relates to IBS symptoms (Drossman *et al.*, 2000a). Previous research has also shown that coping strategies measured by the PCSQ are predictive of pain, psychological function, activity level and physical impairment of patients with chronic pain problems independent of disease severity.

To assess psychiatric comorbidity we use the Structured Clinical Interview for DSM-IV Axis I Disorders (SCID-I; First *et al.*, 2001), a semi-structured interview for obtaining major DSM-IV Axis I diagnoses. Additional psychological self-report measures of our battery tap psychopathology (Brief Symptom Inventory), depression (Beck Depression Inventory), anxiety (STAI), and habitual worry (Penn State Worry Questionnaire).

Because IBS is a chronic condition that can compromise one's emotional, social, and physical well-being, patients are administered the IBS-Quality of Life Measure (IBS-QOL; Patrick *et al.*, 1998), whose 34 items fall into one of seven domains (dysphoria, activity interference, body image, health worry, food avoidance, social relations, sexual activity, intimate relationships) clinically relevant to IBS. Quality of life measures are useful in assessing the extent to which IBS compromises a patient's general sense of happiness and satisfaction in important life domains (e.g. health, recreation, etc.). In comparison to more traditional biological measures that focus on infirmity or disease status, quality of life measures focus on both objective functioning and subjective well-being. These data sources are usually better for assessing the social and emotional outcomes of treatment and disease processes, and proving an overall picture of how treatments or illnesses impact patients' ability to function in life. The IBS-QOL concentrates on the perceived well-being of the patient, not more objective measures of physical functioning (e.g. the activities of daily living). Because there is general consensus that quality of life involves both objective functioning and subjective well-being, we supplement IBS-QOL with information from the MOS 36-Item Short Form (SF-36; Ware & Sherbourne, 1992). The SF-36 assesses eight health dimensions (Stewart & Ware, 1992) that the IBS-QOL does not directly assess, including: (a) limitations in physical activities because of health problems; (b) limitations of social activities because of health or emotional problems; (c) limitations in usual role activities because of health problems; (d) bodily pain; (e) general medical health (psychological distress and well-being); (f) limitations in usual role activities because of emotional problems; (g) vitality (energy and fatigue); and (h) self-evaluation of general health status. The SF-36 has been used to measure health-related quality of life in IBS patients (Hahn *et al.*, 1999).

While these assessment measures provide clear description of symptoms, they do not inherently shed light on the means by which factors control behavior. An important tenet of behaviorism is that a full understanding of behavior is best achieved not simply through describing its "topography" or form, as in the diagnostic tradition, but through a detailed specification of its relationship to the context in which it occurs (Nelson, 1987). After all, the topography of a given behavior may be uniform across patients, but the causes or functions of a behavior or symptom may differ. Focusing on the topography therefore may yield limited information about the situational controlling variables needing modification. On the other hand, if the variables controlling a behavior are identified and modified, the target response stands to change (Haynes & O'Brien, 1999).

Determining the situational controlling variables is achieved through a functional analysis. The functional analysis is the "identification of important controllable causal functional relationships applicable to specified behavior for an individual" (Haynes & O'Brien, 1999, p. 654). Simply put, the functional analysis is a working model that tells a story about the patient's problems as a function of causal variables and underlying causal mechanisms from relevant biological, environmental, cultural, and cognitive domains in a way that enhances clinical decision making (e.g. reduce bias) and informs treatment planning structured around these factors. The functional analysis does not intend to specify or integrate every conceivable causal variable and problem. Instead, it places a premium on situational-controlling variables that precede the response (antecedent), consequent stimuli that follow the response (consequences), and organism variables (biological attributes, cognitive processes, demographic variables, learning, etc.) that mediate the relationship between stimulus and response (Haynes & O'Brien, 1999). The functional analysis subordinates uncontrollable causal influences to controllable causal ones because the latter yield the most useful information for designing a treatment program with the greatest chance of success. A history of sexual abuse, prior infection, and antibiotic use may have important explanatory value in understanding IBS. Although these and other historical variables (e.g. family history of IBS) may have explanatory value, they have limited immediate clinical utility to the extent that they cannot be directly modified. Historical factors are, however, addressed insofar as they influence current modifiable causal relations. For example, while traumatic experiences cannot be reversed, they may have important sequelae that maintain a target problem. A traumatic experience can challenge one's view of the world and fundamental assumptions about life. Common assumptions held by trauma victims may include that they are vulnerable to further harm in a world that is unsafe, and that they lack coping resources to manage stressors. To the extent that trauma-induced sequelae trigger IBS symptoms, then treatment could be directed toward challenging and disputing maladaptive belief patterns that influence IBS and related distress.

Beyond causal and controllable variables, a functional analysis emphasizes important variables. A problem behavior may be caused by multiple factors whose modification requires alternative treatment strategies that differ in efficacy, cost, side-effect profile, speed of action, and acceptability. A major assumption of the functional analytic case formulation approach is that treatments derive their effectiveness by targeting the most important causal variable for the patient's problem (Haynes & Williams, 2003). This approach too often deviates from practice patterns of practitioners whose estimation of the importance of causal relations is informed by their theoretical orientation, available skills, techniques, and competencies as opposed to an objective estimation of the relative degree of impact of a factor on a problem. This is seen when a physician pursues a strict biomedical approach for IBS symptoms that are predominantly driven by psychological triggers, or when a mental health provider imposes a psychological treatment for symptoms with strong biological etiology (e.g. abnormal GI motility). In both cases, the theoretical orientation and existing skill sets of the practitioner run the risk of overestimating the degree of importance of objectively weak causal variables, distorting clinical judgment and decision making, and leading to an inefficient and questionably effective treatment course. Because of the complexity of a functional analysis, the results can be diagrammatically represented using what Haynes calls a functional analytic causal model (e.g. O'Brien & Haynes, 1995). The FACM uses vector diagrams to depict the relationships between a target problem and its causal mechanisms across multiple dimensions (e.g. directionality of causal relationships, the degree of modifiability of causal variables, the interrelationships between problems and their respective causal variables). By quantifying properties of the functional analysis (e.g. causal relations between variables), the FACM attempts to reduce the biases in judgment and decision making that complicate efficient and effective treatment design. An example of a FACM for the case example presented here is shown in Figure 8.1.

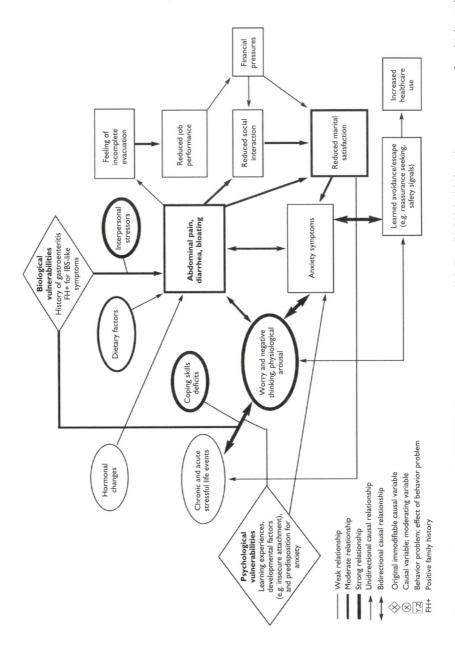

Figure 8.1 A functional analytic causal model (FACM) of a patient with severe IBS. The FACM highlights the importance of multiple problems, multiple causal variables, modifiable and nonmodifiable causal variables, and the directionality and strength of causal relationships.

Case study

Crisanne is a 28-year-old Caucasian, married female advertising executive referred to the SUNY Buffalo Medical School Behavioral Medicine Clinic for evaluation and treatment for a five-year history of IBS. Her assessment was conducted during two sessions as part of the pretreatment phase of an NIH-funded clinical trial of a group-based cognitive therapy program for IBS. Crisanne's primary complaints were abdominal pain associated with diarrhea. On the McGill Pain Inventory, she described typical pain intensity as moderate to severe with stabbing sharp cramping sensations in the lower left abdominal quadrant, and characterized the pain as exhausting, sickening, and tiring. Pain is relieved when she has a bowel movement, passes gas, or stretches. Bowel movements are sometimes accompanied by rectal mucus. After a bowel movement, Crisanne feels she has not completely evacuated all the fecal matter and sometimes notices blood spots on the toilet paper. As a result, she may return to the bathroom two or three times before she heads to work, which leads to her often arriving late at work. Abdominal pain worsens a short time after she experiences psychological stress and, to a lesser extent, following meals. She describes pain as episodic, worse in the morning on arising, and during menstruation. She also experiences diarrhea three to four times a week, which she treats by eating "tons of fiber", but conceded that it has limited benefit. Diarrhea worsens with certain foods (milk, pizza, broccoli, and pasta), strong negative emotions, interpersonal conflicts, and menstruation, and is frequently preceded by a sudden strong urge to defecate. Daily bloated feelings are so intense that she cancels social events that require her to sit for prolonged periods. At pretreatment, her IBS symptoms occurred four to five times weekly.

Her physicians had treated her diarrhea using the predominant symptom approach described above, including antidiarrheal agents such as loperamide, and low dosages of antidepressants for pain control, which reportedly provided approximately 10 per cent relief. Six weeks before our evaluation, she reported some benefit from Lotronex, a 5-HT receptor antagonist used to treat IBS in female patients with diarrhea as the predominant symptom. Lotronex blocks serotonin signals from the brain, decreasing abdominal pain and colon transit alterations, such as diarrhea. Because Lotronex was temporarily withdrawn from sale due to numerous adverse event reports, at the time of her evaluation Crisanne was rationing her supply for "high risk" situations only, but carrying the drug in her purse because it made her feel safer.

Crissane reported no history of fever, weight loss, bloody or black tarry stools, anemia, or physical or sexual abuse. Her symptoms rarely interfered with sleep. In addition to IBS, she had a history of migraine headaches for which she was treated with Imitrix. She reported a family history of GI-related medical problems (mother: diverticulitis, IBS; maternal uncle: colon cancer; brother: IBS).

Clinical history

The clinical picture that emerged from the diagnostic interview and assessment battery is of a patient with a complex IBS profile. GI complaints began in 1997 during a honeymoon to Mexico, where she developed abdominal pain, vomiting, diarrhea, muscle aches, and a low-grade fever. She returned home early because of worsening symptoms, and her physician diagnosed gastroenteritis, an inflammatory condition of the digestive tract. He assured her that the condition was benign and time limited, and prescribed clear fluids. On this diet, she noticed that bowel function was returning to normal within six weeks after onset. Her pain decreased and her stools were less loose and watery, and no longer had the pale white characteristic of gastroenteritis.

Approximately two months later, Crisanne's mother was diagnosed with Alzheimer's disease. Crisanne took complete care of her mother, which led to her being forced to reduce her work hours to part time. One day, whilst waiting at her mother's physician's office, she happened to read a brochure on colorectal cancer, and realized that she experienced six of the nine listed symptoms (diarrhea, fatigue, abdominal pain, gas, bloating, incomplete evacuation). She became worried that her GI complaints were part of a more serious undiagnosed condition, and consulted a gastroenterologist, who after having conducted various medical tests (sigmoidoscopy, stool examination for blood, parasites and ova, lower GI series, and hydrogen breath test), found nothing abnormal. While the results relieved some of her anxiety, her concern returned after a flare-up. She called her physician for reassurance, who told her the problem was benign and "nothing to worry about . . . probably just your nerves". He offered her a Xanax prescription that she never filled as she thought doing so would be a tacit acknowledgement that her problem "was in her head". Crisanne conceded that she had grown increasingly anxious regarding her health, her mother, her job, her marital relationship, and her financial pressures. Her worries were accompanied by restlessness, sleep difficulties, and muscle tension. Racing thoughts and uncomfortable physical symptoms were making it difficult to concentrate on her work – something she, as an advertising executive, could ill afford.

As her anxiety increased, so did her GI symptoms, particularly diarrhea, bloating and pain. At the same time, the unexplained nature of her symptoms felt occasionally overwhelming. The stressors she faced were either beyond her control or not as controllable as she preferred. She experienced a diminished quality of life based on her responses to the IBS-Quality of Life Measure. She and her husband had always enjoyed a satisfying sex life, but her GI symptoms made her feel unattractive and diminished her sexual desire. As sexual relations grew less frequent and satisfying, she and her husband experienced the first sign of real relationship strain since they had begun dating 15 years ago in high school. Their social life was increasingly restricted to familiar restaurants with "gut friendly" menus and accessible bathrooms.

Her medical history was essentially benign, except for tension headaches and shoulder/neck pain which she attributed to prolonged computer work without opportunity for rest. On the SCID, she met DSM-IV diagnostic criteria for generalized anxiety disorder (GAD) and subthreshold diagnosis for social anxiety disorder. During SCID testing she reported a significant traumatic experience: her younger sister had been shot at a fast food restaurant during a failed robbery.

Case formulation

The case formulation is based on a biopsychosocial model that recognizes that genetic, biological, cultural and other developmental factors interact with a person's cognitive, behavioral, and emotional resources to influence symptom patterns, their emotional unpleasantness, illness behaviors, function, and quality of life (Drossman, 1998). As a diathesis-stress model, the biopsychosocial conceptualization of IBS emphasizes a set of biological and psychological factors that contribute to vulnerability of IBS. Psychological vulnerability factor included a history of insecure childhood attachment experiences that occurred after Crisanne's sister was killed. Specifically, Crisanne's history shows a pattern of parent–child role reversal. Parent–child role reversal involves the interchange of traditional role behaviors between a parent and child, with the child adopting some of the behaviors traditional assumed by parents. As noted above, Crisanne as a child assumed many caretaking responsibilities for her grief-stricken and incapacitated mother. Such parent–child role reversal has been implicated as both a risk factor for anxiety problems (i.e. GAD) common among IBS patients. Cassidy et al. (1994) writes that assuming the role of the responsible parent may heighten attentiveness to threat cues, so that patients see the world as a dangerous place whose demands exceed their coping resources and necessitates hypervigilance to potential danger. Hypervigilance to threat cues is also considered a key factor in conceptualizations of IBS (Naliboff, 1999).

Physical vulnerability risk factors include a history of acute gastroenteritis, which was conceptualized as a vulnerability factor that increased her risk factor for developing IBS. The risk of developing irritable bowel syndrome is much higher (ten times more likely) among those who have suffered from bacterial gastroenteritis (Rodriquez & Ruigomez, 1999). Furthermore, the risk of developing IBS is higher in patients with gastroenteritis who have higher levels of hypochondriasis, and who experience a greater number of life events – particularly interpersonal stressors – in the year preceding the onset of gastroenteritis (Gwee et al., 1996). Although Crisanne's level of pre-IBS hypochondriasis is unknown, within three months of her gastroenteritis, she experienced multiple interpersonal stressors including the unexpected death of her father, her mother's diagnosis of Alzheimer's, altered role functioning, and financial pressures. Stressors had a destabilizing effect on Crisanne.

She complained of a number of physical symptoms (e.g. chest pain, fatigue, neck/shoulder pain, headache) with strong autonomic mediation.

Her thinking patterns were characterized by an anxious apprehension about life circumstances, a tendency to think the worst and jump to conclusions, and low confidence in her ability to manage stressors. Although Crisanne excelled at her job, she frequently worried about job security and feared that her performance was never "good enough". Her worries also included her health, her mother's welfare, financial pressures, and her marriage. These worries were supported by negative "core beliefs" regarding herself and the world that included perfectionism, need for approval, a tendency to assume responsibility for others, and an exaggerated illusion of control. Because of this, she often criticized herself for making mistakes she would ignore in others, and was prone to envision negative outcomes if events did not unfold as desired or predicted. She relied on passive coping strategies to manage her symptoms.

It was hypothesized that heightened physiological reactivity, negatively skewed thinking patterns, and avoidance behaviors fueled one another in multiple ways that contributed to IBS symptoms. Increased anxiety about negative life circumstances predisposed her to interpret stressors in a threatening manner and doubt her ability to cope effectively. These thinking patterns elicited physiological arousal, which triggered IBS symptoms whose unpleasantness, unpredictability, and uncontrollability reinforced irrational thought patterns such as catastrophizing, dichotomous thinking, and worry. This in turn disrupted her routines and strengthened her sick role behavior.

At the same time, physiological arousal associated with stressors distorted her capacity to process information accurately, particularly during periods of anxiety, stress, and pain. Threat appraisal produced a state of nervous apprehension, which in turn increased attentional self-focus, amplified unpleasant physical sensation, and contributed to feelings of hopelessness, helplessness and loss of self-esteem. Lacking an adequate repertoire of active self-care skills, she responded to symptoms by seeking reassurance from her physician. On the one hand, his reassurance that her condition was benign decreased her anxiety and desire for more invasive diagnostic testing. However, reassurance provided only temporary relief and was maintained by negative reinforcement (i.e. immediate reduction in distress). Thus, we saw her reassurance seeking as a subtle form of avoidance (i.e. reliance on safety cues) that helped her feel temporarily comfortable but maintained anxiety by reinforcing illness behaviors, preventing her from learning that her health anxiety was unwarranted, and sensitizing her to pain stimuli (Philips, 1987). The case formulation is represented in the FACM in Figure 8.1. As the FACM shows, physiological arousal, dietary triggers, hormonal changes, and cognitive variables were identified causes of IBS symptoms. Of these variables, cognitive variables (inflexible coping response repertoire, threat appraisals) were in comparison to other physiological factors (e.g. dietary, hormonal changes) conceptualized as exerting the strongest influence on IBS symptoms. The primacy of cognitive variables lent itself to a trial of cognitive therapy.

Treatment

Crisanne participated in a ten-session, group-based treatment program offered as part of our current outcome trial. She was randomly assigned to a cognitive therapy condition. The theoretical foundation of treatment is rooted in social learning theory (Bandura, 1977) in which human behavior is explained in terms of a three-way, dynamic reciprocal interaction among personal factors, environmental influences, and behavior. Social learning theory recognizes that external stimulus events (e.g. operant conditioning) shape human behavior, but posits that their influence on individuals is mediated largely by cognitive processes, which in turn are affected by the social and environmental consequences of behavior (Wilson & O'Leary, 1987). Simply put, the way people perceive their environment influences their behavior, affect, and to a significant extent their physiological reactivity. IBS symptoms are an overlearned physiological stress response mediated by a faulty information-processing style that is predisposed to making threat appraisals. Although diarrhea and pain have survival value in the face of a life-threatening physical danger, they are maladaptive in the face of psychological challenges that comprise most stressful experiences of daily life. The cognitive-based treatment for IBS – described more fully in Blanchard (2000) – is designed to teach patients to identify and correct maladaptive beliefs and information-processing errors with the goal of reducing GI symptoms and related distress. Cognitive interventions consisted of (a) increasing patients' awareness of the association among stressors, thoughts, and IBS symptoms; (b) training patients to identify and modify their cognitive appraisals and interpretations of situations, thoughts, and behaviors; and (c) changing underlying depressive or threatening schema or life scripts.

Crisanne met with five other IBS patients for ten weekly sessions (90 minutes long) in a small group setting with a single therapist. During the first session, IBS was described as a multifaceted problem with cognitive, behavioral, and physiological components. Patients are told that treatment will focus on how thoughts influence GI symptoms through the brain–gut axis. The discussion of the psychophysiological basis of IBS is an important part of cognitive restructuring insofar as it challenges patients' disease conviction, fosters a sense of symptom predictability, and cultivates a positive treatment expectancy that enhances motivation and commitment. Patients learn that cognitive processes affect IBS symptoms, and unlike other triggers (e.g. hormonal fluctuations) can be modified to decrease GI symptoms.

Discussion of the physiology of IBS sets the stage for formal cognitive restructuring which is conceptualized as occurring on two levels: overt difficulties (i.e. IBS-like symptoms), and underlying psychological problems. At the first level, cognitive treatment focuses on helping the patient identify, categorize and modify negative automatic thoughts that occur in specific situations when the patient experiences an attack of IBS symptoms or related distress. Patients record internal and external triggers accompanying thoughts or appraisals, and consequent responses (physical and emotional symptoms). A review of Crisanne's dysfunctional thought records identified high-risk situations that typically elicited the negative automatic thought of "I'm going to be sick." These beliefs in turn triggered both physical and emotional responses.

At the second level were a set of "core beliefs" – global, deeply ingrained assumptions individuals hold regarding the world. Whereas automatic thoughts are a moment-by-moment "snapshot" of a patient's perspective, core beliefs are the lens through which a patient sees the world. There is a distinction between autonomic thoughts and core beliefs. Crisanne's autonomic thought of "I'm going to get sick" during social events is an example of a number of thinking errors (jumping to conclusions, overestimating the probability of harm, "mind reading"). However, her tendency to think the worst was driven by a set of underlying core beliefs or assumptions, such as "I need to be in control all the time" and "Situations I can't control are dangerous and make me feel vulnerable."

The initial focus of treatment was directed at identifying and monitoring negative automatic thought, feelings, behaviors, and situations that were stressful and exacerbated IBS symptoms. Once she could identify and record automatic thoughts, the therapist taught her to categorize IBS-related cognitive errors (e.g. all-or-nothing thinking, mind reading, personalization, and so forth), following the procedures devised by Beck and colleagues (e.g. Beck *et al.*, 1979) for depression, or Borkovec and Roemer (1994) for anxiety. When Chrisanne understood that her automatic thoughts reflected and supported cognitive errors, the therapist repeatedly pointed out examples of maladaptive thinking and helped her generate more realistic, adaptive alternatives. Because her IBS symptoms were often tied to anticipated anxiety regarding future threat and worry that reflected inaccurate predictions of a catastrophic outcome, Crisanne's cognitive restructuring exercises targeted maladaptive expectations. She was taught evidence-based logic techniques geared toward helping her identify the evidence for the accuracy of threat-negative predictions; generating alternative explanations for those cognitions; and learning to associate a more adaptive cognitive response when GI distress was detected.

As Crisanne grew more proficient in challenging IBS-related automatic thoughts, the cognitive restructuring component shifted to modifying dysfunctional assumptions or "core beliefs" (e.g. perfectionism, exaggerated sense of control over life events). Using the downward arrow technique (Burns, 1980), Crisanne learned to elicit dysfunctional assumptions and core beliefs which she challenged by applying a number of cognitive restructuring exercises (e.g. reversing positions, reframing, reality testing) learned in the first part of treatment.

The final major component of cognitive therapy is problem-solving training, which is based on the work of Nezu *et al.* (e.g. 1989). This emphasizes formal training in five problem-solving processes (defining the problem, generating alternative solutions, weighing their relative value and costs, decision making; verification) to improve patients' ability to manage and prepare more effectively for problems. Where our approach with IBS patients may differ is in the focus of problem solving. Traditionally, problem-solving training has emphasized the acquisition of a set of action-oriented skills designed to "solve a particular problem successfully" (D'Zurilla & Nezu, 2001). This strict focus on action-oriented problem-solving skills may fall short of therapeutic objectives with functional GI disorder patients who apparently have a rigid pattern of responding and overreliance on problem-solving strategies in situations whose uncontrollability necessitates emotion-focused coping responses (Cheng *et al.*, 2000). An overly rigid coping response (overreliance on either emotion-focused coping responses for controllable events or problem-solving response for uncontrollable events) is not only maladaptive but may generate sufficient negative affect to exacerbate symptoms. Therefore, our problem-solving component emphasizes the value of teaching patients variability and flexibility in the way they cope with different IBS-related stressors. Patients are assigned the task of asking themselves: "Is there anything I can do about this problem?" before they generate problem-solving options. For situations appraised as "uncontrollable", patients are taught the value of responding by using emotion-focused coping responses that emphasize managing the emotional unpleasantness of stressful situations through such cognitive techniques as acceptance/resignation, "letting go", reinterpretation, minimization, distancing, and de-catastrophizing. Our experience is that IBS patients often have less difficulty generating an action-oriented response than accurately appraising the controllability of IBS-related stressors and using an appropriate coping response that helps them cope with pain and distress associated with IBS.

Outcome

At the end of treatment, Crisanne had significantly reduced her GI symptoms (see follow-up data in Table 8.1). At her two-week post-treatment, her symptoms had decreased by approximately 75 per cent and she reported global improvement. Whereas moderate to severe symptoms occurred four to five times weekly at pretreatment and caused significant distress and diminished function, after treatment once-weekly episodes of abdominal pain were rated as mild and non-disabling. Improvements in pain control were accompanied by decreased episodes of bloating (once weekly) and diarrhea, neither of which interfered with function or quality of life. As her

Table 8.1 IBS symptom severity, emotional distress, and quality of life at pre-treatment, post-treatment and follow-up assessments

Outcome measure	Pre-treatment	Post-treatment	Three-month follow-up	Twelve-month follow-up
GI symptom Monitoring index	0.88	0.29	0.32	0.27
State anxiety[a]	49	42	46	46
Trait anxiety[a]	63	48	49	48
Depression[b]	16	5	4	6
Quality of life[c]	74	46	29	30
Role limitations-emotional[d]	80	45	45	48
Pain[d]	79	68	46	41
Social functioning[d]	84	64	57	60
Mental health[d]	75	49	44	56

Note
[a] State-trait Anxiety Inventory (standard scores);
[b] Beck Depression Inventory (raw score);
[c] Irritable Bowel Syndrome Quality of Life Inventory;
[d] SF-36 (T-scores). SF-36 and IBS-QOL are scored inversely such that lower scores reflect improved outcomes.

self-management skills improved, Crisanne's use of medications and reassurance decreased. Her symptoms were rated as "markedly improved" by an independent gastroenterologist blind to her treatment.

She also demonstrated improvement in broader health status. Post-session evaluation for Axis I indicated that she no longer met full DSM-IV criteria for generalized anxiety disorder. At 3-month and 12-month post-follow-up, she had experienced no significant exacerbation of GI symptoms, mood disturbance, or functional limitations

Conclusion

This chapter has focused on the case formulation of irritable bowel syndrome from the perspective of a behavioral analytic perspective, which we believe represents an empirically derived, systematic method for individualizing treatment for complex IBS patients. Because this approach is essentially "atheoretical", it lends itself to formulating cases involving psychophysiological problems influenced by social, environmental; biological, and psychological factors. The behavioral analytic approach does not focus strictly on the "psychological mechanism underlying the patient's problems" (Persons, 1989) and therefore has advantages over other case formulation approaches that presume that psychological factors (e.g. dysfunctional beliefs) are inherently more powerful causal agents than biological or environmental influences. As the foregoing case makes clear, we do not see any inherent conflict between the value we attach to both manualized treatments and case formulation. We recognize that case formulation advocates' emphasis on the value of case formulation can – and has – come across as resistance to empirically derived treatments identified through nomothetic research. This is unfortunate. We believe that a case formulation approach can be used constructively within the structure and format of manualized treatments in clinical trials and private practice. The case formulation approach can help the therapist (and the patient) understand the variables underlying the presenting problem, sequence treatment around the most powerful variable, enhance positive treatment outcome expectancy for both patient and therapist, causal variable(s) with the highest magnitude of effect, and anticipate sources of treatment resistance that may compromise treatment success. At the time, we do not accept unequivocally Wilson's argument (1997) that case formulation approaches are necessarily inherently flawed and potentiate reliance on biased clinical decision making. The practitioner does not require a case formulation approach to exercise flawed clinical judgments (Elstein, 1988). A well-designed, rational case formulation – one based on sound theoretical principles and informed by quality nomothetic research – has the potential to minimize sources of decision-making bias and facilitate the efficient implementation of empirically validated treatments. Advocates of empirically based treatments and manualized protocols sometimes lose sight of the fact that the practice of evidence-based medicine/mental health requires more than knowledge of a diagnosis and skills in the application of a corresponding set of empirically validated treatments. Diagnosis and knowledge about empirically validated treatments are but two (albeit important) judgments that affect clinical decision making. A case formulation synthesizes a broad array of important information regarding causal variables (causal directionality, respective magnitudes of effect for causal variables, etc.) and their interrelationship to a presenting problem in a way that supports the empirically derived treatments for complex problems like irritable bowel syndrome.

Acknowledgements

Preparation of this chapter was supported in part by National Institutes of Health Grant DK-54211. The authors would like to acknowledge the assistance of Stephen Haynes who helped construct the FACM.

References

Adams, P.F, & Benson, V. (1991). Current estimates from the National Health Interview. *Vital Health Statistics, 10*, 83, 92–1509.

Agreus, L., Talley, N.J., & Nyren, O. *et al.* (1998). Natural history of reflux, dyspepsia and irritable bowel syndrome over 7 years in the general population. *Gastroenterology 114*, A-917.

Almy, T.P., Kern, F.J., & Tulin, M. (1949). Alternation in colonic function in man under stress: Experimental production of sigmoid spasm in healthy persons. *Gastroenterology, 12*, 425–436.

Bandura, A. (1977). Self-efficacy: Toward a unifying theory of behavioral change. *Psychological Review, 84*, 191–215.

Bazzocchi, G., Ellis, J., Villanueava-Meyer, J., Jing, J., Reddy, S.N., Mena, I., & Snape, W.J. (1990). Postprandial colonic transit and motor activity in chronic constipation. *Gastroenterology, 98*, 686–693.

Beck, A. T., Rush, A., Shaw, B., & Emery, G. (1979). *Cognitive therapy of depression.* New York: Guilford Press.

Bennet, E.J., Tennant, C.C., Piesse, C., Badcock, C.A., & Kellow, J.E. (1998) Level of chronic life stress predicts clinical outcome in irritable bowel syndrome. *Gut, 43*, 256–261.

Blanchard, E. (2000). *Irritable bowel syndrome: Psychosocial assessment and treatment.* Washington, DC: APA.

Borkovec, T. D., & Roemer, L. (1994). Cognitive behavioral treatment of generalized anxiety disorder. In R. T. Ammerman & M. Hersen (Eds.), *Handbook of prescriptive treatments for adults* (pp. 261–281). New York: Plenum.

Burns, D.D. (1980). *Feeling good: The new mood therapy.* New York: Morrow.

Cassidy, J., Lichtenstein, J., Borkovec, T.D., & Thomas, C. (1994). *Generalized anxiety disorder: Connections with self-reported childhood attachment.* Unpublished manuscript.

Chang, L., Heitkemper, M.M., & Carter, E. (2000). A national survey of irritable bowel syndrome (IBS) in females: Physician and patient perspectives. *Gastroenterology, 118*, 852.

Cheng, C., Hui, W.M., & Lam, S.K. (2000). Perceptual style and behavioral pattern of individuals with functional gastrointestinal disorders. *Health Psychology, 19*, 2, 146–154.

Clouse, R. (1988). Anxiety and gastrointestinal illness. *Psychiatric Clinic of North America, 11*, 399–417.

Crombie, I.K., Croft, P.R., Linton, S.J., LeResche, L., & Von Korff, M. (1999). *Epidemiology of pain.* Washington, DC: IASP Press.

DePonti, F., & Malagelada, J.R. (1998). Functional gut disorders: from motility to sensitivity disorders. A review of current and investigational drugs for their management. *Pharmacological Therapy, 80*, 1, 49–88.

Drossman, D.A. (1994). Irritable bowel syndrome. *The Gastroenterologist, 2*, 315–326.

Drossman, D.A. (1997). *A biopsychosocial approach to irritable bowel syndrome: Improving the physician–patient relationship.* Ontario: Zancom.

Drosssman, D.A. (1998). Presidential address: Gastrointestinal illness and the biopsychosocial model. *Psychosomatic Medicine, 60*, 258–267.

Drossman, D.A. (1999). Review article: An integrated approach to the irritable bowel syndrome. *Ailment Pharmacological Therapy, 13*, 3–14.

Drossman, D.A., Zhiming, L., Andruzzi, E., *et al.* (1993). US householders' survey of functional gastrointestinal disorders: Prevalence, sociodemography, and health impact. *Digestive Diseases and Sciences, 38*, 1569.

Drossman, D.A., Talley, N.J., Olden, K.W., *et al.* (1995). Sexual and physical abuse and gastrointestinal illness: Review and recommendations. *Annual Internal Medicine, 123*, 782–794.

Drossman, D.A., Whitehead, W.E., & Camilleri, M. (1997). Irritable bowel syndrome: A technical review for practice guideline development. *Gastroenterology, 112*, 2120–2137.

Drossman, D.A., Li, Z., Leserman, J., Keefe, F.J., Hu, Y.J., & Toomey, T.C. (2000a). Effects of coping on health outcome among female patients with gastrointestinal disorders. *Psychosomatic Medicine, 62*, 309–317.

Drossman, D.A., Whitehead, W. E., Toner, B. B., Diamant, N., Hu, Y. J., Bangdiwala, S. I., *et al.* (2000b). What determines severity among patients with painful functional bowel disorders? *American Journal of Gastroenterology, 95*, 4, 974–980.

D'Zurilla, T.J., & Nezu, A.M. (2001). Problem-solving therapies. *Handbook of cognitive-behavioral therapies*. New York: Guilford Press.

Elstein, A. (1988). Cognitive processes in clinical inference and decision-making. In D.C. Turk & P. Salovey, (Eds.), *Reasoning, inference and judgment in clinical psychology*. New York: Free Press.

First, M.B., Spitzer, R.L., Gibbon, M., & Williams, J. (2001). *Structured clinical interview for DSM-IV-TR Axis I Disorders, Research Version, Non-patient Edition (SCID-I/NP)*. New York: New York State Psychiatric Institute, Biometrics Research.

Gershon, M. (1998). *The second brain*. New York: HarperCollins.

Gwee, K.A., Leong, Y.L., Graham, C., McKendrick, M.W., Collins, S.M., Walters, S.J., Underwood, J.E., & Read, N.W. (1999). The role of psychological and biological factors in postinfective gut dysfunction. *Gut, 44*, 400–406.

Hahn, B.A., Yan, S., & Strassels, S. (1999). Impact of irritable bowel syndrome on quality of life and resource use in the United States and United Kingdom. *Digestion, 60*, 77–81.

Haynes, S. (1998). The assessment-treatment relationship and functional analysis in behavior therapy. *European Journal of Psychological Assessment, 14*, 26–35.

Haynes, S.N., & O'Brien, W.H. (1999). *Principles and practice of behavioral assessment*. New York: Kluwer Academic/Plenum Publishers.

Haynes, S.N., & Williams, A.W. (2003). Clinical case formulation and the design of treatment programs: Matching treatment mechanisms to causal variables for behavior problems. *European Journal of Psychological Assessment, 19*, 164–174.

Haynes, S.N., Leisen, M.B., & Blaine, D.D. (1997). Design of individualized behavioral treatment programs using functional analytic clinical case models. *Psychological Assessment, 9*, 4, 334–348.

Hislop, I.G. (1971). Psychological significance of the irritable colon syndrome. *Gut, 12*, 452–457.

Lackner, J.M., Mesmer, C., Morley, S., Dowzer, C., & Hamilton, S. (2004). Psychological treatments for irritable bowel syndrome: A systematic review and meta-analysis. *Journal of Consulting and Clinical Psychology, 72*, 6, 1100–1113.

Lang, P. (1968). Fear reduction and fear behavior: Problems in treating a construct. In J. M. Shleien (Ed.), *Research in psychotherapy, III*. Washington, DC: APA.

Lang, P.J., Levin, D.N., Miller, G.A., & Kozak, M. (1983). Fear behavior, fear imagery, and the psychophysiology of emotion: The problem of affective response integration. *Journal of Abnormal Psychology, 92*, 276–306.

Latimer, P.R. (1983). *Functional gastrointestinal disorders: A behavioral medicine approach*. New York: Springer.

Lynn, R.B., & Friedman, L.S. (1993). Irritable bowel syndrome. *New England Journal of Medicine, 329*, 1940–1945.

Mayer, E.A., & Raybould, H.E. (1990). Role of visceral afferent mechanisms in functional bowel disorders. *Gastroenterology, 99*, 1688–1704.

Meissner, J.S., Blanchard, E.B., & Malamood, H.S. (1997). Comparison of treatment outcome measures for irritable bowel syndrome. *Applied Psychophysiology and Biofeedback, 22*, 1, 55–62.

Melzack, R. (1975). The McGill Pain Questionnaire: Major properties and scoring methods. *Pain, 1*, 277–299.

Mertz, H. (2001). Review of Rome II. *Gastroenterology, 121*, 1523–1525.

Naliboff, B. (1999). Hypervigilance. In E. A. Mayer, *Evolving pathophysiological models of functional GI disorders*. New York: Health Education Alliance.

Nelson, R. (1987). DSM-III and behavioral assessment. In C. G. Last & M. Hersen (Eds.), *Issues in diagnostic research*. New York: Plenum Press.

Nezu, A. (1996). What are we doing to our patients and should we care if anyone else knows? *Clinical Psychology: Science and Practice, 3*, 160–163.

Nezu, A, Nezu, C., & Perri, M. (1989). *Problem-solving therapy for depression: Theory, research, and clinical guidelines*. New York: Wiley-Interscience.

Nezu, A., Nezu, C., Friedman, S.H., & Haynes, S.N. (1997). Case formulation in behavior therapy: Problem solving and functional analytic strategies. In T.D. Ellis (Ed.), *Handbook of psychotherapy case formulation* (pp. 368–401). New York: Guilford Press.

O'Brien, W.H., & Haynes, S.N. (1995). A functional analytic approach to the conceptualization, assessment, and treatment of a child with frequent migraine headaches. *Psychotherapy in Practice, 1*, 2, 65–80.

Patrick, D.L., Drossman, D.A., Frederick, I.O., DiCesare, J., & Puder, K.L. (1998). Quality of life in persons with irritable bowel syndrome: Development of a new measure. *Digestive Discovery Science, 43*, 400–411.

Persons, J.B. (1989). *Cognitive therapy in practice: A case formulation approach*. New York: Norton.

Philips, H.C. (1987). Avoidance behavior and its role in sustaining chronic pain. *Behavior Research and Therapy, 25*, 273–280.

Scott-Levin (1999). *Physicians Drug and Diagnosis Audit (PDDA)*. Newtown, PA: Scott-Levin.

Rachman, S. (1998). *Anxiety*. Hove, UK: Psychology Press.

Rachman, S., & Hodgson, R. (1974). Synchrony and desynchrony in fear and avoidance. *Behaviour Research and Therapy, 12*, 311–318.

Rodriguez, L.A.G., & Ruigomez, A. (1999). Increased risk of irritable bowel syndrome after bacterial gastroenteritis: A cohort study. *BMJ, 318*, 565–566.

Rosenstiel, A.K., & Keefe, F.J. (1983). The use of coping strategies in chronic low back pain patients: Relationship to patient characteristics and current adjustment. *Pain, 17*, 33–44.

Stewart, A.L., & Ware, J.E. (1992). *Measuring functioning and well-being: The medical outcomes study approach*. North Carolina: Duke University Press.

Sullivan, M.A., Cohen, S., & Snape, W.J. (1978). Colonic myoelectrical activity in irritable bowel syndrome. Effect of eating and anticholinergics. *New England Journal of Medicine, 298*, 878–883.

Talley, N.J., Gabriel, S.E., Harmsen, W.S., Zinsmeister, A.R., & Evans, R.W. (1995). Medical costs in community subjects with irritable bowel syndrome. *Gastroenterology, 109*, 1736–1741.

Turkat, I.D. (1985). Formation of paranoid personality disorder. In I.D. Turkat (Ed.), *Behavioral case formulation*, (pp. 161–198). New York: Plenum Press.

Ware, J.E., & Sherbourne, C.D. (1992). The MOS 36-Item Short Form Health Survey (SF-36). *Medical Care, 30*, 473–483.

Whitehead, W.E., Engel, B.T., & Schuster, M.M. (1990). Perception of rectal distension is necessary to prevent fecal incontinence. *Advanced Physiological Science, 17*, 203–209.

Whitehead, W.E., Holtkotter, B., & Enck, P. *et al.* (1996). Tolerance for rectosigmoid distension in irritable bowel syndrome. *Gastroenterology, 98*, 1187–1192.

Whitehead, W.E., Palsson, O., & Jones, K.R. (2002). Systematic review of the comorbidity of irritable bowel syndrome with other disorders: What are the causes and implications? *Gastroenterology, 122*, 1140–1156.

Wilson, G.T. (1997). Treatment manuals in clinical practice. *Behavior Research and Therapy, 35*, 205–210.

Wilson, G.T., & O'Leary, D.K. (1987). *Behavior therapy: Applications and outcomes.* New York: Prentice-Hall.

Wolpe, J. (1989). The derailment of behavior therapy: A tale of conceptual misdirection. *Journal of Behavior Therapy and Experimental Psychiatry, 20*, 3–15.

Chapter 9

Epilepsy
An approach to case formulation

Sallie A. Baxendale

Introduction

People with epilepsy are frequently referred for psychological intervention in both neuropsychological and clinical psychology settings. Although epilepsy is a neurological disorder, the psychological effects of living with seizures can be far reaching. In order to generate an appropriate formulation on which to base a clinical intervention it is important that the psychologist understands both the nature of epilepsy and the impact it can have on psychological health. This chapter is divided into four parts. The first part presents some basic facts and figures about epilepsy and explains some of the more common terminology that people with epilepsy and neurologists may use. The second part examines the psychological impact of living with epilepsy and explores some of the developmental factors that may underlie the issues raised in psychological referrals. The third part brings together these neurological and psychological factors and presents an approach to formulation in epilepsy. A framework for assessment is presented and clinical interventions are discussed. This approach to formulation in epilepsy is illustrated with a case study in the final part of the chapter.

Epilepsy: some facts and figures

Epidemiology

Epilepsy is the term used for a group of central nervous system (CNS) disorders that have a common symptom – seizures. Since many factors including trauma, infection, stroke, tumours and degenerative processes can cause disordered electrical activity within the brain, epilepsy is the most common serious neurological disorder and approximately 30 per cent of people with epilepsy have an additional neurological disorder (Nashef, 1996). Up to 80 per cent of the people who have been given a diagnosis of epilepsy may be in remission, that is they may not have experienced a seizure for more than two years (Goodridge & Shorvon, 1983; Elwes *et al.*, 1988). However the possibility of a recurrence of seizures remains and this unpredictability can continue to exert a powerful impact on quality of life.

At the other end of the scale, a minority of people with epilepsy may experience more than one seizure a week. People with epilepsy therefore form a very heterogeneous group, differing in the types, frequency and individual experience of seizures. The psychological impact of a diagnosis of epilepsy will depend on the aetiology of the seizures, the prognosis of any associated neurological disorder and the region of the brain involved. All of these factors mean that the experience of having epilepsy is unique to each individual. However, epilepsy is normally classified by seizure type and the region of the brain involved. It is therefore very important that the psychologist understands the classification of seizures and is familiar with epilepsy terminology. Table 9.1 presents a brief glossary of common epilepsy terms.

Seizure type

The International League Against Epilepsy (ILAE) currently classifies three types of seizures, broadly based on the extent of disordered electrical activity (International League Against Epilepsy, 1989):

1   *Partial (focal, local) seizures.* Partial seizures are those in which the first clinical and electroencephalographic (EEG) changes indicate the disruption of a system of neurons limited to part of one cerebral hemisphere. Partial seizures are further subdivided into simple partial seizures (SPS) and complex partial seizures (CPS).
2   *Generalised seizures (convulsive or non-convulsive).* Generalised seizures are those in which the first clinical and EEG changes indicate the involvement of both hemispheres
3   *Unclassified epileptic seizures.* This includes all seizures that cannot be classified because of incomplete data and some that do not easily fit into the partial and generalised classifications.

These terms supersede the older terms of 'grand mal' and 'petit mal', although many people with epilepsy continue to describe their seizures using these classifications, particularly if these terms were used when they were first diagnosed. The term 'ictal' refers to the seizure itself. For example, ictal behaviour is the behaviour that occurs during the seizure. Post ictal refers to the events that occur after the seizure has finished, for example, post ictal psychosis. Inter ictal refers to events or problems that occur between seizures.

In a simple partial seizure (SPS), consciousness is not impaired. The region of the brain affected dictates the subjective experience of the seizure. Simple partial seizures may therefore range from motor symptoms (involuntary movements), sensory or somato-sensory symptoms (for example, unusual

Table 9.1 Brief glossary of epilepsy terms

Term	Description
Aura	Another term for SPS, often used when the SPS precedes a CPS
CPS: complex partial seizure	Partial seizure with impairment of consciousness
Cryptogenic epilepsy	The cause of the epilepsy is presumed to be symptomatic but the aetiology is not known
EEG	Electroencephalogram
GS: generalised seizure	First clinical and EEG changes suggest the involvement of both hemispheres at the beginning of the seizure Consciousness is usually impaired in a generalised seizure
Grand mal	Outdated term for generalised seizure
Ictal	Seizure related
Idiopathic epilepsy	No clear underlying cause other than hereditary disposition to seizures
Laterality	Side of the brain affected by the seizure
Partial seizure	The first clinical and EEG changes indicate that the seizure activations are limited to part of one cerebral hemisphere
Petit mal	Outdated term for complex partial seizure
Post ictal	Period following the seizure
Reflex epilepsy	Seizures triggered by specific stimuli
Seizure focus	Site in the brain that the seizure originates from. This may be a damaged existing brain structure, e.g. the hippocampus, or the site of a foreign lesion e.g. tumour
Semiology	Pattern of behaviours associated with habitual seizure
SPS: simple partial seizure	Partial seizure where consciousness is not impaired
Status epilepticus	Prolonged seizure that does not 'self-limit'
SUDEP	Sudden unexpected death in epilepsy
Symptomatic epilepsy	Epilepsy is the consequence of a known disorder of the central nervous system
Temporal, frontal, parietal, occipital	Lobe of the brain affected by the seizure, often the lobe where the seizure focus is located

tastes, smells or epigastric feelings) or psychological disturbances including déjà vu, jamais vu (a feeling of unfamiliarity) and intense feelings of ecstasy, fear or anger. Simple partial seizures are also sometimes termed 'auras' or 'warnings' since they may precede a complex partial seizure or generalised convulsion. Because consciousness is not impaired during a SPS, people with epilepsy can sometimes use the warning to prepare for the impending loss of consciousness associated with a complex partial seizure (CPS) or generalised seizure.

Consciousness is impaired in a complex partial seizure. Depending on the region of the brain involved there may be no other features or the seizure may manifest itself very dramatically with shouting and posturing. Since consciousness is impaired, the individual does not take in or act on external information in an appropriate way during the seizure. This can place them and others in extreme danger. In a CPS the people with epilepsy will be oblivious to the dangers of the external environment such as traffic, water or heat and they may not respond to pain. CPS may also be associated with 'automatisms'. These can include orofacial movements such as lip smacking and chewing, over-learnt behaviours such as dressing or undressing, fiddling with hands or clothes, walking, running, circling or the repetition of a single word or phrase. The person with epilepsy will be amnesic for the events that have occurred during a CPS.

A generalised seizure involves a loss of consciousness and both hemispheres are involved. Generalised seizures include convulsive seizures, but can also be nonconvulsive and include absences, myoclonic seizures and atonic seizures (sometimes termed drop attacks). Muscular aches and intense fatigue often follow generalised convulsions.

Most seizures are self-limiting and last less than five minutes. During this time it is important to try to keep the individual safe but no further action is normally necessary. The exception is when a seizure does not stop. This state is called status epilepticus and is dangerous. Status epilepticus can be fatal in up to 8 to 10 per cent of cases (Oxbury & Whitty, 1971), although fortunately this percentage is dropping as treatment becomes more effective (Aicardi, 1986; Maytal *et al.*, 1989). Unremitting seizure activity can cause permanent brain damage after just 30 minutes (Walker M.C., & Shorvon, 1996). Immediate medical attention should be sought if a seizure does not appear to coming to an end after ten minutes.

Epilepsy-related death refers to death that arises as a direct result of having epilepsy rather than the underlying cause of the epilepsy. Epilepsy-related deaths include accidents that occur during seizures, seizures themselves, status epilepticus and sudden unexpected death in epilepsy (SUDEP). Sudden unexpected death is a non-traumatic death that occurs within minutes or hours of the onset of a seizure. Newly diagnosed patients and those with convulsive epilepsy are at higher risk of SUDEP (Cockerell, 1996).

The first stage of the psychological formulation in a referral of someone with epilepsy must therefore be the establishing of exactly what kind of epilepsy the individual has. Whilst there are some very detailed formal assessments of seizure type and severity available, such as the Chalfont Seizure Severity Scale (O'Donoghue *et al.*, 1996), Liverpool Seizure Severity Scale (Scott-Lennox *et al.*, 2001), Hague Seizure Severity Scale (Carpay *et al.*, 1997) and others (see Cramer, 2001 for a review), these may not always be to hand in everyday clinical practice. Nevertheless it is not enough simply to have the patient's diagnosis, for example, left temporal lobe epilepsy. This simply tells you that the left temporal lobe houses the suspected seizure focus. Although this may indicate some neuropsychological problems, specifically memory disturbance, it does not give any indication of the impact of the epilepsy on everyday life. In order to assess this impact it is necessary to generate a clear picture of the type, frequency and severity of seizures. A brief schedule of relevant questions is presented in Box 9.1.

Box 9.1 Five stages for formulation in epilepsy

Stage 1: Assessment of seizure type and severity

1   When did the seizures start?
2   Is there a known aetiology?
3   How many different types of seizure does the individual experience? For each type:
    • How often do they occur?
    • Are there any clear precipitants? (ABC analysis)
    • What happens during the seizure (ideally speak to someone who has witnessed the patient's habitual seizure)?
    • How long does it take to recover completely?

Stage 2: Psychological impact of living with seizures

1   Assess developmental impact:
    • How old was the patient when they were first diagnosed?
    • What was the impact on schooling?
    • What was the impact on social development/family dynamics?
    • What was lost at the time of diagnosis? (What has been lost since?)
    • Are there any very traumatic events associated with past seizures (for example, near death, injury, embarrassment)?
2   Assess impact on current psychological health:
    • Anxiety
    • Depression
    • Coping style.

Stage 3: Neuropsychological assessment

1   Should involve a broad screen of abilities looking for strengths and weaknesses.
Battery should be designed to help to set realistic goals in terms of education, employment, independent living, Address under/over-expectations.

2   Be aware of medications:
   •   Careful and appropriate test selection.

3   Neuropsychological assessment can give details on:
   •   lateralisation/localisation of seizure focus (in conjunction with MRI)
   •   seizure spread (post ictal testing)
   •   long-term effects of seizures.

4   Repeat testing can give useful information on cognitive decline associated with:
   •   seizures
   •   episodes of status epilepticus
   •   head injuries
   •   medication change.

Stage 4: Consolidation

Pulling together of all the information from the previous stages to build a comprehensive picture of the relevant psychological issues associated with living with epilepsy. Useful distinctions in this process include:

•   What is past? What is present?
•   What is fixed? What can be changed?
•   Are problems individual or situational or environmental?
•   What features should be borne in mind when planning interventions (e.g. poor memory, concentration, etc.)

Stage 5: Plan treatment

List detailed and specific treatment goals and corresponding interventions.
In full consultation with the client create the order in which each goal to be tackled based on:

•   desirability of goal
•   achievability of goal
•   nature of intervention.

Psychological impact of living with epilepsy

Epilepsy is a neurological condition. Medical interventions, most commonly in the form of anti-epileptic medications or neurosurgery, form the frontline in the treatment of seizures. However, psychological approaches can be used both to directly target seizure frequency and improve quality of life in epilepsy. Often approaches directed at improving quality of life have an indirect beneficial impact on seizure frequency. The importance of this latter approach should not be underestimated since it may not be the seizures themselves that cause the greatest problems for many people with epilepsy. Frequently the fear of having a seizure and the anticipation of its consequences can be as great or greater a disruption to everyday life than the seizure itself. This fear may be unrelated to the frequency of seizures and may be as great in someone who experiences one seizure a year as in someone who experiences weekly events.

Psychological approaches that directly target seizure frequency

For the majority of people with epilepsy, it is not possible to predict when seizures will occur. It is precisely this sudden and unexpected loss of control that causes many of the physical dangers and psychological difficulties associated with epilepsy. However, up to 5 per cent of people with epilepsy can identify very specific triggers for their seizures. These are termed reflex epilepsies (see Beaumanoir, 1998 for a history of reflex epilepsies). The triggers can include sensory stimuli such as flashing lights in photosensitive epilepsy (Zifkin & Kasteleijn-Nolst, 2000), music in patients with musicogenic seizures (Brien & Murray, 1984), or hot water in hot water epilepsy (Argumosa et al., 2002). Although rare, tactile stimuli such as tooth brushing or rubbing can also induce seizures in some people (Kanemoto et al., 2001).

Some reflex epilepsies can be triggered by higher cognitive functions such as reading or mental arithmetic (Karlov et al., 1995). Systematic desensitisation, avoidance and relaxation techniques can all be used to reduce seizure frequency in people with reflex epilepsies. For example, Ganga et al. (1988) describe a 17-year-old boy in whom the seizures precipitated by eating had been prevented by giving him some alerting stimuli during the meal.

Psychological approaches with an indirect impact on seizure frequency

A number of psychological approaches have been shown to have an indirect impact on seizure frequency. Whilst most people with epilepsy cannot identify a clear trigger for their seizures, many can identify certain situations in which a seizure is more likely. Anxiety, stress, hunger and tiredness may all make a seizure more likely. Diet, exercise, relaxation and yoga have also been shown in some studies to have an impact on seizure frequency.

As a general rule, moderate physical exercise is as beneficial to the person with epilepsy as everyone else in the general population and may have the additional benefit of reducing seizure frequency. Many people with epilepsy, particularly those with uncontrolled seizures, live a sedentary life and have a low level of physical fitness. Nakken (2000) found that regular physical exercise may have a moderate impact on seizure frequency in up to one-third of this patient population. However, strenuous physical exercise may induce seizures in some patients, particularly those who are very unfit, or who have symptomatic epilepsy. Counselling on this topic should therefore be individualised, taking into account both epilepsy-related variables and overall level of physical fitness. Some sports are specifically contra-indicated, including physical contact sports where head injuries may be frequent and unsupervised swimming or diving activities. See Cordova (1993) for guidelines for epilepsy and sport.

Some people with epilepsy may be able to pinpoint a specific food that may trigger a seizure or make one more likely. Alcohol consumption can also increase the likelihood of seizures in some patients. However, most of the research that has focused on diet in epilepsy has looked at the impact of special dietary regimes on seizure frequency. The most popular of these is the ketogenic diet. The ketogenic diet is a high fat (90 per cent), low carbohydrate (3 per cent) diet used to treat refractory seizures most commonly in children but also in adults. It has recently regained popularity. There are few large-scale systematic studies of the efficacy of the diet but some meta-analyses suggest a beneficial reduction of seizure frequency in over half of the children who stick to the diet with a complete cessation of seizures in 16 per cent (Lefevre & Aronson, 2000). Similar results have been found in adults, although compliance is a significant problem (Sirven et al., 1999). Although the ketogenic diet may be effective in controlling seizures in some people with epilepsy, its use in children should be monitored extremely closely. Cardio-myopathies, kidney stones, basal ganglia injuries and growth retardation have all been associated with the diet in young children (Bergqvist et al., 2003; Erickson et al., 2003; Kossoff et al., 2002; Vining et al., 2002).

Psychological approaches aimed at reducing anxiety and improving coping mechanisms may have an indirect impact on seizure frequency (Jacoby et al., 1996). Although relaxation therapies do not appear to have a significant impact on seizure frequency (Ramaratnam et al., 1903), there is some evidence that yoga can reduce seizure frequency in some patients (Ramaratnam & Sridharan, 2000). Psychological approaches can also be used to increase compliance with an anti-epileptic medication regime. Increased compliance can have a very dramatic impact on the reduction of seizures (Thompson, 1988; Irving et al., 1999).

After establishing what kind of epilepsy the patient has, an important stage in the psychological formulation should be establishing whether there is any scope for a psychological approach in the reduction of seizure frequency. This will include a detailed assessment of any direct or situational triggers for the seizures. Diet, exercise, compliance with anti-epileptic regimes and general levels of stress and anxiety should all be assessed as part of this process. This involves a very detailed assessment of when and where seizures occur (see Box 9.1). A behavioural ABC analysis (antecedent, behaviour, consequence) with the seizure as the behaviour is often helpful at this stage.

Psychological adjustment to living with epilepsy

Although psychological approaches can be used in the ways described previously to reduce seizures, they are most commonly employed to help psychological adjustment to living with the disorder. People with epilepsy may have both cognitive and affective problems associated with the disorder. Clinical levels of anxiety are reported in up to one in four people with epilepsy (Swinkels *et al.*, 2001). This is due to the suddenness and unpredictability of seizures and the associated loss of control. Ictal behaviour such as undressing, drooling and incontinence can lead to severe and socially disabling levels of embarrassment. In addition, fear of personal injury or of injuring others can lead to raised anxiety in everyday situations and so significantly restrict normal activities. Finally, increased awareness of sudden unexpected death in epilepsy can understandably elevate anxiety levels even in otherwise generally 'safe' situations. Unfortunately for many people with epilepsy, anxiety reduces their seizure threshold (Little, 1991). This makes seizures more likely to occur and so a vicious cycle is set up (see Figure 9.1).

Depression is also very common in people with epilepsy, and may affect up

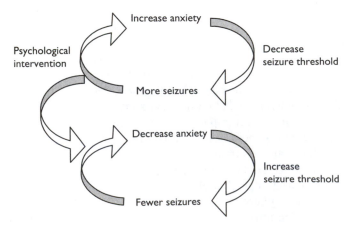

Figure 9.1 Anxiety and seizures.

to one-third of the patient population at some time in their lives (Trimble, 1996). People with epilepsy are at much greater risk than the general population of suffering from depression due to the combination of biological, metabolic and sociological factors. See Harden (2002) for a comprehensive review of the epidemiology, aetiology and treatment of depression in epilepsy. The age of onset of the disorder may have a significant impact on the development of depression. If epilepsy starts in adulthood, an individual's job may be at risk. Although many people with epilepsy continue to work successfully, some jobs are clearly incompatible with the disorder. These include any that involve dangerous machinery or the driving of any kind of vehicle from an aeroplane to a forklift truck. Even if the individual can safely continue their job they will automatically lose their driving licence for at least a year after diagnosis and so consequently may not be able to get to their place of work. If they can continue to work, ignorance about the condition remains common and they may experience unwitting prejudice from friends, family and colleagues. Consequently, the diagnosis of epilepsy in adulthood can have a devastating impact on almost all aspects of life ranging from physical health (anti-epileptic medication side effects) to financial income and close relationships. Unsurprisingly, self-esteem and confidence can plummet and depression can take hold as individuals come to terms with significant losses in many areas of their lives.

Different factors may contribute to the development of depression in people who develop epilepsy in childhood or adolescence. Children are great conformists and can be very unforgiving if they see or sense difference in any way. A single seizure involving incontinence, drooling or any other socially unacceptable behaviour may mark out the young child with epilepsy as different for their entire school career. The fear of having seizures in public may lead to restricted social development as the family tries to protect the child from rejection by their peers. Through adolescence and early adulthood, external restrictions can also hamper social development, such as reliance on public transport and regulatory restrictions in public places such as theme parks and swimming pools. It is not therefore surprising that many young people with epilepsy are very dissatisfied with their social lives. One survey found that two-thirds of young people with epilepsy were severely dissatisfied with their social lives and that they had few interests outside the home (Thompson & Upton, 1992). The same survey found that over 60 per cent of respondents said they had no personal friends, other than friends of the family. This social isolation is a major contributory factor to the development of depression in young people with epilepsy.

Neuropsychological deficits

Cognitive functioning is the process whereby an individual takes in information about the world, makes sense of it and acts upon it. Although they are not discrete functions, cognitive functions are generally divided both conceptually and for assessment purposes into separate categories such as attention, learning, memory, language, perception and executive functions (e.g. planning and decision making).

People with epilepsy are at risk of developing neuropsychological deficits from three sources. The brain damage responsible for the development of the epilepsy, the effects of ongoing seizures (including status epilepticus) and anti-epileptic medications can all contribute to the development of neuropsychological deficits.

The neuropsychological deficit associated with the seizure focus will depend very much on the aetiology of the epilepsy. Very early onset epilepsy may be associated with cortical dysgenesis, an abnormality in the development of the cortex that occurs during the first 12 weeks of gestation (Raymond *et al.*, 1996). Anoxia at birth, which commonly occurs if the cord is wrapped tightly around a baby's neck, may cause extensive hippocampal damage. Head injuries may lead to very focal or widespread diffuse damage, depending on the nature of the injury. Brain infections such as meningitis frequently leave widespread damage. In adults, the onset of epilepsy may be associated with development of both malignant and so-called benign tumours or alcohol abuse. In older adults the underlying aetiology may be widespread or localised vascular disorder (stroke) or a degenerative disease such as Parkinson's or Alzheimer's disease. The nature and extent of the neuropsychological deficit associated with each of these underlying processes will be dictated by:

• the site of the damage within the brain
• the extent and dynamic nature of the damage
• the age at which the insult occurred; some plasticity of function is often seen in people with early insults, particularly those of a developmental nature.

In addition to the underlying aetiology of the seizures, the seizures themselves can also be responsible for the development of additional neuropsychological deficits. Repeated atonic/tonic drop attacks can lead to significant additional brain injury. Although by no means always the case, years of uncontrolled seizures can have a cumulative negative impact on cognitive function (Stafstrom, 1903). Episodes of status epilepticus often lead to permanent additional brain damage (Walker & Shorvon, 1996). Temporary neuropsychological deficits may be evident in the post ictal phase and can also be induced by subclinical epileptiform activity (Casas-Fernandez *et al.*, 2002).

Many anti-epileptic medications have been shown to have a negative impact on cognitive function in group studies (Aldenkamp & Vermeulen, 2002). Cognitive slowing and poor memory appear to be the most common side effects. However, it is important to remember that there can be very individual reactions to anti-epileptic medications with some drug compounds or interactions inducing pseudo-dementias, profound cognitive slowing and significant verbal and intellectual deficits in some patients (Thompson, 1992; Thompson *et al.*, 2000).

Formulation

The previous sections have outlined some of the important neurological and psychological issues in epilepsy. Although epilepsy is a neurological disorder, many of the problems faced by individuals who live with epilepsy fall firmly in the psychological domain. There are at least five stages in the clinical formulation prior to the psychological treatment of someone with epilepsy. These stages are outlined in Box 9.1. The first stage of the formulation is to establish exactly what kind of epilepsy the individual has. This requires a detailed assessment of the type and frequency of seizures in addition to the underlying aetiology. This stage will also involve an assessment of the validity of any psychological approaches to directly target seizure frequency.

The second stage of the formulation involves an assessment of the psychological impact of living with seizures. This will involve a developmental review in addition to an assessment of present psychological difficulties.

The third stage of the formulation involves a detailed assessment of the neuropsychological deficits associated with the disorder. This will give an important insight into the everyday cognitive difficulties experienced by the person with epilepsy and will highlight critical considerations in planning treatments and interventions, such as poor memory and concentration or high impulsivity.

In the fourth stage of the formulation, all of this information is pulled together to build a holistic picture of the impact of epilepsy on an individual's life. A number of issues will emerge. These may include developmental issues such as looking at how living with epilepsy has shaped an individual's personality and coping style. This stage will also yield important information on current levels of anxiety, depression and psychological distress as well as very specific situational difficulties faced by the client on a regular basis.

The fifth and final stage of the formulation is to plan treatment strategies for the issues that have emerged from stage four. Treatments should be planned in full consultation with the client. Stage four of the formulation process will have yielded a number of issues. Long-term psychodynamic approaches may be more appropriate to deal with developmental issues, whilst short-term cognitive behavioural therapies may be more appropriate to deal with social anxiety or agoraphobia. A more educative approach in social skills training or the development of effective coping skills may be useful in helping the client cope with some of the practical problems of living with epilepsy. Sometimes the intervention will not involve the client at all but rather the psychologist attempts to change the environment to reduce difficulties by educating colleagues and peers about epilepsy.

All treatment options and their desired outcomes should be discussed with the client who should be encouraged to place them in a hierarchy and choose which goal they would like to pursue, taking into account the desirability and achievability of the goal and the nature of the planned intervention.

Interventions

A large number of psychological therapies, both stand-alone and in combination, have been offered to people with epilepsy in attempts both to reduce seizure frequency and improve their quality of life. Ramaratnam *et al.* (2001) conducted a comprehensive review of the efficacy of these treatments. Unfortunately, the poor methodologies of most of the studies did not allow for a full meta-analysis of the field, and the authors concluded that in view of methodological deficiencies and limited number of patients studied, there was little roust and substantiated evidence to support the use of these treatments. However, although many psychological treatments have not been tested in robust, double-blind, randomised controlled trials, the literature does suggest that CBT can be effective in treating depression; relaxation and behaviour modification can have a beneficial impact on anxiety; and education can be highly effective in improving compliance with anti-epileptic regimes and social competence (Ramaratnam *et al.*, 2001). These approaches are discussed in more detail below.

Psychodynamic therapeutic approaches may be helpful in aiding the client to understand the effects that the diagnosis of epilepsy has had on their life and psychological style (Williams *et al.*, 1979). These interventions are often long term and the treatment outcomes can be quite diffuse and difficult to monitor. As with many client groups today, cognitive behavioural therapies (CBT) remain some of the most common treatments offered to people with epilepsy. However, psychological interventions for people with epilepsy must be tailored to acknowledge the real risks associated with the disorder. Increased anxiety surrounding everyday activities such as shopping or using public transport may be seen as an entirely adaptive response to the possibility of a seizure and its consequences. Therefore any CBT intervention for anxiety must be tailored to acknowledge real risks and dangers faced by people with epilepsy. A risk management approach is often highly effective. In this approach the client is encouraged to conduct a risk/benefit analysis for each activity and then find ways to reduce the risks. Often a simple change can dramatically reduce risks. Taking someone with the client or letting someone know one has epilepsy can significantly reduce the dangers associated with seizures when out and about.

Different coping strategies can have dramatic effects on anxiety. Social support and a planful problem-solving approach can significantly lower anxiety in people with epilepsy. Therapeutic interventions can be used to improve reliance on these adaptive coping strategies and decrease the use of more unhelpful approaches, such as avoidance. Also increasing the knowledge of the client's own epilepsy can help to reduce anxiety. A seizure diary can help clients identify seizure patterns, precipitants and missed medications (Neugebauer, 1989). This information can suggest situations in which seizures are more or less likely to occur. Introducing just a small element of predictability can have a significant impact on the reduction of anxiety.

Often many of the problems associated with seizures are caused or exacerbated by the lack of understanding of people who witness the event. Since people with epilepsy are generally indistinguishable from others between seizures, the sudden onset of a seizure can produce alarm and suspicion in bystanders. This can further compromise the safety of the person with epilepsy. The decision to tell others about the diagnosis of epilepsy often relies on a fine balance of safety verses privacy/stigma. This balance can often be struck by taking a few individuals into one's confidence; for example, just letting one trusted colleague at work know how to recognise a seizure and what to do if a seizure does occur. In this way the safety of the person with epilepsy is increased whilst the stigma of the disorder is kept to a minimum.

Social skills training can sometimes be helpful in reducing the social isolation of people with epilepsy, but it is more often beneficial to try to find for them appropriate social opportunities in which they can develop their skills without fear of rejection. Psychological interventions can also target the environment. In schools, increased awareness of the condition can reduce the stigma faced by a child with epilepsy. In one case, we conducted a school assembly on epilepsy. This involved a short speech by a very brave 9-year-old girl with complex partial seizures and a brief presentation by her psychologist and neurologist. As a result of the assembly the girl became 'special' rather than different and her life in the school was transformed with the pupils looking out for her and caring for her rather than leaving her in isolation because she was different. In this case, half an hour's intervention with the environment was far more effective than weeks of individual therapy. Similar approaches can also be used in the adult workplace.

Finally, some psychological approaches to coping with the difficulties of living with epilepsy can be very practical in nature. One client was very worried that the stress of her wedding day would lead her to have a seizure. She was understandably concerned that she would become incontinent at the altar in front of all her friends and family and ruin her wedding dress and her big day. In this case we simply advised that she wear incontinence knickers for the event. In that way, even if she did have a seizure and was incontinent, no one would know and her dress would be spared. Her anxiety levels were reduced significantly and the day passed without any seizures. Thus interventions in people with epilepsy can range from long-term psychodynamic psychotherapy to very short-term, one-off practical solutions.

This is why stage four of the formulation process is so important. Treatment goals and approaches should be mixed to give some small short-term successes whilst long-term goals are pursued.

Although neuropsychological difficulties may have an organic basis, there is still scope for psychological intervention and help. Following a neuro-psychological assessment it is very important to give full and frank feedback to the client. This feedback should be tailored to meet the strengths and weaknesses uncovered during the assessment. For example, if the assessment revealed weak concentration skills, shorter sessions might be indicated; someone with a poor memory would benefit from a written summary at the end of each session. Carers and relatives may also benefit from attending feedback sessions, to help them understand some of the more frustrating and opaque neuropsychological difficulties commonly found in epilepsy; for example, post ictal deficits or deficits associated with subclinical events (Bergin *et al.*, 1995). The development of internal memory strategies can be helpful in remediating some of the everyday problems associated with a poor memory as can the use of external aids ranging from drug wallets to post-it notes.

Case study

Referral

> Dear Psychologist,
>
> Rachael is a 29-year-old single mother who experienced a generalised seizure whilst on holiday six months ago and has since experienced a number of auras and two possible complex partial seizures. The return of her seizures has had a devastating effect on her life. She has become very anxious and is afraid of going out. She is also concerned that she will harm her young son (aged 3) and seemed really quite depressed in the clinic today. I wonder if you could help?
>
> A GP

Referrals such as these are common in both neuropsychological and clinical psychology settings. The following sets out the formulation process for this referral.

Stage 1: Assessment of seizure type and severity

Stage 1 of the formulation revealed that Rachael was originally diagnosed with epilepsy at the age of 5. From the age of 3, her mother noticed that Rachael would frequently become unresponsive and fiddle with her clothes. This was thought to be behavioural until a family friend (who was a nurse) witnessed an event and suggested the possibility of complex partial seizures. Rachael was referred to a child neurology service and idiopathic epilepsy was diagnosed. She was started on anti-epileptic medication and her seizure frequency reduced dramatically. Nevertheless she continued to experience approximately three complex partial seizures a year. These tended to occur during times of illness and fever. On one occasion, when she was about 7 years old and suffering from an ear infection, a complex partial seizure generalised and she experienced a generalised tonic clonic convulsion. She and the family were very frightened by this event. Her medication was changed and the frequency of complex partial seizures gradually reduced until the age of 11 when she had her last seizure. She gradually reduced her medication and had stopped taking it by the age of 13. She was then completely seizure free throughout her teenage years and early adulthood.

Sixteen years after her last attack, she experienced a generalised tonic clonic seizure whilst on holiday. She had been drinking alcohol for much of the day and was sunbathing on a hot beach when the seizure occurred. She did not remember anything about the seizure, and only remembered coming round in her hotel over an hour later. Bystanders report a generalised tonic clonic seizure that lasted about five minutes. Her friend reported that Rachael was confused afterwards and could not recall the route back to her hotel. Since that time she has experienced a number of auras involving a strong sense of déjà vu. She also thinks she may have experienced a couple of complex partial seizures, as she has experienced some 'blanks' in her memory for events, once whilst shopping and once at home. The only witness to these events was her 4-year-old son. Her GP has started her on topiramate, one of the newer anti-epileptic drugs.

Stage 2: Psychological impact of living with seizures

Rachael reported that she had never had a seizure at school. Nevertheless, she had been excluded from school swimming lessons and her parents had not allowed her to attend school field trips. As a result she had always felt different and found it difficult to make friends. At the age of 7 she had experienced a generalised seizure whilst at home and came round in hospital. She vividly recalls her parents' fear and concern at this time and remembers her mother crying.

Rachael reported that prior to the return of the seizures, she had felt that her epilepsy was very much in the past. The return of her seizures has had a devastating effect on her life. She has become very anxious and is afraid of going out. She is also extremely concerned that she will harm her young son in a seizure.

Stage 3: Neuropsychological assessment

Neuropsychological assessment revealed some word finding difficulties and deficits in verbal learning and memory in the context of average intelligence.

Stage 4: Consolidation

In this case, the early diagnosis of epilepsy did have an impact on the development of Rachael's personality. Although her peers never witnessed a seizure, she felt different at school and developed a very cautious social style. Although she only experienced one generalised seizure in her childhood, it was a very traumatic event and she developed a strong fear of these seizures. This fear gradually faded as she grew up and her epilepsy became a memory. However, the occurrence of the generalised convulsion on holiday had reawakened all her fears. She was extremely concerned that she would harm her son or frighten him during a seizure. Her memory had deteriorated since she started her medication and she was unsure whether some of her memory lapses were a new kind of complex partial seizure. The possibility that the drugs were not controlling the seizures further increased her anxiety.

Stage 5: Plan treatment

Rachael identified three treatment goals that she wished to work on. These were in order

1   Practical steps to keep her and her son safe.
2   Overall reduction of anxiety.
3   Memory strategies.

The development of practical steps involved the detailed analyses of the everyday activities Rachael feared most. A number of dangerous scenarios were then explored: for example, pouring boiling water from the kettle; her son falling from the bed or changing unit during a nappy change; her son drowning if she had a seizure whilst bathing him. In each scenario, we explored ways in which both Rachel and her son could be kept safe if a seizure occurred. These involved changing nappies on the floor, not carrying her son whilst walking down stairs, use of an adapted kettle requiring two-handed operation to pour liquid and the use of a bath chair for her son.

A combination of CBT and education strategies reduced Rachael's overall anxiety levels. A seizure diary revealed that she had not experienced any seizures since restarting her anti-epileptic medication. In the past she had responded well to AEDs and there was no reason to suggest that this time would be different. There were also many new AEDs and combinations she could try if her current medications were unsuccessful. As her confidence in the treatment grew, her anxiety decreased.

The roots of her great fears surrounding generalised seizures were explored with a CBT approach. By exploring the events surrounding her first generalised seizure, she began to understand that it was the responses of those around her, rather than the seizure itself, that had frightened her as a child. In fact she had never had an entirely unprovoked generalised seizure, the first occurring following a fever, the second occurring when she was probably dehydrated and in the hot sun. Her fear of having a generalised seizure reduced significantly following these sessions.

Rachael was educated about the neuropsychological side effects of some anti-epileptic drugs. Following this session, on balance she felt that some of the memory lapses she had experienced were probably due to a combination of anxiety and drug side effects, rather than a new type of seizure. A number of memory strategies were suggested to help her reduce the nuisance of these memory lapses. Rachael was also encouraged to use her close family network to provide her with both practical and social support.

Rachel underwent eight sessions and was followed up one year after her original referral. She had not experienced any further seizures and her confidence was growing. Although still fearful of the return of her seizures, she felt that her life was returning to normal. She still experienced some memory problems but did not feel that these were complex partial seizures and understood the impact of stress and her medication on neuropsychological function.

Summary

Epilepsy is a neurological disorder with far-reaching psychological effects. Formulation in epilepsy cases involves the synthesis of neurological, psychological and neuropsychological data and frequently requires a developmental perspective. The psychologist should be aware of the nature of any additional underlying neurological condition as this will play an important part in the psychological formulation. A detailed formulation usually yields both short- and long-term goals that can be achieved using a wide range of therapeutic techniques. Although psychological approaches that directly target seizure frequency may be limited, many of the problems associated with living with recurrent seizures respond well to psychological approaches. Improved psychological well-being often has the additional indirect benefit of reducing seizure frequency. This makes people with epilepsy one of the most rewarding neurological client groups to work with in a psychological setting.

References

Aicardi, J. (1986). Consequences and prognosis of convulsive status epilepticus in infants and children. *Japanese Journal of Psychiatry and Neurology, 40*, 283–290.

Aldenkamp, A.P., & Vermeulen, J. (2002). Effects of antiepileptics drugs on cognition. *Revue Neurologique, 34*, 851–856.

Argumosa, A., Herranz, J.L., Barrasa, B.J., & Arteaga, R. (2002). Reflex epilepsy from hot water: A new case and review of the literature. *Revue Neurologique, 35*, 349–353.

Beaumanoir, A. (1998). History of reflex epilepsy. *Advances in Neurology, 75*, 1–4.

Bergin, P.S., Thompson, P.J., Fish, D.R., & Shorvon, S.D. (1995). The effect of seizures on memory for recently learned material. *Neurology, 45*, 236–240.

Bergqvist, A.G., Chee, C.M., Lutchka, L., Rychik, J., & Stallings, V.A. (2003). Selenium deficiency associated with cardiomyopathy: A complication of the ketogenic diet. *Epilepsia, 44*, 618–620.

Brien, S.E., & Murray, T.J. (1984). Musicogenic epilepsy. *Canadian Medical Association Journal, 131*, 1255–1258.

Carpay, J.A., Vermuelen, J., Stroink, H., Brouwer, O.F., Peters, A.C., Aldenkamp, A.P., van Donselaar, C.A., & Arts, W.F. (1997). Seizure severity in children with epilepsy: A parent-completed scale compared with clinical data. *Epilepsia, 38*, 346–352.

Casas-Fernandez, C., Belmonte-Aviles, F., Fernandez-Fernandez, M.V., Recuero-Fernandez, E., Rodriguez-Costa, T., Lopez-Soler, C., Domingo-Jimenez, R., & Puche-Mira, A. (2002). Transient cognitive disorder from subclinical paroxysmal EEG activity. *Revue Neurologique, 35*, S21–S29.

Cockerell O.C (1996). The prognosis of epilepsy. In S.D. Shorvon, F. Dreifuss, D.R. Fish, & D. Thomas, (Eds.), *The treatment of epilepsy* (pp. 97–113). Oxford: Blackwell.

Cordova, F. (1993). Epilepsy and sport. *Australian Family Physician, 22*, 558–562.

Cramer, J.A. (2001). Assessing the severity of seizures and epilepsy: Which scales are valid? *Current Opinion in Neurology, 14*, 225–229.

Elwes, R.D., Johnson, A.L., & Reynolds, E.H. (1988). The course of untreated epilepsy. *BMJ, 297*, 948–950.

Erickson, J.C., Jabbari, B., & Difazio, M.P. (2003). Basal ganglia injury as a complication of the ketogenic diet. *Movement Disorders, 18*, 448–451.

Ganga, A., Sechi, G.P., Porcella, V., Traccis, S., Rosati, G., & Agnetti, V. (1988). Eating seizures and distraction-arousal functions. A case study. *European Neurology, 28*, 167–170.

Goodridge, D.M., & Shorvon, S.D. (1983). Epileptic seizures in a population of 6000. II: Treatment and prognosis. *British Medical Journal (Clinical Research Edition), 287*, 645–647.

Harden, C.L. (2002). The co-morbidity of depression and epilepsy: Epidemiology, etiology, and treatment. *Neurology, 59*, S48–S55.

International League Against Epilepsy (1989). Proposal for revised classification of epilepsies and epileptic syndromes. Commission on Classification and Terminology of the International League Against Epilepsy. *Epilepsia, 30*, 389–399.

Irving, P., Al Dahma, A., Srinivasan, A., & Greenwood, R. (1999). An audit of admissions of patients with epilepsy to a district general hospital. *Seizure, 8*, 166–169.

Jacoby, A., Baker, G.A., Steen, N., Potts, P., & Chadwick, D.W. (1996). The clinical course of epilepsy and its psychosocial correlates: Findings from a UK Community study. *Epilepsia, 37*, 148–161.

Kanemoto, K., Watanabe, Y., Tsuji, T., Fukami, M., & Kawasaki, J. (2001). Rub epilepsy: A somatosensory evoked reflex epilepsy induced by prolonged cutaneous stimulation. *Journal of Neurology, Neurosurgery and Psychiatry, 70*, 541–543.

Karlov, V.A., Zhidkova, I.A., & Vlasov, P.N. (1995). Rare forms of reflex epilepsy – the epilepsy of calculation and the epilepsy of eating. *Zhurnal Nevropatologi Psikhiatri Imeni S S Korsakova, 95*, 13–16.

Kossoff, E.H., Pyzik, P.L., Furth, S.L., Hladky, H.D., Freeman, J.M., & Vining, E.P. (2002). Kidney stones, carbonic anhydrase inhibitors, and the ketogenic diet. *Epilepsia, 43*, 1168–1171.

Lefevre, F., & Aronson, N. (2000). Ketogenic diet for the treatment of refractory epilepsy in children: A systematic review of efficacy. *Pediatrics, 105*, E46.

Little, H.J. (1991). The benzodiazepines: Anxiolytic and withdrawal effects. *Neuropeptides, 19*, 11–14.

Maytal, J., Shinnar, S., Moshe, S.L., & Alvarez, L.A. (1989). Low morbidity and mortality of status epilepticus in children. *Pediatrics, 83*, 323–331.

Nakken, K.O. (2000). Should people with epilepsy exercise? *Tidsskrift for den Norske Laegeforening, 120*, 3051–3053.

Nashef, L. (1996). Definition, aetiologies and diagnosis of epilepsy. In S.D. Shorvon, F. Dreifuss, D.R. Fish, & D. Thomas, (Eds.), *The treatment of epilepsy* (pp. 66–96). Oxford: Blackwell.

Neugebauer, R. (1989). Reliability of seizure diaries in adult epileptic patients. *Neuroepidemiology, 8*, 228–233.

O'Donoghue, M.F., Duncan, J.S., & Sander, J.W. (1996). The National Hospital Seizure Severity Scale: A further development of the Chalfont Seizure Severity Scale. *Epilepsia, 37*, 563–571.

Oxbury, J.M., & Whitty, C.W. (1971). Causes and consequences of status epilepticus in adults. A study of 86 cases. *Brain, 94*, 733–744.

Ramaratnam, S., & Sridharan, K. (2000). Yoga for epilepsy. *Cochrane Database of Systematic Reviews, 3*, CD001524.

Ramaratnam, S., Baker, G.A., & Goldstein, L. (2001). Psychological treatments for epilepsy. *Cochrane Database of Systematic Reviews, 4*, CD002029.

Raymond, A.A., Shorvon, S.D., Fish, D.R., & Sisodiya S.M. (1996). The developmental basis of epilepsy. In S.D. Shorvon, F. Dreifuss, D.R. Fish, & D. Thomas, (Eds.), *The treatment of epilepsy* (pp. 20–54). Oxford: Blackwell.

Scott-Lennox, J., Bryant-Comstock, L., Lennox, R., & Baker, G.A. (2001). Reliability, validity and responsiveness of a revised scoring system for the Liverpool Seizure Severity Scale. *Epilepsy Research, 44*, 53–63.

Sirven, J., Whedon, B., Caplan, D., Liporace, J., Glosser, D., O'Dwyer, J., & Sperling, M.R. (1999). The ketogenic diet for intractable epilepsy in adults: Preliminary results. *Epilepsia, 40*, 1721–1726.

Stafstrom, C.E. (1903). Assessing the behavioral and cognitive effects of seizures on the developing brain. *Progress in Brain Research, 135*, 377–390.

Swinkels, W.A., Kuyk, J., de Graaf, E.H., van Dyck, R., & Spinhoven, P. (2001). Prevalence of psychopathology in Dutch epilepsy inpatients: A comparative study. *Epilepsy Behaviour, 2*, 441–447.

Thompson, P.J. (1988). Psychological aspects of non-compliance. *Epilepsy Research Supplement, 1*, 71–75.

Thompson, P.J. (1992). Antiepileptic drugs and memory. *Epilepsia, 33*, S37–S40.

Thompson, P.J., & Upton, D. (1992). The impact of chronic epilepsy on the family. *Seizure, 1*, 43–48.

Thompson, P.J., Baxendale, S.A., Duncan, J.S., & Sander, J.W. (2000). Effects of topiramate on cognitive function. *Journal of Neurology, Neurosurgery and Psychiatry, 69*, 636–641.

Trimble, M.R. (1996). Psychiatric disorders in epilepsy. In S.D. Shorvon, F. Dreifuss, D.R. Fish, & D. Thomas, (Eds.), *The treatment of epilepsy* (pp. 337–344). Oxford: Blackwell.

Vining, E.P., Pyzik, P., McGrogan, J., Hladky, H., Anand, A., Kriegler, S., & Freeman, J.M. (2002). Growth of children on the ketogenic diet. *Developmental Medicine and Child Neurology, 44*, 796–802.

Walker, M.C., & Shorvon, S.D. (1996). Treatment of status epilepticus and serial seizures. In S.D. Shorvon, F. Dreifuss, D.R. Fish, & D. Thomas, (Eds.), *The treatment of epilepsy* (pp. 269–285). Oxford: Blackwell.

Williams, G.T., Gold, A.P., Shrout, P., Shaffer, D., & Adams, D. (1979). The impact of psychiatric intervention on patients with uncontrolled seizures. *Journal of Nervous and Mental Diseases, 167*, 626–631.

Zifkin, B.G., & Kasteleijn-Nolst, T.D. (2000). Reflex epilepsy and reflex seizures of the visual system: A clinical review. *Epileptic Disorders, 2*, 129–136.

Chapter 10

Chronic pain

Richard W. Hanson

Chronic pain is a widespread problem in western nations. Although prevalence estimates vary across studies, a conservative estimate is that at least 10 per cent of the adult population suffers from some form of chronic benign pain (Verhaak *et al.*, 1998). It should be kept in mind, however, that many of those with chronic pain do not necessarily seek or require specialized pain management services. Some manage their pain mostly outside of the conventional healthcare system, whereas others do use the healthcare system, but are relatively satisfied with the care they receive. Most in the latter group are cared for by a single practitioner who monitors their pain condition, prescribes appropriate medication, and draws upon consulting specialists as needed. A third subgroup includes those chronic pain patients who are not satisfied with the care they receive through the conventional medical system. These individuals complain that their pain is inadequately controlled and often show deterioration in their daily functioning. They are much more likely to have seen a variety of medical specialists and treated unsuccessfully with a variety of medications and physical procedures including surgery and other invasive measures. Such individuals are most likely to be referred to pain specialists, tertiary chronic pain treatment clinics, and multidisciplinary pain centers.

In all likelihood, many persons in the first two groups use healthier psychological coping methods to manage their pain while drawing upon available social supports and other personal resources. They are able to continue meeting most of their normal role expectations with respect to family and work. Those in the first two groups have for the most part accepted the fact that they have a chronic condition and are no longer actively seeking biomedical cure. Instead, their focus is on managing their pain and doing their best to carry on their lives despite chronic pain.

Those in the third group are less accepting of their pain condition and thus place more demands on healthcare providers. In addition to being dissatisfied with their medical care, these individuals are more likely to possess other features of the chronic pain syndrome such as excessive activity intolerance, sleep disturbance, alcohol or drug abuse, family discord, significant emotional distress, and comorbid psychiatric disorders such as major depression. These difficult chronic pain patients present the greatest challenge to the conventional healthcare system and have received the most attention in the chronic pain literature. Some present vague and unusual pain complaints, or complaints that seem out of proportion to medical test findings. As a result, they may be dismissed by their healthcare practitioner as "psychosomatic", exaggerating their pain for "secondary gain", or malingering. Such patients are often assumed to be disability seeking, drug seeking, or attention seeking. However, from the patient's perspective, an often heard complaint is that doctors do not take their pain complaints seriously or dismiss them by suggesting that the pain is "all in their head".

Without question, psychosocial factors such as secondary gain can play a contributing role in the pain complaints of those in the treatment-resistant group. However, it would be a mistake to dismiss all their complaints in this manner. Recently, attention has been called to the fact that chronic pain patients are often undertreated by their physicians, in large part due to misconceptions or overconcerns regarding potential addiction to pain medications (McCaffery & Pasero, 1999). In fact, there has been a shift in attitude among many pain specialists during the past decade toward more aggressive medical management of all types of pain, including chronic, nonmalignant pain. In the past, discontinuance of pain medications, especially opioids, was considered a primary goal of chronic pain management programs (Gildenberg & DeVaul, 1985). Beginning with Melzack's (1990) influential paper on the tragedy of needless pain and advocates such as Portnoy (1990, 1996), it has become much more acceptable and even desirable to treat chronic pain patients with more powerful pain relievers. While use of opioids is becoming increasingly common among pain specialists, many physicians are still very reluctant to utilize these medications due to fears of creating addiction or incurring sanctions by regulatory agencies. Distinctions are now drawn between physical dependence and addiction. The former is a normally occurring pharmacological consequence of taking the drug, whereas addiction is a psychiatric problem characterized by impaired control over drug use, compulsive use, continued use despite harm, and craving. Guidelines are being offered to protect physician and patient alike from possible abuses stemming from use of opioids.

Chronic pain patients who have not responded well to conventional medical management approaches require thorough assessment that takes into account biomedical disease indicators, medical treatments attempted thus far, and psychosocial factors. This comprehensive biopsychosocial assessment becomes the basis for interdisciplinary case formulation and developing appropriate treatment strategies.

Conceptual framework: the biopsychosocial model

Traditional biomedicine has regarded pain as a symptom reflecting physical injury or disease processes. As such, the focus of diagnosis and treatment is primarily on the underlying tissue damage, rather than on the pain itself. It is assumed that once appropriate treatment and/or natural healing occurs, the pain will disappear. While this is indeed the case with acute pain, the assumption does not fit chronic pain. The acute biomedical model is clearly inadequate in addressing the needs of many chronic pain sufferers (Hanson & Gerber, 1990; Turk & Okifuji, 1999). Rather than being viewed merely as a symptom, chronic pain should be treated as a chronic illness in and of itself. That is, when it is no longer possible to correct underlying pathophysiology, the focus of treatment must shift to the pain itself and its effects on the pain sufferer.

Due to shortcomings of the acute biomedical model of pain in addressing these problems, alternative conceptualizations of chronic pain have arisen. Multidimensional, biopsychosocial systems models are considered to be a more appropriate alternative (Hanson & Gerber, 1990; Turk & Monarch, 2002). These expanded models consider not only the pain complaints and associated physical findings, but also many psychological, social, and cultural factors that can contribute to the development of a chronic pain condition, the perpetuation of the pain syndrome, and response to medical treatment. Psychosocial factors include depression and anxiety, personality disorders, defective coping styles, autonomic stress reactions, noncompliance with treatment, somatizing tendencies, disturbances in interpersonal relationships, beliefs about control of pain, self-efficacy and cognitive distortions, and involvement with disability compensation systems (Weisberg & Clavel, 1999). This expanded conceptualization has led to multimodal, multidisciplinary treatment approaches.

Multimodal, multidisciplinary treatment

Most of the early multidisciplinary treatment programs were based upon the realization that behavioural factors play a significant role in the development or maintenance of chronic pain. The behavioural model developed by Fordyce (1976) focused on overt pain behaviour and conceptualized such behaviour as based on either respondent or operant conditioning principles. Respondent pain, controlled by antecedent nociceptive stimuli (e.g. physical injury), became the paradigm for acute pain. Operant pain, controlled by consequent stimuli or environmental reinforcers, became the paradigm for chronic pain. Primary treatment goals included reduction in pain behaviour, increase in activity level (reduction in functional impairment), reduced pain-related healthcare utilization, and promotion of healthy, well behaviour. Treatment programs were largely inpatient, enabling greater control over environmental reinforcers, and utilized the expertise of physical medicine specialists, physical and occupational therapists, as well as psychologists. Involvement of the patient's family was considered important as well. Another common goal of early multidisciplinary programs involved reduction in pain medications (primarily opioids) and tranquilizers through use of the "pain cocktail" where the target drugs where gradually faded out. Several outcome studies have documented the effectiveness of these "operant programs" (Sanders, 2002).

Later, multidisciplinary programs that included a psychological component have incorporated cognitive-behavioural principles and techniques as originally detailed by Turk *et al.* (1983). Rather than limiting the focus to overt pain behaviour, cognitive-behavioural approaches have addressed private events including pain appraisals, beliefs and attitudes, and cognitive coping skills. A number of cognitive-behavioural techniques are now utilized such as relaxation and broader stress-management training, cognitive restructuring, cognitive therapy for depression, problem solving, and training in specific coping skills. Cognitive-behavioural techniques have been utilized with a number of chronic pain conditions and have been subjected to considerable research evaluation. As a result, such methods now enjoy strong empirical support (Morley *et al.*, 1999).

Although the effectiveness of comprehensive, multidisciplinary pain management programs has been demonstrated (Gatchel & Turk, 1999; Okifuji *et al.*, 1999), not all patients require this level of care. Furthermore, with increased emphasis on cost containment, insurers and other governmental funding sources are increasingly reluctant to pay for intensive multidisciplinary treatment (Turk, 2001). Inpatient programs have given way to mostly outpatient treatment. With the development of new pain medications and increased acceptance of opioids in the management of chronic nonmalignant pain, many patients are now being treated primarily with medications. In addition, biomedical pain specialists have developed more sophisticated opioid delivery systems (e.g. spinal administration, implantable pumps) along with other technological procedures aimed at altering neural pathways (e.g. anesthetic nerve blocks, direct neural stimulation, neurolytic techniques).

It has been suggested that specialists in the treatment of chronic pain have evolved largely into two camps that has led to some confusion among consumers (Loeser, 2001). Although these camps are by no means mutually exclusive, there are those who primarily utilize medication and other passive technological procedures, whereas other pain specialists place more emphasis on physical rehabilitative and psychological approaches.

Treatment goals: palliation or functional improvement?

Pain specialists who emphasize use of medications and passive medical procedures are primarily interested in facilitating pain relief, whereas those emphasizing physical rehabilitation and psychological approaches aim more for improved function. Specific functional restoration goals have included return to work, performing household chores, engaging in recreational activities and improved social functioning. The multidisciplinary pain programs, beginning with Fordyce's operant program and later including cognitive-behavioural methods, clearly place greater importance on improvements in functioning, although some patients also report reductions in pain intensity. It was also assumed by the multidisciplinary programs that improvements in daily functioning resulted not only from acquisition of psychological coping strategies and physical reconditioning exercises, but also through decreased reliance on pain medications.

Now that the pendulum is swinging in favor of using pain medications for chronic nonmalignant pain, one of the hot issues today is whether aggressive palliation of pain is associated with commensurate improvements in daily functioning. In other words, if we can significantly reduce a patient's pain intensity through medications, does this mean that the patient will automatically become more active and productive (less disabled)? Moreover, does substantive pain relief also lead to amelioration of the negative psychological consequences of chronic pain (less distressed)? If the answers are yes, aggressive use of medications and other procedures aimed at pain relief would potentially offer a more cost-effective approach to treatment.

Unfortunately, there is currently a lack of research to address these important questions. The use of chronic opioid therapy for chronic nonmalignant pain has recently been reviewed (Harden, 2002; Ballantyne & Mao, 2003). The evidence available thus far indicates that palliation does not automatically lead to improvements in function or mood. In some cases, opioids can interfere with the rehabilitative process (e.g. the patient may be too somnolent to participate in active physical therapies). On the other hand, if a patient is in too much pain to participate in these therapies, rehabilitation and functional restoration are undermined as well. Consequently, what is needed is greater balance between the goals of palliation and functional restoration.

In addition to biases regarding the preferred type of treatment (passive procedures vs. active rehabilitation) and treatment goals (palliation vs. functional restoration), it has been suggested that optimal treatment has been hampered by the "patient uniformity myth" which is the assumption that chronic pain patients in general or even large subgroups of such patients (e.g. those with low back pain) constitute a homogeneous group (Turk & Okifuji, 1998). Rather than basing treatment on the needs of a specific patient, the practitioner's training and preferences often determine the treatment utilized. Furthermore, even multidisciplinary, multicomponent pain treatment programs often use a "shotgun" approach wherein all patients receive essentially the same treatment elements. Turk and Okifuji (1998) argue that empirically derived classification of pain patients based on multiaxial assessment can lead to more specific treatment approaches.

Interdisciplinary case formulation

The essence of case formulation for chronic pain sufferers who are not adequately managed with basic medical care is a determination of which specific treatment procedures and treatment goals are most appropriate for a given patient. Very often this requires assessment from an interdisciplinary, biopsychosocial perspective, as well as genuine collaboration between the patient and treating pain specialists.

The remainder of this chapter will briefly summarize our interdisciplinary approach to case formulation with chronic pain sufferers. In that the focus of this volume is on behavioural medicine, more attention will be given to the psychological portion of the interdisciplinary assessment. Although our own experience with interdisciplinary assessment is primarily with those reporting chronic back pain, a similar process can be used for those with other chronic pain conditions as well. All patients seen in our chronic back pain clinic jointly undergo physical rehabilitation medicine and psychological evaluations. An internal medicine specialist is also part of this clinic. After examining the patient, the physicians and psychologist meet together in case conference to integrate their findings and generate treatment plans.

Medical evaluation

The medical component of the evaluation includes careful review of current pain complaints, history of the pain condition, available medical test data, and medical treatments tried thus far. The physical examination includes observations regarding the patient's posture and gait; range of motion in the neck, trunk and extremities (including movements which cause pain); and palpation of soft tissue (noting occurrence of trigger points, areas of tenderness, or muscle spasms). A brief neurological examination may include assessment of reflexes, pinprick sensation, and muscle strength. During the course of the physical examination, clinicians should observe the occurrence of pain behaviours and signs of emotional distress. Behavioural signs and symptoms that should be noted include vague, ill localized, inconsistent, and unusual complaints that are difficult to explain from known anatomical and pathological mechanisms. Some specific questions to be considered during the medical evaluation are the following:

1   Does the patient present "red flags" suggesting serious organic pathology?
2   Is the patient in need of additional diagnostic testing to clarify the origin of the pain complaints, rule out other serious pathology, or arrive at a working diagnosis?
3   Have all reasonable medical treatments been tried or given a fair trial?
4   Is the patient's pain being adequately controlled with medication?

5   To what extent does the patient's pain complaints and disability corres-
     pond with the medical examination?
6   To what extent is the patient actually seeking pain relief and improve-
     ment in function as opposed to diagnosis, medical validation of pain
     condition, and support of physical disability claims.

Behavioural medicine evaluation

Some chronic pain patients are resistant to the idea of being examined by a
mental health professional. This is particularly the case for those who believe
that their pain complaints have not been taken seriously or there have been
implicit or explicit suggestions that their pain is psychologically based. Care
must be taken in how patients are approached in order to enlist full cooperation and address their complaints in a collaborative manner. We typically
begin the interaction by indicating that we are interested in finding out how
the pain has impacted their lives and how they go about coping with the pain.
Sometimes, when there is clear reluctance to speak with a psychologist, we
inform the patient that our professional involvement is with those presenting
physical pain conditions in contrast to many other psychologists or psychi-
atrists who specialize in treating mental and emotional problems. Most of
our evaluations include both interview and administration of selected tests
and questionnaires. Following are some key issues that we address in our
psychological evaluation of chronic back pain sufferers:

1   A brief history of the chronic pain condition with an emphasis on how
     the patient has come to conceptualize this problem.
2   Perceptions regarding the degree to which the pain interferes with vari-
     ous daily activities along with the types and amounts of activity actually
     engaged in by the patient.
3   Patient's view of medical treatments tried thus far and attitudes regard-
     ing further medical treatment.
4   What the patient does to cope with pain on his/her own and degree of
     perceived control over the pain.
5   Presence of associated psychological/behavioural problems including
     mood disturbance, problems with cognition, characterological problems,
     history of victimization or trauma, ongoing psychosocial stressors, and
     substance abuse.
6   Available social supports and the role these social supports play
     in encouraging healthy functioning as opposed to reinforcing pain
     behaviour.
7   Employment and disability status, attitudes regarding return to work,
     disability seeking behaviour, past and present leisure time activities.
8   Degree of readiness for undertaking psychological pain self-management
     training.

Interview

Much of the above information can be obtained by a thorough interview. We typically begin the interview by focusing briefly on the pain history and reported success with various treatment approaches. To lessen possible defensiveness over the idea of speaking to a mental health professional we attempt to convey through our choice of questions that we are primarily interested in the pain condition and how it has impacted their life. Many end up feeling grateful that a healthcare professional has taken the time to listen to their point of view. After having explored the pain complaints, perceptions of disability, and treatment approaches utilized thus far, we turn our attention to psychosocial issues including work and family information, hobbies and recreation activities, and psychiatric history. In an attempt to identify other major stressful or traumatic life events, we may later ask "Aside from your pain condition what is the worst thing that has ever happened to you, how did you handle it, and is it still affecting you in any way?" It may also be useful to specifically address the question of prior sexual or physical abuse given the growing body of literature that has linked such experiences with later chronic pain conditions (Drossman *et al.*, 1990; Wurtele *et al.*, 1990; Linton *et al.*, 1996; Linton, 2002).

Use of questionnaires

A number of pain-related questionnaires have been developed which can help the clinician to better understand the cognitive, affective, and behavioural aspects of chronic pain (Bradley & McKendree-Smith, 2001; DeGood & Tait, 2001). Since it is far beyond the scope of this chapter to review the large number of questionnaires that are currently available, the focus will be on a few relatively brief instruments that we have found useful in arriving at chronic pain case formulation. These include the Multidimensional Pain Inventory (MPI), Coping Strategies Questionnaire (CSQ), and Survey of Pain Attitudes (SOPA). In addition, we typically include a rating of perceived physical impairments and a Beck Depression Inventory (BDI).

The MPI (Kerns *et al.*, 1985; Turk & Rudy, 1987, 1988) is a 56-item instrument that includes 13 empirically derived scales divided into three sections. The first section assesses (a) pain severity; (b) interference of pain with daily functioning including family and marital functioning; work and social-recreational activities; (c) perceived control over pain and life events; (d) affective distress; (e) perceived support from a spouse or significant other. The second section assesses patients' perceptions regarding how their spouse or significant other responds to displays of pain. Three types of responses measured include (a) punishing responses; (b) solicitous responses; (c) distracting responses. The third section assesses the extent to which the patient engages in various activities including (a) household chores; (b) outdoor work; (c) activities away from home; (d) social activities; (e) a composite rating of general activities.

In addition to scores on each scale, three profile patterns are derived from the MPI. The "dysfunctional" pattern is based on relatively high pain severity, pain interference and affective distress, and low life control and general activity level. The "interpersonally distressed" pattern includes those with low perceived social support along with high punishing responses and low solicitous and distracting responses from significant others. Finally, "adaptive copers" are the opposite of the dysfunctional group and include those with low pain severity, pain interference and affective distress, and high life control and general activity. These three empirically derived groups form the basis of Turk and Rudy's (1990) Multiaxial Assessment of Pain (MAP) system.

The Coping Strategies Questionnaire (Rosenstiel & Keefe, 1983) is a 50-item, rationally derived instrument that assesses six cognitive and two behavioural coping strategies. Cognitive coping strategies include (a) diverting attention; (b) reinterpreting pain sensations; (c) coping self-statements; (d) ignoring pain sensations; (e) praying or hoping; (f) catastrophizing. The two behavioural coping scales are (a) increasing activity level, referring to activities that divert attention away from pain; (b) increasing pain behaviour, which includes pain behaviours that reduce pain sensations. Two additional items concern the patient's perceived control over pain and ability to reduce pain. Although the CSQ has been the most widely used pain coping inventory, a more recent alternative coping measure is the Chronic Pain Coping Inventory (Jensen et al., 1995; Hadjistavropoulos et al., 1999).

The Survey of Pain Attitudes (Jensen et al., 1987; M.P. Jensen et al., 1994) is a 57-item, rationally derived questionnaire that yields scores on seven pain-related beliefs. These include: (a) perceived control over pain; (b) belief in oneself as being disabled by pain; (c) belief in a medical cure for pain and that it is the responsibility of the medical profession to find that cure; (d) belief in the appropriateness of solicitous responses from family members when in pain; (e) belief in the appropriateness of medications to manage pain; (f) belief in the effects of emotions on pain experience; (g) belief that pain indicates damage and that activity can cause harm. Two shorter versions of the SOPA have also been developed containing 30 and 35 items respectively (Tait & Chibnall, 1997; Jensen et al., 2000). We have chosen to continue using the full version due to its greater psychometric reliability (Jensen et al., 2000).

It is also useful to obtain information regarding the impact of pain on the patient's daily physical activities. As indicated above, the MPI provides ratings of perceived interference with daily activities and ratings as to how often the patient engages in various physical activities. In addition, we typically ask patients to rate the extent to which pain interferes with family/home responsibilities, recreation, social activity, work, sexual activity, self-care, and life support activity including eating, sleeping, and breathing.

Assessment of depression is important due to its high comorbidity with chronic pain (Banks & Kerns, 1996). We use the Beck Depression Inventory (BDI-II) for that purpose since it has been widely used in chronic pain research. Some clinicians may also wish to include questionnaires that assess anxiety or anger.

Integrating medical and behavioural medicine evaluations

Following separate evaluations by the pain management physician and behavioural medicine specialist, it is recommended that the evaluators meet in interdisciplinary team conference to discuss findings and formulate a treatment plan. Treatment goals can be developed for medical and physical rehabilitative procedures as well as need for behavioural medicine interventions. This initial case formulation and treatment plan should be followed by a conference with the patient wherein the various recommendations and treatment options can be discussed, patient questions can be answered, and a mutually agreed treatment plan can be developed. It is also often useful to include the patient's family in this discussion. Medical and behavioural medicine aspects of the case formulation are discussed below. Examples will be given for behavioural medicine case formulation.

Medical case formulation

Medical case formulation is largely concerned with the biological component of the biopsychosocial model. Ideally, the examining physician should be somewhat familiar with the chronic pain literature and understand the relative role that biomedical factors play in relation to psychosocial factors for many chronic pain conditions. It is now known that psychosocial variables are often just as important or even more important than so-called objective biomedical indicators. Psychosocial factors can predict who develops chronic pain following acute injuries (Gatchel & Epker, 1999) and can contribute to the perpetuation of the problem. There is also ample evidence that the relationship between biomedical disease indicators and subjective reports of pain and disability are quite variable. This is especially the case when considering chronic low back pain and other musculoskeletal pain conditions. Some patients report significant back pain in the absence of structural spinal abnormalities (Frymoyer, 1988), while several magnetic resonance imaging (MRI) studies of nonsymptomatic ("pain-free") volunteers have indicated the presence of considerable spinal pathology (Boden et al., 1990; M.C. Jensen et al., 1994). Likewise, some chronic pain conditions, such as fibromyalgia, are characterized by the absence of specific disease indicators. As a result, medical practitioners need to be cautious about making too many inferences from either the presence or absence of detectable biomedical disease indictors. With these considerations in mind, decisions should be made regarding the need for:

- additional medical diagnostic tests
- surgical or other specialty medical consultations
- changes in the medication regimen
- physical rehabilitative approaches
- special pain management procedures
- supplemental prosthetic devices.

Although decisions regarding these medical issues are primarily dependent on the expertise of the examining physician, interdisciplinary collaboration with a behavioural medicine specialist may be important as well. This is especially relevant when considering use of opioid analgesics, spinal surgery, and other costly and invasive pain control procedures. A stepwise biopsychosocial approach to screening for such procedures is summarized by Gatchel (2001).

One frequently encountered component of medical case formulation relates to medication management. It should be determined whether the patient is receiving the most appropriate type and amount of analgesic medication. Selection of analgesics should always consider the following goals: (a) reduction in pain intensity to a manageable level; (b) improvement in daily functioning; (c) minimizing adverse side effects. Here it is useful to follow the basic three-step analgesic ladder beginning with non-opioids and reserving more potent opioids for severe pain. Decisions regarding initiation, modification, or discontinuance of opioid therapy are best made following collaboration with the behavioural medicine specialist. Actual or potential misuse of opioid medication is a particular problem issue that needs to be addressed. Patients with substance abuse histories in particular require special consideration. Issues involved in the screening of patients who are at risk for opioid abuse have been discussed by Robinson et al. (2001). When opioid therapy is initiated, the use of a written opioid agreement between patient and prescribing physician is recommended. Such agreements spell out the treatment goals, risks, patient responsibilities, and other required conditions for continued treatment. Additional guidelines for using opioid therapy with chronic nonmalignant pain patients may be found elsewhere (Irving & Wallace, 1996; Merskey & Moulin, 1999). Along with analgesics, decisions should be made regarding use of adjuvant or co-analgesic medications. These may include antidepressants, anticonvulsants, skeletal muscle relaxants, corticosteroids, sedatives and hypnotics, topical agents, etc.

Along with medications, consideration may be given to use of special pain management interventions including trigger point and other local injections, acupuncture, anesthetic nerve blocks (e.g. epidural steroid injections), intraspinal drug infusion including implanted opioid delivery systems, spinal cord electrical stimulation and other forms of neurostimulation, nerve destruction approaches, etc. Although some of these procedures are relatively benign, decisions regarding use of other more invasive and costly procedures such as implantable pain modalities should involve interdisciplinary assessment and collaboration. As discussed by Prager and Jacobs (2001), behavioural factors should always be considered in the pre-screening process for such procedures.

Physical rehabilitative procedures are often part of the overall treatment plan for chronic pain patients. Passive procedures aimed at symptomatic relief include massage, heat therapies, cryotherapy, transcutaneous electrical nerve stimulation (TENS), ultrasound and diathermy, and spinal manipulation among others. Since many chronic pain patients suffer from significant deconditioning associated with activity reduction and disuse, we prefer development of a more active exercise regimen including joint mobilization (stretching), muscle toning, and aerobic exercises. Recommendations regarding active physical exercise may also serve as one component of a weight reduction plan as it is well known that obesity can serve a contributing role for several chronic pain conditions. Along with exercise, patients may require instruction in improving their posture, using proper body mechanics, activity pacing, and work simplification procedures.

Behavioural medicine case formulation

The first issue to be considered is whether or not further behavioural medicine treatment is indicated. In some cases, psychological treatment approaches are simply not indicated, while in other cases psychological pain management is indicated but rejected by the patient. For those in the former group, the medical and physical rehabilitative treatment options listed above may be sufficient for their needs. This is especially true for those who have not yet received adequate medical pain management and show little evidence that psychological factors are contributing to their pain condition. In the later group are those who could potentially benefit from behavioural medicine approaches, such as training in psychological pain coping skills, but are unwilling to even consider these approaches. Some patients view their problems in strictly medical terms, are only interested in medical treatment, and are resistant to viewing their condition from a biopsychosocial perspective. Although these individuals are initially reluctant to consider psychological approaches, an attempt should be made to educate patients regarding their potential value before assuming that they are not appropriate candidates for such approaches.

Many chronic pain patients are amenable to and can profit from behavioural medicine treatment. At one end of the spectrum are those individuals who are functioning reasonably well but are interested in learning non-pharmacological pain management alternatives. At the other end are those presenting significant psychological and interpersonal problems that interfere with their daily functioning. Those in the former group may show relatively little evidence of psychological distress and be classified as "adaptive coper" on the Multidimensional Pain Inventory. Nevertheless, they may still benefit from behavioural medicine treatment aimed at expanding their personal repertoire of pain coping skills. Such treatment may include bio-feedback training, hypnotic procedures, guided imagery, relaxation and medi-tation exercises, and instruction in other cognitive and behavioural coping techniques:

> Ms. A is a 48-year-old, divorced, employed woman who was referred to the pain clinic because of chronic low back pain. Medical evaluation indicated the presence of mechanical back pain probably associated with MRI findings of degenerative disk disease. The patient had already tried chiropractic manipulation, acupuncture, and passive physical therapy modalities with short-term pain relief. She was not interested in surgery or any other invasive treatments. Although both non-opioid and opioid pain relievers had been prescribed, she expressed a reluctance to rely too heavily on pain medication due to concerns about adverse side effects. Psychological evaluation found no evidence of clinically signifi-cant depression or anxiety; however, she did report some stress stemming from her work demands. Aside from receipt of psychological counseling around the time of her divorce, she reported no history of psychiatric problems, including alcohol or drug abuse. Her two young adult children were doing well and she reported having good social supports. At team conference it was agreed that no additional medical treatments or changes in her medication regimen were indicated. Since the patient had expressed some interest in learning better self-management techniques for both stress and pain control, it was decided to offer her training in relaxation and other stress management techniques to which she agreed.

Chronic pain patients who do present psychosocial problems that cause distress and/or interfere with adaptive functioning require careful consider-ation. Examples of such problems include clinical depression, post-traumatic stress and other anxiety disorders, difficulties with anger control, substance abuse and dependence, marital and family discord, and problems coping with psychosocial stressors. These comorbid psychological and interpersonal problems may require special attention and focused treatment aside from or in addition to pain self-management training. At times, assessment may sug-gest that these psychological problems even overshadow the chronic pain complaints.

During the interview process, an attempt should be made to determine the link between these psychological problems and the chronic pain condition. As part of behavioural medicine case formulation, decisions will have to be made whether to primarily target the pain condition as the focus of treatment or the specific psychological problems. In some cases the psychological prob-lem appears to stem directly from the pain condition whereas in other cases it is due more to non-pain-related factors. For example, a patient who is abusing alcohol may be doing so because the analgesics that have been prescribed are insufficient to reduce the pain. Another patient may present problems with alcohol dependence that are longstanding and appear to be independent of the pain condition. Likewise a patient who is significantly depressed may be reacting to the frustrations of trying to cope with severe intractable pain and perceived inability to perform many valued activities. Another patient's depression may stem from life problems that have little to do with the pain condition. When it appears that the psychological problems result directly from difficulties coping with the pain condition, the appropriate focus may be finding ways to better manage the pain through more aggressive medical management and/or training in self-management techniques. In such cases it is hoped that with improved pain management the psychological problems will automatically decrease. Patients who abuse alcohol due to insufficient pain medication will no longer need to do so once appropriate medications are given. Patients whose depression results from the disabling consequences of uncontrollable pain will become less depressed as they are given more effective methods to manage the pain, whether those methods are medical or psychological.

Two specific psychological problems in particular have been identified in the chronic pain literature as being associated with increased distress and maladaptive coping. These are catastrophizing and fear avoidance. Catastrophizing as applied to pain refers to a cognitive process wherein one has excessive or exaggerated negative expectations regarding the pain condition or ability to cope with it. Catastrophizing, as assessed by the Coping Strategies Questionnaire and other instruments, has been associated with higher levels of psychological distress, poorer physical function and disability, higher ratings of pain intensity, reports of greater interference of pain with daily activities, lower levels of general activity, higher rates of psychosocial dysfunction, and reduced ability to work (specific research studies cited by Boothby et al., 1999). Recent evidence indicates that catastrophizing is predictive of psychological distress, pain intensity, and disability independent of actual physical impairment (Severeijns et al., 2001). Pain patients who report high levels of catastrophizing are clearly in need of alternative cognitive strategies or restructuring techniques that promote more realistic appraisals, or decentering techniques that help reduce the emotional impact of catastrophic cognitions.

Fear avoidance represents another significant psychological problem identified in the chronic pain literature (see review by Vlaeyen & Linton, 2000). This problem refers to excessive avoidance of movements or activities thought to be associated with pain as a result of fear. This pattern not only interferes with adaptive coping but also contributes to the development of chronic pain and disability following acute injury (Fritz et al., 2001). In addition to emotional distress from pain-related fears, this pattern is associated with increased self-reported disability and avoidance of physical activity. Prolonged avoidance of activity leads to further deconditioning through disuse, decreased pain/activity tolerance, and greater functional impairment. Patients with such fears tend to score high on the Harm Scale of the Survey of Pain Attitudes. Other instruments that can be used to specifically assess this problem are the Fear and Avoidance Beliefs Questionnaire (FABQ) by Waddell *et al.* (1993) and the Tampa Scale for Kinesiophobia by Kori *et al.* (1990). Patients who present these pain-related fears and avoidance behaviours can benefit from multidisciplinary treatment with two primary objectives. First, they must be provided with clear education, preferably from a physician, regarding the effects of activity and inactivity on their pain condition and general physical health. In particular, patients need to be taught that their pain actually represents a relatively common and benign condition that can be self-managed rather than a serious condition that needs careful protection. Second, they require graded exposure to those physical activities and movements that have come to be viewed as dangerous or threatening (Vlaeyan *et al.*, 2002). Working together, a psychologist and physiotherapist can help the patient develop a hierarchy of specific physical activity goals or exercises which can be pursued in a step-by-step manner (Linton, 1994). For other examples of chronic pain programs that combine physical therapy and psychological self-management approaches, see Moore *et al.* (1999) and Siegel *et al.* (2001).

> Mr. B is a 52-year-old, married, unemployed gentleman with a 25-year history of chronic low back pain. Although he had successfully coped with the pain during most of this time, he reported that pain had become much more severe during the past two years. As a result, he had quit his job, stopped most of his prior social and recreational activities, and become extremely inactive. During the physical exam he showed significant pain behaviour along with bracing and slow, guarded movements. An MRI indicated the presence of degenerative disk disease in the lumbar spine. There were no "red flags" suggesting the presence of significant medical problems. The psychological evaluation indicated that he believed that pain was significantly interfering with his life activities and that he had very little control over the pain or its consequences. He admitted feeling frustrated, depressed, and irritable. He denied any past history of psychiatric problems. Further assessment indicated significant fear avoidance regarding physical activity along with deconditioning syndrome. At team conference it was agreed that the patient needed clear medical feedback regarding the status of his back and the fact that a progressive physical reconditioning program would be beneficial rather than detrimental. It was also agreed that the patient would benefit from a multidisciplinary treatment approach combining active physical rehabilitation with training in psychological self-management approaches.

Some patients present significant psychological problems that seem to be due to factors other than their pain condition. These primary psychological problems may have been present prior to the onset of pain or be attributed to situations and events that have little to do with chronic pain or its consequences. Stated otherwise, these problems would likely persist even if the pain magically disappeared. For example, in our own work with US military veterans, we encounter a number of individuals with non-military-related pain conditions who also suffer from post-traumatic stress disorder stemming from their combat experiences during wartime. Others with chronic pain suffer residual effects of having been repeatedly abused or victimized as children. Some present significant family stressors, socio-economic problems, personal losses, or other major health problems. Still others present longstanding characterological problems such as antisocial, borderline, or narcissistic personality disorders. As part of the behavioural medicine case formulation process, decisions will have to be made whether to separately target these non-pain-related problems for treatment. This becomes most relevant in those cases where the psychological and social problems have an adverse impact on the person's ability to cope with chronic pain, exacerbate the degree of distress associated with pain, or interfere with response to medical treatment. We inform patients that they must be psychiatrically stable before we can initiate pain management training. For example, patients who are actively abusing alcohol or are acutely suicidal should have these issues addressed first.

Ms. C is a 34-year-old, recently separated woman with a history of multiple pain complaints and uncertain etiology. She was recently given a diagnosis of fibromyalgia and chronic fatigue syndrome. During the medical evaluation, she expressed considerable dissatisfaction with previous treating doctors whom she felt did not take her problems seriously. During the physical examination she expressed significant pain complaints including a number of tender areas upon palpation, and muscle weakness in all extremities. Laboratory tests and imaging studies were within normal limits. She had already tried a number of analgesics (non-opioid and opioid) but found none of them helpful. The psychological evaluation found evidence of significant depression including suicidal thoughts, dysfunctional pain coping, and ongoing psychosocial stressors. She was going through a divorce after having been involved in an abusive relationship and had recently lost her job due to excessive absenteeism. Further exploration revealed a history of sexual molestation by her alcoholic father and grief over her inability to bear children following a hysterectomy two years previously. She reported no prior psychiatric treatment. It was agreed during interdisciplinary team conference that psychosocial factors were playing a significant contributing role to her physical complaints and that she was in need of both antidepressant medication and individual psychotherapy to help her better manage her immediate life stressors as well as her previous traumas. It was also agreed that she could benefit from physical therapy and referral to an agency for social assistance. When presenting the treatment plan to the patient, care was taken to accept the validity of her pain complaints while stressing the need to use a multifaceted, multidisciplinary approach to her chronic pain condition.

Case formulation with such difficult and challenging patients must consider available treatment options to address these additional problem issues. Such options may include psychopharmacological treatment, stress management training, individual or group psychotherapy, marital or family counseling, chemical dependence treatment, vocational rehabilitation training, and referral to appropriate community resources including support groups and social welfare agencies.

Conclusion

Pain is a common problem and a frequent reason for physician visits. Despite the existence of a variety of effective treatment options, many persons with chronic nonmalignant pain conditions are not well managed and continue to suffer needlessly. The focus here has been on that subgroup of chronic pain sufferers who are not well managed and are dissatisfied with the care they have received.

This chapter has endeavored to make two key points. First, in order to arrive at effective treatment strategies, chronic pain must be viewed from a multidimensional, biopsychosocial perspective. Attempts to compartmentalize chronic pain as either physical (requiring only medical treatment) or psychological (requiring only psychological intervention) are misguided and do the patient a disservice. Furthermore, treatment goals should be broadly considered and include not only reduction in pain intensity but also improvement in daily functioning. In many cases it is necessary to address associated psychological and social problems that impact the pain condition and response to treatment.

Second, in order to determine the most effective course of treatment for a given individual, an interdisciplinary evaluation and case formulation approach is highly recommended. At a minimum, this should include medical and psychological evaluations by professionals who are familiar with the chronic pain literature, including the potential contributions of both physical and psychosocioeconomic factors. After discussing and integrating the findings, an appropriate treatment plan can be developed which may include some combination of pharmacological, physical rehabilitation, and psychological approaches. In some cases, more invasive medical pain control procedures may be recommended. However, even in these instances, psychological factors should be considered as they may play an important role in eventual outcome.

Finally, it is important that interdisciplinary case formulation and treatment recommendations be reviewed with the patient and family members in a collaborative manner. Efforts should be made to respond to patient questions, obtain their informed consent, and enlist their full cooperation prior to embarking on any treatment option. Patient cooperation and commitment to a course of therapy can often be enhanced by allowing choice within an array of treatment options. For example, patients vary considerably with respect to their relative interest in pharmacological as compared to non-pharmacological interventions. Pain clinicians need to be sensitive and receptive to patient preferences rather than try to impose their preferred treatments onto the patient.

References

Ballantyne, J.C., & Mao, J. (2003). Opioid therapy for chronic pain. *New England Journal of Medicine, 349*, 1943–1953.

Banks, S.M., & Kerns, R.D. (1996). Explaining high rates of depression in chronic pain: A stress-diathesis framework. *Psychological Bulletin, 119*, 95–110.

Boden, S.D., Davis, D.O., Dina, T.S., Patronas, N.J., & Wiesel, S.W. (1990). Abnormal magnetic-resonance scans of the lumbar spine in asymptomatic subjects: A prospective investigation. *Journal of Bone and Joint Surgery, 72*, 403–408.

Boothby, J.L., Thorn, B.E., Stroud, M.W., & Jensen, M.P. (1999). Coping with pain. In R.J. Gatchel & D.C. Turk (Eds.), *Psychosocial factors in pain: Critical perspectives*. New York: Guilford Press.

Bradley, L.A., & McKendree-Smith, N.L. (2001). Assessment of psychological status using interviews and self-report instruments. In D.C. Turk and R. Melzack (Eds.), *Handbook of pain assessment* (2nd ed.). New York: Guilford Press.

DeGood, D.E., & Tait, R.C. (2001). Assessment of pain beliefs and pain coping. In D.C. Turk & R. Melzack (Eds.), *Handbook of pain assessment* (2nd ed.). New York: Guilford Press.

Drossman, D.A., Leserman, J., Nachman, G., Zhiming, L., Gluck, H., Toomey, T.C., & Mitchell, C.M. (1990). Sexual and physical abuse in women with functional or organic gastrointestinal disorders. *Annuals of Internal Medicine, 113*, 828–833.

Fordyce, W.E. (1976). *Behavioral methods for chronic pain and illness*. St. Louis: Mosby.

Fritz, J.M., George, S.Z., & Delitto, A. (2001). The role of fear-avoidance beliefs in acute low back pain: Relations with current and future disability and work status. *Pain, 94*, 7–15.

Frymoyer, J.W. (1988). Back pain and sciatica. *New England Journal of Medicine, 318*, 5, 291–300.

Gatchel, R.J. (2001). A biopsychosocial overview of pretreatment screening of patients with pain. *Clinical Journal of Pain, 17*, 192–199.

Gatchel, R.J., & Epker, J. (1999). Psychosocial predictors of chronic pain and response to treatment. In R.J. Gatchel & D.C. Turk (Eds.), *Psychosocial factors in pain: Critical perspectives*. New York: Guilford Press.

Gatchel, R.J., & Turk, D.C. (1999). Interdisciplinary treatment of chronic pain patients. In R.J. Gatchel & D.C. Turk (Eds.), *Psychosocial factors in pain: Critical perspectives*. New York: Guilford Press.

Gildenberg, P.L., & DeVaul, R.A. (1985). *The chronic pain patient: Evaluation and management*. Basel: Karger.

Hadjistavropoulos, H.D., MacLeod, F.K., & Asmundson, G.J.G. (1999). Validation of the Chronic Pain Coping Inventory. *Pain, 80*, 471–481.

Hanson, R.W., & Gerber, K.E. (1990). *Coping with chronic pain: A guide to patient self-management*. New York: Guilford Press.

Harden, R.N. (2002). Chronic opioid therapy: Another reappraisal. *APS Bulletin, 12*, 1, 1–12.

Irving, G.A., & Wallace, M.S. (1996). *Pain management for the practicing physician*. New York: Churchill Livingtone.

Jensen, M.C., Brant-Zawadzli, M.D., Obucowski, N., Modic, M.T., Malkasian, D., & Ross, J.S. (1994). Magnetic resonance imaging of the lumbar spine in people without back pain. *New England Journal of Medicine, 331*, 2, 69–73.

Jensen, M.P., Karoly, P., & Huger, R. (1987). The development and preliminary validation of an instrument to assess patients' attitudes toward pain. *Journal of Psychosomatic Research, 31*, 393–400.

Jensen, M.P., Turner, J.A., Romano, J.M., & Lawler, B.K. (1994). Relationship of pain-specific beliefs to chronic pain adjustment. *Pain, 57*, 301–309.

Jensen, M.P., Turner, J.A., Romano, J.M., & Strom, S.E. (1995). The Chronic Pain Coping Inventory: Development and preliminary validation. *Pain, 60*, 203–216.

Jensen, M.P., Turner, J.A., & Romano, J.M. (2000). Pain belief assessment: A comparison of the short and long versions of the Survey of Pain Attitudes. *Journal of Pain, 1*, 138–150.

Kerns, R.D., Turk, D.C., & Rudy, T.E. (1985). The West Haven–Yale Multidimensional Pain Inventory (WHYMPI). *Pain, 23*, 345–356.

Kori, S.H., Miller, R.P., & Todd, D.D. (1990). Kinesiophobia: A new view of chronic pain behavior. *Pain Management*, 35–43.

Linton, S.J. (1994). Chronic back pain: Integrating psychological and physical therapy. *Behavioral Medicine, 20*, 101–117.

Linton, S.J. (2002). A prospective study of the effects of sexual or physical abuse on back pain. *Pain, 96*, 347–351.

Linton, S.J., Larden, M., & Gillow, A.M. (1996). Sexual abuse and chronic musculo-skeletal pain: Prevalence and psychological factors. *Clinical Journal of Pain, 12*, 215–221.

Loeser, J.D. (2001). The future: Will pain be abolished or just pain specialists? *APS Bulletin, 11*, 6, 1–10.

McCaffery, M., & Pasero, C. (1999). *Pain: Clinical manual* (2nd ed.). St. Louis: Mosby.

Melzack, R. (1990). The tragedy of needless pain. *Scientific American, 262*, 27–33.

Merskey, H., & Moulin, D. (1999). Pharmacological treatment in chronic pain. In A.R. Block, E.F. Kremer, & E. Fernandez (Eds.), *Handbook of pain syndromes*. Mahwah, NJ: Lawrence Erlbaum Associates, Inc.

Moore, J.E., Lorig, K., Von Korff, M., Gonzalez, V.M., & Laurent, D.D. (1999). *The back pain helpbook*. Reading, MA: Persius.

Morley, S., Eccleston, C., & Williams, A. (1999). Systematic review and meta-analysis of randomized controlled trials of cognitive behavior therapy and behavior therapy for chronic pain in adults, excluding headache. *Pain, 80*, 1–13.

Okifuji, A., Turk, D.C., & Kalauokalani, D. (1999). Clinical outcome and economic evaluation of multidisciplinary pain centers. In A.R. Block, E.F. Kremer, & E. Fernandez (Eds.), *Handbook of pain syndromes*. Mahwah, NJ: Lawrence Erlbaum Associates, Inc.

Portnoy, R.K. (1990). Chronic opioid therapy in nonmalignant pain. *Journal of Pain and Symptom Management, 5*, S46–S62.

Portnoy, R.K. (1996). Opioid therapy for chronic nonmalignant pain: A review of the critical issues. *Journal of Pain and Symptom Management, 11*, 203–217.

Prager, J., & Jacobs, M. (2001). Evaluation of patients for implantable pain modalities: Medical and behavioral assessment. *Clinical Journal of Pain, 17*, 206–214.

Robinson, R.C., Gatchel, R.J., Polatin, P., Deschner, M., Noe, C., & Gajraj, N. (2001). Screening for problematic prescription opioid use. *Clinical Journal of Pain, 17*, 220–228.

Rosenstiel, A.K., & Keefe, F.J. (1983). The use of coping strategies in chronic low back pain patients: Relationship to patient characteristics and current adjustment. *Pain, 17*, 33–44.

Sanders, S.H. (2002). Operant conditioning with chronic pain: Back to basics. In D.C. Turk & R.J. Gatchel (Eds.), *Psychological approaches to pain management* (2nd ed.). New York: Guilford Press.

Severeijns, R.M., Vlaeyen, J.W.S., van den Hout, M.A., & Weber, W.E.J. (2001). Pain catastrophizing predicts pain intensity, disability, and psychological distress independent of the level of physical impairment. *Clinical Journal of Pain, 17*, 165–172.

Siegel, R.D., Urdang, M.H., & Johnson, D.R. (2001). *Back sense*. New York: Broadway Books.

Tait, R.C., & Chibnall, J.T. (1997). Development of a brief version of the Survey of Pain Attitudes. *Pain, 70*, 229–235.

Turk, D.C. (2001). Management of pain: Best of times, worst of times? *Clinical Journal of Pain, 17*, 107–109.

Turk, D.C., & Monarch, E.S. (2002). Biopsychosocial perspective on chronic pain. In D.C. Turk & R.J. Gatchel (Eds.), *Psychological approaches to pain management: A practitioner's handbook* (2nd ed.). New York: Guilford Press.

Turk, D.C., & Okifuji, A. (1998). Directions in prescriptive chronic pain management based on diagnostic characteristics of the patient. *APS Bulletin, 8*, 5, 5–11.

Turk, D.C., & Okifuji, A. (1999). Pain. Assessment of patients' reporting of pain: An integrated perspective. *Lancet, 353*, 1784–1788.

Turk, D.C., & Rudy, T.E. (1987). Towards a comprehensive assessment of chronic pain patients. *Behaviour Research and Therapy, 25*, 237–249.

Turk, D.C., & Rudy, T.E. (1988). Toward an empirically-derived taxonomy of chronic pain patients: Integration of psychological assessment data. *Journal of Consulting and Clinical Psychology, 56*, 233–238.

Turk, D.C., & Rudy, T.E. (1990). The robustness of empirically derived taxonomy of chronic pain patients. *Pain, 43*, 27–35.

Turk, D.C., Meichenbaum, D., & Genest, M. (1983). *Pain and behavioral medicine: A cognitive-behavioral perspective*. New York: Guilford Press.

Verhaak, P.F.M., Kerssens, J.J., Dekker, J., Sorbi, M.J., & Bensing, J.M. (1998). Prevalence of chronic benign pain disorder among adults: A review of the literature. *Pain, 77*, 231–239.

Vlaeyen, J.W.S., & Linton, S.J. (2000). Fear-avoidance and its consequences in chronic musculoskeletal pain: A state of the art. *Pain, 85*, 317–332.

Vlaeyan, J.W.S., de Jong, J., Sieben, J., & Crombez, G. (2002). Graded exposure *in vivo* for pain-related fear. In D.C. Turk & R.J. Gatchel (Eds.), *Psychological approaches to pain management: A practitioner's handbook* (2nd ed.). New York: Guilford Press.

Waddell, G., Newton, M., Henderson, I., Somerville, D., & Main, C. (1993). A Fear-Avoidance Questionnaire (FABQ) and the role of fear-avoidance beliefs in chronic low back pain and disability. *Pain, 52*, 157–168.

Weisberg, M.R., & Clavel, A.L. (1999). Why is chronic pain so difficult to treat? Psychological considerations from simple to complex care. *Postgraduate Medicine, 106*, 141–164.

Wurtele, S.K., Kapalan, G.M., & Keairnes, M. (1990). Childhood sexual abuse among chronic pain patients. *Clinical Journal of Pain, 6*, 110–113.

Chapter 11

Case conceptualisation in chronic fatigue syndrome

Vincent Deary and Trudie Chalder

Explaining the unexplained

> An explanation is a description mapped onto a tautology.
> (Bateson, 1980)

How did the client sitting before you get to where they are today? This is the question a case conceptualisation attempts to answer. In the form of a structured explanation, it provides the bridge between assessment and treatment, forms the basis of a good rationale and provides the fundamental ingredient of engagement – a demonstrated and shared understanding of the client's predicament. This chapter will provide the reader with a structure on which to build case conceptualisations in chronic fatigue syndrome (CFS) and then flesh this structure out with research and case examples.

What turns raw data into a clinical picture, a description into an explanation? Obviously having the right information is crucial, and we will return to that presently. However, something needs to come even before the assessment. The assessment, the information we gather, needs somewhere to go, a kind of mental filing system, otherwise it is just disorganised facts. Any explanation ultimately rests on a pre-existent structure, in our case a model that can help us understand symptoms for which there are no immediately apparent medical cause. The structure is actually very simple and very general too, and it applies to much more than our subject matter. CFS can be conceptualised in terms of:

- the factors that predisposed the person to be vulnerable to it
- the factors that precipitated the current period of illness
- the factors that are now maintaining it.

Let us look at the elements of the structure in turn, and relate them to how we would structure an assessment. In so doing, it will become clearer that the case conceptualisation structures our interaction from the start, and the assessment is best seen as having this explicit purpose.

It is often said that we do not know much about CFS. It is fashionable to classify it as a "medically unexplained illness". Whilst preferable to previous designations such as "psychosomatic illness" or "hysteria", it promulgates the idea of CFS as a "mystery illness". This is not entirely true. Over the last few years a body of evidence has been collected as to what some of the factors involved in causing and maintaining it may be. The notion of a multi-factorial condition is key. Many sufferers, and many professionals and lay people, have an implicit understanding of illness that is based on a cause–cure model. We assume that any illness has a unique cause, determining a patho-physiological process. We cure the illness by identifying and reversing this process. However, it is rarely that simple. Take, for instance, heart disease or type 2 diabetes. There may be some predisposing genetic vulnerability to develop them, but that in itself will not be enough. To precipitate an actual experience of illness we will need several other factors, and these will vary between individuals. Diet, life style, personality, viral infections, degree of physical fitness, life events and stresses will interact in complex, unique ways to determine both the occurrence, the experience and the outcome of the illness. CFS is no different. Let us review some of the factors we do know play a part in the development of this condition.

Predisposition

Personality

> Whoever thinks a faultless piece to see,
> Thinks what ne'er was, nor is, nor e'er shall be.
> (Alexander Pope, *An Essay on Criticism*,
> 1711, 1.253)

Our personality, in that it is a stable state, determines our habitual way of tackling life, and different styles will have a different impact upon the indi-vidual, their life and their health. One factor that consistently emerges from the CFS literature is perfectionism, and more recent studies have high-lighted the so-called negative aspects of this trait (White & Schweitzer, 2000; Deary, 2001).

Perfectionism is the desire to do or produce things to an exactingly high standard. As the quote above correctly notes, complete perfection is unattainable, it is an ideal. Doing things well is not only potentially highly rewarding, it is also sometimes essential. However, there is a downside. The research seems to show that those individuals who both (over?)value high standards for achievement and are extremely critical and doubtful about their own efforts and abilities are more prone to fatigue. It is intuitively obvious how a desire to do too many things too well, or to meet impossible standards, is potentially exhausting. If one attempts to maintain these standards in the face of increasing exhaustion, a negative and demoralising spiral is easily entered.

Another possibly related trait is action proneness or "ergomania", characterised by an overly active life style (Van Houdenhove, 1999). Again this makes intuitive sense and fits with common client descriptions of their premorbid life. We could stretch this notion further to Jeff Young's hypothesised "other directed" schemas in which there is a repetitive tendency to prioritise the needs of others over one's own well-being (Young, 1999). Although this fits with clinical experience, this specific hypothesis remains untested.

Neuroticism is another factor that emerges from the research as significant. The term has required a pejorative overtone, which is unfortunate. In essence it means a fairly stable tendency to experience more negative emotions, specifically anxiety and depression. People who score high on this trait are likely to be more vulnerable to both physical symptoms and emotional distress (Watson & Pennebaker, 1989).

Social desirability

There is some evidence for a subtler mechanism at work. Many will attest that socialising is an energetic, not infrequently tiring activity. Being with people takes energy. We value those interactions where we don't have to try, where we can relax and be ourselves. If there is an element of performance in social interaction (and the sociologist Goffman would argue that all interaction is best understood as a dramatic performance (Goffman, 1959)) then the more energy the performance requires, the more exhausting it will be. Cresswell and Chalder's (2001) study appears to show that this is the case. People who greatly value social desirability (what Goffman would call presenting a good face) but have to suppress a lot of negative emotion, particularly anxiety, to achieve it, are more prone to fatigue. These may be people who we habitually think of as "copers" – stoic, uncomplaining people who are there for others, but never seem to require support themselves. The cost of "putting a brave face on things" is potentially high.

Childhood factors

The perfectionist study above (Deary, 2001), although retrospective, demonstrated that people certainly experience their parents as more critical than non-sufferers. It could be that in some people adult perfectionism is predicated on early acquired beliefs that one is never quite good enough. Fisher and Chalder's study (2003) highlights another possible factor. Using a parental bonding instrument, adults with CFS reported that they were overprotected in their childhood. It could be that this overprotection contributed to unhelpful ways of coping with distress in adulthood.

Life style, life events and previous life experience

Fitness appears to be a factor in this illness. People who were previously very fit are, it seems, more vulnerable to delayed recovery after severe infection (MacDonald *et al.*, 1996). This could simply be that they have more to lose. Through enforced inactivity, fit people will physically decondition fairly rapidly and experience symptoms of pain and fatigue at relatively low levels of activity once they resume it. This could in turn lead to more rest and more deconditioning. We will return to this dynamic later.

There is strong evidence that people are more likely to have gone through stressful life events in the year prior to developing chronic fatigue (Chalder, 1998). They are also more likely to have experienced prior psychological distress, periods of anxiety and/or depression. Chronic stress appears to be another vulnerability factor (Salit, 1997). Although the precise mechanisms whereby these experiences are translated into physical symptoms are unclear, the burgeoning field of psychoneuroimmunology would lead us to the conclusion that stress has a physiological impact that affects both the immunological and central nervous systems. This possibly leaves people more vulnerable to the incidence and effects of infections.

So these are some of the factors that may make one more vulnerable to developing chronic fatigue. In medical terms, this is the diathesis, the inherent or acquired vulnerability to develop a certain condition. However, diathesis in itself is not enough. It requires a stressor to trigger an episode. Let us look at some of the possible triggers that may precipitate the initial crisis of CFS.

Precipitating factors

As with most hard and fast distinctions, the border between predisposing and precipitating factors is somewhat blurred. Typical onsets of CFS often have the feel of prolonged low level trauma: there is too much happening for too long. It could be that taking away any one of these stressors, or curtailing the period of time over which they are acting, could have averted the final crisis. In this tangled web of factors, distinguishing predisposition and precipitation is like trying to decide which straw it was that broke the camel's back. The obvious answer is "the last one" and the final straw of CFS is generally a virus. But it is worth remembering that without the accumulated weight of the other factors it would (probably) not have had the effect that it did.

Viruses

There is a good evidence that people are about four times more likely to develop chronic fatigue and CFS after a bout of glandular fever caused by the Epstein Barr virus (White *et al.*, 1995). This certainly fits with our lay conceptions of illness. We "know" that glandular fever is a serious infection, and that people are generally "wiped out" by it for some time. However, this finding is more complicated than it appears.

Response to being ill

The standard medical advice to people with glandular fever is bed rest. Indeed a cursory glance at the medical advice on the internet still shows this to be standard advice. However, a recent study looked at a different approach to managing the illness – a graded reintroduction of physical activity (Candy *et al.*, 2002). Those who followed this path were much less likely to develop chronic fatigue than those who were offered treatment as usual. This fits in with other findings that show that more than the severity of the virus, it is the length of period of convalescence that predicts fatigue (Hotopf *et al.*, 1996). Given that the length of this period will be mediated by, amongst other factors, medical advice and lay illness beliefs, the virus equals fatigue picture is not as uncomplicated as it looks. It also blurs another distinction, that between what precipitates the condition and what maintains it. It is not just the crisis – it is also the response to the crisis.

Maintaining factors

In CFS there will be a complex interplay of factors maintaining a disabling experience of illness. Physical, behavioural, emotional, cognitive, social, financial and interpersonal issues interplay and, over time, inter-tangle in an increasingly complex weave of maintaining factors that it becomes evermore difficult to see a way out of. Below we will indicate some of the more common factors, but bear in mind, when it comes to a conceptualisation, that each individual will have their own unique mix.

Hypocortisolism

One of the most consistent physical findings in CFS is lowered levels of cortisol (Cleare *et al.*, 1995; Scott *et al.*, 1999). This is also found in chronic stress and post-traumatic stress disorder (PTSD). A normal cortisol response is crucial in responding to stress (the so-called flight or fight reaction) and it has been hypothesised that lower levels of cortisol increase the individual's vulnerability to the effects of stress and also partly mediate symptoms such as sleep disturbance and light and noise sensitivity. Hypocortisolism may represent a "burn-out" of the stress response in the client; an indication that they were under stress for a prolonged period and have thus become less able to deal with it.

Sleep disturbance

A disturbance of the normal sleep–wake cycle is almost a defining character-istic of CFS. Typically individuals will have poorer quality, unrefreshing sleep, an inconsistent sleep routine and frequent daytime sleep. Often people will sleep much more than premorbidly (so-called hypersomnia). Again this is intuitively the right thing to do – if one is more tired, one should surely sleep more. However, hypersomnia in itself will lead to more fatigue. The disturbed circadian rhythms of an inconsistent sleep routine and daytime sleeping also produce more fatigue and yet more disturbed sleep (Neyta & Horne, 1990).

Avoidance

Increasingly there is evidence that rest is not a cure but in fact provokes the very symptoms it intends to reduce. On the face of it this is counter-intuitive. When we are ill we usually become more tired, we rest, we feel better. This may work in acute conditions, but rest over a prolonged period actually has quite profound physiological consequences (Greenleaf & Kozlowski, 1982). Loss of muscle strength, loss of cardiovascular fitness, circulatory changes, changes in mood, etc. Most importantly, it produces more fatigue and more susceptibility to pain. This puts the CFS sufferer in a tricky position. Our usual response to fatigue and pain is to avoid activity. However, prolonged avoidance produces more of these symptoms, which in turn produces avoid-ance. One can become quickly locked into a vicious circle. Illness beliefs have a key role in this.

Beliefs

One belief emerges from the literature as being a key maintaining factor – the belief that activity which provokes symptoms is harmful (Deale *et al.*, 1998). It is easy to see how this plays into the avoidance circle. It also plays a key role in one of the characteristic behavioural patterns of CFS – the boom and bust cycle. On good or relatively symptom-free days, some sufferers will "blow their windfall of energy", catch up on all the stuff they could not previously do. Almost inevitably, this will be followed by a crash in the next day or two, resulting in a self-perpetuating cycle. The "hurt–harm" belief is the most important one to identify and address in treatment.

Symptom focus, anxiety and misinterpretation

In CFS, clients often become very symptom focused, not however through choice. In the absence of a clear explanation, new or persistent symptoms remain a source of preoccupation because it is not clear what they signal – imminent relapse, business as usual and/or something new (Warwick &

Salkovskis, 1990). Anxiety and worry have profound physical effects. Muscle tension will amplify pain, increased adrenaline will increase heart rate and breathing leading to feelings as diverse as chest pain, headache, dizziness, nausea, etc. Particularly if a symptom is (mis)interpreted as the sign of imminent collapse, a spiral of anxiety is produced that becomes a self-fulfilling prophecy. This whole mechanism is also very exhausting to endure.

Self-expectations

Personality does not radically alter just because someone has become ill. Standards that may have predisposed someone to becoming ill often remain in operation during illness. With the literature's emphasis on activation and graded exercise it is easy to think that recovery in CFS is all about doing more. Often this is not the case. There is evidence that maintaining a high degree of conscientiousness in the face of fatigue leads to more fatigue (Deary, 2001). As we shall see in the case conceptualisation example, this behaviour is often maintained by self-expectations which are unreasonably high. A defining characteristic of perfectionism is "all or nothing thinking" in which things are achieved with excellence or not at all. Again, maintaining this pattern in the face of overwhelming fatigue will be both frustrating and exhausting.

Emotional factors

Mood

CFS is not depression. Depression and CFS have different neurochemical profiles, with depression characterised by raised cortisol (Cleare *et al.*, 1995). CFS and depression "feel" very different in clinical work. This is not to say that people with CFS do not get depressed – indeed people with CFS seem more prone to experiencing depression (Wessely & Powell, 1989). However, the conditions remain distinct. Depression that has progressed to the extent where it impedes working on recovery (for which the client needs a fair degree of self-motivation), certainly needs to be addressed independently, and there is a good argument for antidepressants in these cases. However, the depression associated with CFS – and most clients are clear that their depression is secondary to their fatigue – is often of a particular kind, principally characterised by loss, frustration at lack of achievement, and hopelessness about recovery.

Loss

Loss is an underestimated part of CFS. Many of the roles by which we define ourselves will have been profoundly altered, or lost entirely to CFS. Work roles and social positions, our place in the family and our relationships with friends and partners, parents and children – none remain unaltered and many are lost. Perhaps more devastating is loss of time. Many sufferers in their twenties and thirties will have spent much or most of their adult lives trying to manage an illness, at the expense of the career building and relationship formation that most of us devote those years to. There is also loss of future – the career and personal goals that structure most of our life journeys are lost in the blank horizon of ongoing illness. Many sufferers complain of their lack of ability to plan for the next day, the next week, let alone planning and building a future. The prospect of building one's life from scratch in adulthood is daunting and beyond the ability of many.

The fatigue trap

Many clients live in a state of precarious status quo. They will often talk in terms of a tightly rationed energy budget. They have so much energy to divide between, say, shopping, keeping on top of the housework and looking after their families. Any increase in expenditure in one area takes precious reserves from another. Unexpected demands – life events, applying for state benefits, other illness, relationship problems – can wipe out existing reserves at a stroke. Only by very carefully pacing themselves can they maintain their current commitments.

Clients can be stuck in the energetic equivalent of the poverty trap – a fatigue trap. To work on getting out of CFS requires expenditure of energy – precisely the commodity that is in short supply. Consequently doing things at all differently is inherently very risky with relapse being an ever-present threat. Some clients get to the point where it is as difficult to stay where they are as it is to change the situation. This will lead to understandable feelings of helplessness and hopelessness, which in turn will amplify the present symptoms.

Social and culture factors

I can't get better if I have to prove that I am ill.
(A CFS sufferer)

The chronic fatigue syndrome sufferer is constantly having to prove his or her illness. It is hard to imagine how anyone confronted with a sufferer of CFS could fail to be convinced by the reality of their symptoms. Most of the people we see have had to fight long and hard to get a diagnosis and referral, and typically will have encountered numerous health professionals who will have been quite explicit in their disbelief. This is further amplified by an often hostile or confusing media that one day will dismiss CFS as "yuppie flu" only to declare it a "real" condition the next; one that can be cured by fish oils (BBC1 News, 2002).

Part of the blame can be directed, and often is, at Descartes. From him and his Enlightenment descendants we inherit the idea of the person as an animated corpse, a purely material body inhabited and animated by a non-physical, abstract mind/soul. As a framework for explaining illness this model has serious limitations, particularly when confronted by illness which has no clear physical origin. Within this dualist framework, if there is nothing wrong physically then there is only one other place to look – in your mind. Add a dash of Freud and we have the completely unsubstantiated but amazingly pervasive notion that medically unexplained physical symptoms must be the expression of unconscious psychological distress. All we then need do is convince the patient that they are really depressed or personality disordered to effect "a cure".

However, Descartes cannot take all the blame. As we discussed above, another kind of simplistic thinking is at work here – cause–cure dualism. Like most other illnesses, CFS does not fit this model, as should be becoming clear. However, CFS differs from other diseases in one crucial way, it contains a perpetuating ingredient that no other contains – disbelief. The perpetual battle for validation that most sufferers of CFS are caught in is literally, physiologically exhausting, depressing and dispiriting. It affects the course of the illness. No other sufferer of chronic illness has to fight this bizarre battle to have the facts that they live with every day legitimised by a hostile authority. As long as CFS has to prove itself, that much longer will sufferers suffer.

Interpersonal factors

Letting go of support

It is obvious why too little social support would be a contributing factor to illness chronicity and severity. Attempting to keep going on one's own is obviously exhausting. Less obviously, the research has shown that too much support is also associated with disability (Chalder, 1998). Consider, however, an analogy from recovery from heart disease. As with CFS, many heart disease sufferers have built up an infrastructure of support, a coping network, to help them manage their illness. If over-concerned friends and relatives within this network increasingly "take over" the tasks of daily living for the sufferer, in the well-intentioned but misguided belief that they should rest and be protected from any stress, then the enforced inactivity is likely to have an adverse effect on their health and self-efficacy. Part of recovery from both heart disease and CFS can involve gradually dismantling the scaffolding of social support that is built up around the illness.

Toxic relationships

One of the potential blindspots of cognitive behavioural therapy (CBT) is that by locating the problem in the individual and their interpretation of the world, we can easily forget the effect of the network of relationships in which they live their lives. This was dramatically illustrated by one client. For 12 sessions she had come along with her partner, who was apparently very supportive, and together they had done everything right. Pacing, consistency, sleep management and graded increases in activity were all done by the book, but the client did not improve. She missed the next session and did not contact us for a month. Then she phoned: "I've left my partner. I don't have a clue what I am doing or what I'm going to do, I'm scared as hell, but I'm not fatigued anymore." This change persisted, and what emerged in subsequent sessions was that for years she had felt stuck in a relationship that was emotionally and physically draining, but that she felt too ill to leave.

Of course this is an extreme case, but it alerts us to another factor we could easily miss out of our fatigue equation. Unless clients feel they can trust us, and unless we explore, without prying, their network of relationships, their interpersonal styles, we can miss vital information.

Domestic factors

If we have been ill for a while, and we are responsible for the daily running of the house, it is amazing how quickly things pile up – the washing, the dusting, the washing up, the bills, the work commitments, the social obligations. Imagine then having been ill for several years. Many clients describe living in an environment which is literally out of control. Having not been able to keep order for some time, order has gone out of the window. The ensuing chaos is so daunting, so out of proportion to their current ability to manage it, that it becomes yet worse. This of course produces yet more exhaustion – a mountain of washing up is much more daunting than one morning's teacups.

Work and money – the benefit trap

Many clients are dependent on benefits, from the state or from private insurance. Currently in Britain it is very difficult to make a smooth transition out of benefit dependence, to "wean oneself off it". If one is deemed fit for work, benefits are abruptly stopped. Of course, the only way to become fit for work is to gradually ease oneself back into it, but often as soon as a first step is made the whole benefit is threatened. This is the famous benefit trap, and it is as real for CFS sufferers as for any other unemployed person. There is good evidence that being on benefits is a predictor of poor outcome (Bentall *et al.*, 2002). As therapists, the least we can do is be aware of this as a potential factor in our clients' lives.

A case conceptualisation example

We now have the framework, fleshed out with research, of a case conceptualisation and some of the factors that are likely to play a part in it. Let us take this one stage further by presenting a case, a composite of actual clients.

Presenting problem

Doris is a 45-year-old widow, currently on incapacity benefit. Her principle symptom is profound physical fatigue, the kind of fatigue associated with a bad flu. In addition she has severe muscle pain, particularly in her neck and shoulders and in her legs. She also has dizziness, which is for her the most unpleasant symptom, as she frequently feels nauseous with it, though she is never actually sick. Her concentration is impaired and she cannot even follow a half-hour episode of her favourite soap without becoming confused. She also complains of great sensitivity to noise and light and finds, for instance, that having to deal with more than one person, or a noisy environment, is confusing and overwhelming.

The impact of these symptoms on her life is severe. She spends most of her day either sitting or lying down. She will "potter" about the house for a few minutes at most, but feels very unsteady on her feet. She only leaves the house in a wheelchair, pushed by friends. She will not walk outside because "I know I would fall over". She sleeps, in fits and starts, for about 12 hours a night, and wakes unrefreshed. She frequently sleeps for long periods of the day. She has an extensive network of friends and acquaintances "from my previous (premorbid) life" who are on a rota and come at least three times a day. They help her with basic domestic maintenance and in looking after her pets – a gerbil, a cat and a dog. She wears a head collar to keep her head static. She avoids looking down and turns over in bed with extreme caution.

Onset

The current problems began five years ago. At the time she had a job as a care worker in an old people's home, doing long hours and shift work. She enjoyed the work, though often found the level of care from other staff frustrating. She also worked for the Samaritans three evenings a week, gave guitar lessons to two friends' children and was an active member of her local church. She "thoroughly enjoyed" her life. Three years ago, her husband died. Doris kept going for six months and seemed to be "coping". She then contracted the flu. She was "completely floored" and spent the next few weeks in bed. Attempts to return to work ended in relapse. Her doctor advised her to rest for at least three months and wrote her a sick certificate. Subsequent attempts to resume activities such as church and teaching were all "too much" and two years ago she settled into her current pattern.

Prior to her current illness she describes herself as cheerful, but a worrier. Her mood is currently low, due to her frustration at her inability to enjoy life. She still misses her husband, but can now think of him fondly rather than with distress.

Relevant history

Doris was the youngest of three daughters. Her mother and father are still alive, and she has a very distant relationship with them both. This is partly because it emerged six years previously that her father had sexually abused the two older daughters. Doris has no memory of abuse herself, but "never trusted" her father. Her mother was a "complainer, a victim" who Doris found it necessary to "look after, keep happy". Even then she was often accused by her of "being selfish" of "not thinking of anyone but herself". Doris was popular at school and "could always make friends easily, still can" and did "good enough" academically. She left school at 16 and was training to be a nurse when she met her husband, a doctor. They married soon after, and she gave up nursing to "set up home" with him. She has no regrets about this, and in her thirties returned to care work, when it became clear that they could not have children. She has some money left from his life insurance, but not enough to live on comfortably without state benefit.

Previous treatment and attributions

Doris is convinced that the flu and "the stress" have permanently damaged her central nervous system. Her doctor, though sympathetic, "doesn't know what to do with her" and has referred her to a neurologist, an immunologist and a psychiatrist who she described as worse than useless. She is particularly upset by the suggestion, which also comes from friends, that she has not got over her husband's death and is "really depressed". She has tried two anti-depressants to no effect. She has also tried myriad alternative therapies, to no great effect. She does not like to give up hope, but cannot see a way forward.

Conceptualisation

The above case is not untypical. Let us put the data from the history onto the framework, beginning with the present picture and then working back.

Maintaining factors

Physical inactivity and sleep disturbance

Doris's current level of fatigue is partly maintained by her very low levels of activity. This will have led to some muscular atrophy and general loss of fitness. More specifically, her neck collar and the resultant lack of head movement and the loss of neck strength mean that she has become more sensitised to the effects of movements (pain and dizziness) when they occur. In addition, she is sleeping almost twice the amount she did premorbidly, which together with the disturbed cycle will be contributing to her fatigue.

Cognitions

Although not explicit, Doris "just knows" that being active when she feels unwell, particularly when she is feeling dizzy, is "an invitation to disaster". Specifically, she is worried that she will fall over and not be able to get up. This belief is partly maintaining her activity avoidance. This means that when she does walk, particularly away from support, she feels anxious (walking equals danger) and this amplifies her dizziness, weakness and unsteadiness. This, in turn, is interpreted as predictive of imminent collapse.

Graded activity has been suggested in the past, but she believes that pushing herself will lead to a worsening of her condition, which will make her unable to do the little she does. She worries particularly about having to give up her animals, whom she loves, and also worries that she may herself end up in a home. Increased activity and increased symptoms have in short become catastrophised and not without cause.

Other symptoms, particularly the cognitive impairment, she interprets as signs of neurological damage, a belief she finds extensive and well-researched support for on the self-help websites. Although this does not directly affect her behaviour, it does make her dubious about recovery and particularly anxious when these symptoms occur.

Emotions

Doris feels frustrated and ashamed by her lack of ability to look after herself, and feels selfish that she "can't give anything back to my friends". This is likely to be maintained by early acquired beliefs that she was a selfish person (see predisposing factors). Despite this her self-esteem is pretty intact and she sees herself as "an essentially kind person in dire straits". Her predominant feeling is anxiety, as she feels her life is in a very precarious balance (see cognitions).

Social

Doris has, by her own admission "never had this much care in my life". Her network of social support is a testament to her value as a friend, and she feels that giving this up and "going it on my own" will be nigh on impossible. Her network, although on one level gratifying, is thus also maintaining her low level of activity and reinforcing reduced self-efficacy.

Financial

Although it is clear that Doris is a long way from being able to be financially independent, she is currently having to fill in a reapplication form for incapacity benefit which may possibly result in another Department of Social Security (DSS) medical. The whole process is gruelling, actively makes her feel exhausted (concentrating on the forms) and puts her in the defensive position of having to "prove that I am ill". This is an active impediment to progress as the latter could be interpreted by the DSS and/or friends that she is either becoming fit for work, or was not really ill in the first place.

Medical

Doris has had no rational explanation for her symptoms, no prognosis and no advice on how to manage her condition. At best she has been listened to, at worst dismissed as depressed. She has thus bought into the medics' hopelessness, reinforced by the self-help sites that there is nothing she can do "except hope it goes away". She thus has no sense of control over her illness, indeed feels that "the ME controls me", and this further fuels her anxiety, her frustration and her symptoms.

Predisposing and precipitating factors

Early experience and acquired beliefs

Early on, Doris acquired the belief that thinking of yourself before others was selfish and that other people were unreliable either because they were weak and needed help, or they were not trustworthy. She also only felt "reinforced" when she was looking after other people, particularly her mother, and thus acquired the belief that in order to be liked it was necessary to give and not to accept anything for oneself. These beliefs received a lot of benign reinforcement in that it made her extremely popular as an adept helper to friends, her husband, her church and eventually her clients as a carer. However, it also meant that she had a permanent "me last" attitude so when she did need support (when her husband died) she found it initially difficult to be perceived as "not coping". This in turn probably meant that she kept going when she should have stopped and thus made herself more physically and emotional vulnerable to the incidence and effect of infection. Her "habitual giving" was not initially problematic, but eventually she was giving so much, to her carers, pupils, her husband, her church and the Samaritans that she was overstretched, so when the crisis did hit, she was already vulnerable to its effects.

It is worth nothing that despite our reliance as therapists on the acquired beliefs model, there is only fairly weak evidence for the effect of parenting on the adult psyche and much stronger evidence that both genetics and our childhood peer group (in descending order of influence) play a far larger part in shaping who we are. It could be that Doris was a natural giver, who found herself in a situation where her talents were in great demand (see Pinker, 2002 for an extensive review of the nature/nurture literature).

The critical incident(s)

Her husband dying was not only traumatic in itself, but it raised a need for support that went directly against her core beliefs about herself and other people. She reported that she had "never lent on my husband", and took pleasure in helping him, by all accounts a worrier. This recalls the dynamic sketched above of "social desirability", with Doris trying to suppress and to some extent repress unpleasant emotions beneath a coping exterior.

It is quite possible that continuing to work through her "stress" resulted in Doris "burning out", i.e. there were doubtless psychoneuroimmunological consequences which could still be in effect. Certainly the crash following the flu – the second critical incident – has in retrospect a kind of inevitability. She had to stop somehow and physical illness was perhaps the only thing that could slow down this habitual coper.

What happens next?

Doris goes through a highly typical cycle post crisis. Attempts to return to work and resume normal activity are met by a recurrence and intensification of symptoms at much lower levels of activity. This leads to further rest, followed by repeated attempts to resume her life, which are each time met by a recurrence of symptoms at increasingly lower levels of activity. All the while, fitness, self-efficacy and key social roles are disappearing. This ever-diminishing boom and bust cycle, over time, will often end up in a more or less stable state of very low level activity. The whole cycle is in turn reinforced by lack of medical advice and management, which only serves to increase the uncertainty and anxiety over symptoms. Having, in the midst of all else, to apply for and become dependent on state benefits is both physically draining and emotionally at odds with her habitual independence.

Treatment plan

In chronic illness with multiple secondary factors, the therapist can, like the client, become overwhelmed with the amount to be dealt with. Two inter-linked questions arise. How much of the case conceptualisation do we share with the client and, most urgently, where do we start?

A rationale for treatment

Our first step, as always in CBT, is to begin with an area in which we can make some changes. Most importantly, in someone as disabled as Doris, our approach is initially necessarily one of rehabilitation. The major maintaining factors are her activity avoidance and her disturbed and excessive sleep. The research is clear on this; if we do not change that, nothing else will change. Essentially to get better she will need to do more and rest less.

As should be clear from the above, this is exactly what Doris does not want to do, and for good reason. Her previous experience confirms her beliefs that activity can have catastrophic consequences. To make any changes she will require extremely plausible reasons for doing so. Does our case conceptualisation provide them?

In part. We have certainly identified and have the research to support our contentions that reduced activity and increased rest and sleep are possibly maintaining factors. We also have the research to know that the way to proceed, particularly in someone as cautious as this, is slowly and at their pace. The reader is referred to the numerous how-to manuals (Chalder, 1995; Sharpe *et al.*, 1997; Deary, 2003) but the starting point is essentially simple – to set targets for consistent graded small increases in activity that the client is willing to engage in.

Given the relatively unambitious nature of our first interventions is the "full monty" case conceptualisation above necessary? Almost certainly not. Indeed, initially, it could be counter-productive. With its weight of other factors it could easily be perceived as a psychological model. Indeed the bulk of the model is speculative if, to us, persuasive. The only thing we really know is that as long as Doris responds to symptoms by ceasing activity, so long will the symptoms reign supreme. From the point of view of engagement and treatment compliance, our initial rationale should be based on this: helping the client gain control of their condition, by establishing an achievable "baseline" routine, which a rehabilitation programme can then be slowly built on.

In Doris's case this initial goal was to take three two-minute walks up and down her corridor every day. She also agreed on a getting up time. She did this because she could see that her legs were weak and that her sleep was excessive (though some education was provided here). She also did it because she thought she could. We anticipated that symptoms would increase initially, but provided the alternative hypothesis that this would be a natural result of increasing activity (like when a sedentary therapist decides to start jogging it, feels bad at first). She was not entirely convinced, but it obviously was not nonsense, and she was willing to try. We tackled the two things we know need tackling – increasing activity (in someone this disabled) and identifying fearful cognitions associated with it. The latter are not so much challenged as given hypothetical non-catastrophic alternatives.

Graded increase in conceptualisation

Only once a solid baseline of activity increase and rest reduction was established, and the inevitable blips were decatastrophised, normalised or problem solved, did we move on to other territories. Trust, and a credible treatment approach having been established, we began to discuss other issues. The first issue we tackled was dismantling some of the social support. Doris knew it would have to happen and took it at her pace, dictating the moves herself. This led on naturally to a discussion of her feelings about helping and being helped, and how her illness experience had already effectively challenged some of these. This in turn led to a discussion of how she had sometimes given too much, to her own detriment, and we wondered about how much this was a factor from her childhood.

In short, we let the conceptualisation unfold at the client's pace. The only part that the therapist initiated was the role of irregular/reduced activity and increased sleep in maintaining her fatigue. The rest, the facts of her life, she knew better than the therapist. The therapist–client discussions merely helped Doris see how some of these beliefs and behaviours may have contributed to her illness, and how working on them might help her recover and protect her in the future. By the end of treatment, back in voluntary work, doing some guitar teaching, walking regularly where she wanted without feeling bad, still on benefits, but active and much happier, her attribution had not changed. She still had or was recovering from ME. She rated herself as much improved.

Conclusion

Many clients become preoccupied with the last straw, the triggering event that precipitated their current predicament. Often, though not always, this is a virus. Our model for conceptualisation does not seek to question this understanding so much as to broaden it. By identifying the predisposing and precipitating factors, the client can begin to make sense of what made them vulnerable to this trigger. To the extent that some of these factors are within their control, we can also provide them with tools and insight to protect them against relapse in the future. By identifying the maintaining factors that are keeping the client stuck in an illness cycle, we provide them, again, with insight and tools to begin to modify their life and move it forward. Our conceptualisation, in short, provides both the means to understand and the strategies to change the situation. For clients who are concerned that this sounds overly "psychological", or for the therapists keen to foist a "psychological" explanation on their clients, it is worth pointing out that this model is in essence a framework for understanding any experience of illness, be it heart disease or schizophrenia. The key is to use this framework to understand what it is that has led this person sitting in front of you to where they are today.

References

Bateson, G. (1980). *Mind and nature – A necessary unity*. London: Bantam.

BBC1 News (2002). *Fish oil tablets 'could fight ME'*. Available HITP <http://news.bbc.co.uk/1/hi/health/2236698.stm> (accessed 04.09.2002).

Bentall, R.P., Powell, P., Nye, F.J., Edwards, E., & Richard H. T. (2002). Predictors of response to treatment for chronic fatigue syndrome. *British Journal of Psychiatry*, *181*, 3, 248–252.

Candy, B., Chalder, T., Cleare, A.J., Wessely, S., White, P.D., & Hotopf, M. (2002). Recovery from infectious mononucleosis: a case from more that symptomatic therapy? A systematic review. *British Journal of General Practice*, *52*, 483, 884–851.

Chalder, T. (1995). *Coping with chronic fatigue*. London: Sheldon Press.

Chalder, T. (1998). Factors contributing to the development and maintenance of fatigue in primary care. Unpublished PhD thesis, London.

Cleare, A., Bearn, J., Allain, T., Wessely, S., McGregor, A., & Keane, V. (1995). Contrasting neuroendocrine responses in depression and chronic fatigue syndrome. *Journal of Affective Disorders*, *35*, 283–289.

Cresswell, C., & Chalder, T. (2001). Defensive coping styles in chronic fatigue syndrome. *Journal of Psychosomatic Research*, *51*, 607–610.

Deale, A., Chalder, T., & Wessely, S. (1998). Illness beliefs and treatment outcome in chronic fatigue syndrome. *Journal of Psychosomatic Research*, *45*, 1, 77–83.

Deary, V. (2001). Personality traits in chronic fatigue syndrome. Unpublished masters thesis, London.

Deary, V. (2003). *Chronic fatigue and chronic fatigue syndrome – a practical self help site*. Available HTTP <http://www.kcl.ac.uk/cfs> (accessed 11.11.2004).

Fisher, L., & Chalder, T. (2003). Childhood experiences of illness and parenting in adults with chronic fatigue syndrome. *Journal of Psychosomatic Research*, *54*, 439–443.

Goffman, E. (1959). *The presentation of self in everyday life*. Garden City, NY: Doubleday.

Greenleaf, J., & Kozlowski, S. (1982). Physiological consequences of reduced activity during bedrest. *Exercise and Sports Science Review*, *10*, 84–119.

Hotopf, M., Noah, N., & Wessely, S. (1996). Chronic fatigue and minor psychiatric morbidity after viral meningitis: A controlled study. *Journal of Neurology, Neurosurgery and Psychiatry*, *60*, 504–509.

MacDonald, K., Osterholm, M., & LeDell, K. (1996). A case control study to assess possible triggers and co-factors in chronic fatigue syndrome. *American Journal of Psychiatry*, *100*, 548–554.

Neyta, N., & Horne, J. (1990). Effects of sleep extension and reduction on mood in healthy adults. *Human Psychopharmacology*, *6*, 173–188.

Pinker, S. (2002). *The blank slate. The modern denial of human nature*. London: Viking Penguin.

Salit, I. (1997). Precipitating factors for chronic fatigue syndrome. *Journal of Psychiatric Research*, *31*, 1, 59–65.

Scott, L.V., Reznek, R., Martin, A., Sohaib, A., & Dinan, T.G. (1999). Small adrenal glands in chronic fatigue syndrome: A preliminary computer tomography study. *Psychoneuroendocrinology*, *24*, 7, 759–768.

Sharpe, M., Chalder, T., Palmer, I., & Wessely, S. (1997). Chronic fatigue syndrome: A practical guide to assessment and management. *General Hospital Psychiatry*, *19*, 3, 185–199.

Van Houdenhove, B., & Neerinckx, E. (1999). Is 'ergomania' a predisposing factor to chronic pain and fatigue? *Psychosomatics*, *40*, 6, 529–530.

Warwick, H., & Salkovskis, P. (1990). Hypochondriasis. In C. Scott, J. Williams, & A. Beck, (Eds.), *Cognitive therapy: A clinical casebook*. London: Croom Helm.

Watson, D., & Pennebaker, J.W. (1989). Health complaints, stress and distress: Exploring the central role of negative affectivity. *Psychological Review*, *96*, 234–254.

Wessely, S., & Powell, R. (1989). Fatigue syndromes: A comparison of chronic 'postviral' fatigue with neuromuscular and affective disorders. *Journal of Neurology, Neurosurgery & Psychiatry*, *52*, 8, 940–948.

White, C., & Scweitzer, R. (2000). The role of personality in the development and perpetuation of chronic fatigue syndrome. *Journal of Psychosomatic Research*, *48*, 515–524.

White, C., Thomas, J., & Amess, J. (1995). The existence of fatigue syndrome after glandular fever. *Psychological Medicine*, *25*, 907–916.

Young, J.E. (1999). *Cognitive therapy for personality disorders: A schema-focused approach*. Sarasota, FL: Professional Resource Press.

Chapter 12

Behavioral medicine interventions in HIV/AIDS

Challenges and opportunities for promoting health and adaptation

Peter A. Vanable and Michael P. Carey

Biomedical advances have led to improvements in quality of life for many individuals living with HIV disease. However, current treatments for HIV are not curative, and a significant proportion of people taking highly active antiretroviral therapies (HAART) do not experience long-term benefits. Psychosocial factors, including mental health adaptation, strict medication adherence, and sustained health behavior change, have become central determinants of long-term outcomes for people with HIV.

Behavioral medicine interventions to improve mental health and self-management of HIV disease hold considerable promise as a means of enhancing health and quality of life among people living with HIV. This chapter provides an overview of the clinical assessment and case formulation process for behavioral medicine specialists working with persons infected with HIV. Following a discussion of the role of behavioral medicine in HIV care, we describe the major assessment and intervention challenges faced by clinicians working with men and women living with HIV. Two case histories are then presented to highlight approaches to HIV case formulation and clinical intervention.

HIV and behavioral medicine in context

More than 20 years have passed since the first cases of AIDS were described in the scientific literature and HIV was found to be the causal agent in AIDS. In the early days of the epidemic, an AIDS diagnosis was synonymous with impending death, and physicians provided palliative treatments only as a means of forestalling opportunistic infections. Psychosocial care for people living with HIV focused primarily on improving coping and mental health adjustment as patients faced adaptation to an incurable, progressively worsening, and ultimately fatal health condition. Much has changed since those early days of the epidemic. HIV remains a leading cause of death and disability among young men and women, but biomedical advances have improved the health outlook for HIV+ people living in developed countries with access to HAART (Detels *et al.*, 1998). With these improvements, HIV now shares some similarities with other serious but chronic health conditions. The current "era of HAART" has prompted new concerns and challenges for HIV+ men and women, and a new set of priorities for behavioral medicine specialists working in HIV care (Kelly & Kalichman, 2002). Patients often require assistance in adapting to demanding behavioral requirements associated with living with HIV, including the need for very high levels of adherence to drug treatments and the need for consistent condom use to avoid STD co-infections and HIV transmission. Similarly, interventions to improve mental health adaptation and coping have become an essential part of HIV care.

Assessment and intervention challenges

Provision of psychosocial care in the context of HIV/AIDS involves working with patients who often face difficult social circumstances and multiple barriers to long-term adaptation. Assessment, case formulation, and intervention require knowledge about psychosocial factors in HIV disease, as well as flexibility in prioritization of intervention foci to maximize clinical outcomes. Several important assessment and intervention domains are described below.

Medication adherence

Overview

Medication adherence is a prominent challenge for many HIV+ patients and constitutes a critical intervention focus for behavioral medicine practitioners (Chesney et al., 1999). Medication adherence in the context of HIV care refers to the act of closely following or "sticking to" the recommended dosage and special instructions for a drug regimen. Patients who are able to take their medications as prescribed often can expect to experience total suppression of HIV viral load to "undetectable levels". Conversely, patients with suboptimal adherence are likely to develop drug resistance and to experience poor clinical outcomes (Paterson et al., 2000).

Data from clinical trials and community-based surveys indicate that adherence difficulties are common, with suboptimal adherence reported by between one-third and one-half of patients taking HAART (Bangsberg et al., 2000; Gifford et al., 2000). Indeed, some patients choose not to fill their medication prescriptions because of mistrust, expense, fear of side effects, or a desire to delay treatment until serious symptoms emerge. Reasons for poor adherence include forgetting, being too busy, being away from home, a change in daily routine, or being asleep (Chesney et al., 2000). Psychosocial barriers, including poor social support, distress, and low self-efficacy beliefs also determine medication adherence (Mostashari et al., 1998; Catz et al., 2000). Patients with additional psychiatric or substance use difficulties are even more vulnerable to adherence difficulties (Paterson *et al.*, 2000). Provider behaviors can also influence adherence. For example, poor communication between care providers and patients regarding medication instructions can lead to misunderstandings, and such difficulties are compounded by high rates of illiteracy among HIV+ patients (Kalichman *et al.*, 1999).

Assessment

There is no standardized protocol or "gold standard" for assessing HIV medication adherence. Research protocols often rely on electronic pill-cap monitoring (medication event monitoring systems or MEMS caps), but these technologies are too expensive and impractical for use in a behavioral medicine referral service. Behavioral medicine clinicians tend to rely on self-report as a means of assessing adherence. Fortunately, self-report data correlate highly with other assessment modalities (Bartlett, 2002), and self-report also has the advantage of capturing patients' attitudes, beliefs about, and experiences with their medications.

Several self-report measures are available to clinicians, including a measure used by the Adult AIDS Clinical Trials Group (Chesney *et al.*, 2000). The ACTG measure includes items assessing the frequency of missed medications in general (e.g. "When was the last time you missed taking any of your medications?"), as well a series of items assessing the frequency of missed medications within specific contexts (e.g. "How often have you missed taking your medication because you were busy with other things?"). Also useful are diaries in which patients record each pill taken on a given day, along with notation regarding compliance difficulties, side effects, and contextual factors that contribute to missed dosages. Interview and self-report based approaches should also include an assessment of the patient's understanding of the medication instructions, experiences with medication side effects, and perceptions regarding barriers to adherence.

Interventions to promote adherence

Clinicians seeking input from the scientific literature will find that intervention trials to promote HIV medication adherence have only recently begun to appear (Bamberger *et al.*, 2000; Tuldra *et al.*, 2000; Frick *et al.*, 2001). Nonetheless, several common strategies have emerged, and are commonly used in practice settings. Initially, patients struggling with medication adherence benefit from increased information about medication instructions (Chesney *et al.*, 1999; Bartlett, 2002). It cannot be assumed that patients understand that even slight deviations from prescribed regimens can lead to treatment failure. Likewise, even higher functioning patients may struggle to understand fully the complex instructions they receive regarding when and how medications are to be taken.

A related issue concerns regimen complexity. If it is determined that a medication regimen is too complex to fit within a person's life circumstances, it is important to consult with the treating physician to determine whether simplification is possible to minimize pill burden, dosing frequency, and dietary restrictions (Bartlett, 2002). Patients must also have clear expectations regarding medication side effects, as adherence is often increased by letting patients know at the outset what side effects to expect.

Once it is clear that patients understand the importance of taking medications as prescribed, the details of the regimen, and anticipated side effects, clinicians can then proceed to intervene within a flexible and compassionate framework to identify useful self-management strategies to promote adherence. Behavioral strategies, including multiple reminders (e.g. daily pill boxes, daily checklists, watch alarms), self-management skills training, and problem solving to facilitate integration of medication regimens into daily activities, are components that are likely to be useful when developing individually tailored adherence interventions (Rabkin & Chesney, 1999). Interventions should also help patients to use social support networks, especially relationship partners, to strengthen self-efficacy for following treatment plans (Catz *et al.*, 2000).

It is important for clinicians to maintain an empathic and supportive posture that allows patients to disclose medication difficulties without fear of rejection. Patients vary considerably in their motivation to adopt new adherence strategies. For this reason, motivational interviewing techniques are often useful as a means of enhancing patients' readiness to improve their medication adherence. Key elements of motivational interviewing that have been identified as active ingredients are summarized by the acronym FRAMES, and can be adopted for use for adherence interventions (Miller & Rollnick, 2002). Specifically, therapists can provide Feedback on personal risks associated with poor adherence, emphasize personal Responsibility for change, provide clear Advice regarding approaches to change when warranted, provide a Menu of change options, offer Empathy to patients for their difficult change efforts, and encourage patients' sense of Self-efficacy and optimism for maintaining improved adherence.

Mental health and substance use

Overview

Psychological adjustment and coping are central to effective HIV disease management. Indeed, positive adjustment and optimistic beliefs about one's prognosis may improve treatment response and extend longevity (Reed *et al.*, 1999; Taylor *et al.*, 2000). Similarly, poor adjustment, psychiatric illness, and substance use have been shown to interfere with medication adherence, increase HIV risk behaviors, and ultimately contribute to poor health outcomes (Kelly *et al.*, 1998b). Thus, all behavioral medicine consultations in the context of HIV should include assessment of psychological adjustment and substance use as part of an initial consultation.

The importance of assessing and treating psychiatric and substance use disorders is reinforced by data indicating that nearly one-half of a nationally representative sample of 30,000 HIV-infected patients in the USA screened positive for a psychiatric disorder in the previous year (Bing *et al.*, 2001). Consistent with other reports in the literature (Rabkin *et al.*, 1996), depression and dysthymia were the most commonly reported disorders, followed by anxiety-related disorders. Approximately one-half of the sample also reported illicit drug use, and 12 per cent screened positive for drug dependence. Rates of heavy drinking were twice those found in the general population (Galvan *et al.*, 2002). Considered within a broader context, elevated rates of psychiatric and substance use problems are of little surprise. In fact, pre-existing mental illness and substance use disorders are risk factors for contracting HIV in the first place (Carey *et al.*, 1997). Further, many patients are vulnerable to acute distress in response to distinct phases of the illness, including initial notification of an HIV+ test result, the initial onset of physical symptoms, a sudden decline in CD4 counts, diagnosis of AIDS, and a first hospitalization all represent potent stressors during the course of HIV illness (Kalichman, 1998; Remien & Rabkin, 2001).Throughout the course of the disease, patients are also confronted with the ongoing challenges associated with coping with a highly stigmatized illness. Discrimination and stigma from employers, friends, and family remain prevalent and undoubtedly contribute to adjustment difficulties (Sowell *et al.*, 1997; Herek *et al.*, 2002).

Disclosure of HIV status also represents a major source of stress for persons living with HIV. Disclosure of HIV status allows couples to make informed choices regarding health risks. However, some HIV+ individuals choose not to disclose their status (De Rosa & Marks, 1998), in part because of fear of partner reprisal or rejection. Beyond the immediate context of close relationships, efforts to conceal one's serostatus limits the availability of social support, and requires that patients live a "double life" involving the need for deception about the reasons for recurrent medical visits, symptoms, and pill taking.

Assessment

It is important for clinicians to distinguish between normal stress reactions in response to disease-specific events and more severe adjustment difficulties. Likewise, it is important to distinguish between somatic symptoms caused by illness or medication side effects (e.g. fatigue and loss of appetite) and symptoms that are more directly linked to depression or other psychiatric disturbance (Remien & Rabkin, 2001). Beyond these considerations, behavioral medicine clinicians will find it helpful to assess mood and anxiety symptoms, as well as current substance use during intake interviews. Clinicians should also assess the broader context of the patient's experience in coping with HIV disease. Thus, the intake should include an assessment of patient's efforts to cope with major stressors, including changes in health status, treatment side effects, social support, relationship functioning, experiences with HIV-related stigmatization, and employment difficulties.

Clinicians may also wish to use brief screening instruments such as the Beck Depression Inventory or the Primary Care Evaluation of Mental Disorders (PRIME-MD; Spitzer *et al.*, 1999). The latter shows promise as a self-report screening tool for use in primary care settings. To screen for alcohol and drug use risk, the Alcohol Use Disorders Identification Test (Saunders *et al.*, 1993) and the Drug Abuse Screening Test (Skinner, 1982) are brief, reliable and valid instruments. If indicated, a more detailed evaluation of substance use based on the principles of motivational interviewing may prove helpful (Miller & Rollnick, 2002).

Coping and substance use interventions

Both pharmacological and cognitive behavioral interventions have been used successfully to treat mood and anxiety disorders among HIV+ individuals. Because cognitive behavioral therapy (CBT) provides generalizable coping skills that may assist patients with disease management, we recommend the use of such strategies either alone or in conjunction with drug therapy. Several recent reports in the literature provide helpful guidance in conducting CBT-based interventions in the context of HIV care. Folkman and Chesney (1991) reported encouraging results from their Coping Effectiveness Training (CET) intervention. This group-based intervention improves coping skills through the use of cognitive behavioral strategies and enhancement of social support. In a study involving 128 HIV+ gay men with depressive symptoms, men receiving the CET intervention showed a significant increase in self-efficacy, and decreased distress compared to participants in the information only group (Chesney *et al.*, 1996).

Antoni and colleagues (Antoni *et al.*, 1991; Cruess *et al.*, 2000) have also developed a cognitive behavioral stress management program (CBSM) that has shown great promise. This program takes a self-management approach to reducing psychological distress and improving health-related outcomes. The CBSM is a ten-week, group-based intervention that includes techniques for building awareness of stress and negative thoughts, cognitive restructuring techniques, relaxation and imagery techniques, coping skills training, interpersonal skills training, and methods for enhancing social support.

Whereas coping and mental health interventions that are tailored to the needs of HIV+ men and women have evolved considerably in recent years, strategies for assisting drug and alcohol dependent HIV+ men and women have only recently begun to appear in the literature (Ferrando & Batki, 2000). For behavioral medicine clinicians, an important initial decision point concerns whether a patient's substance use requires referral to a treatment program or can be managed in the context of a broader coping intervention. In the latter context, motivational interviewing strategies show considerable promise, both for encouraging efforts to reduce substance use, and to reinforce patients' progress in maintaining abstinence (Miller & Rollnick, 2002). For patients with severe dependence, inpatient treatment may be required to assist with initial efforts to abstain from substance use and for management of withdrawal symptoms.

Sexual health

Overview

A central challenge for persons living with HIV involves resumption of healthy, enjoyable, and safer sexual activity. Newly infected individuals commonly experience reduced interest in sex and high levels of anxiety about the prospect of re-initiating sexual activity. Over time, however, most people with HIV resume sexual activity and are faced with the new reality of pursuing romantic relationships despite having a severe, and ultimately fatal, sexually transmittable disease. For many, a return to being sexually active marks the beginning of a commitment to condom use for penetrative sexual behaviors (Weinhardt et al., 1999). However, a substantial proportion of HIV+ individuals struggle to follow safer sex guidelines. Studies of gay men (Vanable et al., 2000), injection drug users (Bluthenthal et al., 2000), and general outpatient samples (De Rosa & Marks, 1998) indicate that between one-third and one-half of persons living with HIV report engaging in unprotected sex on at least a periodic basis (Crepaz & Marks, 2002).

Some HIV+ individuals choose to have unprotected sex only when they are with other HIV+ partners. However, survey findings indicate that risk behavior between seropositive partners may account for less than one-third of those reporting unprotected sex (Marks et al., 1999). Further, unprotected sex between infected partners can pose considerable health risks if such encounters result in co-infections with another STD or contraction of a more virulent HIV strain. Indeed, infection with STDs such as syphilis, gonorrhea, or herpes can accelerate disease progression, and can also increase HIV infectiousness (Phair et al., 1992; Gao et al., 1996; Fox et al., 2001).

Correlates of continued risky sexual behavior among HIV+ individuals include poor negotiation skills (Fisher et al., 1998; Kalichman, 1999; Semple et al., 2000), substance use (Kalichman et al., 1997b; Vanable et al., 2000), and low self-efficacy for coping with high-risk situations (Godin et al., 1996; Kalichman et al., 1997a). An increasingly important factor among HIV+ individuals concerns the role of treatment-related attitudes and perceptions.

Widespread access to antiretroviral therapies has reinforced the optimistic view that HIV is now a survivable illness (Kelly *et al.*, 1998a) and that safer sex may be less important than it once was. Our research with HIV+ MSM supports these observations. Reduced concern about sexual risk behavior stemming from the availability of HAART was a strong predictor of unprotected anal sex across two samples of HIV+ MSM (Vanable *et al.*, 2000, 2003). Given the risks conferred to uninfected sexual partners and the risks associated with STD co-infection for the HIV+ persons, it is imperative that clinicians provide risk reduction counseling as part of their intervention work with HIV+ individuals.

Assessment

Referrals will sometimes indicate concerns about sexual functioning or about continued high-risk sexual behavior. However, patients often avoid disclosure of these concerns in the context of brief exchanges with healthcare providers. It is therefore important to include an assessment of current relationship status, sexual functioning and satisfaction, condom use, and perceptions regarding safer sex, as part of a standard assessment.

Careful listening serves as the cornerstone of the assessment process. Many patients will initially be reluctant to discuss sexual health concerns because of embarrassment, shame, or uncertainty about a provider's response. To facilitate an accurate history, this part of the interview should occur after a basic rapport has been established, and after you have assured the patient of confidentiality. It is also important that clinicians provide a rationale for asking questions about sexual behaviors. For example, one might say that sexual health is assessed for all patients, just as are medication adherence, symptoms, and other important matters. Thus, all patients are asked and no patient will feel singled out as being at unique risk. It is also important to ask questions in a direct fashion, without apology or hesitancy. When assessing sexual behavior, we have found it helpful to adopt some assumptions in order to gather the most accurate information efficiently. These assumptions reflect the preferred direction of error. Thus, for example, we assume a low level of understanding on the part of the patient so that language is directed to the patient in a clear and concrete manner. As the clinician learns more about the patient, these assumptions can be adjusted.

Depending upon the patient and referral context, it may be useful to sequence the inquiry from the least to most threatening questions. Thus, questions about relationship and sexual satisfaction might precede questions about unprotected penetrative sexual behavior. Experience also suggests that it can be helpful to place the "burden of denial" on the patient. That is, rather than ask "if" a patients has engaged in a particular activity, the clinician might ask "how many times have you . . .?" engaged in the activity. Use of this strategy will depend upon the nature of the relationship that has been established with the patient. More detailed guidelines for conducting a careful sexual history can be found in Wincze and Carey (2001).

Interventions to improve sexual health

Given the importance of sexual behavior among HIV+ persons, it is surprising to note the relative paucity of intervention research involving persons living with HIV. Findings from several coping interventions for seropositive individuals suggest that supportive contact alone can be beneficial in terms of reducing sexual risk behavior. For example, Coates *et al.* (1989) reported that participation in an intervention for HIV+ MSM that included relaxation and self-management training was associated with a reduction in number of partners at follow-up. Kelly *et al.* (1993) found that, compared to a control group and a cognitive behavioral coping intervention, participants who received a social support intervention reduced their frequency of unprotected receptive anal intercourse, relative to the other two groups.

Several studies have tested the effects of interventions that focus specifically on sexual risk reduction among HIV+ individuals. For example, Rotheram-Borus and colleagues (2001) reported encouraging results using a multi-session, group-based intervention designed to enhance self-regulatory skills required to cope with high-risk sexual situations among HIV+ adolescents. Results showed that adolescents who received the intervention reduced the number of HIV-negative sexual partners by 50 per cent, and decreased the number of unprotected acts by 82 per cent. In another comprehensive risk reduction intervention for HIV+ adults, Kalichman *et al.* (2001) compared the effectiveness of a five-session, theory-based intervention to a contact-matched support group, in a primary care sample of 233 men and 99 women living with HIV. The group-based risk reduction intervention included skills training to cope with high-risk sexual situations, skills for disclosure of HIV serostatus to partners, and skills for negotiating condom use. Results indicated that the intervention to reduce HIV transmission behaviors resulted in fewer instances of unprotected sex and increased condom use at a six-month follow-up.

For clinicians working with individual patients on sexual risk reduction, the fairly limited literature provides encouraging evidence to suggest that efforts to reduce sexual risk taking can be embedded within the broader context of mental health services. Indeed, because of the personal nature of sexual behavior and the unique challenges facing men and women with HIV, individual sessions may provide an ideal setting to conduct motivational enhancement for sexual behavior change, along with role-playing exercises to improve negotiation of safer sex, and cognitive behavioral strategies to assist patients in coping with high-risk settings often associated with non-condom use (Kelly & Kalichman, 2002).

Integrating assessment data into a case formulation

Behavioral medicine referrals in the context of HIV care involve the development of personalized interventions around challenging and often clinically sensitive problems. Prior to implementing a psychosocial intervention in the context of HIV care, an important goal is to develop a case formulation to guide treatment. A case formulation represents a set of working hypotheses concerning the role of biomedical, psychological, and social factors that serve to maintain problem behavior(s), poor coping, or disease self-management difficulties (Carey *et al.*, 1984). A case formulation should integrate information gathered from the patient's medical record, feedback from the referring physician or nurse practitioner, questionnaire data, and interview data gathered during the intake. In addition, the case formulation may include information gathered through self-monitoring exercises and other homework assignments.

By developing hypotheses about causal mechanisms that serve to maintain problem behaviors or poor adaptation, the case formulation should yield a conceptual "road map" for a subsequent intervention. A case conceptualization also communicates to your patient that their difficulties are understandable and that there is reason for optimism that an intervention will provide benefit and relief in addressing a set of presenting complaints or difficulties noted by a referring physician. To illustrate the assessment, case formulation, and treatment process, we now present two hypothetical cases involving HIV patients referred for behavioral medicine services.

Case I: Ben

Background information

Ben was a 28-year-old, white, gay-identified male who was newly employed as a web designer. Ben lived with his partner, Tom, who was also HIV+, in an apartment in a large urban setting. Ben was referred for evaluation and treatment by an infectious disease physician who had overseen Ben's medical care for the past four years. Ben's physician initiated combination antiretroviral therapy two years prior to the evaluation, following a drop in Ben's CD4 count and a bout with shingles. Results from Ben's most recent blood draw revealed a CD4 count of 300 and a viral load of 200 copies/ml (in the "undetectable" range), indicating that treatments were suppressing the virus as well as could be expected. The referring physician noted that, although Ben's health status was stable, Ben had reported irregularities in medication adherence over the last several visits. The referral also noted that Ben had recently contracted gonorrhea and that Ben seemed "depressed".

Assessment

Ben arrived promptly for his initial intake appointment. He was casually dressed and neat in appearance. The patient was engaging and cooperative throughout the 90-minute intake interview, and indicated that he was glad to have someone to talk to. When asked to describe his understanding of why he had been referred to the behavioral medicine service, he replied that he and his doctor had "not been getting along well lately". Ben reported that, during a recent appointment his doctor asked "a lot of personal questions about my sex life that made me feel uncomfortable". Ben also noted that he had a recurrent conflict with his parents. Although Ben did not initially mention medication adherence difficulties, he acknowledged that he had missed taking his medication on several occasions recently. Ben reported feeling "embarrassed and scared" after learning that he had contracted gonorrhea, and that this revelation had not been well received by his partner, Tom. He and Tom had a "negotiated safety" agreement in which they decided to forgo condom use within their seroconcordant relationship, but to always use condoms when with other partners. However, Ben described having a couple of recent "slips" in the context of heavy drinking occasions. In each instance, Ben reported that he had intended to use protection, but that he was talked into unprotected sex by partners he was very attracted to. When asked about concerns regarding HIV transmission to other partners, he reported that he was "fairly certain" that they were also HIV+, having seen at least one of them at the HIV care clinic he attends. Ben stated that he understood that unprotected sex posed some health risks even with his primary partner (because of concerns about HIV reinfection and possible STD infections), but indicated that he had no interest in using condoms with his primary partner. However, he reported being very motivated to avoid future lapses while with other partners.

Ben reported that he drank infrequently and in moderate quantities while at home. However, when out at bars and parties on weekends, he almost always drank heavily (i.e. six or more drinks), and frequently experienced hangovers. Ben reported occasional use of marijuana and poppers (amyl nitrates), but no other current recreational drug use. Ben did not see his drinking as a big problem and did not wish to consider the possibility of abstaining.

Ben described his mood as "generally okay", but later acknowledged being somewhat upset because of strained relations with his parents. Ben had only recently disclosed his HIV status to them, and it was within this context that he also told his parents that he was gay. Ben reported subsequently having frequent arguments with his parents, who he said were still in a "state of shock" with regard to his illness. He reported that his mother was fairly understanding, but his father had repeatedly made disparaging comments about Ben's "gay life style". Both parents were worried about his illness and – although they never stated it as such – Ben assumed that his parents viewed his HIV diagnosis as a "death sentence". In addition to concerns about his family, Ben also reported feeling upset about having HIV, noting that he had several friends who have been "less fortunate" in terms of responding well to treatment. Ben reported that he wanted to live a full and productive life, but that his HIV treatment regimen served as a constant reminder that his health status could "take a turn for the worse" at any point. He indicated that he had, up until recently, been fairly successful in taking his medications as prescribed. Adherence difficulties began shortly after he started his new job. He reported that he had simply forgotten to take his medication on several occasions while in the midst of working under a tight deadline. He also noted that he had occasionally missed taking his medication because of fears that his co-workers would see his medication and figure out that he is HIV+.

As part of the initial assessment, Ben also completed several self-report questionnaires. He scored in the mild to moderately depressed range on the Beck Depression Inventory (score of 12), and scored in the "elevated risk" range on the AUDIT (score of 9). Ben also kept a detailed diary of his medication usage during the week that followed his initial appointment. He missed taking his medication on two occasions that week (both lapses occurred while he was at work).

Case formulation and intervention

Ben's depressed mood and anxiety symptoms were not of sufficient severity to warrant an Axis I diagnosis, but nonetheless represented an important focus for treatment. Stressors included his strained relations with his parents, chronic concerns about his health and long-term prognosis, and his gonorrhea diagnosis. Alcohol use was also a concern. Ben met criteria for alcohol abuse, and his drinking was clearly contributing to poor choices with sexual partners. Ben's perspective was that drinking was only problematic in the context of his weekend partying at gay bars. He was interested in the possibility of reducing his substance use in sexual contexts but unmotivated to fully abstain from alcohol use.

Ben's recent STD diagnosis put a strain on his relationship with Tom and posed clear health risks for Ben and his sexual partners (several of whom were of unknown serostatus). Ben therefore identified avoiding unprotected sex with non-steady partners as an essential goal. Assessment data suggested at least two related factors were contributing to lapses in condom use and warranted intervention attention: (a) heavy alcohol use in gay bar settings; (b) skills deficits in negotiating condom use with new partners. Although the clinician considered condom use with Ben's primary partner, Tom, to be a worthwhile goal as well, Ben was not interested in such a change. Consistent with a "harm reduction" approach, Ben's plan to focus on reducing risky sex with non-steady partners was considered realistic given Ben's strong commitment to maintaining his negotiated safety agreement with Tom.

Adherence difficulties clearly warranted treatment as well. The clinician established that Ben had a good understanding of his medication regimen and was aware of the possible consequence of not taking his medication. Self-management difficulties and avoidance of stigma in the context of work were deemed to be a central determinant of adherence lapses. An initial plan was to continue self-monitoring of adherence for two weeks to clarify the circumstances of missed doses, and to subsequently implement new strategies that would prevent detection by co-workers.

During the feedback session, the clinician reassured Ben that, in fact, he was coping remarkably well given the range of challenges he was facing. Ben reported that he was "relieved" to be able to talk to someone about his experiences with HIV, and readily agreed to commit to ten sessions of weekly therapy, focusing on mood management, eliminating high-risk sex with non-steady partners, and improved adherence. The therapist adopted a cognitive behavioral perspective in assisting Ben with his coping difficulties and utilized motivational enhancement strategies to assist with Ben's alcohol-related difficulties. Ben was gradually able to identify when illness-related worries set in, and to adopt alternative self-statements that emphasized his own capacity to manage his illness (rather than dwelling on what could go wrong). His therapist also taught him to use breathing techniques as a means of relaxation. He encouraged Ben to rely more on his partner Tom as a source of support, and for the two of them to schedule real "dates" to increase pleasurable interactions. Ben eventually accepted that his relationship with his parents would take time to improve. He identified strategies for discussing his illness with his parents and was able to reassure them that he would likely remain in good health for many years. Ben raised the possibility of inviting his parents for a visit to meet Tom at some point, but thought that such a visit should occur only after he and his parents were getting along better.

Ben's gonorrhea diagnosis proved to be a potent motivator of change with regard to sexual activity outside of his primary relationship. Initial therapy sessions included a focus on identifying strategies for reduced alcohol use in contexts that could involve meeting new partners. Role-playing exercises were used to enhance Ben's assertiveness skills for communicating with new partners. To his therapist's surprise, Ben decided to eliminate bar going altogether and to focus on his relationship with Tom. Over time, however, Ben did return to occasional weekend bar going. He had some success in reducing his alcohol by alternating between alcoholic and non-alcoholic beverages, and by setting a limit at three drinks per drinking occasion. He only had one outside sexual encounter during the initial phase of therapy, and successfully negotiated the use of condoms.

Self-monitoring of medication adherence revealed a few lapses in the timing of his medication while at work and one occasion in which he missed his pills altogether when faced with a tight deadline. Although Ben had rejected the use of a pill planner when his physician first suggested it, he later reconsidered it, and this proved to be very helpful, allowing him to lay out his whole regimen on a weekly basis. Ben also put his computer skills to work by devising a way to use his handheld computer to remind him when his next pills were due to be taken.

After completing ten sessions, Ben reported considerable improvement in his mood and adherence. He decided to continue with individual therapy to maintain gains and to refine his coping skills.

Case 2: Paula

Background

Paula was a single, unemployed, 32-year-old African-American woman who tested positive for HIV seven years ago. She lived in a small apartment with two young children, aged 5 and 8. Both children were HIV-negative. Paula believes that she contracted HIV through sexual contact with a former boyfriend, an intravenous drug user. Her medical record noted a history of occasional cocaine use and occasional sex trading. A note from a recent social work consultation indicated that Paula was currently in an abusive relationship. At the time of the referral, Paula's health status was described as "declining". She was diagnosed with AIDS six months prior to this evaluation, and was recently started on a new drug regimen. Adherence was described as "poor". The referral noted that Paula was depressed and that the treatment team had concerns that she may be demoralized and "losing hope". The referring physician requested a behavioral medicine evaluation as a first step in initiating a comprehensive treatment plan to prevent further deterioration in Paula's mental and physical health.

Assessment

Paula arrived for her first appointment accompanied by her two children. Initially, her eye contact was poor and she provided only brief responses to the clinician's queries. Paula became somewhat more engaged after the clinician showed an interest in her children and provided them with several toys to play with in an adjacent waiting room. Noting that her children are "all that she has", Paula tearfully described that she was fearful of dying and leaving her children. When asked to describe her understanding of why she was referred to the behavioral medicine service, she stated that her doctor "says I'm depressed and not taking good care of myself".

Paula described her mood as "really bad", noting that she had been feeling worse since learning that she had AIDS. The patient stated that she sometimes feels like "giving up the fight" but indicated that she would never harm herself because of her religious beliefs and the effect that would have on her children. She was currently experiencing sleep onset difficulties and early morning awakenings, as well as persistently poor appetite. Paula indicated that she had little energy and that she struggles to find the motivation to get out of bed each day to get her children ready for school. She stated that, apart from her children, she had few sources of pleasure and little to look forward to. She later noted that her faith in God provided some comfort. She stated that she prays that she will one day feel healthy again, but also knows that "things aren't looking too good right now". Paula attends a local church when she can, and reports that her children participate in several youth activities through the church. Her mother lives nearby and helps occasionally with babysitting. Apart from the support she receives from her mother, Paula indicated that other family members avoid talking to her about her illness, but "they all know what I have".

Paula stated that she currently receives a small disability check and lives in subsidized housing. She stated that she had no money to buy clothing for her kids and little money for food. Paula reported that she occasionally had sex with men who stopped by as a way of earning extra spending money. She also reported that she has a regular boyfriend whom she sees several times a week. However, she reported that he is often high on crack cocaine, and shows little interest in her difficulties. Paula reported that she is sexually active with her boyfriend but derives little pleasure from spending time with him. She reported that he is aware of her HIV status but that "he'd never use condoms". On a recent occasion when Paula attempted to refuse sex because she wasn't feeling well, she eventually gave in after her boyfriend slapped her and threatened to do more harm if she continued to refuse sex.

Paula acknowledged occasional cocaine use in the past, but reported that she stopped once she learned that she had AIDS. She denied current alcohol use.

When asked about her HIV medications, she stated that "they make me feel sick". Paula struggled to recall the names of her medication or the details of her regimen, stating that she does "the best she can" to take her pills. She knew that she was supposed to take her medicines several times a day, but had to check her pill bottles to recall the timing of each medication and the dietary requirements. When asked about adherence in the previous week, she reported that she missed taking her pill for two days, because she "ran out" and lacked transportation to the drug store. She expressed some understanding of the importance of taking her medication as prescribed, but reported feeling doubtful that she could improve her adherence.

Case formulation and intervention

Paula's case demonstrates the way in which poverty, demoralization, and poor social support can create seemingly insurmountable barriers to adequate self-care. Paula presents with severe depression, very poor medication adherence, and declining health. Faced with multiple stressors, including the need to care for two young children with little outside help, an abusive relationship, and inadequate financial resources, Paula is understandably pessimistic about her future. She is often immobilized by depression, and her declining health status serves as a reminder that she may not survive to see her children grow up. Notable strengths include Paula's dedication to caring for her children, her use of faith and the church as a means of support, and her strong emotional ties to her mother and other family members.

Based on the complexity of the case, the referring clinician arranged for a case conference to discuss various intervention options with the referring physician, a clinic social worker, and a representative from a local HIV case management service. Those in attendance at the meeting agreed that Paula would benefit from twice weekly home visits by a case manager to assure that medication refills were completed on time, to assist with preparation of her pill planner, and to provide other support services. In addition, the social worker agreed to follow Paula for supportive therapy and to provide psycho-oeducational intervention to improve Paula's understanding of her medication regimen. To further address Paula's depression, the examining clinician recommended a referral to the psychiatry service, as well as participation in a women's HIV support group.

Following this initial meeting, the clinician arranged for an immediate consultation with the psychiatry service, and Paula was started on an SSRI antidepressant. Although Paula had previously declined case management services, she agreed to the home visits, which proved to be beneficial. She also agreed to participate in the support group and to attend weekly meetings with the social worker. Paula's individual therapy focused initially on medication adherence, but broadened to include a focus on improving her circumstances at home. The social worker provided assistance in renewing Paula's eligibility for food stamps and helped to arrange for after-school programs for Paula's children. The social worker also encouraged Paula to become more involved in church-related activities and to arrange for more frequent get-togethers with family. Paula's abusive relationship was discussed often during therapy, and she eventually found the strength to break up with her boyfriend.

As a result of this multidisciplinary intervention, Paula's medication adherence improved somewhat, as did her health status. The antidepressant was helpful in alleviating depressive symptoms, and greater involvement with her church served to provide some additional social support. With these short-term improvements, the treatment team was cautiously optimistic about Paula's longer term prospects.

Concluding remarks

As these cases illustrate, case formulations are an essential starting point for developing collaborative treatment plans to assist HIV+ patients with common presenting concerns, including difficulties with medication adherence and maintenance of safer sex, along with issues related to long-term coping and adaptation to a life-threatening illness. To be effective, treatment providers must remain informed about the latest biomedical advances in what has proven to be a rapidly changing treatment environment. At present, while HAART treatments offer tremendous benefits for some, poor treatment response is all too common, and a true cure or effective vaccine is likely to remain elusive for the foreseeable future. As the global HIV epidemic continues to evolve, behavioral medicine specialists will undoubtedly play an important role in efforts to forestall disease progression and improve the lives of those who are affected by this devastating disease.

References

Antoni, M. H., Baggett, L., Ironson, G., LaPerriere, A., August, S., Klimas, N., et al. (1991). Cognitive-behavioral stress management intervention buffers distress responses and immunologic changes following notification of HIV-1 seropositivity. *Journal of Consulting and Clinical Psychology, 59*, 906–915.

Bamberger, J. D., Unick, J., Klein, P., Fraser, M., Chesney, M., & Katz, M. H. (2000). Helping the urban poor stay with antiretroviral HIV drug therapy. *American Journal of Public Health, 90*, 699–701.

Bangsberg, D. R., Hecht, F. M., Charlebois, E. D., Zolopa, A. R., Holodniy, M., Sheiner, L., et al. (2000). Adherence to protease inhibitors, HIV-1 viral load, and development of drug resistance in an indigent population. *AIDS, 14*, 357–366.

Bartlett, J. A. (2002). Addressing the challenges of adherence. *Journal of Acquired Immune Deficiency Syndrome, 29*, S2–10.

Bing, E. G., Burnam, M. A., Longshore, D., Fleishman, J. A., Sherbourne, C. D., London, A. S., et al. (2001). Psychiatric disorders and drug use among human immunodeficiency virus-infected adults in the United States. *Archives of General Psychiatry, 58*, 721–728.

Bluthenthal, R. N., Kral, A. H., Gee, L., Erringer, E. A., & Edlin, B. R. (2000). The effect of syringe exchange use on high-risk injection drug users: A cohort study. *AIDS, 14*, 605–611.

Carey, M. P., Flasher, L. V., Maisto, S. A., & Turkat, I. D. (1984). The a priori approach to psychological assessment. *Professional Psychology: Research and Practice, 15*, 515–527.

Carey, M. P., Carey, K. B., & Kalichman, S. C. (1997). Risk for human immunodeficiency virus (HIV) infection among persons with severe mental illnesses. *Clinical Psychology Review, 17*, 271–291.

Catz, S. L., Kelly, J. A., Bogart, L. M., Benotsch, E. G., & McAuliffe, T. L. (2000). Patterns, correlates, and barriers to medication adherence among persons prescribed new treatments for HIV disease. *Health Psychology, 19*, 124–133.

Chesney, M., Folkman, S., & Chambers, D. (1996). Coping effectiveness training for men living with HIV: Preliminary findings. *International Journal of STD and AIDS, 7*, 75–82.

Chesney, M. A., Ickovics, J., Hecht, F. M., Sikipa, G., & Rabkin, J. (1999). Adherence: A necessity for successful HIV combination therapy. *AIDS, 13*, S271–278.

Chesney, M. A., Ickovics, J. R., Chambers, D. B., Gifford, A. L., Neidig, J., Zwickl, B., et al. (2000). Self-reported adherence to antiretroviral medications among participants in HIV clinical trials: The AACTG adherence instruments. *AIDS Care, 12*, 255–266.

Coates, T. J., McKusick, L., Kuno, R., & Stites, D. P. (1989). Stress reduction training changed number of sexual partners but not immune function in men with HIV. *American Journal of Public Health, 79*, 885–887.

Crepaz, N., & Marks, G. (2002). Towards an understanding of sexual risk behavior in people living with HIV: A review of social, psychological, and medical findings. *AIDS, 16*, 135–149.

Cruess, D. G., Antoni, M. H., Schneiderman, N., Ironson, G., McCabe, P., Fernandez, J. B., et al. (2000). Cognitive-behavioral stress management increases free testosterone and decreases psychological distress in HIV-seropositive men. *Health Psychology, 19*, 12–20.

De Rosa, C. J., & Marks, G. (1998). Preventive counseling of HIV-positive men and self-disclosure of serostatus to sex partners: New opportunities for prevention. *Health Psychology, 17*, 224–231.

Detels, R., Munoz, A., McFarlane, G., Kingsley, L. A., Margolick, J. B., Giorgi, J., et al. (1998). Effectiveness of potent antiretroviral therapy on time to AIDS and death in men with known HIV infection duration. Multicenter AIDS Cohort Study Investigators. *JAMA, 280*, 1497–1503.

Ferrando, S. J., & Batki, S. L. (2000). Substance abuse and HIV infection. *New Directions in Mental Health Service*, 57–67.

Fisher, J. D., Kimble, D., Misovich, S. J., & Weinstein, E. (1998). Dynamics of HIV risk behavior in HIV-infected men who have sex with men. *AIDS and Behavior, 2*, 101–113.

Folkman, S., & Chesney, M. (1991). Translating coping theory into intervention. In J. Eckenrode (Ed.), *The social context of stress* (pp. 239–260). New York: Plenum.

Fox, K. K., del Rio, C., Holmes, K. K., Hook, E. W., 3rd, Judson, F. N., Knapp, J. S., et al. (2001). Gonorrhea in the HIV era: A reversal in trends among men who have sex with men. *American Journal of Public Health, 91*, 959–964.

Frick, P. A., Lavreys, L., Mandaliya, K., & Kreiss, J. K. (2001). Impact of an alarm device on medication compliance in women in Mombasa, Kenya. *International Journal of STDs and AIDS, 12*, 329–333.

Galvan, F. H., Bing, E. G., Fleishman, J. A., London, A. S., Caetano, R., Burnam, M. A., et al. (2002). The prevalence of alcohol consumption and heavy drinking among people with HIV in the United States: Results from the HIV Cost and Services Utilization Study. *Journal of Studies on Alcohol, 63*, 179–186.

Gao, S. J., Kingsley, L., Hoover, D. R., Spira, T. J., Rinaldo, C. R., Saah, A., et al. (1996). Seroconversion to antibodies against Kaposi's sarcoma-associated herpesvirus-related latent nuclear antigens before the development of Kaposi's sarcoma. *New England Journal of Medicine, 335*, 233–241.

Gifford, A. L., Bormann, J. E., Shively, M. J., Wright, B. C., Richman, D. D., & Bozzette, S. A. (2000). Predictors of self-reported adherence and plasma HIV concentrations in patients on multidrug antiretroviral regimens. *Journal of Acquired Immune Deficiency Syndrome, 23*, 386–395.

Godin, G., Savard, J., Kok, G., Fortin, C., & Boyer, R. (1996). HIV seropositive gay men: Understanding adoption of safe sexual practices. *AIDS Education and Prevention, 8*, 529–545.

Herek, G. M., Capitanio, J. P., & Widaman, K. F. (2002). HIV-related stigma and knowledge in the United States: Prevalence and trends, 1991–1999. *American Journal of Public Health, 92*, 371–377.

Kalichman, S. C. (1998). *Understanding AIDS: Advances in research and treatment* (2nd ed.). Washington, DC: American Psychological Association.

Kalichman, S. C. (1999). Psychological and social correlates of high-risk sexual behaviour among men and women living with HIV/AIDS. *AIDS Care, 11*, 415–427.

Kalichman, S. C., Greenberg, J., & Abel, G. G. (1997a). HIV-seropositive men who engage in high-risk sexual behaviour: Psychological characteristics and implications for prevention. *AIDS Care, 9*, 441–450.

Kalichman, S. C., Kelly, J. A., & Rompa, D. (1997b). Continued high-risk sex among HIV seropositive gay and bisexual men seeking HIV prevention services. *Health Psychology, 16*, 369–373.

Kalichman, S. C., Ramachandran, B., & Catz, S. (1999). Adherence to combination antiretroviral therapies in HIV patients of low health literacy. *Journal of General Internal Medicine, 14*, 267–273.

Kalichman, S. C., Rompa, D., Cage, M., DiFonzo, K., Simpson, D., Austin, J., *et al.* (2001). Effectiveness of an intervention to reduce HIV transmission risks in HIV-positive people. *American Journal of Preventive Medicine, 21*, 84–92.

Kelly, J. A., & Kalichman, S. C. (2002). Behavioral research on HIV/AIDS primary and secondary prevention: Recent advances and future directions. *Journal of Consulting and Clinical Psychology, 70*, 626–639.

Kelly, J. A., Murphy, D. A., Bahr, G. R., Kalichman, S. C., Morgan, M. G., Stevenson, L. Y., *et al.* (1993). Outcome of cognitive-behavioral and support group brief therapies for depressed, HIV-infected persons. *American Journal of Psychiatry, 150*, 1679–1686.

Kelly, J. A., Hoffmann, R. G., Rompa, D., & Gray, M. (1998a). Protease inhibitor combination therapies and perceptions gay men regarding AIDS severity and the need to maintain safer sex. *AIDS, 12*, F91–F95.

Kelly, J. A., Otto-Salaj, L. L., Sikkema, K. J., Pinkerton, S. D., & Bloom, F. R. (1998b). Implications of HIV treatment advances for behavioral research on AIDS: Protease inhibitors and new challenges in HIV secondary prevention. *Health Psychology, 17*, 310–319.

Marks, G., Burris, S., & Peterman, T. A. (1999). Reducing sexual transmission of HIV from those who know they are infected: The need for personal and collective responsibility. *AIDS, 13*, 297–306.

Miller, W. R., & Rollnick, S. (2002). *Motivational interviewing: Preparing people for change* (2nd ed.). New York: Guilford Press.

Mostashari, F., Riley, E., Selwyn, P. A., & Altice, F. L. (1998). Acceptance and adherence with antiretroviral therapy among HIV-infected women in a correctional facility. *Journal of Acquired Immune Deficiency Syndrome, 18*, 341–348.

Paterson, D. L., Swindells, S., Mohr, J., Brester, M., Vergis, E. N., Squier, C., *et al.* (2000). Adherence to protease inhibitor therapy and outcomes in patients with HIV infection. *Annals of Internal Medicine, 133*, 21–30.

Phair, J., Jacobson, L., Detels, R., Rinaldo, C., Saah, A., Schrager, L., *et al.* (1992).

Acquired immune deficiency syndrome occurring within 5 years of infection with human immunodeficiency virus type-1: The Multicenter AIDS Cohort Study. *Journal of Acquired Immune Deficiency Syndrome, 5*, 490–496.

Rabkin, J. G., & Chesney, M. (1999). Treatment adherence to HIV medications: The achilles heel of the new therapies. In D. G. Ostrow & S. C. Kalichman (Eds.), *Psychosocial and public health impacts of new HIV therapies* (pp. 61–79). New York: Kluwer Academic/Plenum.

Rabkin, J. G., Wagener, G., & Rabkin, R. (1996). Treatment of depression in HIV+ men: Literature review and report of an ongoing study of testosterone replacement therapy. *Annals of Behavioral Medicine, 18*, 24–29.

Reed, G. M., Kemeny, M. E., Taylor, S. E., & Visscher, B. R. (1999). Negative HIV-specific expectancies and AIDS-related bereavement as predictors of symptom onset in asymptomatic HIV-positive gay men. *Health Psychology, 18*, 354–363.

Remien, R. H., & Rabkin, J. G. (2001). Psychological aspects of living with HIV disease: A primary care perspective. *Western Journal of Medicine, 175*, 332–335.

Rotheram-Borus, M. J., Lee, M. B., Murphy, D. A., Futterman, D., Duan, N., Birnbaum, J. M., *et al.* (2001). Efficacy of a preventive intervention for youths living with HIV. *American Journal of Public Health, 91*, 400–405.

Saunders, J. B., Aasland, O. G., Babor, T. F., de la Fuente, J. R., & Grant, M. (1993). Development of the Alcohol Use Disorders Identification Test (AUDIT): WHO Collaborative Project on Early Detection of Persons with Harmful Alcohol Consumption–II. *Addiction, 88*, 791–804.

Semple, S. J., Patterson, T. L., & Grant, I. (2000). The sexual negotiation behavior of HIV-positive gay and bisexual men. *Journal of Consulting and Clinical Psychology, 68*, 934–937.

Skinner, H. A. (1982). The Drug Abuse Screening Test. *Addictive Behaviors, 7*, 363–371.

Sowell, R. L., Seals, B. F., Moneyham, L., Demi, A., Cohen, L., & Brake, S. (1997). Quality of life in HIV-infected women in the south-eastern United States. *AIDS Care, 9*, 501–512.

Spitzer, R. L., Kroenke, K., & Williams, J. B. (1999). Validation and utility of a self-report version of PRIME-MD: The PHQ primary care study. Primary Care Evaluation of Mental Disorders. Patient Health Questionnaire. *JAMA, 282*, 1737–1744.

Taylor, S. E., Kemeny, M. E., Reed, G. M., Bower, J. E., & Gruenewald, T. L. (2000). Psychological resources, positive illusions, and health. *American Psychologist, 55*, 99–109.

Tuldra, A., Fumaz, C. R., Ferrer, M. J., Bayes, R., Arno, A., Balague, M., *et al.* (2000). Prospective randomized two-arm controlled study to determine the efficacy of a specific intervention to improve long-term adherence to highly active antiretroviral therapy. *Journal of Acquired Immune Deficiency Syndrome, 25*, 221–228.

Vanable, P. A., Ostrow, D. G., McKirnan, D. J., Taywaditep, K. J., & Hope, B. A. (2000). Impact of combination therapies on HIV risk perceptions and sexual risk among HIV-positive and HIV-negative gay and bisexual men. *Health Psychology, 19*, 134–145.

Vanable, P. A., Ostrow, D. G., & McKirnan, D. J. (2003). Viral load and HIV treatment attitudes as correlates of sexual risk behavior among HIV-positive gay men. *Journal of Psychosomatic Research, 54*, 263–269.

Weinhardt, L. S., Carey, M. P., Johnson, B. T., & Bickham, N. L. (1999). Effects of HIV counseling and testing on sexual risk behavior: A meta- analytic review of published research, 1985–1997. *American Journal of Public Health, 89*, 1397–1405.

Wincze, J. P., & Carey, M. P. (2001). *Sexual dysfunction: Guide for assessment and treatment.* (2nd ed.). New York: Guilford Press.

Chapter 13

Cancer

*Arthur M. Nezu, Elizabeth R. Lombardo and
Christine Maguth Nezu*

Introduction

Although cancer continues to be a huge public health problem, considerable medical progress has been made in treating this set of diseases during the past several decades. Many forms are curable and there is a sustained decline in the overall death rate from cancer when one focuses on the impact on the total population (Murphy *et al.*, 1997). Because of improvements in medical science, more people are living with cancer than ever before. However, despite these improved medical prognoses, psychosocial and emotional needs are often overlooked (Nezu *et al.*, 1998). Almost every aspect of one's life can be affected, as cancer engenders many stressors and can lead to significantly compromised quality of life. Even for people who historically have coped well with negative life events, cancer and its treatment greatly increases the stressful nature of even routine daily tasks. Weissman and Worden (1976–77) referred to this situation for cancer patients as an "existential plight", where one's very existence can be endangered. With the advent of the field of psychosocial oncology, increased attention has been paid by mental health professionals to this "plight" (Andersen, 2002; Nezu & Nezu, 2004).

For therapists to be able to optimally help distressed cancer patients, it is important to have a basic understanding of the nature and types of problems such individuals may experience, as well as the types of psychosocial interventions that have been found to be effective for such difficulties. As such, in the next section, we provide answers to the following key questions:

- What are the general psychosocial effects of cancer?
- What are important psychosocial variables that can mediate the impact of cancer?
- What are treatment strategies that are effective in improving the quality of life of such individuals?

In addition, along with describing the course of cancer and its treatment in order to foster a more effective case formulation, we provide various clinical cases that highlight the differing psychosocial issues that can emerge during such pathways. Last, in the appendix, we provide a list of assessment tools that can help the mental health professional to evaluate both symptoms of distress and their psychosocial mediators.

What are the psychosocial effects of cancer?

Estimates suggest a high prevalence of psychological difficulties across cancer diagnoses (Telch & Telch, 1985). For example, in a study of 215 patients with varying types of cancers, nearly half (47 per cent) had clinically apparent psychiatric disorders (Massie & Holland, 1987). Over two-thirds (68 per cent) had reactive anxiety and depression, 13 per cent had major depression, 8 per cent had an organic mental disorder, 7 per cent had personality disorders, and 4 per cent had anxiety disorders. In addition, of the psychiatric disorders observed in this population, 90 per cent were reactions to the disease or its treatment. Common problems of cancer patients include depression, anxiety, suicide, delirium, body image concerns, sexual dysfunctions, and pain.

Depression

Depression is a common experience among cancer patients (Newport & Nemeroff, 1998). Studies utilizing both self-report and clinical observations suggest that major depression affects approximately 25 per cent of cancer patients (Massie & Holland, 1987). Factors associated with greater prevalence of depression include higher levels of physical disability, advanced disease stage, and the presence of pain (Williamson & Schulz, 1995). Higher rates of depression have also been associated with the side effects of medications and treatment for cancer.

Anxiety

Anxiety is also prevalent among cancer patients, in part due to fears regarding "bad news" about diagnoses, prognoses, and treatment options. In addition, cancer treatments themselves can be anxiety provoking and may contribute to the cancer patient's psychological morbidity. Anxiety disorders appear to be more common in persons with cancer than controls or other chronic illnesses in the general population. Maguire *et al.* (1978), for example, found moderate to severe anxiety in 27 per cent of a sample of breast cancer patients as compared to 14 per cent in a control sample. In addition, some researchers have suggested that cancer survivors may respond to the psychological distress and uncertainty about the future by manifesting post-traumatic stress disorder-like symptoms similar to those experienced by victims of war or environmental disasters (Cordova *et al.*, 1995).

Suicide

Some studies estimating the prevalence of suicide among cancer patients suggest that it is two to ten times greater than that of the general population (Whitlock, 1978). The risk for suicide may be greater in the advanced stages of the illness and with patients experiencing significant fatigue. Cancer patients are at an increased risk for suicide during hospitalization, immediately after discharge, and at the time of recurrence and/or treatment failure. However, it is important to recognize that suicide risk in patients with cancer may be at its highest after successful treatment or as one's depression lifts. As depression and hopelessness have been found to be causally linked to suicide (Beck *et al.*, 1975), the degree to which cancer patients experience such feelings may increase their vulnerability to suicide. In addition, the fear of death or recurrence of cancer may develop into suicidal ideation.

Delirium

Delirium is a common psychiatric problem among cancer patients due to the direct effects of cancer on the central nervous system (CNS) and the indirect CNS complications of the disease and medical treatment. Delirium can often go unrecognized because it mimics signs of depression. Symptoms consist of agitation, impaired cognitive function, altered attention span, and a fluctuating level of consciousness. Those at an increased risk for delirium are inpatients, elderly patients, and those with an advanced or terminal disease.

Body image problems

Negative body image is one of the most profound psychological consequences from cancer treatments affecting patients with a variety of disease sites. The scars and physical disfigurement serve as reminders of the painful experience of cancer and its treatment. The stress and depression which may be a result of body image concerns can further impact other areas of the patient's and family's lives, such as sexual intimacy, psychological distress, and self-esteem. In women who have had breast surgery, concerns range from distress over scars to feelings of decreased sexual attractiveness and restrictions of use of certain items of clothing. In a study of women who had breast conserving surgery, 25 per cent had serious body image problems (Sneeuw *et al.*, 1992).

Sexual functioning difficulties

Estimates of sexual functioning problems range depending on the type of cancer, but appear to be common across cancer sites (Andersen *et al.*, 1989). For example, in a study of cancer patients undergoing a bone marrow transplantation, 47 per cent were found to have a global sexual dysfunction and 60 per cent had abnormalities of at least one parameter of sexual dysfunction (Marks *et al.*, 1996). Common sexual functioning problems among cancer patients include loss of sexual desire in both men and women, erectile dysfunction in men, and dyspareunia in women. Studies suggest that sexual dysfunctions continue one to two years post-treatment, indicating a large impact on a patient's quality of life (Marks *et al.*, 1997). Cancer treatment itself can further contribute to a patient's sexual dysfunctions.

Pain

The prevalence of psychiatric disorders is especially high in patients experiencing pain as a result of cancer and its treatment. In the Psychosocial Collaborative Oncology Group study (Derogatis *et al.*, 1983), 39 per cent of those who received a psychiatric disorder were experiencing significant pain. The psychiatric diagnosis of such patients was predominantly adjustment disorder with depressed mood (69 per cent), and 15 per cent of the patients with significant pain had symptoms of major depression.

What important psychosocial variables mediate the impact of cancer?

Although the type of tumor, treatment, diagnosis, and prior quality of life greatly determine the course of the disease, there are certain psychosocial variables that can significantly influence the adaptation process (Burgess *et al.*, 1988; Nezu *et al.*, 1999). When facing a stressful life event such as cancer, various coping skills, as well as the quality of one's social support, can be valuable in maintaining adequate functioning and can actually moderate the negative impact of such traumatic events on physical, social, and emotional functioning. Coping variables include avoidance/denial, fighting spirit/ optimism, problem solving, and monitoring/blunting.

Avoidance/denial

The research literature has yielded conflicting results regarding the impact of denial on adjustment to cancer. For example, Watson *et al.* (1984) found that those who initially denied the seriousness of cancer reported less mood disturbance as compared to patients who initially accepted the implications of the disease and admitted fears of death. However, Carver *et al.* (1993) found avoidance coping to be positively correlated with emotional distress. Further, two separate studies by C. M. Nezu *et al.* (1999) found that increased use of avoidance coping was strongly correlated with increased levels of anxiety and depression and more frequent cancer-related problems.

Fighting spirit/optimism

Individuals with cancer who demonstrate more of a confrontational coping style, optimism, and a fighting spirit have been found to have improved psychological adjustment compared to those with passive acceptance, helplessness, anxious preoccupation, avoidance, and denial (Van't Spiker *et al.*, 1997). In general, the construct of optimism has been associated with less distress in individuals facing a diagnosis of cancer. For example, C. M. Nezu *et al.* (1999) found a positive orientation towards coping with stress to be negatively correlated with emotional distress among adult cancer patients.

Problem solving

Deficits in social problem-solving ability (i.e. the ability to effectively resolve real-life problems) have been found to be strongly correlated with psychological distress in general (Nezu, 2004). With regard to patients with cancer, C. M. Nezu *et al.* (1999) reported that cancer patients who were characterized by less effective problem-solving ability were found to report higher levels of depressive and anxiety symptomatology, as well as more frequent cancer-related problems. Furthermore, poorer problem-solving ability was also found to predict emotional distress among a sample of breast cancer survivors who had undergone surgery between 1 and 13.3 years previously.

Monitoring and blunting

Miller and her colleagues (2001) have developed a cognitive-social health information processing model that outlines how two types of coping styles – monitoring and blunting – predict reactions to a cancer diagnosis. Individuals who dispositionally scan for threatening cancer cues or information are considered "monitors", whereas "blunters" are individuals who dispositionally attempt to distract themselves from and minimize threatening cancer-related information. Monitors are characterized by greater perceptions of threat, lower self-efficacy expectations, and greater cancer-related distress. The importance of attempting to identify such coping styles lies in the manner in which information should be provided to the differing "types" of patients. For example, framing cancer-related information in a less negative, non-threatening manner can lead to reduced distress among monitors.

Social support

Social support has also been found to have an important impact on patients' sense of well-being when confronting the stress of cancer and its treatments. Social supports are the resources provided by people in an individual's social network, such as spouses, family members, friends, co-workers, fellow patients, or professionals. These sources are helpful in times of stress (e.g. dealing with an illness) and may consist of instrumental aid, expressive or emotional aid, and informational aid. The beneficial effects of social support can be both direct (i.e. positive social interactions can directly increase positive cognitions, emotions, and behaviors), as well as indirect (i.e. buffers stress through the provision of various coping resources, such as emotional or practical support) (Helgelson *et al.*, 1998).

What are effective psychosocial treatment strategies for cancer patients?

To address the negative consequences of cancer and its treatment, a variety of effective psychosocial interventions have been developed (Baum & Andersen, 2002). Such approaches include educational interventions, cognitive-behavioral strategies, and group therapy approaches.

Educational interventions

The major goal of educational strategies is to reduce cancer patients' distress and improve their sense of control that may be engendered by lack of knowledge and feelings of uncertainty. The topics covered include technical aspects of the disease and its treatment, potential side effects, navigating the medical system, and the physician–patient relationship. Research suggests that providing such information can lead to beneficial effects, such as decreases in depression and anxiety (Nezu *et al.*, 2003c).

Cognitive-behavioral interventions

Cognitive-behavior therapy (CBT) incorporates a wide array of intervention strategies that attempt to change behavioral, cognitive, and affective variables that mediate the negative effects of cancer and its treatment. Many strategies under the CBT umbrella are theoretically based on principles of respondent and operant conditioning, such as contingency management (e.g. changing the consequences of behavior to change the behavior), biofeedback, relaxation training, and systematic desensitization, whereas other strategies are more cognitive in nature and include techniques such as cognitive distraction, cognitive restructuring, guided imagery, and problem-solving therapy. Applications of CBT for cancer patients have addressed both specific negative symptoms (e.g. anticipatory nausea, pain), as well as overall distress and quality of life.

CBT for anticipatory nausea

Clinically, a negative side effect of chemotherapy is anticipatory nausea and vomiting. From a respondent conditioning conceptualization, this occurs when previously neutral stimuli (e.g. smells, colors, and sounds associated with the treatment room) acquire nausea-eliciting properties due to repeated association with chemotherapy treatments and its negative after-effects. Research has found various CBT approaches, such as progressive muscle relaxation, guided imagery, and systematic desensitization, to be effective in reducing anticipatory nausea and vomiting (Nezu *et al.*, 2003c). Systematic desensitization is a procedure whereby over repeated pairings of anxiety-provoking stimuli with a relaxation-inducing response, such stimuli lose their anxiety-engendering properties as feelings of relaxation rather than tension become associated with such events.

CBT for pain

CBT strategies that have been found to be effective in reducing cancer-related pain include relaxation, guided imagery and distraction, and cognitive coping and restructuring. Cognitive coping and restructuring strategies teach individuals to change those negative thoughts and beliefs (e.g. "I'll never get better." "This is the absolute worst thing that can happen to me!") that evoke or intensify negative stressful reactions, such as pain and distress.

CBT for emotional distress

Most of the empirical studies involving CBT interventions with cancer patients tend to address general goals of decreasing their psychological distress and improving their overall quality of life. For example, behavioral stress management strategies (e.g. relaxation training, guided imagery) have been found to be especially effective in achieving such goals (e.g. Antoni *et al.*, 2001). Guided imagery is a CBT strategy that provides structured means of focusing on pleasant (e.g. favorite vacation place) or mastery (e.g. scenes of successfully coping with distress) images as a means of fostering a relaxation response. A review of the literature suggests that multi-component CBT protocols (i.e. combining several different CBT techniques) tend to be the norm. For example, the seminal study conducted by Fawzy and his colleagues (1990) included four components – health education, behavioral stress management, problem-solving training, and group support.

CBT-oriented interventions have also included family members in treatment as a means of enhancing the positive effects of this approach by capitalizing on a patient's positive social support network. For example, Nezu *et al.* (2003b) provided training in problem-solving skills to cancer patients along with their family caregivers (e.g. spouse, adult son or daughter). Problem-solving therapy helps individuals to better cope with stressful life events by improving their ability to be optimistic, identify why situations are problems, generate a variety of possible solutions, make effective decisions as to which solutions to carry out, and monitor the consequences of implemented solutions (Nezu *et al.*, 2003a). In this study, the investigators found that including a significant other fostered improved well-being above and beyond the positive effects of problem-solving therapy alone.

Group therapy approaches

The potential strengths of group psychotherapy for cancer patients are three-fold: (a) it can provide for a milieu in which people with similar experiences can provide emotional support to each other; (b) it is cost effective for the patient; (c) it is time efficient for the mental health professional. On a cautionary note, research suggests that group therapy programs which focus primarily on providing peer support and emphasize the shared expression of emotions are less effective than either educational protocols or programs that teach coping skills (Helgeson *et al.*, 1998).

The cancer experience: the course of cancer and its treatment

The clinical pathways, or timing of the cancer onset and course of treatment, can significantly influence the psychosocial stressors that someone with cancer may face. Such stages include: (a) receiving the diagnosis; (b) becoming a cancer patient; (c) ongoing cancer treatment; (d) the road to recovery; (e) living as a cancer survivor. In addition, if the cancer treatment is not effective, a different pathway would involve dealing with death and dying. As a means of helping the reader to develop a better case formulation when working with cancer patients, we briefly provide a series of case examples of cancer patients experiencing problems at each of these stages.

The diagnosis

The cancer experience at times begins even before an "official" diagnosis. Consider the case of Sara, a 31-year-old female, who found a lump in her breast one morning during a shower. She put off going to the doctor, discounting the lump because of her age. However, following her routine gynecological appointment, Sara was diagnosed with stage II breast cancer. Upon hearing this diagnosis, Sara was shocked. She recalled hearing the words "You have cancer", but could not remember anything else her doctor said. Her initial reactions fluctuated from denial to depression with questions of "Why me?"

Sara went to a psychologist at the recommendation of her oncologist because of indecisions and anxiety regarding treatment. While her doctor was requesting that she make a prompt decision, Sara was feeling overwhelmed about differing treatment options. She expressed difficulty remembering what her doctor had explained to her. Like many other women with breast cancer,

Sara was experiencing a variety of psychological distress symptoms including anxiety regarding her diagnosis and future treatment, anger at herself for not having the lump checked out earlier, and guilt that she will give cancer to her two daughters. In addition, she found herself crying often, had difficulties with sleep, and was unable to engage in previously enjoyable activities.

During the first session, her therapist asked Sara what cancer "meant to her". As is common, Sara equated cancer with death. With vivid images of a frail, decrepit body, she recounted her aunt's slow, painful death from cancer when Sara was a young child. Moreover, Sara, a Catholic, had an abortion several years ago and attributed her cancer to "being a punishment from God for this act". She rationalized, "I always lived a healthy life, so what else could it be?"

Sara and her therapist developed a problem list of areas to address in therapy. Themes included Sara's depressive symptoms, dysfunctional thoughts, sense of being overwhelmed, difficulties making treatment decisions, and strained marital relations. In an effort to address these problems, several therapeutic interventions were implemented. First, Sara's therapist "normalized" her distress. As part of an educational intervention, he provided her with research findings indicating that emotional distress is not uncommon after receiving a diagnosis of cancer, but often diminishes.

Next, CBT (cognitive therapy and problem-solving therapy) was conducted in an effort to help Sara improve her depressive mood and to change the depressogenic maladaptive thoughts (e.g. attributing the "only" cause for her cancer to be her previous abortion; believing that she would "definitely give" her daughters breast cancer). This treatment approach eventually led to significant decreases in depressive symptoms and distress, as well as an increase in Sara's sense of control. Problem-solving strategies were also used to help Sara regarding her treatment decisions. Applying the problem-solving skills, Sara was able to devise a list of questions to ask her oncologist and make well-informed decisions regarding her treatment.

Becoming a cancer patient

Becoming a cancer patient usually presents experiences that are novel to the individual. Chemotherapy, radiation, surgery, altered customary roles, changes in work, family, and leisure activities, and numerous occasions of loss, are only some of the more common stressors that can exist at this stage of the cancer experience.

As an illustration, consider George, a correctional officer. After being diagnosed with leukemia without forewarning during a routine blood test, George was advised to start high-dose chemotherapy immediately in preparation for a bone marrow transplant. He was hospitalized in a controlled environment requiring physical isolation. In addition to being away from his wife and young children, he was faced with an incredible sense of loss, independence, and control. As an officer in a prison and the head of the household, George was used to "giving, rather than following, orders". Constraints were forced upon him, such as not being able to leave his small room and being barred from smoking his habitual daily cigar. Furthermore, in reaction to the medical treatment, George developed an agonizing rash that consumed his attention.

George was having difficulty adjusting. In reaction to the cancer and its ensuing treatment, he became angry and verbally aggressive, resulting in adverse effects on himself and the oncology staff. George frequently objected to those entering his room and often refused medical treatment. With regard to a mental health consult, the initial barrier was his critical view of psychology. At the initial consultation, he explained to the therapist, "I am not crazy, I don't need a shrink." Needless to say, establishing a beneficial rapport with George was the therapist's primary treatment goal. She accomplished this by staying away from what he viewed as "psycho-babble" (e.g. "Tell me about your deepest thoughts and feelings") and asking him more benign questions (e.g. "What would you be doing if you were at work now?"). This allowed the therapist to gain a better understanding of George (e.g. his history of aggressive behavior and the purpose it served him) and permitted him to feel more comfortable disclosing information to, and receiving constructive feedback from, the therapist.

The next goal of treatment was to decrease George's anger and aggressive behavior as a means of improving not only his quality of life, but that of his family and the oncology staff as well. His anger was conceptualized as being related to his lack of perceived control and sense of helplessness, his rash, and his fears surrounding the cancer. To address this sense of helplessness, George and his therapist developed a list of activities over which he could still execute some control. For example, prior to therapy, George would angrily yell at anyone who entered his room when he wanted to be alone (e.g. while sitting on the bedside commode). As such, it was subsequently established with George and the oncology staff that any "visitors" would knock before entering George's room. In addition, while young ones were not typically permitted to visit the unit, George's children were granted visitation privileges every Sunday (a day George usually spent with his family) as long as everyone wore protective masks. The therapist recommended that they "make a game of it" to help decrease tension associated with the medical costume.

As George started to feel more comfortable with his therapist, he became more amenable to additional psychological interventions. George loved martial arts films and had taken a few karate classes in the past. "Borrowing" from martial arts philosophy, George was instructed in mindful meditation approaches, deep (diaphragmatic) breathing exercises, and focusing his attention on a "peaceful center in the face of adversity" (e.g. his rash, his anger). In addition, he and his therapist developed a list of activities in which he could engage to help distract him, given his constraints of hospitalization and adverse effects of treatment (e.g. surfing the web, reading car magazines, watching movies). These therapeutic strategies resulted in an increased sense of control, decreased aggressive acts, and less complaints about his rash.

Ongoing cancer treatment

Continuing cancer treatment can produce a multitude of new stressors. This is often a time when the individual with cancer attempts to have his or her life return to normal despite ongoing medical treatment. Attending outpatient appointments while trying to return to previous activities, coping with reactions from others (e.g. seemingly too little or too much attention), and strained social relationships are not uncommon. In addition, some individuals are faced with new cancer decisions, such as pursuing prophylactic treatment.

Lisa, for example, was a 33-year-old married administrative assistant with no children who was receiving ongoing outpatient therapy for gynecological cancer. Upon entering psychotherapy, her stressors were centered on her continued oncology treatments, work, and personal life. She was experiencing increased depressive and anxiety symptoms, similar to many women with the same type of cancer. Regarding her cancer treatment, Lisa was undergoing radiation therapy and chemotherapy. Related to the chemotherapy, she was also experiencing anticipatory nausea and emotional distress. Further, Lisa's radiation was causing her to feel fatigued.

In addition, Lisa was very concerned about how her cancer treatment would affect her ability to have children in the future. She had always wanted children and was feeling guilty for not having started a family earlier. Her anguish regarding this matter caused her to avoid speaking about it with her doctor. She was also experiencing a sense of worthlessness (e.g. "What good am I if I can't give my husband any children?") and hopelessness.

Having returned to her job, Lisa was experiencing numerous stressors associated with work. For example, the physical demands of her job were taxing and she was having difficulty engaging in her previous level of activity. Work was even more straining on days she received treatment due to the adverse side effects and the added time commitment of the medical therapies. Further, she believed her boss was too demanding and "heartless – she's just setting me up to fail so she can fire me".

In contrast, within her personal life, Lisa considered her husband to be too pampering. She complained, "He thinks I'm incompetent. He never lets me do anything and looks at me like I'm going to die." In addition, Lisa was experiencing a decreased interest in sex.

Multiple strategies were implemented to help Lisa learn skills to cope more adaptively. Due to her difficulties at managing a hectic schedule, the therapist initially helped Lisa establish priorities. Cognitive therapy was implemented to address dysfunctional thoughts (e.g. assuming her own infertility and equating that with "dishonor") and unrealistic expectations (e.g. the need to return to her previous level of activity). Time management and goal-setting skills were taught to help address the numerous tasks she was attempting (e.g. work, care for home, doctors' appointments). As a function of this therapy, Lisa was able to give herself permission to decrease her current level of activity, resulting in decreased distress and fatigue. Assertiveness and communication skills training further resulted in improved interactions between Lisa and her boss, her husband, and her doctor (i.e. about fertility options).

Finally, specific therapeutic interventions were conducted to help with some of the adverse effects of her cancer treatment. Relaxation training and systematic desensitization were implemented to address Lisa's anticipatory nausea. In addition, Lisa participated in group therapy with other women receiving radiation therapy, resulting in further decreased emotional and physical distress.

The road to recovery

Recovering from cancer brings an array of emotions, from delight that treatment is now complete, to distress associated with a host of additional stressors. Despite less frequent medical appointments, side effects from treatment can prevail, resulting in discomfort and possible body image concerns. Worry about recurrence, problems returning to previous activities, difficulty with relationships now that the patient is "well", and financial strain (e.g. from treatment, not working) can result in psychological distress.

For example, consider Allison, who was diagnosed with colon cancer. She was a 39-year-old single woman. At the time of therapy, Allison had undergone surgery and chemotherapy. She was having difficulty coping with some of the adverse effects of treatment, particularly her hair loss and need for a colostomy bag. She was also having difficulties with her body image. Allison's distress was so strong that she was unable to undress or shower with the lights on, which hindered her ability to properly wash and care for her colostomy.

Allison had moved in with her parents when treatment started and was still residing with them. While appreciative of their help, Allison was feeling inundated with her mother's "doting" over her. Furthermore, Allison was feeling pressure to spend time with her parents, despite wanting some time to herself. Her friends, on the other hand, had stopped calling and visiting as much as they had before. Despite overwhelming previous support from friends and co-workers, offers to help Allison had significantly decreased. Termination of treatment appeared to have been interpreted as an end to her need for support. Allison was troubled by not being included in social outings and felt as though her friends had given up interest in her.

Allison was also experiencing difficulties with her boyfriend, Tom. She complained that he did not want to talk about the cancer, expressing "Let's not dwell on the past." He did not understand Allison's depressive mood or her decreased libido. Because of her distress regarding her colostomy, she shied away from any sexual act, although she felt unable to explain this to Tom.

Psychological treatment centered on addressing Allison's body image and her ineffective communication. As with any loss, Sara needed to "mourn" the loss of her previous body. While her hair would grow back, its absence was a constant reminder of her cancer. Furthermore, Allison needed to accept the need for the colostomy. The doctors had noted that a surgical reversal might be possible in the future, but for now she had to cope with it. Normalizing her sadness regarding this loss of her physical appearance, and providing a safe milieu to address her thoughts and feelings, promoted the "bereavement process".

Regarding her difficulties with undressing and bathing herself, numerous interventions were implemented, including cognitive restructuring and graded exposure. The therapist helped Allison address her fears about seeing her colostomy. Eventually Allison was able to undress with the lights on and properly care for her wound sight and bag.

In an effort to help Allison interact with others, communication training was implemented. Allison learned skills to speak more effectively with her parents about her need for some solitude and her friends regarding her desire to re-engage in social activities. She also gained skills to speak more honestly with her boyfriend. Allison and Tom were able to voice their thoughts and feelings, resulting in enhanced interactions.

Living as a survivor

A cancer patient is generally identified as a "survivor" after being cancer-free for five or more years. Certainly the time distancing oneself from the cancer may help decrease distress associated with it. However, certain cancer-related stressors can continue to arise. For example, concerns about recurrence, potential long-term side effects (e.g. osteoporosis from steroids), and having a different perspective of life and goals can present difficulties in the lives of cancer survivors.

Consider Alan, a 59-year-old man diagnosed with prostate cancer approximately seven years previously. While perhaps unrelated, Alan was experiencing persistent gastrointestinal (GI) disturbances at the time of his diagnosis. Thus, he associated the stomach irritation with his cancer. For his cancer treatment, Alan underwent surgery and radiation, and was subsequently told he was cancer-free.

Upon entering psychotherapy, Alan was hypervigilant regarding physical symptoms, particularly those associated with the GI tract. He consistently believed any GI discomfort was a signal that the cancer was recurring. Furthermore, Alan had learned from the internet that people who had cancer are at increased risk for developing secondary cancer. This understandably resulted in additional fears.

Alan was in a long-term relationship with Rick. Although Rick had been emotionally supportive, Alan thought his partner was "getting tired of me – he calls me paranoid" because of his vigilance toward his physical symptoms. Alan was also experiencing much fatigue and difficulty engaging in activities he and Rick used to do together. Moreover, Alan was suffering from erectile dysfunction. He felt too embarrassed to talk to Rick, placing additional strain on their relationship.

Prior to his cancer diagnosis, Alan was a partner in a law firm, working 80 to 100 hours each week. Since his cancer treatment, he was reconsidering his choice of occupation and life style, expressing that "life is too short to waste it at work". He often felt distressed and confused about how he wanted to spend the rest of his life (e.g. returning to work, gaining new employment, retiring with less money than he had originally planned).

The major goals in Alan's treatment were to reduce his worry associated with his physical health, enhance communication with his partner, and assist him in making decisions about his future. Education was an important component of therapy to address the first goal. The therapist normalized Alan's concerns, sharing with him research indicating that adverse psychosocial consequences often extend past treatment and that fear of cancer recurrence, as well as increased somatic concerns, often prevail. In addition, cancer-related fatigue, associated with negative effects on physical, psychosocial, and financial areas of the lives of both the patient and caregiver often continue for more than five years following treatment.

Alan's therapist then provided psychoeducation regarding the reciprocal relationship between somatic symptoms and distress (i.e. worry increases his GI symptoms, which in turn increases his worry). Cognitive therapy was implemented to decrease such maladaptive automatic thoughts (e.g. "I know I will get cancer again") and replace them with more adaptive thinking (e.g. "While I may be at increased risk for cancer as compared to the general population, I am leading a healthy life style and am consistently getting medical check-ups to objectively ensure I am healthy"). Such cognitive changes resulted in decreased hypervigilance and psychological distress.

Cognitive therapy was also applied to address Alan's difficulty discussing his sexual difficulties with his partner. The therapist shared with Alan that sexual problems are not uncommon among cancer survivors, particularly those with prostate cancer. After exploring the barriers to disclosing his sexual difficulties, Alan role played talking to Rick about this problem. These interventions facilitated better communication between the couple.

To help Alan decrease his maladaptive thinking about his work and make decisions about his future, the therapist applied problem-solving therapy. With such training, Alan was able to accept that his priorities in life had changed as a result of his experience with cancer. He was able to generate numerous alternatives and eventually decided to get involved in legal work for a large non-profit cancer organization. This permitted him to engage in an activity he thought meaningful while still making money for retirement.

When cancer treatment does not work

Cancer patients in the terminal phases of illness are especially vulnerable to both psychiatric and physical complications. Suicide tends to be more prevalent during such advanced stages. Patients may actually go through a grieving process as they face their own mortality and the impact of their death on family and friends. Some patients may experience emotional distress including symptoms of guilt, anger, depression, and anxiety. Often it is the process of dying (e.g. loss of functioning, persistent pain), more than death itself, which is feared most by cancer patients. Such fears often prevent patients from discussing these concerns with their physicians or others.

Consider Jim who was diagnosed with stage IV lung cancer that was deemed inoperable and for which chemotherapy and radiation therapy had been ineffective. Jim was married with four children ranging in ages from 2 to 15. His wife wanted Jim to participate in a clinical trial of an experimental chemotherapy agent, but Jim was not interested. His doctor had mentioned "something about hospice" but Jim did not know what that meant.

During the initial interview with a therapist, Jim described a wide range of emotions including sadness, guilt, anger, and anxiety. He conveyed a sense of confusion regarding the future. On one hand, he was tired of treatments that were not only not working, but fraught with side effects that were "worse than the cancer itself". He recounted the fatigue, nausea, diarrhea, and discomfort that resulted from previous treatments that kept him in bed or the bathroom and away from his family. He did not know how to tell his wife this, who kept saying "You have to do everything you can to stay alive for the kids."

Conversely, Jim had strong fears about death and dying. He was extremely concerned about how his wife and children would cope after he passed away. Jim, the habitual breadwinner, had apprehensions about who would care for his family both financially and emotionally (e.g. "Who will teach little Jimmy how to throw the football?"). Further, Jim and his wife were concerned about how to tell their children about Jim's health.

Psychotherapy centered on issues related to death and dying, communication, and treatment decisions. The therapist helped Jim explore his fears about the dying process. This is a topic that is often on the minds of people with cancer, particularly at this stage, but is frequently not discussed because it can engender feelings of discomfort for all parties involved. Jim expressed a sense of relief that his therapist brought up this topic, explaining he felt as though, in spite of its strong possibility, people around him avoided talking about it. In examining his distress, he realized that, in addition to being troubled about his family, he was anxious about the dying process and fearful of the potential pain. He felt unable to talk about such fears because he did not want his wife to be more afraid.

Couples therapy was implemented in an effort to help enhance communication between Jim and his wife. Specific topics included each spouse's views about Jim's cancer, treatment, and death. Jim's wife expressed a fear that Jim was giving up on her and their children. Jim was able to explain to her that it was time not to give up, but to accept that treatment was not helping and to change the focus on enhancing his quality of life so that he could spend "quality" time with his family until his death.

After the couple had begun to accept this next stage of their lives, the therapist taught the couple problem-solving skills to help make decisions about Jim's treatment and plans for the family's future. Jim and his wife decided on palliative care at home to help decrease pain and spend as much time as possible together as a family. The couple gained the skills to address issues such as end-of-life decisions (e.g. code status, establishing a will), financial planning, and assistance with childcare. Furthermore, saddened by the prospect of missing major milestones in his children's lives, Jim wrote cards to each of his children for their future graduations and weddings, expressing his love and delight for them.

In addition, the therapist helped the couple devise a plan regarding how to discuss Jim's health with their children. Specifically, the therapist recommended they encourage an open dialogue with their children, providing age-appropriate information and answering the children's questions. Children often have vivid imaginations that can lead to unrealistic fears if not addressed. As children often blame themselves, attributing their bad behavior to causing a parent's illness, the couple was encouraged to consistently remind the children that Jim's cancer was not because of something they did. Further, the psychologist suggested having the older children take over some of Jim's more simple household responsibilities in an effort to permit them to feel useful. Finally, the therapist encouraged the couple to engage in "fun activities" as a family to help the children keep their minds off the negative aspects of their father's health.

Appendix

The following is a brief list of measures that have been applied to various cancer populations that can be useful for assessment purposes.

Measures of psychological distress

- Brief Symptom Inventory (BSI, Derogatis, 1993)
- Profile of Mood States (McNair et al., 1992)

Measures of quality of life and cancer-related problems

- Cancer Rehabilitation Evaluation System (CARES, Schag & Heinrich, 1989)
- Functional Assessment of Cancer Therapy Scale (Cella *et al.*, 1993)

Measures of coping

- Dealing with Illness Coping Inventory (Billings & Moos, 1981)
- Mental Adjustment to Cancer (MAC, Watson *et al.*, 1988)
- Social Problem-Solving Inventory-Revised (SPSI-R, D'Zurilla *et al.*, 2002)

Measures of social support

- Interpersonal Support Evaluation List (Cohen *et al.*, 1985)

References

Andersen, B. L. (2002). Biobehavioral outcomes following psychosocial interventions for cancer patients. *Journal of Consulting and Clinical Psychology, 70*, 590–610.

Andersen, B. L., Anderson, B., & DeProsse, C. (1989). Controlled prospective longitudinal study of women with cancer: I. Sexual functioning outcomes. *Journal of Consulting and Clinical Psychology, 57*, 683–691.

Antoni, M. H., Lehman, J. M., Kilbourn, K. M., Boyers, A. E., Culver, J. L., Alferi, S. M., Yount, S. E., McGregor, B. A., Arena, P. L., Harris, S. D., Price, A. A., & Carver, C. S. (2001). Cognitive-behavioral stress management intervention decreases the prevalence of depression and enhanced benefit finding among women under treatment for early-stage breast cancer. *Health Psychology, 20*, 20–32.

Baum, A., & Andersen, B. L. (Eds.). (2002). *Psychosocial interventions for cancer.* Washington, DC: American Psychological Association.

Beck, A. T., Kovacs, M., & Weissman, A. (1975). Hopelessness and suicidal behavior: An overview. *Journal of the American Medical Association, 234*, 1146–1149.

Billings, A.G., & Moos, R. (1981). The role of coping responses and social resources in attenuating the stress of life events. *Journal of Behavioural Medicine, 4*, 139–157.

Burgess, C., Morris, T., & Pettingale, K. W. (1988). Psychological response to cancer diagnosis: II. Evidence for coping styles (coping styles and cancer diagnosis). *Journal of Psychosomatic Research, 32*, 263–272.

Carver, C. S., Pozo, C., Harris, S. D., Noriega, V., Scheier, M. F., Robinson, D. S., Ketchamn, A. S., Moffat, F. L., & Clark, K. C. (1993). How coping mediates the effect of optimism on distress: A study of women with early stage breast cancer. *Journal of Personality and Social Psychology, 65*, 375–390.

Cella, D.F., Tulsky, D.S., Gray, G., Sarafan, B., Linn, E., Bonomi, A., Silberman, M., Yellen, S.B., Winicour, P., & Brannon, J. (1993). The Functional Assessment of Cancer Therapy Scale: Development and validation of the general measure. *Journal of Clinical Oncology, II*, 570–579.

Cohen, S., Mermelstein, R.J., & Kamarch, T. (1985). Measuring the fundamental components of social support. In I.G. Sarason and B.R. Sarason (Eds.), *Social support: Theory, research and applications*. Dordrecht: Martinus Nijhoff.

Cordova, M. J., Andrylowski, M. A., Kenady, D. E., McGrath, P. C., Sloan, D. A., & Redd, W. H. (1995). Frequency and correlates of PTSD-like symptoms following treatment for breast cancer. *Journal of Consulting and Clinical Psychology, 63*, 981–986.

Derogatis, L.R. (1993). *Brief Symptom Inventory (BSI) administration, scoring and procedures manual*. Minneapolis, MN: National Computer Systems.

Derogatis, L. R., Morrow, G. R., & Fetting, J. (1983). The prevalence of psychiatric disorders among cancer patients. *Journal of the American Medical Association, 249*, 751–757.

D'Zurilla, T.J., Nezu, A.M., & Maydeu-Olivares (2002). *Social Problem-Solving Inventory-Revisited (SPSI-R)*. North Tonawanda, NY: Multi-Health Systems.

Fawzy, F. I., Cousins, N., Fawzy, N. W., Kemeny, M. E., Elashoff, R., & Morton, D. (1990). A structured psychiatric intervention for cancer patients: I. Changes over time in methods of coping and affective disturbance. *Archives of General Psychiatry, 47*, 720–725.

Helgelson, V. S., Cohen, S., & Fritz, H. L. (1998). Social ties and cancer. In J. C. Holland (Ed.), *Psycho oncology* (pp. 99–109). New York: Oxford University Press.

McNair, D.M., Lorr, M., & Droppleman, L.F. (1992). *EdITS manual for the Profile of Mood States*. San Diego, CA:EdITS.

Maguire, G. P., Lee, E. G., & Bevington, D. J. (1978). Psychiatric problems in the first year after mastectomy. *British Journal of Medicine, 1*, 963–965.

Marks, D. I., Crilley, P., Nezu, C. M., & Nezu, A. M. (1996). Sexual dysfunction prior to high-dose chemotherapy and bone marrow transplantation. *Bone Marrow Transplantation, 17*, 595–599.

Marks, D. I., Friedman, S. H., DelliCarpini, L., Nezu, C. M., & Nezu, A. M. (1997). A prospective study of the effects of high dose chemotherapy and bone marrow transplantation on sexual function in the first year after transplant. *Bone Marrow Transplantation, 19*, 819–822.

Massie, M., & Holland, J. (1987). The cancer patient with pain: Psychiatric complications and their management. *Medical Clinics of North America, 71*, 243–257.

Miller, S. M., Fang, C. Y., Diefenbach, M. A., & Bales, C. B. (2001). Tailoring psychosocial interventions to the individual's health information-processing style. In A. Baum & B. L. Andersen (Eds.), *Psychosocial interventions for cancer* (pp. 343–362). Washington, DC: American Psychological Association.

Murphy, G. P., Morris, L. B., & Lange, D. (1997). *Informed decisions: The complete book of cancer diagnosis, treatment, and recovery*. New York: Viking.

Newport, D. J., & Nemeroff, C. B. (1998). Assessment and treatment of depression in the cancer patient. *Journal of Psychosomatic Research, 45*, 215–237.

Nezu, A. M. (2004). Problem solving and behavior therapy revisited. *Behavior Therapy, 35*, 1–33.

Nezu, A. M., & Nezu, C. M. (2004). Cancer: Psychosocial treatment. In N. B. Anderson (Ed.), *Encyclopedia of health and behavior* (pp. 129–133). New York: Sage.

Nezu, A. M., Nezu, C. M., Friedman, S. H., Faddis, S., & Houts, P. S. (1998). *Helping cancer patients cope: A problem-solving approach*. Washington, DC: American Psychological Association.

Nezu, A. M., Nezu, C. M., Houts, P. S., Friedman, S. H., & Faddis, S. (1999).

Relevance of problem-solving therapy to psychosocial oncology. *Journal of Psychosocial Oncology, 16*, 5–26.

Nezu, A. M., Nezu, C. M., & Lombardo, E. (2003a). Problem-solving therapy. In W. O'Donohue, J. E. Fisher, & Hayes, S. C. (Eds.), *Cognitive behavior therapy: Applying empirically-supported techniques in your practice* (pp. 301–307). New York: Wiley.

Nezu, A. M., Nezu, C. M., Felgoise, S. H., McClure, K. S., & Houts, P. S. (2003b). Project Genesis: Assessing the efficacy of problem-solving therapy for distressed adult cancer patients. *Journal of Consulting and Clinical Psychology, 71*, 1036–1048.

Nezu, A. M., Nezu, C. M., Felgoise, S. H., & Zwick, M. L. (2003c). Psychosocial oncology. In A. M. Nezu, C. M. Nezu, & P. A. Geller (Eds.), *Health psychology* (pp. 267–292). New York: Wiley.

Nezu, C. M., Nezu, A. M., Friedman, S. H., Houts, P. S., DelliCarpini, L. A., Nemeth, C. B., & Faddis, S. (1999). Cancer and psychological distress: Two investigations regarding the role of problem solving. *Journal of Psychosocial Oncology, 16*, 27–40.

Schag, C.A.C., & Heinrich, R.L. (1989). *The Cancer Rehabilitation Evaluation System (CARES): Manual*. Los Angeles: CARES Consultants.

Sneeuw, K. C., Aaronson, N. K., Yarnold, J. R., Broderick, M., Regan, J., Ross, G., & Goddard, A. (1992). Cosmetic and functional outcomes of breast conserving treatment for early stage breast cancer. 2: Relationship with psychosocial functioning. *Radiotherapy Oncology, 25*, 160–166.

Telch, C. F., & Telch, M. J. (1985). Psychological approaches for enhancing coping among cancer patients: A review. *Clinical Psychology Review, 5*, 325–344.

Van't Spiker, A., Trijsburg, R. W., & Duivenvoorder, H. J. (1997). Psychological sequelae of cancer diagnosis: A meta-analytical review of 58 studies after 1980. *Psychosomatic Medicine, 59*, 280–293.

Watson, M., Greer, S., Blake, S., & Shrapnell, K. (1984). Reaction to a diagnosis of breast cancer: Relationship between denial, delay, and rates of psychological morbidity. *Cancer, 53*, 2008–2012.

Watson, M., Greer, S., Young, J., Inayat, Q., Burgess, C. & Robertson, B. (1988). Development of a questionnaire measure of adjustment to cancer: The MAC scale. *Journal of Health and Social Behaviour, 18*, 203–209.

Weissman, A. D., & Worden, J. W. (1976–1977). The existential plight in cancer: Significance of the first 100 days. *International Journal of Psychiatric Medicine, 7*, 1–15.

Whitlock, F. A. (1978). Suicide, cancer, and depression. *British Journal of Psychiatry, 132*, 269–274.

Williamson, G., & Schulz, R. (1995). Activity restriction mediates the association between pain and depressed affect: A study of younger and older adult cancer patients. *Psychology and Aging, 10*, 369–378.

Chapter 14

Miscarriage

Conceptualisation and treatment of the psychological sequelae

Ana V. Nikčević

Introduction

Miscarriage is the commonest pregnancy complication. Although the majority of women are able to adjust to this experience without major psychological difficulties, for some, psychological assistance may be of help in facilitating the integration of this experience and its psychological aftermath. This chapter outlines the process of formulation and treatment of psychological difficulties of women who have suffered pregnancy loss, from within a cognitive-behavioural perspective.

The chapter is divided into three parts. In the first part, after presenting some basic facts and figures concerning the miscarriage, the psychological impact of this event is examined, and the needs of women who have suffered this type of loss are reviewed. In the second part, the cognitive-behavioural perspective on bereavement is outlined, and the issues concerning assessment and formulation of psychological difficulties following pregnancy loss are discussed. Two case studies are presented in the third part to illustrate the process of clinical formulation and intervention.

Miscarriage: the problem, its impact and the women's needs

Facts and figures

Early pregnancy failure, often referred to as miscarriage, occurs in approximately 15 per cent to 20 per cent of all recognised pregnancies (Kline & Stein, 1990). Miscarriage is usually defined as a spontaneous loss of pregnancy before 24 completed weeks of gestation (Farquharson, 2002). However, there is considerable variation in the upper limit of gestation in the definition of miscarriage, in different countries or studies, including 20, 24 or 28 weeks (Kline & Stein, 1990). When a pregnancy loss occurs in the first trimester (i.e. up to 14 weeks) it is usually referred to as an early miscarriage. Miscarriages that occur in the second trimester (i.e. between 14 and 24 weeks) are described as late miscarriages, whilst the loss of a baby after 24 weeks is referred to as stillbirth.

Miscarriage is the commonest pregnancy complication. Most miscarriages occur early, before 14 weeks gestation, and are due to fetal chromosomal abnormalities. Other possible causes include uterine abnormalities, immunological and hormonal factors. However, even with detailed investigations, the cause remains unknown in about 40 per cent of cases. Although the overall risk of a pregnancy ending in failure after one or two miscarriages is unchanged, i.e. 15 to 20 per cent, the risk increases substantially by age. The loss of three or more consecutive pregnancies before 24 weeks of gestation is often referred to as recurrent miscarriage. Approximately 1 per cent of women of childbearing age experience recurrent miscarriage (Clifford *et al.*, 1994).

The first indicators of early pregnancy failure are vaginal bleeding and abdominal pain. Often, the bleeding can become quite profuse and women are hospitalised for a surgical removal of the pregnancy. Surgery is usually performed under general anaesthesia, and is called a D&C (dilatation and curettage) or an ERPC (evacuation of the retained products of conception). Late losses usually involve delivery of a baby which, due to its immaturity, is unlikely to be alive at birth.

Physical and psychological impact of miscarriage

For many women, miscarriage is physically and psychologically a traumatic experience. Because miscarriage involves sudden and unexpected bleeding, pain, and passing of tissue, it is reported that fear is a common reaction to pregnancy loss (Graves, 1987; Moulder, 1990). Furthermore, rapid hospitalisation and undergoing of surgical procedures such as dilatation and curettage (D&C) are often unfamiliar, painful and distressing, and they contribute to the stressfulness and the traumatic nature of the experience (Cecil, 1994; Lee & Slade, 1996). In some settings, miscarriage may pose a serious threat to the life of a woman (Saraiya *et al.*, 1999).

Psychologically, for the majority, the loss of a desirable pregnancy will be marked by a range of grief-related emotions such as feelings of sadness, tearfulness, sense of loss, yearning for the baby, anger at what happened, the desire to talk about the loss and to find meaningful explanations for it, and pain at seeing pregnant women (Beutel *et al.*, 1995; Nikčević *et al.*, 1999a). Both the intensity and range of feelings of grief experienced following a miscarriage have been identified to be similar to those after a loss of a close relative or a friend (Nikčević *et al.*, 1999a). Additionally, miscarriage represents the loss of a baby, a future child, of motherhood, and women's self-esteem and confidence in own procreative capacities may be undermined. Both late miscarriage and, more recently, early pregnancy loss have increasingly been viewed as "perinatal bereavement", which can have negative impact not only on a woman but on other family members as well.

It is generally expected that mourning which follows bereavement subsides after six months to a year (Parkes, 1985), although some grief-related emotions may last for several years. In contrast with normal grief which gradually decreases with time after loss, pathological mourning or pathological grief does not subside with time and/or interferes with the day-to-day behaviour and emotional state of the person (Bowlby, 1980). Two types of pathological grief reactions have been described: prolonged or 'chronic' grief and absent or 'inhibited' grief. Prolonged grief is also called adjustment disorder with depression or unresolved grief (mourning). This grief initially appears normal but it fails to resolve within the expected period of time, continuing to have a disabling effect on the person. Absent grief is a failure to display symptoms of grief in the first few weeks after loss. However, the grief may later manifest through severe anniversary reactions (delayed grief), or the later development of anxiety symptoms (masked grief) (Condon, 1986; Hughes, 1998).

There are great individual differences in the levels of grief experienced by women following a loss of a desired pregnancy, with some showing intense grief reactions and others reporting few grief-related emotions shortly after the loss (Beutel et al., 1995; Paton et al., 1999). Although the levels of grief for the majority of women who suffer a miscarriage will decrease substantially within the first six to twelve months after loss (Lasker & Toedter, 1991; Beutel et al., 1995), it appears that, for a minority of women the grief may actually increase with time. In a study by Lasker & Toedter (1991), 17 per cent of women had higher scores on the Perinatal Grief Scale (PGS) after two years than they had two months after loss. Case studies of women presenting with complicated/pathological grief reactions in clinical settings have also been described in the literature (e.g. Corney & Horton, 1974).

Bereavement after miscarriage is complex and can be difficult for a number of reasons. The death is sudden and unexpected, there are no memories or shared life experiences and, where the loss occurred early, there is no visible child to mourn (Lee & Slade, 1996). In addition, women who miscarry often lack social and emotional support, both from hospital staff and friends and family, which is provided with other types of bereavement (Lasker & Toedter, 1991). Thus there is a lack of recognition of the significance of such loss by society (Rajan & Oakley, 1993). Women may also be subjected to insensitive and negative attitudes related to others' perceptions of what the "normal recovery time" after a pregnancy loss should be. Both lack of support from one's immediate environment and societal attitudes may lead to an increase in stress and long-term emotional consequences (Lee & Slade, 1996).

Apart from grief, empirical research studies in the area have also reported on a number of psychiatric symptoms experienced by women in the aftermath of miscarriage. Miscarriage is associated with an increased incidence of major and minor depression (Neugebauer et al., 1997; Klier et al., 2000). Elevations in depressive symptoms may last as long as one year after loss (e.g. Robinson *et al.*, 1994; Beutel *et al.*, 1995), and childless women and those with a history of major depression may be more vulnerable (Neugebauer *et al.*, 1992, 1997). It has also been reported that suicidal thoughts and attempts could be present in as many as 10 per cent of women because of grief and guilt over the miscarriage (e.g. Friedman & Gath, 1989; DeFrain, 1994).

Risk for anxiety and post-traumatic disorder are also elevated. High levels of anxiety, intrusion and avoidance feature in women's responses shortly after miscarriage and they may be as high as in people who sought psychotherapy following personal injuries (Lee *et al.*, 1996). Engelhard *et al.* (2001) reported that at one month post-miscarriage up to 25 per cent of women may be suffering from acute stress disorder. At four months after loss, a decline in PTSD symptoms has been reported (Lee *et al.*, 1996; Engelhard *et al.*, 2001; Walker & Davidson, 2001). Elevations in anxiety after miscarriage are likely to be related to the traumatic nature of the experience (Lee & Slade, 1996), to the feelings of grief about the lost pregnancy (Nikčević *et al.*, 1999a), lack of knowledge and understanding concerning the impact of miscarriage on their health and reproductive lives and to the worries concerning future attempts at reproduction (Nikčević *et al.*, 1999b).

It is also not surprising or unusual for women to experience a range of somatic complaints after miscarriage. Some of these, such as pain and tiredness, may be related to the physical trauma of pregnancy loss. Other complaints, such as difficulty sleeping, irritability, loss of appetite, weight gain or loss are likely to be manifestations of psychological distress. These somatic complaints can limit women's daily functioning. It has been reported that up to 77 per cent of women may exhibit such an increase in somatic complaints shortly after miscarriage (Zaccardi *et al.*, 1993), with levels remaining high at four to six months afterwards (Janssen *et al.*, 1996; Engelhard *et al.*, 2001) and normalising at around 12 months after loss (Janssen *et al.*, 1996).

The needs of women who have suffered a miscarriage

There are several major issues that women who have suffered a miscarriage report and identify as their primary concerns post loss. These include concerns regarding reasons for the failure of their pregnancy, worries concerning future pregnancy outcomes and risks of it happening again, and the intensity and duration of the emotional impact of the event (Nikčević *et al.*, 1998b). The majority of women want follow-up care after miscarriage and indicate that such care should be provided by a doctor (their general practitioner or an obstetrician; Nikčević *et al.*, 1998b). Currently, there is no routine offer of miscarriage follow-up care in the UK, despite growing recognition that miscarriage is a stressful life experience for many women and their partners. A follow-up offered to all women shortly after miscarriage would represent a forum where women's worries and concerns could be addressed, relevant information provided and uncertainties arrayed. Such follow-up care with a woman's general practitioner may be associated with a decrease in their anxiety levels (Nikčević *et al.*, in review).

Apart from a follow-up which should be routinely offered to all women after a miscarriage, some women are likely to benefit from a further special-ised psychological input to help them deal with the emotional consequences of their loss. In a survey of women's desires and needs for follow-up care after miscarriage, Nikčević *et al.* (1998b) reported that women who expressed the need for psychological services were those suffering higher distress levels inclusive of anxiety, depression and grief. Clinical attention in the early weeks after miscarriage may help offset more serious long-term psychological consequences, inclusive of those which may occur in pregnancies subsequent to a miscarriage.

Psychological interventions

Despite the fact that many obstetric services in the western world provide bereavement counselling/psychological interventions for women/families after perinatal death (inclusive of stillbirth, neonatal death or termination of pregnancy for fetal anomaly) there is almost a complete paucity of random-ised controlled trials examining the effectiveness of such interventions (Chambers & Chan, 1998).

The majority of studies reporting on the effects of psychosocial interven-tions in women post-miscarriage are descriptive and anecdotal (e.g. Leppert & Pahlka, 1984; Hamilton, 1989). These reports have suggested that for a healthy resolution of grief it is necessary for women to ventilate and work through their feelings concerning the miscarriage (e.g. Leppert & Pahlka, 1984; Ney, 1987). Beneficial effects of such bereavement counselling interven-tions have been reported in a number of uncontrolled studies (Leppert & Pahlka, 1984; Hamilton, 1989; Neugebauer *et al.*, 1992).

Several controlled studies utilising various interventions (e.g. grief counsel-ling, psychological debriefing) have reported no significant impact of such psychological counselling on women's distress levels (Lee *et al.*, 1996; Swanson, 1999). More recently, Nikčević *et al.* (in review) carried out an evaluation of the benefits of a single session of psychological counselling offered to women as an adjunct to a medical consultation. A single counsel-ling session with a psychologist, lasting on average one hour, was broadly based on a cognitive therapy framework. The main aims were: encourage-ment of the expression of feelings regarding the loss, normalisation of such expressed emotions, exposure to the memories (e.g. to the images of the initial ultrasound scan when diagnosis of miscarriage was made, and the events that took place subsequently by going over them and describing them in detail), cognitive restructuring (where evidence of self-blame for the event was apparent), and reframing and reorganising of the experience in the con-text of the available information about the miscarriage. Worries concerning future attempts at reproduction were also discussed. Psychological counselling, in addition to the medical consultation, was superior to both medical counselling, as well as to the control group of 'untreated' women, in bringing about decreases on several distress outcomes (e.g. grief, self-blame and worry about future pregnancy).

All women suffering from any form of perinatal loss should be informed about the emotional sequelae of perinatal bereavement. Specific psychological interventions may be offered to those exhibiting higher distress levels. Whilst for some a single session of psychological counselling may be beneficial in helping them to reconstruct and facilitate processing of their loss, for others several sessions are needed which need to be tailored to accommodate individual differences.

Cognitive-behavioural perspective on bereavement: assessment and formulation issues

Theoretical framework

According to the cognitive-behavioural perspective, negative life events such as bereavement are likely to cause a threat to a person's 'assumptive world'. This assumptive world is a conceptual system that allows people to classify and predict the world around them, to guide interactions and generally enable them to function effectively (Janoff-Bulman, 1992). Three core assumptions are threatened by the negative events: beliefs about the benevolence and meaningfulness of the world and beliefs about the worthiness of self (Janoff-Bulman, 1992). The process of 'adjustment' to adverse life events can be defined as an intrapsychic and interpersonal journey that individuals strive to negotiate with and which results in a 'personal transition' or shift in the individual's core assumptions (Brennan, 2001). The symptoms experienced by the bereaved person (e.g. shock, restlessness, anxiety) are suggestive of the difficulties a person has in integrating the changes brought about by the trauma. On a cognitive level, these difficulties in adjustment often appear in the areas of: beliefs about the self or the future, processing of information or the combination of both (Gluhoski, 1995).

For a clinician, problems in adjustment following a loss can best be described by an application of a combined anxiety/depression model, with grief appearing like a low-grade post-traumatic stress disorder (Kavanagh, 1990). Such a model incorporates most of the features that are observed in normal and pathological grief. Cognitive-behavioural interventions for grief should be targeting these difficulties through an individualised approach to the formulation of distress. Such individually tailored interventions are necessary as factors maintaining specific psychological difficulties differ between individuals.

This cognitive-behavioural perspective on bereavement is adopted as a basis for the conceptualisation of the experiences of women who have suffered a miscarriage, and for guiding specific interventions.

Assessment and formulation issues

Many obstetric departments now have specialist counselling services for women who experience perinatal loss. However, whilst patients with stillbirth or neonatal death typically have an established relationship with their obstetric team and are often routinely offered specialist bereavement counselling through their hospitals, women who have suffered a miscarriage are unlikely to be referred to such services. Typically, the general practitioner is the main point of contact for women who suffer adverse emotional impact of pregnancy loss and he or she is most likely to refer them for psychological treatment because of very intense grief reactions, persistent distress, and difficulty coping with day-to-day activities.

Assessment of the person's difficulties is the crucial stage in the process of individual problem formulation. Loss of a desired and longed for pregnancy/ baby can trigger a range of psychological difficulties ranging from acute distress as a manifestation of normal grief/mourning, prolonged intense grief, to reoccurrence of depression or obsessive-compulsive disorder (OCD) from which the person has suffered in the past, anxiety and PTSD, and interpersonal problems. The person who attends for miscarriage counselling is usually acutely distressed and overwhelmed by emotions related to the loss of pregnancy. The role of the therapist in the initial stages of problem formulation is to understand the range of problems the person is experiencing, but at the same time to allow the person to express her distress and to acknowledge her loss. Empathic listening and reflection are core skills necessary at this stage. At the same time, a careful list of difficulties which have occurred since the loss is compiled, and the most bothersome problem identified.

A range of psychological instruments may assist in the process of assessment of a person's difficulties and symptoms. For the assessment of grief the Perinatal Grief Scale (PGS; Lasker & Toedter, 1991), and the Texas Grief Inventory Adjusted for Miscarriage (TGI; Nikčević et al., 1999a) can be used. The PGS is particularly suited for the assessment of grief in those who have suffered a late loss. It has two subscales "Difficulty Coping" and "Despair", the high scores on which indicate problems with adjustment and complicated grief responses. For the assessment of depression, the depression subscale of the Hospital Anxiety and Depression Scale (HADS; Zigmond & Snaith, 1983) is a useful tool which assesses cognitive and affective dimensions of depression. The Beck Depression Inventory (BDI; Beck et al., 1996), can also be used when the woman complains of somatic problems and to examine the presence of suicidal thoughts. For the assessment of anxiety, either the anxiety subscale of the HADS (Zigmond & Snaith, 1983) or the State Trait Anxiety Inventory (STAI; Spielberger et al., 1970) are good measures. For the assessment of PTSD symptoms either Horowitz's Impact of Event Scale (IES; Horowitz *et al.*, 1979), which assesses the severity of intrusions and avoidance related to the traumatic event, i.e. miscarriage, or the Post-traumatic Stress Diagnostic Scale (PDS; Foa *et al.*, 1993), which allows the clinician to make a clinical diagnosis as well as assess the intensity of PTSD symptoms can be used. Depending on the presenting complaints, other instruments may need to be employed at this stage (e.g. for the assessment of marital difficulties, OCD, etc.).

Apart from the assessment of the range and intensity of psychological distress responses, a range of factors which are often implicated in the maintenance of distress in women who have lost a pregnancy can be explored. These could be grouped into factors in the area of: beliefs about the self, world or the future, processing of information, coping skills, and vulnerability factors.

Beliefs about the self which have been identified as negatively associated with adjustment involve feelings of blame and personal responsibility for the miscarriage, blame of others and feelings that others are blaming them for the miscarriage (Robinson *et al.*, 1994; James & Kristiansen, 1995; Nikčević, *et al.*, 1998a). Women with lower levels of self-esteem and self-efficacy are more likely to generate self-blaming attributions for the loss and in turn these are likely to lower their mood and maintain their distress (Nikčević *et al.*, 1998a). Examples of such beliefs are: "I know that I must have caused the loss because I continued jogging in pregnancy." "It's my fault I know. I'm being punished because I didn't want the baby in the first instance." Feelings of self-blame for the loss can be assessed through the use of a three-item measure of feelings of self-blame and personal responsibility for the loss (Nikčević *et al.*, 1999b): "I blame myself for the pregnancy loss", "I feel personally responsible for the miscarriage", and "I worry that I might have done something that caused the miscarriage" to which respondents either mostly disagree (1) to mostly agree (5).

Thoughts and beliefs related to the future often involve doubts concerning one's ability to have a child, one's ability to cope with another pregnancy loss, feelings of vulnerability not only about oneself but also about other close people (e.g. children, partner). Research indicates that women with perceptions of high personal control over the future (e.g. "I've quit smoking and my next pregnancy is going to be fine") are more likely to experience higher anxiety (Tunaley *et al.*, 1993) and depression (Madden, 1988) than those with low feelings of personal control. Thus, in this context, acceptance of uncertainty and unpredictability of future pregnancy outcomes is seen as a more adaptive and realistic attitude towards the future.

The aftermath of miscarriage is also characterised by cognitive processes which aim at developing some kind of meaning, or developing some understanding as to why the loss occurred. This search for meaning can be seen as a part of the normal adjustment process. However, in some cases, processing of information related to the loss is hindered through the use of maladaptive cognitive and/or behavioural strategies. The examples of these would be: cognitive and behavioural avoidance of stimuli associated with the loss (e.g. avoiding to think and talk about the loss and pregnancy-related issues, avoiding other pregnant women and all reminders of the loss). Such avoidant responses are utilised in order to avoid the distress associated with the original trauma. Whilst such responses shortly after loss may be part of a normal process of adaptation, protracted use of such avoidant strategies is likely to hinder processing of the loss and negatively impact women's long-term adjustment. Similarly, excessive and persistent ruminations about the loss, its causes, and the tendency to focus on negative feelings will exacerbate and prolong distress (Nolen-Hocksema *et al.*, 1997).

Closely linked to the above is the exploration of the woman's coping skills. Whilst the majority of women who experience a miscarriage are likely to have in their repertoire of coping skills those necessary to deal with the disappointment and the trauma of a pregnancy loss, some may engage in unhelpful coping strategies which are likely to hinder their adjustment to miscarriage. The examples of these would include passive coping strategies such as social withdrawal and wishful thinking which have been identified to be associated with more depressive responses (James & Kristiansen, 1995). It is useful to explore how the woman has coped with past stress, especially stress related to bereavement, and to identify successful coping strategies that she may have utilised since the miscarriage. Mobilisation of social support, primarily from one's partner, close friends or relatives, is of crucial importance in the process of adaptation to the trauma of miscarriage. Women who lack social support and those who feel that their partner or significant others are blaming them for the loss are more likely to experience difficulties in the process of adjustment following the loss of a baby.

In addition to the above, awareness of vulnerability factors may be helpful in the formulation of the individual's problems. Both history of previous psychological difficulties and complicated obstetric histories (e.g. difficulties conceiving and/or previous perinatal loss) are likely to be associated with more adverse psychological outcomes to miscarriage (for a review see Slade, 1994).

An exploration of the cognitive and behavioural strategies used by the woman to deal with the distress which is made during the initial assessment stages can be aided through the use of a diary to record the thoughts and the associated cues. The use of a functional analysis may also be helpful to identify factors that trigger and maintain specific psychological difficulties.

Integration of the gathered information should result in a problem formulation. This in turn will inform the adopted treatment approach. For some, the intervention will focus on the ventilation of feelings, encouragement of the exploration of the meaning of the loss and its impact on future pregnancies. For others, the intervention will be a compromise between aspects that encourage exploration of the loss and ones that moderate the depressive response, anxiety, symptoms of PTSD and/or interpersonal difficulties. The examples given below will illustrate the differences in the approaches to treatment based on different formulations of women's difficulties following miscarriage. The two women described in the case studies were seen in a dedicated Miscarriage Follow-up clinic developed in the Harris Birthright Research Centre for Fetal Medicine, at King's College Hospital, London. The number of sessions of psychological therapy were limited to seven.

Case studies

Helen

Background information and assessment

Helen (a pseudonym) was a 44-year-old woman who attended for an ultrasound scan at ten weeks of gestation because of bleeding and pain. The scan revealed a miscarriage and she had a D&C to remove the pregnancy. No complications following the D&C procedure were experienced. Approximately ten days after the D&C she contacted the Miscarriage Follow-up clinic because of distress and desire to talk to someone about her loss.

Helen arrived at the clinic in a highly distressed state. She was a head teacher in a local school, married, with two children aged 14 and 11 from a previous marriage. She had been with her second partner for three years. Prior to the current pregnancy, she had lost two others within the space of two years. Helen expressed that this was their last attempt for a pregnancy and she was finding it difficult to accept the loss, and the fact that she will not be able to have a baby with her husband. Helen's partner was compassionate and supportive towards her, but she expressed that he was not nearly as upset by the loss as she was. She described their relationship as "very good". Her children were not aware of the fact that she had lost a pregnancy. Helen described that she was worried about the impact of her emotional state on her children, yet felt unable to communicate to them what had happened. She had taken time off work and was feeling unsure as to when she would be able to go back due to her distressed state. This also upset her further.

During the first session Helen expressed that she was feeling uncomfortable and upset about the fact that she had to ask for help (from a psychologist) as she described "I am always in control. I can cope with emotional things, yet now I feel so helpless and so overwhelmed by my grief." She also stated that she had never felt as upset and sad, not even after the death of her father. This was the first time she had asked for psychological support. Helen described that, since her loss, she could not concentrate on anything, that she felt like crying all the time and staying in bed, and felt "unbearable pain". She felt she could not express completely how deep her pain was in front of her partner.

Her children kept asking her why she was so tearful and upset but she was unable to talk to them openly.

Helen completed several questionnaires to assess her symptoms of mood and grief. She scored very highly on the measure of grief (TGI score = 75, range: 17–85). Her scores for anxiety and depression were clinically significant (Hospital Anxiety Scale (HAS) score = 13; range: 0–21; Hospital Depression Scale (HDS) score = 19, range: 0–21). The score on the self-blame scale was low (SBS = 5, range: 3–15).

Problem formulation and intervention

Helen was an educated woman with a supportive family environment. Prior to her miscarriage, she was well adjusted and appeared to have adequate resources to cope with bereavement and other life stressors. Her current high levels of depression, anxiety and grief were manifestations of the acute phase of mourning. Her grief was not only about the lost pregnancy/baby but also about the loss of reproductive capacity. Her distress seemed to have been exacerbated by the negative self-appraisals and excessively rigid beliefs she had about herself ("Why am I so upset? I should not feel like this. I am completely out of control. Maybe I will never get over this. I am so weak"). Thus, the psychological intervention/therapy involved exploration of issues related to the meaning of the loss, ventilation and normalisation of her feelings, and exploration of the impact of this loss on her views of self and the future. This involved accepting the self as more vulnerable and challenging her belief that she had to be in control at all times. She was encouraged to share her feelings of loss with her children and we planned in the session how she would go about it and how she would deal with their questions. Although she described her partner as "very supportive", we explored the barriers to her sharing with him her sense of loss and disappointment. This again involved exploration of her beliefs about herself as "always strong and always there for the others" and challenging the belief that the loss and pain she was experiencing were proofs of her weakness. Gradually, Helen became less tearful during the sessions, and was able to start planning activities with her children and her return to work. The last session involved exploration of how she was going to deal with people at work asking about her miscarriage, and rehearsing her answers. At the end of the five weekly sessions, she reported feeling better and wishing to end therapy. She did however state that the pain and sense of loss would be with her for a long time. She refused the offer of follow-up, stating that she would be fine. At the end of the therapy sessions she was given several questionnaires to complete and mail back. Her scores on all the measures indicated a general decrease in distress (HAS = 6, HDS = 8, TGI = 58).

Carol

Background information and assessment

Carol (a pseudonym) was a 39-year-old woman who called for an appointment at the Miscarriage Follow-up clinic approximately eight weeks after her pregnancy loss. She worked as an accountant for a large financial organisation. She was married with no children and had a history of prior pregnancy loss which occurred approximately six months previous to her recent miscarriage.

Carol was very distressed on her arrival at the clinic. She was diagnosed with a miscarriage during a routine ultrasound examination at 14 weeks of pregnancy. She planned to have a D&C but in the meantime, whilst waiting for her appointment, she miscarried at home. Carol described this as a very traumatic experience as she was not prepared for a huge loss of blood and pain. The experience left her somewhat numb and traumatised, but as she expressed she had a very demanding job and had to get on with her life and not let herself be upset too much. She wanted to forget about the experience and concentrate on getting pregnant again. She felt that she was coping fine with the miscarriage until her best friend gave birth to a baby a couple of weeks prior to her contacting us. She went to see her friend and the baby, managed to "keep the face" during the occasion, but felt completely overwhelmed with grief, jealousy, hurt and anger after the visit. She realised that she had not got over her loss as she previously thought and decided to contact the Miscarriage clinic to help her "sort out" her emotions. She described that her relationship with her husband had not been very good for some time, roughly from around the time when she had the first miscarriage. At the time he was made redundant and "behaved in a strange way" (he bought a new car after he lost his job). Carol described that their sexual relationship was not very good (due to her lack of desire towards her husband) and stated that this worried her as she was "aware of the biological clock" and desperately wanted to get pregnant as soon as possible.

Carol described a range of difficulties, some of which she could trace back to the earlier miscarriage and which had become worse since the second miscarriage: difficulty concentrating, breathing difficulties, occasional panic attacks, intrusive thoughts about the miscarriage, feelings of emptiness, difficulty falling asleep, fatigue, irritability, relationship difficulties, loss of interest in her work activities and doing things as if on automatic pilot. Since seeing her friend and the baby she had felt very angry with her husband, herself and fate; she experienced intense feelings of jealousy and longing for a baby. She feared that she would run out of time and would never have a child. Carol also felt guilty for having postponed planning a family for so long because of her career. She reported no previous psychiatric or medical history. In terms of goals of therapy, she expressed that she wanted to feel more in control of her feelings and less upset about the miscarriage so that she could start trying for another baby. Although she recognised that her sexual and general marital relationship were not very good she wanted to deal primarily with her feelings related to her miscarriages.

The assessment of mood and current difficulties revealed that her anxiety levels were high: HAS = 19 (range: 0–21), somewhat lower for depression: HDS = 12 (range: 0–21), and her score on the measure of grief was also high: TGI = 71 (range: 17–85). The IES scores were clinically significant (IES intrusion = 20; range: 0–21; IES avoidance = 21; range 0–23).

Functional analysis of her current difficulties revealed that she predominantly used avoidance strategies to deal with all reminders, thoughts and intrusions concerning her losses. Typically, as soon as the memories were activated, she would suppress all related thoughts and would avoid all reminders of the loss. She often experienced intrusions concerning the future outcomes (e.g. "I will never be able to have a child") which caused her a lot of anxiety (e.g. breathing difficulties, restlessness before falling asleep and occasional panic attacks). She was also irritated and angry towards her husband. Carol was aware that her strategy of dealing with her loss was not working and that she needed some help in getting over her losses.

Problem formulation and intervention

The main features of Carol's presenting difficulties (i.e. intrusions, avoidance, anxiety) were best explained by applying the anxiety/post-traumatic stress model. Processing of information related to the loss seemed to have been incomplete due to the use of avoidance strategies (e.g. avoiding thinking about the impact and meaning of the loss, getting back to work immediately after the miscarriage, avoiding discussing her feelings of loss with her husband or close relatives and friends). Such strategies were hindering effective communication with her husband and contributing to her irritable and angry outbursts towards him. It was hypothesised that an exposure programme would be beneficial as it would enable Carol to "work through" her loss-related feelings, allow her to express the disappointment and anger that she felt, and that this could also have an indirect positive impact on the relationship with her husband. Some breathing retraining and cognitive restructuring could address her breathing difficulties and catastrophic interpretations of future pregnancy outcomes.

The "treatment phase" was initiated by providing Carol with an explanation of people's common responses to traumatic events, and on the role of avoidance in the maintenance of her distress and presenting difficulties. Following the rationale, Carol agreed to an exposure programme: for homework she was to write about her experience of miscarriage over several consecutive days for several weeks of treatment, inclusive of both memories of the actual experience, as well as about her feelings and the meaning that her pregnancy losses had for her. She was instructed to read through the written account each day before starting to write again. Carol's exposure programme lasted three weeks. She read her written account of the experience over three sessions; during each session she was tearful and upset. She described her sense of helplessness and horror when she lost the second baby, the bleeding, pain and the visible fetus she saw in the loo. She expressed regret that she and her husband decided to flush the toilet instead of having some form of burial for the baby. These memories were particularly distressing and she was asked to hold in her mind the image of the fetus she saw and to describe it in detail. During the fifth session of treatment she was less tearful and upset. She talked about her fears for the future, worries about future pregnancies and her marital difficulties. Breathing retraining was practised in the session to address her anxious response (breathing difficulties) to catastrophic interpretations of future ("I will never be able to have a baby"), and more rational responses to such cognitions were discussed.

In the final session she felt that her emotions were more under control and she felt optimistic about the future. Her relationship with her husband was somewhat improved through the fact that she was less irritable and angry with him. She was able to appreciate her husband's "good points" more, but she still felt lack of sexual desire towards him. I offered to refer them for treatment of marital difficulties elsewhere but she was reluctant to accept the offer. Her scores on all the measures taken at the beginning of the treatment were considerably reduced and were not clinically significant at the end of the treatment (HAS = 8, HDS = 5, TGI = 55, IES intrusion = 12, IES avoidance = 3). Four months after the end of therapy Carol was pregnant again.

Summary

Miscarriage is the commonest complication of pregnancy which can, for some women, have long-lasting negative psychological effects and interfere with their daily functioning. Difficulties in adjustment to the loss and fears about future pregnancy outcomes can be conceptualised within a cognitive-behavioural framework. The interventions derived should be targeting presenting difficulties through an individualised approach to formulation of distress and grief experienced by the person. Such an individualised approach to understanding meanings attributed to the experience of miscarriage is likely to foster a good therapeutic relationship and lead to a more effective treatment plan.

References

Beck, A.T., Steer, R.A., & Brown, G.K. (1996). *BDI-II, Beck Depression Inventory Manual* (2nd ed.). Boston, MA: Harcourt, Brace.
Beutel, M., Deckardt, R., von Rad, M., & Weiner, H. (1995). Grief and depression

after miscarriage: Their separation, antecedents, and course. *Psychosomatic Medicine, 57*, 517–526.

Bowlby, J. (1980). *Attachment and loss. Vol. 3: Loss: Sadness and depression*. London: Hogarth Press.

Brennan, J. (2001). Adjustment to cancer – coping or personal transition? *Psycho-oncology, 10*, 1–18.

Cecil, R. (1994). Miscarriage: Women's views of care. *Journal of Reproductive and Infant Psychology, 12*, 21–29.

Chambers, H.M., & Chan, F.Y. (2000). Support for women/families after perinatal death (Cochrane Review). *The Cochrane Library*, 1.

Clifford, K., Raj, R., Watson, H., & Regan, L. (1994). An informative protocol for the investigation of recurrent miscarriage: Preliminary experience of 500 consecutive cases. *Human Reproduction, 9*, 1328–1332.

Condon, J.T. (1986). Management of established pathological grief reaction after stillbirth. *American Journal of Psychiatry, 143*, 987–992.

Corney, R.T., & Horton, F.T. (1974). Pathological grief following spontaneous abortion. *American Journal of Psychiatry, 131*, 825–827.

DeFrain, J. (1991). Learning about grief from normal families: SIDS, stillbirth and miscarriage. *Journal of Marital and Family Therapy, 17*, 215–232.

Engelhard, I.M., van den Hout, M.A., & Arntz, A. (2001). Posttraumatic stress disorder after pregnancy loss. *General Hospital Psychiatry, 23*, 62–66.

Farquharson, R.G. (2002). Recurring miscarriage – investigation and classification. In R.G. Farquharson (Ed.), *Miscarriage*. London: Mark Allen.

Foa, E.B., Riggs, D.S., Dancu, C.V., & Rothbaum, B.O. (1993). Reliability and validity of a brief instrument for assessing post-traumatic stress disorder. *Journal of Traumatic Stress, 6*, 459–473.

Friedman, T., & Gath, D. (1989). The psychiatric consequences of spontaneous abortion. *British Journal of Psychiatry, 155*, 810–813.

Gluhoski, V.L. (1995). A cognitive perspective on bereavement: Mechanism and treatment. *Journal of Cognitive Psychotherapy, 9*, 75–84.

Graves, W.I. (1987). Psychological aspects of spontaneous abortion. In M.J. Bennett & D.K. Edmonds (Eds.), *Spontaneous and recurrent abortion*. Oxford: Blackwell.

Hamilton, S.M. (1989). Should follow-up be provided after miscarriage? *British Journal of Obstetrics & Gynecology, 96*, 743–745.

Horowitz, M.J., Wilner, N., & Alvarez, W. (1979). Impact of Event Scale: A measure of subjective stress. *Psychosomatic Medicine, 41*, 209–218.

Hughes, P. (1998). Psychological effects of stillbirth and neonatal loss. In S. Clement, (Ed.), *Psychological perspectives on pregnancy and childbirth*. Edinburgh: Churchill Livingstone.

James, D.S., & Kristiansen, C.M. (1995). Women's reactions to miscarriage: The role of attributions, coping style, and knowledge. *Journal of Applied Social Psychology, 25*, 59–76.

Janoff-Bulman, R. (1992). *Shattered assumptions: Towards a new psychology of trauma*. New York: Free Press.

Janssen, H.J.E.M., Cuisinier, M.C.J., Hoogduin, K.A.L., & de Graauw, K.P.H.M. (1996). Controlled prospective study on the mental health of women following pregnancy loss. *American Journal of Psychiatry, 153*, 226–230.

Kavanagh, D.J. (1990). Towards a cognitive-behavioural intervention for adult grief reactions. *British Journal of Psychiatry, 157*, 373–383.

Klier, C.M., Geller., P.A., & Neugebauer, R. (2000). Minor depressive disorder in the context of miscarriage. *Journal of Affective Disorders, 59*, 13–21.

Kline, J., & Stein, Z. (1990). The epidemiology of spontaneous abortions. In H.J. Huisjes & T. Lind (Eds.), *Early pregnancy failure*. Edinburgh: Churchill Livingstone.

Lasker, J.N., & Toedter, L. J. (1991). Acute versus chronic grief: The case of pregnancy loss. *American Journal of Orthopsychiatry, 61*, 510–522.

Lee, C., & Slade, P. (1996). Miscarriage as a traumatic event: A review of literature and new implications for intervention. *Journal of Psychosomatic Research, 40*, 232–245.

Lee, C., Slade, P., & Lygo, V.E.N. (1996). The influence of psychological debriefing on emotional adaptation in women following early miscarriage: A preliminary study. *British Journal of Medical Psychology, 69*, 47–58.

Leppert, P.C., & Pahlka, B.S. (1984). Grieving characteristics after spontaneous abortion: A management approach. *Obstetrics & Gynecology, 64*, 119–122.

Madden, M.E. (1988). Internal and external attribution following miscarriage. *Journal of Social and Clinical Psychology, 7*, 113–121.

Moulder, C. (Ed.). (1990). *Miscarriage: Women's experiences and needs*. London: Pandora.

Neugebauer, R., Kline, J., O'Connor, P., Shrout, P., Johnson, J., Skodol, A., Wicks, J., & Susser, M. (1992). Depressive symptoms in women in the six months after miscarriage. *American Journal of Obstetrics & Gynecology, 166*, 104–109.

Neugebauer, R., Kline, J., Shrout, P., Skodol, A., O'Connor, P., Geller, P.A., Stein, Z., & Susser, M. (1997). Major depressive disorder in the 6 months after miscarriage. *JAMA, 277*, 383–388.

Ney, P.G. (1987). Helping patients cope with pregnancy loss. *Contemporary Obstetrics & Gynecology, 117*, 117–130.

Nikčević, A.V., Kuczmierczyk, A., & Nicolaides, K.H. (1998a). Personal coping resources, responsibility, anxiety and depression after early pregnancy loss. *Journal of Psychosomatic Obstetrics and Gynecology, 19*, 145–154.

Nikčević, A.V., Tunkel, S.A., & Nicolaides, K.H. (1998b). Psychological outcomes following missed abortions and provision of follow-up care. *Ultrasound in Obstetrics & Gynaecology. 11*, 123–128.

Nikčević, A.V., Kupek, E., Snijders, R., & Nicolaides, K.H. (1999a). Some psycho-metrics properties of the Texas Grief Inventory adjusted for miscarriage. *British Journal of Medical Psychology, 72*, 171–178.

Nikčević, A.V., Tunkel, S.A., Kuczmierczyk, A.R., & Nicolaides, K.H. (1999b). Investigation of the cause of miscarriage and its influence on women's psycho-logical distress. *British Journal of Obstetrics & Gynecology, 106*, 808–813.

Nikčević, A.V., Kuczmierczyk, A.R., & Nicolaides, K.H. (in review). The impact of medical and psychological interventions on women's distress after miscarriage.

Nolen-Hoeksema, S., McBride, A., & Larson, J. (1997). Rumination and psycho-logical distress among bereaved partners. *Journal of Personality and Social Psychology, 72*, 855–862.

Parkes, C.M. (1985). Bereavement. *British Journal of Psychiatry, 146*, 11–17.

Paton, F., Wood, R., Bor, R., & Nitsun, M. (1999). Grief in miscarriage patients and satisfaction with care in a London hospital. *Journal of Reproductive and Infant Psychology, 17*, 301–315.

Rajan, L., & Oakley, A. (1993). No pills for heartache: The importance of social support for women who suffer pregnancy loss. *Journal of Reproductive & Infant Psychology, 11*, 75–87.

Robinson, G.E., Stirtzinger, R., Stewart, D.E., & Ralevski, E. (1994). Psychological reactions in women followed for 1 year after miscarriage. *Journal of Reproductive and Infant Psychology, 34*, 191–198.

Saraiya, M., Green, C.A., Berg, C.J., Hopkins, F.W., Koonin, L.M., & Atrash., H.K. (1999). Spontaneous abortion: Related death among women in the United States, 1981–1991. *Obstetrics and Gynaecology, 94*, 172–176.

Slade, P. (1994). Predicting the psychological impact of miscarriage. *Journal of Reproductive and Infant Psychology, 12*, 5–16.

Spielberger, C.D., Gorsuch, R.L., & Lushene, R.E. (1970). *The State-Trait Anxiety Inventory (test manual)*. Paolo Alto, CA: Consulting Psychologists Press.

Swanson, K.M. (1999). Effects of caring, measurement, and time on miscarriage impact and women's well-being. *Nursing Research, 48*, 288–298.

Tunaley, J., Slade, P., & Duncan, S.B. (1993). Cognitive processes in psychological adaptation to miscarriage: A preliminary report. *Psychology and Health, 8*, 369–381.

Walker, T.M., & Davidson, K.M. (2001). A preliminary investigation of psychological distress following surgical management of early pregnancy loss detected at initial ultrasound scanning: A trauma perspective. *Journal of Reproductive and Infant Psychology, 19*, 7–16.

Zaccardi, R., Abbott, J., & Koziol-McLain, J. (1993). Loss and grief reactions after spontaneous miscarriage in the emergency department. *Annals of Emergency Medicine, 22*, 799–804.

Zigmond, A.S., & Snaith, R.P. (1983). The Hospital Anxiety and Depression Scale. *Acta Psychiatrica Scandinavica, 67*, 361–370.

Index

Note: page numbers in **bold** refer to information contained in tables, pager numbers in *italics* refer to diagrams.